The Religious Enlightenment

JEWS, CHRISTIANS, AND MUSLIMS
FROM THE ANCIENT TO THE MODERN WORLD

Michael Cook, William Chester Jordan, and Peter Schäfer
Series Editors

The Religious Enlightenment

PROTESTANTS, JEWS, AND CATHOLICS
FROM LONDON TO VIENNA

David Sorkin

PRINCETON UNIVERSITY PRESS

PRINCETON AND OXFORD

Copyright © 2008 by Princeton University Press

Published by Princeton University Press, 41 William Street, Princeton, New Jersey 08540

In the United Kingdom: Princeton University Press, 6 Oxford Street, Woodstock, Oxfordshire OX20 1TW

Library of Congress Cataloging-in-Publication Data

Sorkin, David Jan.

   The religious Enlightenment: Protestants, Jews and Catholics from London to Vienna/David Sorkin.

      p. cm.—(Jews, Christians, and Muslims from the ancient to the modern world)
   Includes index

   ISBN 978-0-691-13502-1 (hardcover: alk. paper)

   1. Europe—Church history—17th century.   2. Europe—Church history—18th century.   3. Enlightenment—Europe. I. Title.

   BR735.S67 2008

   274'.07—dc22   2007040965

British Library Cataloging-in-Publication Data is available

This book has been composed in Palatino

Printed on acid-free paper. ∞

press.princeton.edu

Printed in the United States of America

10   9   8   7   6   5   4   3   2   1

In memory of George L. Mosse

L'abus du savoir produit l'incrédulité; . . .
L'orgueilleuse philosophie mène au fanatisme.
Évitez ces extrémités.

The abuse of knowledge produces unbelief; . . .
A haughty philosophy leads to fanaticism.
Avoid these extremes.

—Rousseau, *Émile* (Book IV)

Contents

List of Illustrations

List of Maps

Preface

THIS BOOK had its distant origins in a graduate seminar the late Martin Malia taught at the University of California–Berkeley in 1978. While reading the (then) major scholarship on the Enlightenment—that by Ernst Cassirer, Paul Hazard, and Peter Gay—I felt, from what I knew about Jewish history, that religious thinkers and ideas received short shrift. I decided I would someday write about the Enlightenment from the perspective of religion. That idea remained a mental note while I wrote a book on German Jewish history, though there were a few occasions when my imagination caught fire. I distinctly remember the afternoon in the glass-floored stacks of Doe Library when I found a monograph on the Anglo-Catholic Enlightenment.

My mental note became a full-time occupation when a fellowship at the Oxford Centre for Hebrew and Jewish Studies and St. Antony's College enabled me to spend long hours at the Bodleian and British Museum Libraries. I started writing about Protestants and Catholics in German-speaking Europe. When I was invited to write a book on Moses Mendelssohn, I put those chapters aside. I seized the chance to study a central figure of the tradition I knew best, and to indicate, however provisionally, his affinities with thinkers of other confessions. Surprisingly, examining those affinities required emphasizing Mendelssohn's neglected Hebrew works.

An unexpected invitation to deliver the Sherman Lectures in the Department of Religions and Theology at the University of Manchester gave me a chance to dust off my chapters in order to extricate the Berlin Haskalah (Jewish Enlightenment) from its conventional parochial setting by comparing it to developments among German Protestants and Catholics. Because of my commitment to Jewish history, then, I was preoccupied throughout most of the 1990s with the religious Enlightenment's implications for our understanding of the Haskalah. Indeed, the late Isaiah Berlin once quipped that my project was to discover whether there was a "Haskalah" among Protestants and Catholics.

A reader might well ask, why should a scholar of Jewish history devote years to studying Christian thought? My answer is that this book emerged from my studies of Jewish history. Alert to the ways, subtle and not, in which Jews and Judaism were excluded from histories of Europe, I quickly sensed the extent to which scholars had arbitrarily defined the Enlightenment. I realized that if I were to restore religion to the Enlightenment, I would have to cross the boundaries that had hitherto supported artificial conceptions.

Despite its protracted parturition, this book does not purport to offer a definitive account of the religious Enlightenment. It is neither comprehensive (it examines only six figures) nor geographically inclusive (it does not treat Italy, Spain, Scotland, Scandinavia, Eastern Europe, and the Americas); it also does not address such crucial subjects as art, music or architecture. Instead, it aims to identify some new landmarks as a way to reorient the compass of Enlightenment studies. The reorientation is that the Enlightenment could be reverent as well as irreverent, and that such reverence was at its very core.

I cannot forget the morning in the domed reading room of the former British Library when I received some volumes of German Reform Catholic theology from the 1780s whose pages were uncut. That they had gone unread for some two centuries affirmed my commitment to this project. I am grateful to the Bodleian Library; the British Museum Library; the Codrington Library, All Souls College; Christ Church College Library; Bayerische Staatsbibliothek; Bibliothèque National Française; Niedersächsische Staats- und Universitätsbibliothek; Doe Library, the University of California–Berkeley; Princeton University Library; Northwestern University Library; Hebrew Union College Library, Cincinnati; Indiana University Library; Stiftsbibliothek Kremsmünster; Widener Library, Harvard University; Bibliothèque Publique et Universitaire, Geneva; Stanford University Library; Wiener Stadt- und Landesbibliothek; and the Memorial Library, University of Wisconsin–Madison. Our assiduous bibliographer, Barbara Walden, has been consistently helpful.

There are many colleagues to whom I am indebted. Martin Jay continues to be an exemplary adviser. Phil Harth read the chapter on Warburton. Robert Kingdon wisely suggested that I include Geneva, and then read the chapter on Vernet, as did Helena Rosenblatt. Hans Bödeker has encouraged me with numerous conversations and invitations. Laurence Brockliss, John Robertson, and Jan Spurlock welcomed me into their Enlightenment workshop. Ritchie Robertson suggested the figure of Joseph Eybel, and James Van Horn Melton and Steven Beller read the chapter. Klaus Berghahn's skepticism about Catholic Enlightenment was a goad. Larry Dickey has been my interlocutor on the Enlightenment since I arrived in Madison. Tony Michels read the chapter on Mendelssohn. Alyssa Sepinwall read an early draft of the chapter on Lamourette, and Suzanne Desan helped me rethink it. Chuck Cohen, Jeremi Suri, and Tom Broman helped me sharpen the introduction. Lou Roberts helped make this book more coherent and accessible in numerous ways. Dale Van Kley filled the final stages of writing with inspiring conversation. Chas Camic and Erik Wright pointed me to relevant sociological literature. Matteo Saranzo expertly summarized Daniele Menozzi's book. My project assistants, Maggie Wunnenberg, Greg Shealy and Michelle Wing, saved me time and headaches. Stephan Wendehorst kindly procured a photocopy of a rare book in Vienna.

I could not have completed this project without the generous support of a British Academy travel grant; a National Endowment for the Humanities Fellowship for University Teachers; a Summer Fellowship at the Max Planck Institut für Geschichte, Göttingen; a Visiting Fellowship at All Souls College, Oxford; and a John Simon Guggenheim Memorial Foundation Fellowship. I would especially like to thank the University of Wisconsin–Madison for the Frances and Laurence Weinstein Chair in Jewish Studies, a Kellett Mid-Career Fellowship, and a Senior Fellowship at the Institute for Research in the Humanities, followed by a term as director.

I would like to thank Princeton University Press for publishing this book. Brigitta van Rheinberg was enthusiastic from the start and offered sage editorial advice. Clara Platter, Deborah Tegarden, and Marjorie Pannell have been impressively professional in all respects and a pleasure to work with.

Earlier versions of some chapters have appeared in the following publications. "William Warburton: The Middle Way of 'Heroic Moderation,'" in *Dutch Review of Church History* 82 (2002) 262–300; " Reclaiming Theology for the Enlightenment: The Case of Siegmund Jacob Baumgarten (1706–1757)," *Central European Hostory* 36 no. 4 (2003) 503–530; "Geneva's 'Enlightened Orthodoxy': The Middle Way of Jacob Vernet (1698–1789)," *Church History* 74 no. 2 (2005) 286–305. I gratefully acknowledge the journals and their editors for granting permission to use these materials.

Finally, this book is dedicated to the memory of George L. Mosse. His electrifying lectures first aroused my interest in European history. He was a generous mentor who quietly inspired confidence in his students. I cannot predict what George would have thought of this book: even though it echoes some thoughts expressed in early essays, he was contrarian by temperament and conviction. Yet whether he agreed or disagreed with the direction of his students' work, he delighted in it.

The Religious Enlightenment

Introduction

IN THE ACADEMIC as well as the popular imagination, the Enlightenment figures as a quintessentially secular phenomenon—indeed, as
the very source of modern secular culture. Historical scholarship of
the 1960s successfully disseminated this image by propagating the
master narrative of a secular European culture that commenced with
the Enlightenment.[1] This master narrative was the counterpart to
modernization theory in the social sciences. The two shared a trium-
phalist linear teleology: in the social sciences, the destination was urban, industrial, democratic society; in intellectual history, it was secularization and the ascendancy of reason.[2] A wide range of philosophers,
working from diverse and often conflicting positions, reinforced this
image. The Frankfurt School and Alasdair MacIntyre, Foucault and
the post-modernists all spoke of a unitary Enlightenment project
that, for better or worse, was the unquestionable seedbed of secular
culture.[3] Open the pages of virtually any academic journal in the
humanities today and you will find writers routinely invoking the
cliché of a unitary Enlightenment, sometimes as a pejorative, sometimes as an ideal, but invariably as the starting point of secular modernity and rationality.

In recent decades this image of a unitary, secular Enlightenment
project has become a foundational myth of the United States: it has converged with the idea of America's "exceptionalism," or singular place
in the world. Henry Steele Commager argued that whereas Europe

---

[1] Peter Gay, *The Enlightenment*, 2 vols. (New York, 1966–69). A recent restatement is
Louis Dupré, *The Enlightenment and the Intellectual Foundations of Modern Culture* (New
Haven, 2004). For an early critique, see Sheridan Gilley, "Christianity and Enlightenment: An Historical Survey," *History of European Ideas* 1, no. 2 (1981): 103–21. For an effort
to restore the Enlightenment's theological origins and a more complex notion of secularization, see Charles Taylor, *Sources of the Self: The Making of the Modern Identity* (Cambridge, MA, 1989). For nonteleological secularization theory, see David Martin, *On Secularization: Towards a Revised General Theory* (Aldershot, UK, 2005).

[2] Cyril E. Black, *The Dynamics of Modernization* (New York, 1966).

[3] MacIntyre coined the term "enlightenment project" in *After Virtue* (Notre Dame, IN,
1981). Theodor Adorno and Max Horkheimer, *The Dialectic of the Enlightenment*, trans.
John Cumming (New York, 1972); Michel Foucault, "What Is Enlightenment?" in *The
Foucault Reader*, ed. Paul Rabinow (New York, 1984), 32–50. For postmodernism, see
Daniel Gordon, ed., *Postmodernism and the Enlightenment* (New York, 2001). Useful is
James Schmitt, *What Is Enlightenment? Eighteenth-Century Answers and Twentieth-Century
Questions* (Berkeley, 1996).

only "imagined" the Enlightenment, the United States "realized" it; in America "it not only survived but triumphed" and indeed "*was* the American Revolution." Moreover, this was an Enlightenment of "secularism and rationalism," of "Faith in Reason, in Progress, in a common Humanity."[4] Gertrude Himmelfarb has reinforced this view by asserting that America's "exceptionalism" consists in its embodying the Enlightenment's pragmatic "politics of liberty" hostile to rationalist utopias.[5]

This image of a secular Enlightenment has become so pervasive that thinkers regularly invoke it to legitimize partisan positions. A recent writer on the left has appealed to it as representing "cosmopolitan tolerance, economic justice, democratic accountability and the idea of the "'good society,'" or, even more polemically, "a movement of protest against the exercise of arbitrary power, the force of custom and ingrained prejudices, and the justification of social misery."[6] A recent writer on the right has claimed it as an endorsement for "compassionate conservatism" by having "superimposed on the politics of liberty something very like a sociology of virtue."[7]

Finally, the image of a secular Enlightenment has become integral to America's response to twenty-first-century fundamentalism. At home, a secularist versus fundamentalist conflict allegedly threatens to divide us into implacably hostile camps. At the same time, there are serious concerns about America's creeping "national disenlightenment," its renunciation of science and rationality in favor of a "theologization" of politics and a "theological correctness" grounded in millenarian Christianity.[8] Abroad, resurgent fundamentalisms are thought to presage

<hr/>

[4] Henry Steele Commager, *The Empire of Reason: How Europe Imagined and America Realized the Enlightenment* (New York, 1977), xi–xii, 41, 71. For similar views see Howard Mumford Jones, *Revolution and Romanticism* (Cambridge, MA, 1974), 153–59; and Ralf Dahrendorf, *Die Angewandte Aufklärung; Gesellschaft und Soziologie in Amerika* (Munich, 1963).

[5] Gertrude Himmelfarb, *The Roads to Modernity: The British, French, and American Enlightenments* (New York, 2004). For American exceptionalism, see 232. For a differentiated notion of the Enlightenment, see Henry May, *The Enlightenment in America* (New York, 1976). For the distinction between the historical Enlightenment and its legacy, see Donald H. Meyer, *The Democratic Enlightenment* (New York, 1976). A recent literary synthesis is Robert A. Ferguson, *The American Enlightenment, 1750–1820* (Cambridge, 1997).

[6] Stephen Eric Bronner, *Reclaiming the Enlightenment: Towards a Politics of Radical Engagement* (New York, 2004), ix, 7.

[7] Himmelfarb, *Roads to Modernity*, 233–34.

[8] Kevin Phillips, *American Theocracy: The Peril and Politics of Radical Religion, Oil, and Borrowed Money in the 21st Century* (New York, 2006), 103, 217, 226, 236. Cf. Gary Wills, "The Day the Enlightenment Went Out," *New York Times*, Nov. 4, 2004.

seemingly unbridgeable chasms between adherents of different religions or religiously based "civilizations."[9]

This book aims to revise our understanding of the Enlightenment. Contrary to the secular master narrative, the Enlightenment was not only compatible with religious belief but conducive to it. The Enlightenment made possible new iterations of faith. With the Enlightenment's advent, religion lost neither its place nor its authority in European society and culture. If we trace modern culture to the Enlightenment, its foundations were decidedly religious.

This study endeavors to heed the call to "re-historicize the Enlightenment with a vengeance." It attempts to counter all those writers who, in diverse ways and for disparate reasons, have produced "cardboard-character representations of the Enlightenment mind."[10] In bringing the religious Enlightenment to the fore, it undertakes "an exercise in retrieval" to reconceive the historical Enlightenment and understand "modernity aright."[11]

ENLIGHTENMENT OR ENLIGHTENMENTS?

In the last three decades, historians have begun to question the image of a unitary secular Enlightenment project, asserting that it was neither unambiguously secular nor religion's polar adversary.[12] Rather, in the words of J.G.A. Pocock, the Enlightenment was "a product of religious debate and not merely a rebellion against it."[13] The same scholars have further argued that the Enlightenment included a range of positions, from the most thoroughly secular to the most thoroughly religious. For example, Pocock speaks of a "family" or a "plurality" of Enlightenments whose intellectual means, varied and multiple, extended from the genuinely religious to the genuinely antireligious.[14] Jonathan Israel

---

[9] Samuel P. Huntington, *The Clash of Civilizations and the Making of a New World Order* (New York, 1997), presumes the "resurgence" of religion and "la Revanche de Dieu."

[10] David Hollinger, "The Enlightenment and the Genealogy of Cultural Conflict in the United States," in *What's Left of Enlightenment? A Postmodern Question*, ed. Keith Michael Baker and Peter Hanns Reill (Stanford, 2001), 18, 15

[11] Taylor, *Sources of the Self*, xi.

[12] Roy Porter and Mikulás Teich, eds., *The Enlightenment in National Context* (Cambridge, UK, 1981), stimulated such studies.

[13] J.G.A. Pocock, *Barbarism and Religion: The Enlightenments of Edward Gibbon, 1737–1764* (Cambridge, UK, 1999), 5.

[14] Ibid., 9, 138. For "plurality," see Roy Porter, *The Enlightenment*, 2nd ed. (Houndmills, Basingstoke, UK, 2001), 9. For multiple perspectives, see Fania Oz-Salzberger, "New Approaches Towards a History of the Enlightenment: Can Disparate Perspectives Make a General Picture?" *Tel Aviver Jahrbuch für deutsche Geschichte* 29 (2000): 171–82.

confirmed this notion with his bipartite view of a "radical Enlightenment," derived largely from Spinoza, alongside a "moderate," "mainstream," "providential" Enlightenment that inhabited the middle ground.[15]

Although scholars first applied these ideas to Protestant countries, they have since extended them to Catholic ones as well. Jonathan Israel identified both Protestant and Catholic versions of the "moderate" Enlightenment. In their introduction to a collection of articles, James Bradley and Dale Van Kley portrayed two geographical "crescents": a "distinctively Protestant Enlightenment" that "stretched like a crescent from England and Scotland through the Protestant Netherlands and western Germanies only to end in the Swiss cities like Geneva and Lausanne," and a "distinctively Catholic Enlightenment" that "formed another and southern crescent from the Catholic Germanies in the southeast through the north-central Italies, including Rome in the center, and on through the Iberian peninsula in the West."[16]

The authors of these views are to be applauded for providing a fuller account of the Enlightenment's relationship to religion. Yet they do not go far enough. To understand the religious Enlightenment's full scope, we need to consider not just Protestantism and Catholicism but also Judaism, as well as dissenting Protestant and Catholic sects. It would be fundamentally misleading to speak of a Christian Enlightenment, since we would thereby reinstate the Peace of Westphalia's terms (which in 1648 recognized only Calvinism, Lutheranism, and Catholicism) as if they accurately represented Europe's religious composition.[17]

Moreover, it is imperative to compare the various manifestations of the religious Enlightenment. We need to be able to ascertain in what ways they constituted an identifiable entity, in what ways they were disparate, and how they functioned in various settings. This has not

---

[15] Jonathan Israel, *Radical Enlightenment: Philosophy and the Making of Modernity, 1650–1750* (Oxford, 2001), 445–562. Margaret C. Jacob distinguished between a "radical" (materialist, republican, anticlerical) and a "moderate" (Newtonian, Christian) Enlightenment in England and Holland. See *The Radical Enlightenment: Pantheists, Freemasons and Republicans* (London, 1981). Taylor distinguished between a providential Christian deism (Locke, Shaftesbury, Hutcheson) and a radical materialist, utilitarian non-Christian Enlightenment (Helvétius, Bentham, Holbach, Condorcet). See *Sources of the Self.*

[16] James E. Bradley and Dale K. Van Kley, *Religion and Politics in Enlightenment Europe* (Notre Dame, IN, 2001), 15.

[17] For attempts to include Judaism, see Samuel J. Miller, *Portugal and Rome c. 1748–1830: An Aspect of the Catholic Enlightenment, Miscellanea Historiae Pontificiae* 44, (Rome, 1978), 1–2; Bernard Plongeron, "Was ist katholische Aufklärung?" in *Katholische Aufklärung und Josephinismus,* ed. Elisabeth Kovács (Munich, 1979), 39–45; Horst Möller, *Vernunft und Kritik: Deutsche Aufklärung im 17. und 18. Jahrhundert* (Frankfurt, 1986), 100–107; David Sorkin, *The Berlin Haskalah and German Religious Thought* (London, 2000).

been possible, since individual scholars have usually confined themselves to analyzing a single tradition, either Protestant or Catholic, in one country or two. To take a broad view, we need to cross confessional and national boundaries. We need a multinational and comparative history of the religious Enlightenment that emphasizes similarities while recognizing and explicating differences.[18]

Finally, we need to expand the canon of Enlightenment thinkers and literature to include theologians and theology. Only by reclaiming these heretofore ostracized thinkers can we begin to replace the master narrative of a secular Enlightenment with a more historically accurate notion, complex, differentiated, and plural.

To make the religious Enlightenment accessible, I have focused on individuals. I have selected figures who were sufficiently established and centrally positioned to render their respective traditions understandable. As writers and thinkers, agents and actors, they generated and adapted ideas to specific historical situations and circumstances. These figures serve as touchstones, rendering movements and events personal and tangible. They allow us to explore similarities and differences in the religious Enlightenment in particular times and places. Although in historical retrospect these figures were, by and large, decidedly second rank, they were prominent and influential in their day.[19]

This book also suggests a different approach to Europe's religious history. The religious Enlightenment was not confined to any one denomination in one country or group of countries but crossed religious and national borders, encompassing Protestantism, Catholicism, and Judaism in a number of polities. It was perhaps the first development common to Western and Central Europe's religions. To account for the religious Enlightenment requires a comparative history of religion that, while respecting enduring differences, emphasizes shared developments.

THE RELIGIOUS ENLIGHTENMENT

The immediate background to the religious Enlightenment was the century of warfare following the Reformation, which, by inflicting unprecedented devastation and misery, discredited all belligerent, militant, and

---

[18] Nancy Green, "Forms of Comparison," in *Comparison and History: Europe in Cross-National Perspective*, ed. Deborah Cohen and Maura O'Connor (New York, 2004), 41–56.

[19] On individuals as "windows," "agents," "symbols," or "touchstones," see Alyssa Sepinwall, *The Abbé Grégoire and the French Revolution: The Making of Modern Universalism* (Berkeley, 2005), and Hans Erich Bödeker, *Biographie Schreiben* (Göttingen, 2003).

intolerant forms of religion. As one of Montesquieu's Persian travelers put it: "I can assure you that no kingdom has ever had as many civil wars as the kingdom of Christ."[20] Those wars also produced a religious stalemate that undermined the confessional state ideal—the territorial coincidence of church and state. The Peace of Westphalia, agreed to in 1648, recognized the existence of polities with virtual parity between religious groups, polities in which the ruler professed a different creed from the majority of his subjects and polities that included a substantial religious minority. The burning issue was how to establish the toleration, common morality, and shared political allegiance needed to sustain a multiconfessional polity. Finally, those developments coincided with the intellectual revolutions of Newtonian science and post-Aristotelian philosophy: Locke's empiricism and the rationalisms of Descartes, Leibniz, and Wolff.

The religious Enlightenment addressed this situation. In the century from England's Glorious Revolution, which kept the monarchy Protestant and safeguarded fundamental rights, and its Act of Toleration (1689), to the France Revolution and its Civil Constitution of the Clergy (1790), religious enlighteners attempted to renew and rearticulate their faith, using the new science and philosophy to promote a tolerant, irenic understanding of belief that could serve a shared morality and politics. Aiming to harmonize faith and reason, and thinking themselves engaged in a common enterprise with all but the most radical enlighteners, the religious enlighteners enlisted some of the seventeenth century's most audacious, heterodox ideas for the mainstream of eighteenth-century orthodox belief. For Christians, the religious Enlightenment represented a renunciation of Reformation and Counter-Reformation militance, an express alternative to two centuries of dogmatism and fanaticism, intolerance and religious warfare. For Jews, it represented an effort to overcome the uncharacteristic cultural isolation of the post-Reformation period through reappropriation of neglected elements of their own heritage and engagement with the larger culture.

The religious Enlightenment spread across Western and Central Europe in a sequence of cross-confessional and cross-national influence and filiation. Many of its fundamental ideas, Protestant and Catholic, first appeared in the Dutch Republic, which maintained a precarious toleration. The republic, a confessional state with a "public Church" and a dominant clergy whose religious plurality (Mennonites, Lutherans, Catholics, Jews, Socinians, Quakers) was the "unforeseen and unfortunate result of the Reformation and the Dutch Revolt," prioritized

---

[20] *Lettres persanes* (1721), letter 29. Quotation from Montesquieu, *Persian Letters*, trans. C. J. Berrs (Harmondsworth, UK, 1973), 81.

social "concord," preventing either the Reformed Church or the Catholic Church from imposing confessional unity.[21] In this setting, revisions of militant Calvinism and baroque Catholicism flourished, while Judaism engaged with the larger culture.

Among Protestants, Jacobus Arminus (1560–1609) emphasized free will, questioned predestination of the elect, and denied confessional creeds divine authority, initiating Protestantism's central reform theology, Arminianism. Writers such as Johannes Coccejus (1603–69) and Christopher Wittich (1625–87) disputed the literalist Biblical exegesis underpinning Calvinist confessionalism. Hugo Grotius (1583–1645), Simon Episcopius (1583–1643), and Philip van Limborch (1633–1712) championed versions of toleration, while the radical sect of Collegiants went furthest in recognizing freedom of belief by envisaging the Church as a voluntary society.[22]

Catholics championed a new theology and controversial ecclesiology. Cornelis Jansen (1585–1638), bishop of Ypres, by proposing an austere notion of grace, morality, and inward piety opposed to excessive external devotion (baroque Catholicism), launched the movement that eventually bore his name, Jansenism. In response to Dutch circumstances, Catholics advocated local or national (Gallicanism) as opposed to papal control of the Church. The University of Louvain became a stronghold of Jansenism and Zeger Bernard Van Espen (1646–1728), one of its most renowned professors, a proponent of Gallicanism.[23]

Jews in the Dutch Republic, many of them *conversos* from the Iberian Peninsula, enjoyed toleration and even, in some cases, municipal citizenship. The school in Amsterdam (*Ets Hayyim*) represented an ideal in integrating secular subjects into a well-ordered religious curriculum. Amsterdam became a center of Hebrew book publishing, and early Jewish enlighteners (*maskilim*) assembled there. Baruch Spinoza (1632–77), the descendant of a converso family, was educated in Amsterdam

---

[21] Joris Van Eijnatten, *Liberty and Concord in the United Provinces: Religious Toleration and the Public in the Eighteenth-Century Netherlands* (Leiden, 2003), 3.

[22] Andrew Fix, *Prophecy and Reason: The Dutch Collegiants in the Early Enlightenment* (Princeton, 1991), and idem, *Fallen Angels: Balthasar Bekker, Spirit Belief and Confessionalism in the Seventeenth Century Dutch Republic*, International Archives of the History of Ideas 165 (Dordrecht, 1999); Philip S. Gorski, *The Disciplinary Revolution: Calvinism and the Rise of the State in Early Modern Europe* (Chicago, 2003), 39–77; Jonathan I. Israel, *The Dutch Republic: Its Rise, Greatness and Fall, 1477–1806*, 2nd ed. (Oxford, 1998), and idem, *The Enlightenment Contested: Philosophy, Modernity and the Emancipation of Man, 1670–1752* (Oxford, 2006), 27ff.; Wiep van Bunge, ed., *The Early Enlightenment in the Dutch Republic, 1650–1750* (Leiden: Brill, 2003)

[23] Michel Nuttinck, *La vie et l'oeuvre de Zeger-Bernard van Espen: Un canoniste janséniste, gallican et régalien à l'Université de Louvain, 1646–1728* (Louvain, 1969); Nigel Abercrombie, *The Origins of Jansenism* (Oxford, 1936), 125–58.

and, later associating with Collegiants and other radical Protestants, developed his materialist naturalism and critique of scripture that haunted Europe's religious imagination.[24]

Dutch developments were so influential as to comprise the first matrix of religious Enlightenment ideas. Dutch books circulated in the original and in translation throughout northern and Central Europe.[25] Catholics and Protestants from across Europe came to the Netherlands to study the new theology and natural law. Political refugees from England (Locke) and France (Descartes, Bayle) found a safe haven replete with, and receptive to, new ideas. The Dutch Republic, and particularly Amsterdam, served as a model of religious toleration and prosperity.[26]

Nevertheless, neither Armininians and Collegiants nor Jansenist Catholics, let alone Jewish maskilim, became the dominant version of their respective religion and gained state sponsorship—essential features of religious Enlightenment. The Synod of Dort (1618–19) banned Arminian theology; an anti-Trinitarian scare resulted as late as 1653 in a prohibition of Collegiants; and Arminians and Collegiants continually lost members to the Reformed Church during the eighteenth century. The Dutch Catholic Church remained sorely divided until the schism of 1723 formally separated an "Old Catholic" Jansenist Church of Utrecht from the Pope's Vicar-Apostolic, and in subsequent decades the former shrank dramatically.[27] Maskilic Jews were a tiny portion of a minority eager to display its adherence to rabbinic Judaism.[28]

The first fully realized example of religious Enlightenment, and its second matrix of ideas, was the Church of England's "moderation." Moderation emerged in the wake of the Glorious Revolution as a broadly

[24] Shmuel Feiner, *The Jewish Enlightenment* (Philadelphia, 2002), 26, 78; Steven Nadler, *Spinoza: A Life* (Cambridge, 1999); Israel, *Radical Enlightenment*; Miriam Bodian, *Hebrews of the Portuguese Nation: Conversos and Community in Early Modern Amsterdam* (Bloomington, IN, 1997); Daniel Swetschinski, *Reluctant Cosmopolitans: The Portuguese Jews of Seventeenth-Century Amsterdam* (London, 2000).

[25] Israel, *Radical Enlightenment*, 29ff. Cf. G. C. Gibbs, "The Role of the Dutch Republic as the Intellectual Entrepôt of Europe in the Seventeenth and Eighteenth Centuries," *Bijdragen en mededelingen betreffende de geschiedenis der Nederlanden* 86 (1971): 323–49. For the Netherlands and England as the Enlightenment's two sources, see Eduard Winter, *Frühaufklärung: Der Kampf gegen den Konfessionalismus in Mittel- und Osteuropa und die deutsch-slawische Begegnung* (Berlin, 1966), 17.

[26] Israel, *Enlightenment Contested*, 29–30.

[27] Israel, *The Dutch Republic*, 460–64, 911–13, 653–58, 1034–37. See Mordechai Feingold, "Reversal of Fortunes: The Displacement of Cultural Hegemony from the Netherlands to England in the Seventeenth and Early Eighteenth Centuries," in *The World of William and Mary: Anglo-Dutch Perspectives on the Revolution of 1688–89*, ed. Dale Hoak and Mordechai Feingold (Stanford, 1996), 234–61.

[28] Yosef Kaplan, *An Alternative Path to Modernity: The Sephardi Diaspora in Western Europe* (Leiden, 2000).

Arminian alternative to Catholicism and "inner light" enthusiasm. As one historian has put it, "If Popery was the epitome of despotism, imposed from above, Puritanism was anarchy incarnate, breaking out from below."[29] Founded on Locke's philosophy and Newton's science, Moderation was not a fixed set of ideas but an ethos or disposition, ranging from the low church to the high, that concerned all aspects of religious life. William Warburton (1698–1779), bishop of Gloucester and author of highly influential works on church-state relations and historical theology, represents Moderation (chapter 1).

English Moderation became a model for "enlightened Orthodoxy" in Calvinist Geneva. Enlightened Orthodoxy emerged over two generations as theologians endeavored to replace Calvinist rigorism with a tolerant doctrine of reason, natural religion, and revelation. Jacob Vernet (1698–1789), the dominant theologian of his age, was inspired by Descartes's philosophy, Arminian theology, and English moderation (chapter 2).

The English model and Dutch precedents also influenced the "theological Enlightenment" among German Lutherans, which was poised between militant orthodoxy and enthusiastic Pietism. Its first phase (ca. 1700–40) consisted of disparate attempts to use the new science and philosophy to renew Lutheranism. In the most important of those efforts, theologians used Christian Wolff's rationalist method to reformulate Lutheran belief ("theological Wolffianism"). Siegmund Jacob Baumgarten (1706–57), professor of theology at Halle, was the preeminent scholar of his generation, dubbed by Voltaire "the jewel in the crown of German scholarship" (chapter 3).

The German Protestant theological Enlightenment influenced the Haskalah (Jewish Enlightenment), which presented a middle way between Judaism's dominant intellectual traditions in early modern Europe: monolithic Talmudism buttressed by mysticism (Kabbalah), and Maimonidean rationalism. The early Haskalah (ca. 1700–70) was a cultural tendency of individuals who attempted to expand the curriculum of Ashkenazic (or Central and East European) Jewry by reviving the disciplines of biblical exegesis and philosophy in Hebrew and Hebrew language study, as well as by introducing contemporary science and philosophy. Becoming a public movement of societies centered around a journal in the 1770s and 1780s, the Haskalah politicized the earlier effort to broaden Judaism's curriculum. A participant in its early phase and pivotal in its later one, Moses Mendelssohn (1729–86) was the Haskalah's

---

[29] Roy Porter, *The Creation of the Modern World: The Untold Story of the British Enlightenment*, (New York, 2000), 51.

foremost thinker. He was conversant with various versions of the Protestant religious Enlightenment (chapter 4).

Reform Catholicism in the southern German states and Habsburg lands was an indigenous effort at intellectual and religious renewal. Drawing inspiration from Catholic humanism, and especially the works of the Italian theologian and historian Ludovico Muratori (1672–1750), it was a "counter-Counter-Reformation" that navigated between Jesuit baroque piety and the controversial Jansenist movement. Reform Catholicism proffered an alternative to the Jesuit curriculum by altering not the content but the method of expounding belief, employing science (Copernicus, Newton), philosophy (Leibniz, Wolff, Locke, and eventually Kant) and historical study (scripture, patristics, church history). At first (ca. 1720–50) attempting to renew rather than replace the scholastic method, it eventually (ca. 1750–80) embraced an eclectic version of Wolff's philosophy. Joseph Valentine Eybel (1741–1805) was a sometime professor who promoted natural law theory and gained fame advocating and administering Emperor Joseph II's reforms (chapter 5).

Finally, France. In Roy Porter's words, France was "the great anomaly" whose peculiar configuration of politics, religion, and culture long precluded Reform Catholicism.[30] The French monarchy, by choosing to suppress rather than sponsor Jansenism, the key movement for religious reform, generated a concatenation of momentous developments. It pushed some Jansenists into the arms of enthusiasm. It fostered a dispute between Jansenists and Jesuits which, from mid-century, the *philosophes* made three-sided, and that three-sided dispute introduced a polarization between enlightenment and religion.[31] Dominating Louis XV's reign (1715–74), this situation thwarted Reform Catholicism. In the 1780s, Adrien Lamourette (1742–94), a Lazarist priest and seminary professor, attempted to devise a Reform Catholic theology by combining the ideas of reasonable religion and Rousseauist sentiment on the

---

[30] Porter, *The Enlightenment*, 55. See also Ernst Cassirer, *The Philosophy of the Enlightenment* (Princeton, 1951), 134; Lester G. Crocker, "The Enlightenment: Problems of Interpretation," in *L'età dei Lumi: Studi Storici sul Settecento Europeo in onore di Franco Venturi* (Naples, 1985), 23; W. R. Ward, *Christianity under the Ancien Régime, 1648–1789* (Cambridge, 1999), 171; and MacIntyre, *After Virtue*, 37. For France's centrality, see Robert Darnton, *George Washington's False Teeth: An Unconventional Guide to the Eighteenth Century* (New York, 2003), and Norman Hampson, *The Enlightenment* (Harmondsworth, UK, 1968).

[31] See Lamourette: "in the eighteenth century Philosophy has become the opposite of Christianity, and [philosophy] needed to be impious and blasphemous to merit the honor of figuring in the [mental] picture of the wise." *Les Délices de la Religion, ou le pouvoir de l'Évangile pour nous rendre heureux* (Paris, 1788), ix; cf. *Pensées sur la Philosophie de l'Incrédulité, ou Reflexions sur l'esprit et le dessein des philosophes irréligieux de ce Siècle* (Paris, 1786), 253, 263.

basis of a moderate fideist skepticism. As constitutional bishop of Lyon and a delegate to the Legislative Assembly, he avidly supported the revolution and what would have been Reform Catholicism's greatest triumph, the Civil Constitution of the Clergy, until, along with other patriotic clergy, he was sent to the guillotine (chapter 6).

By studying the religious Enlightenment through six figures in six historical contexts, this book highlights intellectual similarities while recognizing national differences.[32] This approach allows us to define the religious Enlightenment according to four characteristics. The first two are clusters of ideas, the last two social and political attributes. First, religious enlighteners searched for the middle way of reasonable belief grounded in the idea of "natural religion" and the exegetical principle of accommodation. Second, they embraced toleration based on the idea of natural law. Third, the public sphere was central: the religious Enlightenment was an important component of it, while religious enlighteners engaged in multiple pursuits in it. Fourth, the religious Enlightenment gained the sponsorship of states and, using natural law theory, advocated a state church.

REASONABLENESS

The religious Enlightenment constituted a conscious search for a middle way between extremes. William Warburton spoke of a "heroic moderation," Baumgarten called his theological position "the true middle way," Jacob Vernet wrote that "the middle way . . . constitutes the true religion," and Lamourette suggested that "the philosophes of our century have shown themselves to be too *anti-Theologian,* and our theologians have perhaps been a bit too *anti-Philosophes.*"[33]

The religious enlighteners identified the middle way with "reasonableness" or "reasonable" belief. Joseph Eybel defined his ideal reader as being neither a freethinker nor an unthinking enthusiast but a "reasonable and well-instructed Christian."[34] The terms *reasonable* and *reasonableness* were already current when Locke popularized

---

[32] For "two contexts, one Enlightenment," see John Robertson, *The Case for the Enlightenment: Scotland and Naples, 1680–1760* (Cambridge, 2005), 9, 377.

[33] William Warburton, *Divine Legation of Moses Demonstrated,* in *The Works of the Right Reverend William Warburton, D.D.,* 12 vols. (London, 1811), 4:12; Siegmund Jacob Baumgarten, *Siegmund Jacob Baumgartens Kleine Teutsche Schriften* (Halle, 1743), 77, 301, 346; Jacob Vernet, *Instruction chrétienne, divisée en cinq volumes; seconde edition, retouchée par l'Auteur & augmentée de quelques pièces,* 5 vols. (Geneva, 1756), 1:177; Adrien Lamourette, *Pensées sur la Philosophie de la foi* (Paris, 1789), xviii–xix. Cf. Joseph Eybel, *Göttergespräche gegen die Jakobiner* (Linz, 1794), 435–37, 572–73.

[34] Joseph Eybel, *Was ist der Pabst?* (Vienna, 1782), 6.

them in his 1695 treatise, *The Reasonableness of Christianity*. Reasonable should be distinguished from *rational*, the term scholars commonly employ to assert the Enlightenment's primary if not exclusive reliance on reason. We should follow contemporaries by thinking of reasonable in relationship to unreasonable. To religious enlighteners, unreasonable meant an exclusive embrace of either reason or faith. Faith untempered by knowledge, or combined with excessively partisan forms, produced intolerant, dogmatic, or enthusiastic religion. They had in mind "inner light" Puritanism, Pietism, or convulsionary Jansenism; the polemical, scholastic theology of the major Christian denominations (Lutherans, Calvinists, and Catholics) in the seventeenth century; or, in the case of Judaism, an exclusivist and casuistic (*pilpul*) method of studying the Talmud.[35] At the same time, religious enlighteners thought that unaided reason engendered immoral skepticism and unbelief. They were certain that morality without belief was neither desirable nor possible.

Reasonable, in contrast, signified a balance between reason and faith. Reasonable belief meant the coordination of reason and revelation; they did not contradict because by definition, as the two God-given "lights," they could not. As Lamourette put it: "Reason and revelation get along infinitely better than their interpreters. . . . These two torches are taken from . . . the same light; they never spoil each other and conflict except in the hands of man."[36] Reasonable or reasonableness meant acknowledging reason as a criterion of judgment in the narrow sense derived from the respective philosophical culture: in England, Locke; in French-speaking Europe, Descartes or Malebranche; in the German lands, Christian Wolff. Yet it also meant reason in the sense of admitting criteria such as testimony, the credibility of tradition or miracles that were indispensable to recognizing the authority of scripture. In other words, reason was defined broadly to maintain the common ground of philosophy and theology.[37]

This broad understanding of reason had two important consequences. It became common practice among the religious enlighteners

---

[35] William Bouwsma, *The Waning of the Renaissance, 1550–1640* (New Haven, 2000), 232–45. For enthusiasm, see Michael Heyd, *"Be Sober and Reasonable": The Critique of Enthusiasm in the Seventeenth and Early Eighteenth Centuries* (Leiden, 1995), and Lawrence Klein and Anthony J. La Vopa, eds., *Enthusiasm and Enlightenment in Europe, 1650–1850* (San Marino, CA, 1998).

[36] Lamourette, *Pensées sur la Philosophie de la foi*, xviii–xix. Cf. *Pensées sur la Philosophie de l'Incrédulité*, 253, 263, and *Les Délices*, ix.

[37] Gerard Reedy, *The Bible and Reason: Anglicans and Scripture in Late Seventeenth-Century England* (Philadelphia, 1985), 34–40, 54–55, 140–41. For changing notions of reason vis-à-vis scripture, see Heyd, *"Be Sober and Reasonable,"* 165–90.

first to show what reason could teach about a particular doctrine, then to draw on scripture to certify, augment, and refine that knowledge. In addition, the religious enlighteners endorsed the distinction that revelation could not contain truths contrary to reason (*contra rationem*) yet did include truths above reason (*supra rationem*), namely, the truths of revelation not accessible to, but in harmony with, reason.

The idea of natural religion epitomized this coordination of reason and faith. Natural religion consisted in the truths accessible to unassisted reason, which usually meant a belief in God, His providence, and the rewards and punishments of a future life. Libertines and deists (notably Herbert of Cherbury, 1583–1648) had first promoted the idea of natural religion in the seventeenth century in opposition to revealed religion. Most Enlightenment thinkers adopted it, since, by transcending confession, it could guarantee a common morality and be the foundation of a multireligious polity. Natural religion emphasized not dogma or precise formulations of belief as represented in creeds or symbolic books but practice and morality.[38]

Religious enlighteners coopted the idea of natural religion to revealed religion, thereby making a radical idea of the seventeenth century entirely conventional in the eighteenth. They treated natural religion as a necessary but insufficient foundation for belief. Natural religion alone was incapable of teaching morality and true belief. Only reason and revelation in tandem were equal to the task.

This sort of argument was so common that it structured religious Enlightenment tracts. They typically began with a consideration of natural religion, proceeded to Judaism as the first revealed religion and Christianity as its successor, and concluded with a consideration of the author's particular Christian creed.

Since reasonableness confirmed revelation, it also entailed a defense of exegetical methods. Religious enlighteners renewed inherited forms of exegesis, asserting their ability to derive revelation from scripture's inspired texts. An understanding of revelation rested on an awareness of history. Most of the religious enlighteners employed the exegetical principle of accommodation, namely, that in dealing with humankind, God "accommodated" or "condescended" to time, place, and particular mentalities. This principle enabled them to contend that whereas aspects of scripture were historically bound, its true content transcended history. The religious enlighteners thus acknowledged history but

---

[38] Christoph Link, "Christentum und moderner Staat: Zur Grundlegung eines freiheitlichen Staatskirchenrechts im Aufklärungszeitalter," in *Christentum, Säkularisation und modernes Recht*, ed. Luigi Lombardi Vallauri and Gerhard Dilcher (Baden-Baden, 1981), 859–61.

rejected any attempt to relativize revelation or deny its universal valid-ity by limiting it to a particular time or place. They were historical but not historicist, insisting on the capacity of reason to apprehend revela-tion through the medium of the text.

Whereas the idea of reasonableness rested heavily on scripture, the religious enlighteners argued that scripture was not the supreme source of all knowledge. They did not expect the Bible to serve as a textbook of science or politics. They understood its scope to be lim-ited to salvation and man's relationship to God: science was not in its purview, as expressed in the saying Galileo made famous, "the Bible tells us how to go to heaven and not how the heavens go."[39] These were intellectual strategies, drawing on the principle of accommodation as well as the historical approach, that aimed to defend revelation's authority without relativizing it.

TOLERATION

The religious Enlightenment was distinguished by its commitment to toleration of competing religions and dissenting sects. In the sixteenth and seventeenth centuries, the idea of toleration had largely been the preserve of heterodox sects, humanists, and proponents of raison d'etat. By trying to transform the militant and intolerant orthodoxies of the Reformation and Counter-Reformation era into tolerant forms of belief, the religious enlighteners brought the idea of toleration to the center of the established religions. Some English-language accounts present toleration as primarily a creation of Protestants in England, the Netherlands (especially Huguenots), and Switzerland. In fact, it was neither exclusively Protestant nor concentrated in Western Eu-rope. Catholics, Jews, and German-speaking Europe also had a hand in creating it.[40]

---

[39] Klaus Scholder, *The Birth of Modern Critical Theology: Origins and Problems of Biblical Criticism in the Seventeenth Century* (London, 1990), 57–61. Galileo was quoting Cardinal Baronius.

[40] For a recent example, see Perez Zagorin, *How the Idea of Religious Toleration Came to the West* (Princeton, 2003). Important accounts are Wilbur K. Jordan, *The Development of Religious Toleration in England*, 4 vols. (Cambridge, 1932–40); Joseph Lecler, *Toleration and the Reformation*, 2 vols. (New York, 1960); and Henry Kamen, *The Rise of Toleration* (New York, 1967). For revisionist views, see John Laursen and Cary Nederman, eds., *Beyond the Persecuting Society: Religious Toleration Before the Enlightenment* (Philadelphia, 1998), and Ole Peter Grell and Roy Porter, eds., *Toleration in Enlightenment Europe* (Cambridge, 2000). For a survey, see Michael Walzer, *On Toleration* (New Haven, 1997).

The religious enlighteners used ecclesiastical versions of natural law theory known as collegialism, derived from the dissenting Dutch Calvinist sect, and territorialism, which put more emphasis on the "territorial" state's authority, both of which were based on the individual's autonomy and freedom of conscience. Their common point of departure was the individual's relationship to the church or synagogue. Religious enlighteners first defined the church or synagogue as a separate society (or collegium) of equal individuals, and then used that same criterion to define state and society. They linked these notions to the idea of natural religion. Religious opponents in the seventeenth and eighteenth centuries claimed that toleration would promote indifference and skepticism. Religious enlighteners addressed that fear by using collegialism or territorialism to justify toleration on the basis of belief.[41]

This toleration was decidedly selective: every thinker and denomination had their respective limits. Such selectivity was characteristic of virtually all theories of toleration at the time. Locke, it should be remembered, would not tolerate atheists because their oaths were not credible and Catholics because of their loyalty to the Pope.[42] Most religious enlighteners, including Warburton, Baumgarten, and Mendelssohn, shared Locke's attitude toward atheists. The religious enlighteners also had other limits. Vernet would extend toleration to other Protestants but not to Catholics, let alone Jews (neither Catholics nor Jews were admitted to Geneva in Vernet's lifetime). Eybel, like other Reform Catholic advocates of toleration, maintained the crucial Catholic distinction between civil and theological toleration: he granted the former, hoping for reunification with Protestants and the Jews' conversion. Baumgarten's unwavering commitment to freedom of conscience made his idea of toleration virtually universal, yet he retained the ultimate aim of converting the Jews. Aside from excluding atheists, Mendelssohn enunciated the most comprehensive theory of toleration because of his metaphysical commitment to religious pluralism. Despite these limitations, we should not underestimate the achievement: here were representatives of the established religions advocating toleration as essential to faith.

---

[41] Fix, *Prophecy and Reason*; Klaus Schlaich, *Kollegialtheorie: Kirche, Recht und Staat in der Aufklärung* (Munich, 1969).

[42] John Marshall, *John Locke, Toleration and Early Enlightenment Culture: Religious Intolerance and Arguments for Religious Toleration in Early Modern and "Early Enlightenment" Europe* (Cambridge, 2006); and Israel, *Enlightenment Contested*, 135–63.

The Public Sphere

There has been a strong tendency among scholars to see the eighteenth-century public sphere as increasingly if not distinctly secular. This was not the case. The religious Enlightenment and the religious enlighteners were an integral part of the emerging public sphere; indeed, without the public sphere, the religious Enlightenment was inconceivable. The public sphere made it possible for the religious Enlightenment to arise among multiple religions in a number of countries and become the first common development of Western and Central Europe's religions. This could not have occurred a century earlier.[43]

The religious Enlightenment was a functioning aspect of the public sphere. The absolute number of religious works published in the eighteenth century increased, even if their percentage of overall book production declined. There were established networks of travel, correspondence, and book production to transmit and propagate the religious Enlightenment. Many religious enlighteners studied or visited in its two original matrices of ideas, Holland and England, and also met kindred spirits in other countries. There was a republic of letters that enabled scholars to exchange ideas through correspondence within and between confessions. Finally, there was a library of the religious Enlightenment. In the course of the eighteenth century a collection of books emerged—by Anglican Moderates and Dutch Collegiants and Arminians, German Protestant and Gallican church historians and theorists, and works of ecclesiastical natural law—from which one could absorb the religious Enlightenment.[44]

---

[43] Jürgen Habermas, *The Structural Transformation of the Public Sphere: An Inquiry into a Category of Bourgeois Society*, trans. Thomas Burger (Cambridge, 1989). On Habermas's neglect of religion, see James Van Horn Melton, *The Rise of the Public in Enlightenment Europe* (Cambridge, 2001), 48, 87–88.

[44] On the clergy's participation in German periodicals (*Berlinische Monatsschrift, Allgemeine Deutsche Bibliothek*), see Horst Möller, *Aufklärung in Preußen: Der Verleger, Publizist und Geschichtsschreiber Friedrich Nicolai* (Berlin, 1974), 252–53, 266–67 and Roger Kirscher, *Théologie et Lumières: Les Théologiens Éclairés autour de la revue de Friedrich Nicolal, Allgemeine Deutsche Bibliothek, 1765–1792* (Villeneuve-d'Ascq, 2001). From 1695 to 1785 the production of religious books in France multiplied by a factor of 3.6 yet dropped as a percentage of total output (from 44 percent to 30 percent). See J. Quéniart, *Culture et société urbaines dans la France de l'Ouest au XVIIIe siècle* (Paris, 1978), 319–24. Theological works constituted at least 18.2 percent (perhaps as much as 24.4 percent) of books published between 1780 and 1782 in the German states. See Helmuth Kiesel and Paul Münch, *Gesellschaft und Literatur im 18. Jahrhundert: Voraussetzungen und Entstehung des literarischen Markts in Deutschland* (Munich, 1977), 186–87. For a religious Enlightenment library, see *Verzeichniß der auserlesenen Büchersammlung des seeligen Herrn Moses Mendelssohn* (Berlin, 1786).

Furthermore, religious enlighteners participated in the apparently secular aspects of the public sphere. They wrote history, geography, philosophy, belles lettres, and political tracts because they discerned no barriers between these pursuits and their religious beliefs. In fact, they were convinced of the opposite: they thought the two contributed equally to what they believed were the compatible if not identical goals of Enlightenment and faith. Since the religious enlighteners recognized no unmistakable let alone unpassable boundaries between the secular and the religious, being a man of letters and a man of belief were entirely consistent. It was therefore common to find religious enlighteners who were as well if not better known for their "secular" as their religious works.

The religious enlighteners were not opportunists or "trimmers" who, by engaging in seemingly secular pursuits, were philosophes in disguise or only doing the philosophes' work.[45] Then and now, this view invoked the metaphor of a slippery slope, asserting that once these figures repudiated orthodoxy, they inevitably slid through a series of compromised positions into deism or unbelief. The slippery slope metaphor is fundamentally mistaken in its point of departure, by erroneously investing one formulation or period of religious thinking with normative status, and in its destination, by supporting a linear notion of secularization. It assumes that, aside from "orthodoxy," there were no viable theological positions. In this view, the repudiation of orthodoxy results, among Protestants, in an unavoidable slide through Arminianism to Socinianism and on to deism; or among Catholics, that aside from Tridentine doctrine there was no other legitimate standard for practice and belief; or among Jews, the rejection of monolithic Talmudism was tantamount to antinomianism. This view is patently false: Arminianism was a tenable Protestant theology, not a way station; Jansenism, conciliarism, and the ideal of the early church were an alternative to, or indeed an alternative realization of, Trent; and in Judaism there were alternative textual traditions available, primarily from Sephardi Jewry.[46]

The religious enlighteners were not trimmers but sincere believers and apologists who mounted an energetic attack in the public sphere on deists and unbelievers in order to defend the faith, and that defense included their writings in other fields. They had an extensive knowledge of history and were aware of the competing versions of

---

[45] Gay, *The Enlightenment: An Interpretation*, 1:359ff.

[46] Pocock criticized the "slippery slope" theory as "Whiggish" and "Catholic" (inevitable secularization). See "Enthusiasm: The Antiself of Enlightenment," in *Enthusiasm and Enlightenment in Europe, 1650–1850*, 12.

their respective traditions. They understood the repudiation of orthodoxy as enabling them to restore or fashion true belief.

STATE NEXUS

The state nexus defined the politics of the religious Enlightenment. The state and the resources at its disposal were a crucial factor in the Enlightenment's genesis and the religious Enightenment's character: the growth of the state mechanism in large part made possible the public sphere in which the Enlightenment took root and flourished. That public sphere comprised a broad coalition of elites whose differences prevented it from being monolithic, affording significant freedom.[47] The religious Enlighteners belonged to those elites, and in the course of the eighteenth century they gained the sponsorship of states seeking political stability (England, Geneva) or pursuing reform from above (Prussia, Habsburg empire). The rulers of these polities saw a "reasonable" interpretation of religion as a means to further their own efforts to promote the irenicism and toleration that allowed politics and state building to replace theological controversies and the ideal of the confessional state.

Religious enlighteners recognized constituted authority, whatever its form, yet wanted to change the terms of state-church relations. In opposition to the confessional state's extremes of state (Erastian) or church (theocratic) rule, including papal monarchy (curialism), they sought a middle way in the idea of a state church based on ecclesiastical natural law theory (Collegialism, Territorialism). They envisaged the church shedding its corporate characteristics in order to integrate into the state's growing administrative mechanism. They envisaged the state guaranteeing individual freedom of conscience and the church's institutional independence by limiting its jurisdiction to those religious matters that impinged on the civil order. Religious enlighteners did not advocate radical alternatives to the confessional state, such as separation of church and state or civil religion. Rather, they devised a moderate reform by making autonomy in matters of faith, for the individual and the church, the price of accepting the bureaucratic state's authority.[48]

---

[47] Robert Wuthnow, *Communities of Discourse: Ideology and Social Structure in the Reformation, the Enlightenment and European Socialism* (Cambridge, MA, 1989), 160–164, 178.

[48] Link, "Christentum und moderner Staat"; Fix, *Prophecy and Reason*; Schlaich, *Kollegialtheorie*; T. J. Hochstrasser, *Natural Law Theories in the Early Enlightenment* (Cambridge,

It was no accident that the religious Enlightenment coincided with the Whig supremacy in England and patrician rule in Geneva, both of which attempted to refine existing state churches (chapters 1 and 2), or enlightened absolutism in Prussia and the Habsburg empire, both of which aimed to create state churches (chapters 3 and 5). The religious Enlightenment was an integral element of those political constellations. Similarly, the mature Haskalah aimed to turn the Jewish community into a voluntary society that could exist alongside a state church, thereby qualifying the Jews for emancipation (chapter 4). And the French Revolution designed a model state church in the Civil Constitution of the Clergy (chapter 6).

THE ENLIGHTENMENT SPECTRUM

What are the implications of the existence of a transnational and multi-confessional religious Enlightenment? We should replace the notion of a unitary, secular Enlightenment project with the concept of an Enlightenment spectrum. We should resist the impulse to hypostatize the religious Enlightenment as a separate entity and rather see it as one position on that spectrum.

Following Jonathan Israel's account, the conventional figures of the Enlightenment—Newton and Locke, Descartes and Montesquieu, Leibniz and Wolff—constituted a moderate version at the spectrum's center that espoused a sort of providential deism including "belief in Creation, divine Providence, the divine origin and absolute validity of morality, the special role of Christ, and the immortality of the soul." This moderate mainstream "was overwhelmingly dominant in terms of support, official approval, and prestige practically everywhere except for a few decades in France from the 1740s onwards." It had "three rival versions": "Neo-Cartesianism, Newtonianism (reinforced with Locke) and Leibnizian-Wolffianism." All three relied on "physico-theology" or the "argument from design," which, the "strongest single intellectual pillar buttressing the moderate mainstream Enlightenment," was often combined with a defense of miracle. By the middle of the eighteenth century, the neo-Cartesian version had largely exhausted itself, leaving the field to the rival Newtonian-Lockean and Leibnizian-Wolffian versions.[49] The moderate Enlightenment was flanked on one side, Israel further contends,

---

2000), 24–29; Ian Hunter, *Rival Enlightenments: Civil and Metaphysical Philosophy in Early Modern Germany* (Cambridge, 2001).

[49] Israel, *The Enlightenment Contested*, 11, and idem, *The Radical Enlightenment* (Oxford, 2001), 471, 477, 456–61, 556.

by a "radical" enlightenment that was materialist, democratic, egalitarian, anti theological, and favored absolute freedom of thought; its three principal architects were Spinoza, Bayle, and Diderot. Although "a tiny fringe in terms of numbers, status and approval ratings," it was "remarkably successful not just in continually unsettling the middle ground . . . but also in infiltrating popular culture and opinion." In the nineteenth and twentieth centuries socialists and Marxists claimed this materialist tradition, guaranteeing that liberal and conservative scholars would disdainfully ignore it. The historians who have recently focused on it wish to reclaim Spinoza's hitherto unrecognized importance, as well as the Enlightenment's anti-imperialism.[50]

If we follow this argument, then flanking the moderate Enlightenment on the other side, and significantly overlapping with it, was the religious Enlightenment. It consisted of multiple movements across Europe that found institutional expression and state patronage. In a variety of philosophical idioms—Cartesian, Lockean, or Wolffian— religious enlighteners championed ideas of reasonableness and natural religion, toleration and natural law that aimed to inform, and in some cases reform, established religion. Religious enlighteners were theologians, clergy, and religious thinkers who were fully committed partisans and reformers of their own tradition. The religious Enlightenment developed largely within the institutional confines of the respective religious tradition even as its members were active participants in the public sphere.[51]

The Enlightenment consisted of its radical, moderate, and religious versions as they developed across Europe from the mid-seventeenth century to the end of the eighteenth century. We must renounce the temptation, however intellectually seductive or politically expedient, to designate any one version, either in any one place at any one time, or in any one cultural or religious tradition, *the* Enlightenment.[52] The entire spectrum across Europe during the entire period constituted the Enlightenment.

---

[50] Israel, *The Radical Enlightenment*; idem, *The Enlightenment Contested*, 11–12, 42; Margaret Jacob, *The Radical Enlightenment*; Sankar Muthu, *Enlightenment Against Empire* (Princeton, 2003); Lynn Hunt and Margaret Jacob, "Enlightenment Studies," in *Encyclopedia of the Enlightenment*, ed. Alan Charles Kors, 4 vols. (New York, 2003), 1:426.

[51] For the Counter-Enlightenment, see Darrin McMahon, *Enemies of the Enlightenment: The French Counter-Enlightenment and the Making of Modernity* (New York, 2001), and Joseph Mali and Robert Wokler, eds., *Isaiah Berlin's Counter-Enlightenment* (Philadelphia, 2003).

[52] This was the point of Roy Porter's and Mikulás Teich's seminal *The Enlightenment in National Context*. Peter Gay idealized Voltaire and Hume, Robert Darnton the Parisian Enlightenment, Jonathan Israel Spinoza, Bayle, and Diderot.

We should discard the facile yet tenacious notion that as a result of the Enlightenment, religion lost its power and influence in eighteenth-century society. The religious Enlightenment gained state sponsorship. It was at the heart of the eighteenth century: it may have had more influential adherents and exerted more power in its day than either the moderate or the radical version of the Enlightenment. The religious Enlightenment represented the last attempt by European states to use reasonable religion—as opposed to romantic, mystical, or nationalist interpretations—as the cement of society.

We need to imagine our way back into a world in which the secular and religious were not distinct and fixed categories but so fundamentally intertwined as to be inseparable. The Enlightenment spectrum boasted a constant interaction and intersection between the religious and secular. Alongside the philosophe and the *Aufklärer*, the Enlightenment's personnel included the religious enlightener—the Anglican Moderate, the Genevan enlightened Orthodox, the Prussian Lutheran theological enlightener, the Jewish maskil, the Reform Catholic in the Habsburg empire and, for a short time, in France—who propagated the Enlightenment on his own terms, the terms of faith. The religious-secular dichotomy first became dominant with the French Revolution and in fact destroyed the religious Enlightenment.

Contrary to the secular master narrative of the Enlightenment, modern culture also has religious roots. Since religious enlighteners argued on religious grounds for such ideas as reasonableness and natural religion, natural law and toleration, the eighteenth-century roots of political liberalism are as much within organized religion as in opposition to it. The Enlightenment origins of modern culture were neither secular nor religious but a complex amalgam.

Opposite: William Warburton. Frontispiece, *The Works of the Right Reverend William Warburton, D.D., Lord Bishop of Gloucester*, 12 vols. (London, 1811). Courtesy of Memorial Library, University of Wisconsin–Madison.

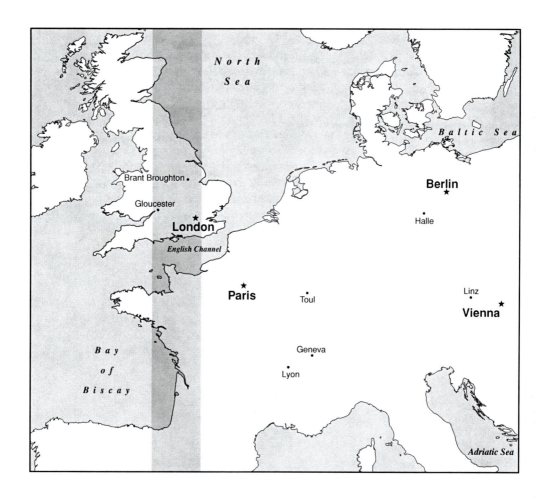

CHAPTER ONE

Brant Broughton, London, Gloucester

William Warburton's "Heroic Moderation"

From the civil war (1642) to the Hanoverian Succession (1714), England was racked by incessant political strife and intermittent warfare, in part owing to conflicts over religion. The Glorious Revolution had brought William and Mary (1689) to the throne to preclude the renewal of domestic turmoil that James II's Catholicism seemed to threaten. The Act of Settlement (1701), by ensuring that no Catholic could reign in England, had paved the way for George I and the Hanoverian Succession. Yet how was the country to achieve harmony with an established Church, jealous of its power and prerogatives, beset by Protestant dissenters and a resurgent Catholicism? Some resolution among the contending religious forces was indispensable to political stability, and the version of Anglicanism known as Moderation succeeded in proffering it.[1]

William Warburton (1698–1779) made his reputation as an apologist for a "heroic moderation" that supported the revolution settlement.[2]

---

[1] J. H. Plumb, *The Growth of Political Stability in England, 1675–1725*, 3rd ed. (London, 1977), Theodore K. Rabb, *The Struggle for Stability in Early Modern Europe* (New York, 1975).

[2] *Divine Legation of Moses Demonstrated*, in *The Works of the Right Reverend William Warburton, D.D.*, 12 vols. (London, 1811), 4:12: "that HEROIC MODERATION so necessary to allay the violence of public disorders; for to be MODERATE amidst party-extremes, requires no common degree of patriotic courage." Warburton lamented the human tendency to embrace extremes. See *Divine Legation*, in *Works*, 3:248–49, 6:310, and *The Alliance between Church and State*, 7:24, 218.

Locke's version of Christianity was a middle way between predestination and natural religion. See *The Reasonableness of Christianity as Delivered in the Scriptures*, in *Works of John Locke*, 11th ed., 10 vols. (London, 1812), 7:4. He used "just and moderate government" to describe a tolerant state. See *A Letter Concerning Toleration*, in *Works of John Locke*, 6:49–50.

Edmund Gibson argued "that true Christianity lies in the middle way between ["lukewarmness" and "enthusiasm"]." See *The Late Bishop of London Dr. Gibson's Five Pastoral Letters to the People of His Diocese* (London, 1751), 285. Gilbert Burnet so described the Latitudinarians ("They wished things might have been carried with more moderation"). See O. W. Airy, ed., *History of my Own Time*, 2 vols. (Oxford, 1897), 1:334. For titles of books, see Edward Fowler, *The Principles and Practices of Certain Moderate Divines of the Church of England* (London, 1670); Charles Leslie, *The New Association of Those Called, Moderate-Church-Men* (London, 1702); and Benjamin Hoadly, *A Moderate Church-Man* (London, 1710).

See John Walsh and Stephen Taylor, "Introduction: The Church and Anglicanism in the 'Long' Eighteenth Century," in *The Church of England c. 1689– c. 1833: From Toleration to Tractarianism*, ed. John Walsh, Colin Haydon, and Stephen Taylor, (Cambridge, 1993), 51–61.

His career came at the highpoint of the Church of England's effort to shape the ideas to champion an established Church limited by Corporation and Test Acts. Drawing inspiration from Anglo-Dutch Arminianism, Locke, and Newton, he provided an important rearticulation of Protestant belief that included an enduring defense of church-state relations and a historical interpretation of Christianity. Generally ranked among the secondary figures of the period, Warburton devised a potent renewal of English Protestantism that belonged to the first full-fledged instance of the religious Enlightenment.[3]

Born in Newark in Nottinghamshire, Warburton's childhood and early adolescence coincided with Moderation's militant period (1689–1714), in which the High Church and Moderate parties emerged to struggle over the future of the Church. He began his career in the period of Moderation's ascendancy (1714–30) and spent the bulk of it in Moderation's triumph (1730–60).

The High Church and Moderate parties represented less a discrete set of ideas than an ethos or disposition. The High Churchmen tended to view the world as a fixed hierarchy in which a divinely ordained (jure divino) order ruled church and state. They regarded the accession of William and Mary as a "Glorious Revolution" because God had providentially saved England from Catholicism and arbitrary government. Yet they also saw the Church in danger from the old threat of dissenters, as well as the new one of deists and other unbelievers. For the sake of religious comprehension, High Churchmen opposed tampering with the liturgy or sacraments; for the sake of religious uniformity, they often endorsed coercion. There was good reason that High Churchmen were often dubbed "Tories at prayer."[4]

---

[3] Warburton's rough manner prevented his works getting serious attention. Mark Pattison stressed his "career of antagonism." See "Life of Bishop Warburton," in *Essays by the late Mark Pattison*, ed. Henry Nettleship (Oxford, 1889). Similarly, Leslie Stephen, *History of English Thought in the 18th Century*, 3rd ed., 2 vols. (London, 1902), 1:344–71. Better on controversies than ideas are A. W. Evans, *Warburton and the Warburtonians: A Study in Some Eighteenth-Century Controversies* (London, 1932), and B. W. Young, *Religion and Enlightenment in Eighteenth-Century England: Theological Debate from Locke to Burke* (Oxford: Clarendon, 1998), 167–212.

A fairer assessment is Richard Hurd, "A Discourse by Way of General Preface: Containing Some Account of the Life, Writings and Character of the Author," *Works* 1:1–127. For Warburton as one of the period's five or six most influential theologians, see Ernest C. Mossner, *Bishop Butler and the Age of Reason* (New York, 1936), 186.

[4] Jeffrey S. Chamberlain, *Accommodating High Churchmen: The Clergy of Sussex, 1700–1745* (Urbana and Chicago, 1997), 13–30. On coercion, see Mark Goldie, "The Theory of Religious Intolerance in Restoration England," in *From Persecution to Toleration: The Glorious Revolution and Religion in England*, ed. O. P. Grell, Jonathan Israel, and Nicholas Tyacke (Oxford, 1991), 331–68.

In contrast, the Moderates (including the so-called Latitudinarians) rejected the notion of a fixed, divine order in church and state. They saw the state as a convention rather than a divinely ordained institution; they could normally accept William and Mary or the Hanoverians without recourse to providential design (although the future archbishop John Tillotson employed the notion of "divine right by Providence"). While many of them embraced episcopacy, they could also entertain other possibilities. Similarly, they had some sympathy for dissenters and were willing to consider changes in the liturgy and sacraments to foster comprehension. In any case, they favored conversion by example rather than coercion, emphasizing liberty of conscience rather than control and authority. The Moderates generally allied with the Whigs.[5]

These schematic characterizations suggest two distinct groups with sharply demarcated boundaries. The reality was more complex, and the complexity grew over time. The Moderates at first

---

[5] A pejorative from its inception, Latitudinarianism remains identified with deism and unbelief, political opportunism, and craven servility. See Mark Pattison, "Tendencies of Religious Thought in England, 1688–1750," in *Essays and Reviews*, 9th ed. (London, 1861). On the identification of Latitudinarianism with deism, see Stephen, *History of English Thought*, and G. R. Cragg, *From Puritanism to the Age of Reason* (Cambridge, 1966).

For Latitudinarianism's rehabilitation, see Donald Greene, "The Via Media in an Age of Revolution: Anglicanism in the 18th Century," in *The Varied Pattern: Studies in the 18th Century*, ed. Peter Hughes and David Williams, (Toronto, 1971), 297–320; Roger L. Emerson, "Latitudinarianism and the English Deists," in *Deism, Masonry and the Enlightenment*, ed. J. A. Leo Lemay (Newark, 1987), 19–48; John Spurr, "'Rational Religion' in Restoration England," *Journal of the History of Ideas* (1988): 563–85, and idem, *The Restoration Church of England, 1646–1689* (New Haven, 1991); John Marshall, "The Ecclesiology of the Latitude-men, 1660–1689: Stillingfleet, Tillotson and 'Hobbism,'" *Journal of Ecclesiastical History* 36 (1985): 407–27; Martin Fitzpatrick, "Latitudinarianism at the Parting of the Ways: A Suggestion," in *The Church of England c. 1689– c. 1833: From Toleration to Tractarianism*, 209–27; W. M. Spellman, *The Latitudinarians and the Church of England, 1660–1700* (Athens, 1993); and Gerard Reedy, "Socinians, John Toland and the Anglican Rationalists," *Harvard Theological Review* 70 (1977): 285–304, and idem, *The Bible and Reason: Anglicans and Scripture in Late Seventeenth-Century England* (Philadelphia, 1985).

The perpetuation of the Pattison-Stephen identification of Latitudinarianism with deism can be found in Martin I. J. Griffin, *Latitudinarianism in the Seventeenth-Century Church of England* (Leiden, 1992); Isabel Rivers, *Reason, Grace and Sentiment: A Study of the Language of Religion and Ethics in England, 1660–1780* (New York, 1992); Irene Simon, *Three Restoration Divines: Barrow, South, Tillotson. Selected Sermons*, 3 vols. (Paris, 1967–1976); and Ronald Paulson, *The Beautiful, Novel and Strange: Aesthetics and Heterodoxy* (Baltimore, 1996).

Margaret C. Jacob, *The Newtonians and the English Revolution, 1689–1720* (Ithaca, 1976), imputes undue coherence to Latitudinarianism.

attempted to defend the status quo by advocating ideas such as natural right, natural religion, and Newtonian science, in addition to liberty of conscience—ideas they supposed, or hoped, were common to all Protestants and a bulwark in their two-front war against Roman Catholicism ("popery") and Puritan "inner light" enthusiasm. The Moderates would later use these same ideas to defend the faith, in rapid succession, against High Churchmen, the deists, and then the Methodists. The appearance of new adversaries, such as the deists, highlighted the significant common ground between Moderates and High Churchmen. Moreover, time and circumstance would similarly alter the High Churchmen, making possible unforeseen alliances.

The Moderates first moved into positions of power when, thanks to the Earl of Nottingham, Daniel Finch (1647–1730), William and Mary discovered a number of clergymen who, out of opposition to James II, had left Cambridge fellowships for London livings (John Tillotson, 1630–94; Simon Patrick, 1626–1707; Edward Stillingfleet, 1635–99), and elevated some of them to the episcopacy (from 1689) and, a few years later, one, Tillotson, to the primacy (1691).[6] These fashioners of militant Moderation had experienced the full force of the interregnum and the Glorious Revolution; they were keenly aware of the dire political and social consequences of religious extremism. They aimed at a comprehensive Church that, bolstered by the dissenters, could successfully resist the Catholic menace. The first generation of Moderates saw themselves as the "legitimate heirs of orthodox Anglican tradition," navigating between extreme Calvinism and resurgent Catholicism. In a new "plain style" of preaching they expounded such inherited doctrines as original sin, salvation, and the need for moral reform.[7]

When a Tory–High Church opposition coalesced to defend the status quo ante against the Crown's alliance with the Whigs (ca. 1695), the battle lines sharpened. The zenith of contention came during the reign of Queen Anne under the slogan "the Church in danger." It had two foci. The impeachment (1708–10) of the High Churchman Henry

---

[6] John Gascoigne, *Cambridge in the Age of Enlightenment: Science, Religion and Politics from the Restoration to the French Revolution* (Cambridge, 1989), 40–67; G. V. Bennett, "King William III and the Episcopate," in *Essays in Modern English Church History in Memory of Norman Sykes*, ed. G. B. Bennett and J. D. Walsh (London, 1966), 104–31; H. G. Horwitz, *Revolution Politicks: The Career of Daniel Finch, Second Earl of Nottingham, 1647–1730* (Cambridge, 1968).

[7] Spellman, *The Latitudinarians and the Church of England*, 12; Griffin, *Latitudinarianism in the Seventeenth-Century Church of England*, 14. For Tillotson's sermons, see Gerard Reedy, "Interpreting Tillotson," *Harvard Theological Review* 86 (1993): 81–103.

Sacheverell (1674–1724) for his venomous attacks on the Latitudinarians as "false brethren" provided High Churchmen with a martyr and saint. In contrast, Convocation (1702–5, 1710–14) constituted a virtual High Church counterrevolution in which the lower house of parish clergy vied with the upper house of bishops.[8]

In this militant period, the Boyle Lectures (from 1692), founded by the natural philosopher Robert Boyle (1627–91) to counter heterodoxy and unbelief, became a prominent forum for Moderates.[9] Boyle lecturers such as Richard Bentley (1662–1742), Samuel Clarke (1675–1729), William Whiston (1667–1752) and William Derham (1657–1735) belonged to Moderation's second generation. These were turn-of-the-century men whose experience of political upheaval was restricted to 1688–89, though some were too young even for that. Shaped by the revolution settlement, they were among the first to popularize Newtonian science, construing it as compelling proof of God's handiwork (the argument from design).

The fires of counterrevolution began to dampen with George's accession and the Whig victory (1714). Moderation gained the ascendant as the Hanoverians strove to create a Church-Whig alliance. The issues fueling the High Church cause gradually dissipated, and the dissenters declined in numbers and significance.[10] Over time, the Whigs proved their loyalty to the Church. Moreover, the new threat of various heterodoxies, increasing with the press's freedom after the Licensing Act's lapse in 1695, encouraged the former adversaries to join forces.[11] Patronage also played a role. From the moment of his appointment as bishop of London in 1723, Edmund Gibson worked with the government to appoint bishops loyal to the Protestant succession, important not least because of their votes in the House of Lords.[12]

The High Church–Tory cause died a slow death. Convocation was suppressed through indefinite prorogation (1717). The Occasional Conformity and Schism Acts, infringements on the Act of Toleration enacted during the reign of Queen Anne, were repealed (1719). And a respected leader such as Francis Atterbury (1662–1732) lost credibility

---

[8] G. Holmes, *The Trial of Doctor Sacheverell* (London, 1973); G. Straka, *The Anglican Reaction to the Revolution of 1688* (Madison, 1962).

[9] Jacob, *The Newtonians and the English Revolution*, 32–33, 143–200, John J. Dahm, "Science and Apologetics in the Early Boyle Lectures," *Church History* 39 (1970): 172–86.

[10] Michael Watts, *The Dissenters from the Reformation to the French Revolution* (Oxford, 1978), 371–93.

[11] Chamberlain, *Accommodating High Churchmen*, 8–9, 67–105.

[12] D. R. Hirschberg, "The Government and Church Patronage in England, 1660–1760," *Journal of British Studies* 20 (1980): 109–39; Norman Sykes, *Edmund Gibson: Bishop of London, 1669–1748. A Study in Politics and Religion in the Eighteenth Century* (London, 1926).

when he cast his lot with the Jacobites in 1716, and, when he went into voluntary exile in 1723, accepted defeat.[13]

Moderation was truly triumphant for some three decades after 1730. The High Church party was increasingly disarmed since the Church was patently not in danger. Indeed, the ideological boundaries had so blurred that one could find High Church Whigs as well as Low Church Tories. The Jacobite invasion of 1745 elicited a united front that further welded High Churchmen to the Hanoverian Succession and the Whig ascendancy. Moreover, patronage rested in the hands of the decidedly Whig Duke of Newcastle (Thomas Pelham-Holles [1693–1768], who also played an important role at Cambridge, first as steward and then as chancellor).[14]

Moderation was an integral element of England's "conservative Enlightenment" that clergy and clerisy propagated with the aim of upholding the "constitution in Church and State": in politics the revolution settlement and the Protestant succession, in religion toleration, an established Church and Test Acts.[15] Warburton became one of the most notable advocates of Moderation's third generation, those ecclesiastics who, having grown up in the eighteenth century's relatively stable politics and social relations, defended the status quo in good conscience.

Warburton was well equipped to take up the cudgels on behalf of Moderation. The second of five children whose father (an attorney) died before he completed his eighth year, Warburton was able to attend school until the age of sixteen, when he was articled to an attorney.[16] After successfully finishing his five-year stint, Warburton convinced his family that his heart was with history, antiquity, and literature, and that to be able to continue his studies he should enter the Church. With the help of the local schoolmaster he made up deficiencies in Greek and Latin. In 1723 he was ordained deacon, in 1727 priest. Through family connections he gained preferment: in 1727 a small living at Greasley, Nottinghamshire, and the next year a comfortable one at Brant Broughton, Lincolnshire. In that same year, Warburton's patron

---

[13] G. V. Bennett, *The Tory Crisis in Church and State, 1688–1730: The Career of Francis Atterbury, Bishop of Rochester* (Oxford, 1975).

[14] Gascoigne, *Cambridge in the Age of Enlightenment*, 72–113; Hirschberg, "The Government and Church Patronage in England," 132–38; Chamberlain, *Accommodating High Churchmen*, 79–86; Reed Browning, *The Duke of Newcastle* (New Haven, 1975), 78–79, 186–88.

[15] J.G.A. Pocock, "Clergy and Commerce: The Conservative Enlightenment in England," in *L'Età dei Lumi: Studi Storici sul Settecento Europeo in Onore di Franco Venturi*, 2 vols. (Naples, 1985), 1:523–61.

[16] Richard Hurd, "A Discourse by Way of General Preface," *Works*, 1:1–4.

managed to get his name on George II's visitation list for a master of arts at Cambridge. Finally, he received some additional livings from the Duke of Newcastle (1730).[17]

Warburton spent eighteen years at Brant Broughton in virtually uninterrupted study. The breadth of his reading was legendary: he reportedly had read classical authors known by name alone to Oxford and Cambridge dons. In Dr. Johnson's famous interview with the king, upon being asked whether he had read a great deal, Johnson replied "that he had not read much compared with Dr. Warburton."[18] Yet, as was typical of many autodidacts, his learning was not systematic. Richard Bentley, the distinguished if petulant classicist, said that Warburton "had a voracious appetite for knowledge, but . . . doubted whether he had a good digestion."[19]

During his years at Brant Broughton, Warburton published the two works that established his reputation and his place in the religious Enlightenment: *The Alliance between Church and State* (1737), and *The Divine Legation* (volume 1 appeared in 1738, volume 2 in 1741).

NATURAL RIGHT AND TOLERATION

In the *Alliance between Church and State*, Warburton championed a via media. In his characteristically vituperative style, he depicted the extremes as a catalogue of follies:

> The PAPIST makes the state a creature of the church; the ERASTIAN makes the church a creature of the state; the PRESBYTERIAN would regulate the state on church ideas; the HOBBEIST, the church, on reasons of state: And, to compleat the farce, the QUAKER abolishes the very being of a church; and the MENNONITE suppresses the office of the civil magistrate.[20]

Warburton's via media was a justification of the status quo. He followed the tradition of apologetic for the status quo as a systematic disquisition from first principles as represented by Richard

[17] Hurd, "A Discourse by Way of General Preface"; Evans, *Warburton and the Warburtonians*.

[18] George Birkbeck Hill and L. F. Powell, eds., *Boswell's Life of Johnson*, 6 vols. (Oxford, 1934–50), 2:36.

[19] Quoted in Evans, *Warburton and the Warburtonians*, 18.

[20] *Alliance*, 7:41. His earlier works were *Miscellaneous Translations in Prose and Verse from Roman Poets, Orators and Historians* (1723) and *A Critical and Philosophical Enquiry into the Causes of Prodigies and Miracles as Related by Historians* (1727). See Evans, *Warburton and the Warburtonians*, 10–27.

Hooker (1553–1600; *The Laws of Ecclesiastical Polity*).[21] Warburton aimed

> To furnish every Lover of his country with reasonable principles, to oppose to the destructive Fancies of the Enemies of our happy Establishment. Not to reform the fundamental Constitutions of the State, but to show they needed no reforming.[22]

His account of church-state relations therefore closely resembled the actual, or presumed actual, conditions of Hanoverian England:

> In England alone, the original terms of this convention are kept up so exactly, that this account of Alliance between church and state, seems rather a copy of the Church and State of England, than a theory, as indeed it was, formed solely on the contemplation of nature, and the unvariable reason of things.[23]

For Warburton, the revolution settlement and the Protestant succession were the foundation for "our happy constitution, where gospel-light and civil liberty go hand in hand."[24] He used the natural law arguments usually pitted against establishment and a test law to defend them (the book's subtitle reads *The Necessity and Equity of an Established Religion and a Test Law*).

Warburton's tract was acutely political.[25] Dissenters actively campaigned to get the Corporation and Test Acts repealed during the 1730s. The agitation began with Irish Presbyterians requesting relief from having to "conform" (take annual Communion in the Church of England to hold political office) and resulted in a pamphlet war in which dissenters asserted that the Corporation and Test Acts violated natural rights. The bishop of London, Edmund Gibson, defended the test law and became the focal point of subsequent

[21] W.D.J. Cargill Thompson, "The Philosopher of the 'Politic Society': Richard Hooker as a Political Thinker," in *Studies in the Reformation: Luther to Hooker* (London, 1980), 140–44. For Hooker and the Moderates, see Spellman, *The Latitudinarians and the Church of England*, 16–17, 64–66, 74–77, 157–58. For Warburton arguing from first principles, see *Alliance*, 7:242.

[22] *Alliance*, 7:289–90.

[23] Ibid., 7:166. For the discrepancies between his account and the Church, see R. W. Greaves, "The Working of the Alliance: A Comment on Warburton," in *Essays in Modern English Church History in Memory of Norman Sykes*, ed. G. B. Bennett and J. D. Walsh (London, 1966), 163–79. Cf. Norman Sykes, *Church and State in England in the Eighteenth Century* (Cambridge, 1934), and Walsh, Haydon, and Taylor, eds., *The Church of England c. 1689– c. 1833: From Toleration to Tractarianism*.

[24] Warburton, "The Edification of Gospel Righteousness," in *The Principles of Natural and Revealed Religion, Works*, 9:184.

[25] See the 1765 dedication of the *Divine Legation* at 4:6–7.

debate.[26] Influential dissenters then took the campaign to Parliament, proposing a motion to repeal the Corporation and Test Acts in March 1736 that was soundly defeated. Undeterred, they continued to organize, and even commissioned pamphlets from two sympathetic Anglican clergy (Bishop Hoadly wrote one).[27] A second motion introduced in Parliament was defeated in March 1739 by an insuperable majority.

Warburton defended establishment and a test law with ideas derived largely from the Anglo-Dutch Collegialist tradition. Collegialist theory was at the heart of the seventeenth-century reform of the Reformation, the transition from Reformation militance, especially Calvinist, to tolerance and confessional pluralism. The Reformation had produced the so-called two-kingdom theory according to which church and state, ruled by revelation, were understood to be equal parts of one community.[28] Collegialist thought emerged from the failure to realize the two-kingdom theory and establish a confessional state in Holland in the 1630s and 1640s. Collegialist thinkers denied the notion of a single community ruled by revelation, positing instead that the Church was an independent society or association voluntarily constituted through contract (attesting to the "triumph of natural law in Calvinist speculation").[29] Collegialists advocated the separation of church and state based on the distinction between the spiritual (internal, ecclesiastical) and the civil (external, temporal), promoted a secular understanding of the state by recognizing it to be a human organization with political and civil purposes, and introduced toleration while safeguarding the Church's independence. The Collegialists' retreat from supernatural theories was a renunciation

[26] Richard Burgess Barlow, *Citizenship and Conscience: A Study in the Theory and Practice of Religious Toleration in England during the Eighteenth Century* (Philadelphia, 1962), 57–97; N. C. Hunt, *Two Early Political Associations: The Quakers and the Dissenting Deputies in the Age of Sir Robert Walpole* (Oxford, 1961), 130–53. For the dissenters, see Gerald R. Cragg, *Reason and Authority in the Eighteenth Century* (Cambridge, 1964), 205–13. For Warburton, see Stephen Taylor, "William Warburton and the Alliance of Church and State," *Journal of Ecclesiastical History* 43 (1992): 271. Gibson's pamphlet was *The Dispute Adjusted about the Proper Time of Applying for a Repeal of the Corporation and Test Acts by Shewing That No Time Is Proper* (London, 1732). See Sykes, *Edmund Gibson*, 280–91.

[27] Robert Seagrave, *Observations upon the Conduct of the Clergy* (London, 1738); Benjamin Hoadly, *The Objections against the Repeal of the Corporation and Test Acts Considered* (London, 1739).

[28] W.D.J. Cargill Thompson, "The 'Two Kingdoms' and the 'Two Regiments': Some Problems of Luther's *Zwei-Reiche-Lehre*," in *Studies in the Reformation: Luther to Hooker*, 42–59.

[29] Douglas Nobbs, *Theocracy and Toleration: A Study of the Disputes in Dutch Calvinism from 1600 to 1650* (Cambridge, 1938), 269–70. Cf. Klaus Schlaich, *Kollegialtheorie: Kirche, Recht und Staat in der Aufklärung* (Munich, 1969).

of the Calvinist pretension of supremacy in church and state. Colle-gialist thought became a mainstay of the religious Enlightenment, being used by Protestant, Jewish, and Catholic thinkers as it migrated from Holland and England to the German states and Habsburg lands.

Warburton readily absorbed Collegialism since it coincided with Anglican notions of the Church as a society. For instance, Richard Hooker, Warburton's great predecessor in apologetics, had understood the Church to be a "politic society" that combined natural and super-natural elements.[30] In addition, advocates of toleration from John Mil-ton (1608–74) to Thomas Barlow (1607–91) and John Owen (1616–83) had also treated church and state as separate societies. John Locke was a major figure in this regard: his exile in Holland and his familiarity with Collegialist and Arminian literature epitomized the Anglo-Dutch symbiosis.[31]

Warburton formulated his views of the Church as an independent society vis-à-vis Hooker. Warburton thought Hooker had committed a fundamental error: although he recognized the Church as a "politic society," he collapsed church and state by arguing that they were two names for one society. In opposition to the Puritans, Hooker voiced a version of the very two-kingdom theory that the Collegialists had disputed (Hooker supported royal supremacy, the Dutch Calvinists supported church supremacy). Warburton disagreed, asserting that a nation has the capacity to create an infinite number of independent societies, each with its own ends and contracts. For him, "religion nat-urally and necessarily composes a society, sovereign and independent of the civil."[32] Warburton regarded Hooker as an object lesson in fail-ing to secure the via media:

> Hooker saw plainly, that the Puritan principle . . . necessarily brought in that absurd and fatal evil in politics, an *imperium in imperio*. . . . To combat this principle, which makes the *state a slave to the church*, HOOKER ran into the opposite extreme, which makes the *church a slave to the state*.[33]

---

[30] Cargill Thompson, "The Philosopher of the "Politic Society."

[31] Barlow, *Citizenship and Conscience*, 26–42. Cf. G. C. Gibbs, "The Role of the Dutch Republic as the Intellectual Entrepôt of Europe in the Seventeenth and Eighteenth Centuries," *Bijdragen en mededelingen betreffende de geschiedenis der Nederlanden* 86 (1971): 323–49.

[32] *Alliance*, 7:171. Cf. 7:116, 215, 211–12. Warburton cited Pierre de Marca (1594–1662) at *Alliance*, 7:212.

[33] Ibid., 7:218.

On behalf of the status quo, Warburton enlisted the natural right and contract theory which, since the mid-seventeenth century, opponents had regularly used against government and establishment. He argued that civil society arises from a compact: at first "constituted for the sake of living," it is, echoing Aristotle, "carried on for the sake of happy living." Following in Locke's tradition of negative rather than positive liberty, Warburton understood the social contract as a restraint: "society" was "invented for a remedy against injustice" rather than to attain some imagined ideal. Civil society required an additional force that could oblige its members to observe "the duties of *imperfect obligation*, which human Laws overlook," and "those duties of *perfect obligation* which human Laws cannot reach, or sufficiently enforce."[34] Religion is that force through its "sanction of rewards." Civil society cannot function without religion.

Warburton's argument was also informed by the Collegialist distinction between body and soul, action and opinion. The state's jurisdiction extends only to men's bodies, its power to their actions; the state can punish sins but not opinions. Because religion's end is "to procure the Favour of God" and "to advance and improve our own intellectual Nature," it has the right to promote morality through the gift of ultimate rewards. Just as civil society needs the protection of the state, so religion needs the Church. The Church can attain "purity of Worship," its "immediate end," through the power of excommunication. Its "ultimate end, the salvation of souls," is not susceptible to coercion. The Church can best serve its function if constituted as "an independency without coercive power."[35]

Warburton followed the Collegialists and Locke in distinguishing between acceptable and unacceptable forms of excommunication. To preserve "uniformity," he vouchsafed the Church the minor ban, namely, excluding individuals from worship. The major ban was indefensible since, by excluding the individual from society, it impinged on civil standing and infringed natural law.[36]

Warburton deliberately abjured divine right (jure divino) arguments. Divine right arguments on behalf of the state gradually gave way after 1689 to notions of "providential right" and "right by conquest." The Hanoverian Succession largely put such arguments to rest. Divine right

[34] *Alliance*, 7:38. Cf. 7:27, 25. For positive and negative liberty, see Isaiah Berlin, *Two Concepts of Liberty* (Oxford, 1958). For the distinction between perfect (enforceable) and imperfect (unenforceable) rights, see Pufendorf, *De jure naturae et gentium* (1672), bk. 1, chap. 7, sec. 7. My thanks to Johann P. Sommerville for this reference.

[35] *Alliance*, 7:71. Cf. 7:55, 7:66.

[36] Ibid., 7:69.

arguments on behalf of the church were similarly contested by Whigs, Erastians, and Low Churchmen, with Edmund Gibson's famous compilation of ecclesiastical law (1713) being perhaps the most authoritative assault. Nonetheless, the High Church party continued to proffer such arguments until mid-century or later. Warburton thought the supposedly irresistible claims of divine right arguments resulted in intolerance. He instead thought church-state relations combined the human and divine: everything God-given had to be made usable by man.[37]

Warburton's opponents thought establishment and a test law were "the two great solecisms in modern politics." He tried to show that they were the "the instruments of an enlightened liberty" by guaranteeing toleration and liberty of conscience.[38]

Having separated church and state in theory as independent associations, Warburton connected them in practice: he advocated a "coalition" or "artful insertion" of the two. "The Church should serve the State, and the State protect the Church." This end is best reached through the church's establishment, a "free convention" that requires "joint consent" and accords with natural law. The state can "improve the natural efficacy of religion" by assuming responsibility for clerical salaries, giving the Church the right to vote in the House of Lords, and protecting it with a test law. The state, in turn, derives two benefits from such an alliance. It neutralizes the Church as a source of sedition and faction by linking the clergy to itself. In addition, it acquires "supremacy in matters ecclesiastical" by retaining power over church appointments, the convocation of synods, and the execution of writs of excommunication.[39]

The Church's establishment resulted in the state gaining the power to curtail opinions that impinged on the commonweal. To be sure, Warburton had already maintained that the magistrate should have power over opinions relating to "natural religion"—which he identified as God, providence, and the essential distinction between good and evil—since these are "the very foundation and bond of Civil Policy." Yet he went further. Even though granting the magistrate power over opinions would seem to fly in the face of Collegialism's division between action and opinion, Warburton defended it by pointing

[37] Ibid., 7:23, 39. For divine right theory, see Gerald Straka, "The Final Phase of Divine Right Theory in England, 1688–1702," *English Historical Review*" 77 (1962): 638–58, and idem, *Anglican Reaction to the Revolution of 1688* (Madison, WI, 1962), 81. For the theory's persistence, see J.C.D. Clark, *English Society, 1688–1832: Ideology, Social Structure and Political Practice during the Ancien Régime* (Cambridge, 1985), 119–98. Gibson's book was *Codex juris Ecclesiastici Anglicani* (1713).

[38] *Alliance*, 7:21. See Greaves, "The Working of the Alliance," 166.

[39] *Alliance*, 7:40, 164, 89, 160, 153.

to the differing purposes of civil society and religion. Civil society aims to help man attain happiness *here*, whereas "the means of his happiness *hereafter* is contemplation." Should the two conflict, then the opinions involved must be either "no truths, or truths of no importance." Warburton here voiced an assumption underpinning his entire argument: "truth and utility do necessarily coincide." So long as a government is legitimate and has the consent of the people, then "to abridge a citizen of his civil rights for matters of opinion which affect society, is no violation of justice or natural equity."[40]

Warburton claimed that an alliance between church and state was not Erastianism in disguise. The "Church by law established" arises from a free compact and remains a free subject: the Alliance "takes off their [the clergy's] independency, and makes them free subjects, but not the tools of civil power." Nevertheless, Warburton maintained that the state's utility is uppermost: "the true end for which religion is established is, not to provide for the true faith, but for civil utility." In keeping, he claimed that the alliance with the church is "perpetual but not irrevocable." The state chooses the church whose adherents comprise a majority; should the church lose its majority, the state can transfer its alliance.[41] Yet Warburton also insisted that no disjunction existed between church and state: "public utility and truth do coincide."

That utility is the basis of establishment is of cardinal importance, since it justifies toleration. Were religion established by a claim to absolute and exclusive truth, great "mischief"—persecution—would ensue.[42] In the Restoration period, High Churchmen vindicated intolerance: using force did not constitute coercion if, linked to edification and conducted with pastoral concern, it was directed to the will rather than to understanding. These writers drew on such Catholic sources as Augustine and Aquinas.[43] Warburton renounced such Reformation-style assertions of "true religion" because they contradicted the law of nature: restraints would turn to punishment of opinions and civil rights would be violated. Warburton criticized Hooker on this very score: his theory led to "persecution for opinions."[44] Warburton defended an established church based on utility rather than on absolute truth, since it served as a bulwark of toleration. He offered similar utilitarian justifications for a test law. It aimed to keep hostile sectarians from gaining entrance to offices that had power over the Church of

[40] Ibid., 7:45, 264–67.
[41] Ibid., 7:99, 287, 243.
[42] Ibid., 7:275, 283ff.
[43] Goldie, "The Theory of Religious Intolerance in Restoration England," 331–68.
[44] *Alliance*, 7:285, 222.

England; it served as a "restraint" against civil rather than doctrinal evils: "the pain inflicted by a test-law is no more than just necessary to repel *the evil of diversity of sects when got into the administration*; and, consequently, that it is a *restraint only*."[45] Were its aim the "extension" of the established church through the inclusion of sectarians, then the test law would be a form of coercion and a violation of natural rights. In fact, its aim was the "protection" of the "national church."[46]

Warburton's sources are noteworthy. In addition to Anglo-Dutch Collegialism, Hooker, and Locke, Warburton also relied on two of the most prominent proponents of the Gallican church, Pierre de Marca (1594–1662) and Jacques-Benigne Bossuet (1627–1704) (their works also influenced Reform Catholic thinkers, including Eybel and Lamourette). Warburton cited them in regard to such ecclesiastical issues as the nature of the established church and excommunication. Warburton could use these Catholic thinkers, since their defense of Gallican or state-church prerogatives freed them from the taint of popery.[47] Warburton's Moderation characteristically included varied strands of thought.

In later editions of the *Alliance*, Warburton made special efforts to criticize Rousseau. In the *Contrat social* (1762), Rousseau had taken issue with Warburton's contention that Christianity could be beneficial to the state, asserting that its influence could only be pernicious. Warburton argued that Rousseau "instead of the *spirit of Christianity* has given us the *spirit of Popery*." While Rousseau's arguments might hold for Roman Catholicism, they did not apply to the rest of Christianity, least of all to the Church of England.[48]

The *Alliance between Church and State* made Warburton's reputation; "an obscure country parson residing upon his cure" had articulated a model natural rights vindication of the status quo.[49] Recognized as nearly authoritative, the book became a point of reference for all parties to the discussion of establishment and a test law.[50] For example,

---

[45] Ibid., 7:256.

[46] Ibid., 7:260.

[47] Warburton cited de Marca at 7:29, 107, 157, 161–62, 167–68. The work, *De concordia sacerdotti et imperii: Epistola ad Cardinalem de Richielieu* (1641), appeared on the Papal Index, and de Marca recanted. Warburton cited Bossuet at 7:69–70, 87.

[48] *Alliance*, 7:207. See 7:175–208. Rousseau's *Contrat social* was published in 1762; these criticisms were not in the earliest editions. See Evans, *Warburton and the Warburtonians*, 47.

[49] See Greaves, "The Working of the Alliance," 163.

[50] For the importance of the *Alliance*, see Barlow, *Citizenship and Conscience*, 55; Evans, *Warburton and the Warburtonians*, 46–47; and Sykes, *Church and State*, 318–26. For Warburton's arguments being "personal and idiosyncratic," see Taylor, "William Warburton and the Alliance of Church and State," 271–86.

Blackstone cited Warburton in his famous compendium of English law (1769); dissenters attacked him in the 1760s and 1770s when again trying to repeal the Test Act; and during the early years of the French Revolution, Nicolas Bonneville (1760–1828), a key Girondin, criticized Warburton's understanding of the relationship between state and religion.[51]

This aspect of Warburton's "heroic moderation" could not have been more successful. Yet it would be a mistake to follow the commentators who have seen his book as a fundamentally secular approach to church-state relations. Warburton's sources alone demonstrate the *Alliance*'s religious character. The case is stronger still. Warburton conceived of the book as the first part of the monumental work, *The Divine Legation of Moses Demonstrated*, which began to appear the next year. Warburton's *Alliance* belongs to his historical theology.[52]

HISTORY

The Divine Legation of Moses Demonstrated was one of the most erudite and influential treatises of eighteenth-century historical theology. Warburton attempted to reclaim the ideas the deists had used to discredit Christianity: the method of history and the ideas of natural religion and natural right. He also employed history to defend established religion. At the same time, he aimed to correct some of the mistaken notions about Judaism and Christianity that believers had articulated in debate with the deists. He waged a two-front battle on behalf of a middle way of justification by faith and morality.[53]

To reclaim history from the deists, Warburton set out to prove that scripture remained its definitive source. By renewing inherited exegetical methods, he tried to demonstrate that the relationship between

---

[51] Sir William Blackstone, *Commentaries on the Laws of England* (London, 1769), 4:53. On Warburton's uses, see Barlow, *Citizenship and Conscience*, 137, 160, 164, 167, 188. For Bonneville, see *De l'esprit des religions* (Paris, 1791), and Hans Maier, *Revolution and Church: The Early History of Christian Democracy, 1789–1901*, trans. Emily M. Schossberger (Notre Dame, IN, 1965), 130–31.

[52] For the secular view, see Barlow, *Citizenship and Conscience*, 16. In contrast, see Hurd, "A Discourse by Way of General Preface," *Works*, 1:21; and Evans, *Warburton and the Warburtonians*, 31.

[53] Critics pointed out the work's inordinate length (2,300 pages of text and notes in the 1811 edition) and numerous digressions and polemics. Warburton asserted it was not "an indigested and inconnected heap of discourses, thrown out upon one another to disburthern a commonplace." *Divine Legation*, in *Works*, 6:104.

natural and revealed religion could be understood only on the basis of scripture's "internal" evidence.[54]

Warburton's central argument, a syllogism, rested on a so-called "omission": Judaism lacked a concept of the future life. For this reason it had to have functioned under a special providence:

> Whatever Religion and Society have no future state for their support, must be supported by an extraordinary providence;
> The Jewish Religion and Society had no future state for their support; therefore the Jewish Religion and Society were supported by an extraordinary Providence.[55]

Warburton wanted to defend Judaism's divine origin and its inextricable link to Christianity. Some deists had attacked Christianity by disparaging its Jewish foundations; some believers had severed Judaism from Christianity in order to defend the latter. Warburton objected that all such reconfigurations were untrue to history and God's plan: they lose "all true conception of that divine harmony which inspires every part, and runs through the whole of God's great Dispensation to Mankind."[56] Warburton tried to establish Judaism and Christianity's true nature by delineating their relationship to natural religion.

Warburton recognized that the deists had stolen some of the Moderates' best arguments. The very ideas of natural religion, natural law, and reasonableness that the Moderates had used against enthusiasts, the deists turned into a stick with which to beat the Church: clerical corruption first distorted pristine natural religion and then became the basis for civil oppression. The deists believed that claims to jure divino authority in the church were inseparable from those in the state and responsible for civil and clerical tyranny. Historically explicated clerical authority was one of deism's defining issues.[57]

Its other defining issue was the elevation of reason and nature above revelation. Most of the deists held "the light of nature" and reason to be adequate sources of knowledge: while they acknowledged the existence of God, they claimed that the natural religion found in the Bible was sufficient to ground morality and, if conjoined with natural right

---

[54] *Divine Legation*, 1:193–97, 5:156; cf. the appendix to the first edition of the *Alliance between Church and State*, 7:299–304.

[55] *Divine Legation*, 3:332.

[56] Ibid., 5:293.

[57] For deism and history, see Richard Popkin, "The Deist Challenge," in *From Persecution to Toleration: The Glorious Revolution and Religion in England*, ed. Ole Peter Grell, Jonathan Israel, and Nicholas Tyacke (Oxford, 1991), 195–215, and Jonathan Sheehan, *The Enlightenment Bible: Translation, Scholarship, Culture* (Princeton, 2005), 27–53.

in a civil theology, to establish society. For many of them Christianity represented merely a "republication" of natural religion.[58]

In the debates of the 1720s and 1730s, the Moderates' challenge was to find a middle way to refute the deists without giving ground to either enthusiasts or High Churchmen. The answer lay in history.

Throughout the seventeenth century, the deists had found ways to evade the censor and circulate manuscripts or publish books—as early as the 1670s clergymen had felt the need to address the specter of deism. With the lapse of the last Licensing Act (1695), deism found its public voice: deist publications proliferated, and a debate began that peaked in the 1720s and 1730s.[59]

Numerous Anglican apologists weighed in, employing various strategies. Some of the earliest apologists, especially the Boyle lecturers, used Newtonian science to defend revealed religion. Samuel Clark put forward philosophical arguments inspired by the mathematical method: he tried to demonstrate natural religion's credibility as well as Christianity's necessity. Many apologists tried to put Locke's sensationalist epistemology in the service of belief. Bishop George Berkeley took another approach in developing an immaterialist philosophy to attack the "freethinkers." Perhaps the most enduring philosophical apology was Bishop Joseph Butler's *Analogy of Religion, Natural and Revealed* (1736): he argued that probability should make any reasonable man a believer in revelation and the Christian dispensation.[60]

Warburton's apologetic was historical: he showed that the concept of natural religion neither questioned nor qualified the validity of

---

[58] Emerson, "Latitudinarianism and the English Deists," 19–48. Useful, despite identifying Latitudinarianism with deism, are Robert Sullivan, *John Toland and the Deist Controversy: A Study in Adaptation* (Cambridge, MA, 1982), and Cragg, *From Puritanism to the Age of Reason*, 136–56. For deism as a radical Protestant and often republican extension of Erastianism that engendered anticlericalism but not unbelief, see J.A.I. Champion, *The Pillars of Priestcraft Shaken: The Church of England and Its Enemies, 1660–1730* (Cambridge, 1992), and Henning Graf Reventlow, *The Authority of the Bible and the Rise of the Modern World* (Philadelphia, 1985). Tindal introduced the idea of Christianity as a "republication" in *Christianity as Old as the Creation* (London, 1730).

[59] Bishop Stillingfleet, *Letter to a Deist, in Answer to Several Objections against the Truth and Authority of the Scriptures* (London, 1677). On the deist debate, see Roland Stromberg, *Religious Liberalism in 18th-Century England* (Oxford, 1954), 52–89.

[60] For the Boyle Lectures, see Jacob, *The Newtonians and the English Revolution*; Cragg, *From Puritanism to the Age of Reason*, 87–113; and John Dahm, "Science and Apologetics in the Early Boyle Lectures," *Church History* 39 (1970): 172–86. For Samuel Clark, see *A Demonstration of the Being and Attributes of God* (London, 1705) and *A Discourse Concerning the Unchangeable Obligations of Natural Religion and the Truth and Certainty of the Christian Revelation* (London, 1706). For Locke and Anglican apologetics, see John W. Yolton, *Locke and the Way of Ideas* (Oxford, 1956), 181–202. See Berkeley's dialogue, *Alciphron* (1732). For Butler, see Mossner, *Bishop Butler and the Age of Reason*.

revelation. From the outset, mankind was subject to natural religion. By instilling reason in Adam and Eve, God had given them the rudiments of natural religion and natural law. They lived by that law until their admission to paradise, at which point they lived under God's will. Adam and Eve's fall cost mankind immortality. According to Warburton, "Faith alone justifieth, or, in other words, is the *sole condition* of recovering the possession of what we lost by Adam."[61]

Warburton gave natural religion a Christian definition by arguing it was not inherently connected to the idea of a future life. The usual association with the future life (the triad of God, Providence, and the future life) was merely accidental. Rather, he quoted St. Paul to assert that natural religion consists of two beliefs: "that *God is, and he is a rewarder of them who seek him.*"[62]

Warburton understood natural religion on the basis of "scripture history." The corruption after the Fall resulted in mankind's loss of natural religion, including the idea of the one God. God chose the Jews as the medium to restore the ideas of natural religion and His unity. "The *Mosaic Religion* was a republication of *natural Religion* to the Jews."[63] God delivered the Mosaic religion in an "extraordinary" manner, albeit without vouchsafing any new knowledge. The Mosaic legislation acknowledged the creator and rewards, and the rewards were given in this world:

> When God separated a chosen People, he gave them, for their Belief, the principles of NATURAL RELIGION (*republished* by the Ministry of Moses) in its ORIGINAL and most perfect Form, under an *equal Providence . . .* which sets it far above its PUBLICATION amongst the Gentiles by natural light.[64]

Jesus first restored to mankind the gift of immortality Adam had lost. Christianity agrees with yet transcends natural religion by offering definite knowledge of a future state—an argument Moderates had made at the end of the seventeenth century.[65] For Warburton, two mistaken assumptions had become commonplace: that a future state is

---

[61] *Divine Legation*, 6:305, 246–47.

[62] Ibid., 3:338. Cf. 3:350–51. Warburton defined natural religion as "the being of a God; his providence over human affairs; the natural essential difference of moral good and evil." Cf. *Divine Legation*, 7:45.

[63] *Divine Legation*, 3:350. See *Alliance*, 7:171: "The Jewish religion was, like the true natural, which it ratified. . . ."

[64] *Divine Legation*, 3:351.

[65] Ibid., 1:286. Spellman, *The Latitudinarians and the Church of England*, 89–111.

integral to natural religion and that it is the same one the Gospel promised:

> Natural light discovers to us nothing of the Nature of that [future] State; and therefore leaves the mind in that situation in which an indefinite reward puts it. The Gospel, indeed, defines a future state so fully, as to enable the doctrine to purify and spiritualize the Mind, above all modes of Religion.[66]

Warburton had stolen the deists' thunder. He conceded that the content of revealed religion can be a mere "republication" of the religion of nature, yet insisted this applied to Judaism, not Christianity. At the same time, the manner in which Judaism received knowledge was "extraordinary." He thereby used natural religion to defend the revealed religions ("Let the Friends of Revelation, however, constantly and uniformly hold the inseparable connexion between the two Dispensations") as well as to show Christianity's superiority.[67] He had demonstrated "the divine harmony which inspires every part, and runs through the whole of God's great Dispensation to Mankind."

Warburton's refutation of deism required him to defend Judaism. One of the deists' central objections was Judaism's claim to an exclusive revelation. How could God have revealed Himself to one people rather than all mankind? Was an exclusive revelation not opposed to universal knowledge of God? Did this particularism not disprove the claims to revelation?[68]

Warburton answered this objection by arguing that God chose the Jews in order to prepare the way for His revelation to all mankind through Jesus. Judaism was "good" in its time, whereas Christianity is good for everyone at all times:

> It [Judaism] was *relatively good* . . . as it fully answered the design of God who gave it; which was, to preserve a chosen People, separate from the rest of mankind, to be a repository for the doctrine of the UNITY; and to prepare the way for the further Revelation of a Religion *absolutely good*, or a Religion for the use of all Mankind.[69]

---

[66] *Divine Legation*, 3:353. Locke had Jesus introducing a future state. See *Reasonableness of Christianity*, in *Works of John Locke*, 7:149.

[67] *Divine Legation*, 6:43.

[68] Tindal, *Christianity as Old as the Creation*. See also John Toland, *Christianity Not Mysterious* (London, 1696).

[69] *Divine Legation*, 3:339.

In other words, "the Jewish Religion was the great mean, employed by Providence of bringing *all men to* Christ."[70]

To make the Jews the "mean[s]" entailed freeing them from the idolatry and paganism they had absorbed in Egypt as well as subjecting them to a special administration to prevent recidivism.[71] With this goal in mind, God instituted the Mosaic legislation.

The Mosaic legislation was informed by God's practice of "accommodat[ing] his Institutions to the state, the condition and contracted habits, of his creatures." God introduced an intricate and detailed ritual that outwardly resembled the practices the Jews had acquired in Egypt, yet in design and intent was contrary to them. This combination of conformity and opposition was the pedagogic device by which God hoped to free the Jews from idolatry and lead them to true belief. Warburton asserted that when cast in this light, the "ritual law . . . is seen to be an Institution of the most beautiful and sublime contrivance."[72]

Yet God went still further to liberate the Jews from idolatry. He established a theocracy, a polity that appealed to the Jews since it resembled the Egyptian practice of worshipping "tutelary" deities. Therefore, "the Almighty . . . in condescension to the prejudices of the Israelites, assumed the title of a tutelary local God, and chose Judea for his peculiar regency."[73]

In this theocracy, God was the judge who punished the people's "transgressions with severity."[74] The Jews received their just deserts in this world; there was no need for future rewards and punishments. Theocracy was the "extraordinary" Providence that made it possible for the Jews to conform to "natural religion" without knowledge of a future life. Theocracy constituted a unique form of government:

> a Policy differing from all the Institutions of mankind; in which the two Societies, civil and religious, were perfectly incorporated, with GOD ALMIGHTY, AS A TEMPORAL GOVERNOR, at the head of both.[75]

Theocracy aimed to eradicate idolatry by being "the reverse of Paganism: for there Kings became Gods; whereas here, God condescended to become King."[76]

---

[70] Ibid., 3:342. Cf. 4:22.

[71] Ibid., 4:22.

[72] Ibid., 4:301. Cf. 4:323, 329.

[73] Ibid., 5:51.

[74] Ibid., 5:30. See also 5:37, 51, 169.

[75] Ibid., 5:1. The Jewish theocracy was "a form of government different in kind from all human policies whatsoever" and "peculiar and singular." See *Alliance*, 7:51, 217. He rued Protestants' attempts, especially Puritans, to imitate it. See *Divine Legation*, 7:51–52.

[76] *Divine Legation*, 5:37.

Two aspects of this theocracy recall Warburton's *The Alliance between Church and State*. Theocracy perfectly accorded with natural law. The severe laws that kept the Jews from idolatry would have been unjust were they civil laws a magistrate administered. In a theocracy, however, control over opinions as well as severe punishments were entirely appropriate. Similarly, God did not trespass on the people's natural rights in appointing Himself king or, later, in appointing a human king as His deputy. God's actions always left "the rights of mankind inviolate."[77]

By construing theocracy to be historically specific, Warburton rejected the Calvinists' presumption to it, a presumption that was fresh in contemporaries' minds in, for example, Holland, Geneva, and Cromwell's commonwealth. In *The Alliance between Church and State*, Warburton called these Calvinist experiments examples of "the Jewish dispensation ill understood" that threatened to turn Protestantism into popery.[78]

Warburton's frequent use of the words "accommodation" and "condescension" shows that he answered the deists' objections by giving a new twist to the venerable exegetical principle of accommodation. The notion that God had to "condescend" to make His infinite wisdom comprehensible to finite human understanding, "accommodating" it to the circumstances of human life, permeated Christian and Jewish Biblical exegesis from the time of the Church fathers and the early rabbis. Christians used it to explain how the older Jewish forms of worship had been superseded and thus to assert, in intramural debates, the appropriate form of Christian worship and belief. Jewish exegetes used the principle to explain the pedagogic function of the law and biblical anthropomorphisms. Thinkers such as Augustine and Maimonides used it to reconcile history and revelation.[79]

Warburton acknowledged his debt to "the great Maimonides" on two counts. The Mosaic legislation (especially sacrifices) was God's way of accommodating the Jews' prejudices while weaning them from idolatry, and it belonged entirely to this world.[80] Warburton used the

---

[77] Ibid., 5:23. Cf. 5:22–23, 84, 93.

[78] *Alliance*, 7:51–52.

[79] Stephen D. Benin, *The Footprints of God: Divine Accommodation in Jewish and Christian Thought* (Albany, NY, 1993); Amos Funkenstein, *Theology and the Scientific Imagination from the Middle Ages to the Seventeenth Century* (Princeton, 1986), 213–70. Locke used it in *The Reasonableness of Christianity* at 7:2 ("condescencion to our understanding"), 7:152 ("accommodated to our notions and prejudices"), and 7:154 ("proper accommodations to the apprehensions of those they were writ to").

[80] *Divine Legation*, 4:362. Warburton included Maimonides in the curriculum he designed for students of theology. See "Directions for the Study of Theology," in *Works*, 10:361–62. For the popularity of Maimonides' chapter on the sacrifices in his *The Guide of the Perplexed*, see Frank E. Manuel, *The Eighteenth Century Confronts the Gods* (Cambridge, MA, 1959), 8.

principle of accommodation to redefine theocracy: the Jews could live without knowledge of a future life because they were under an extraordinary providence that, in its policies and approaches, was tailored to their time and place.[81] Warburton thereby fashioned a middle way between the deists' and Christians' misconceptions.[82]

Despite his tribute to Maimonides, Warburton's notion of accommodation was closer to that of John Spencer (1630–93), the principle's greatest early modern expositor. The medieval exegetes had been content to show the correspondence between pagan practice and Mosaic precept. In contrast, Spencer attempted to reconstruct the pagan mentality. Despite his Christian disdain for pagan Egypt, he recognized it as the source of Judaism, regarded Moses as an Egyptian-educated Hebrew, and devoted considerable effort to a detailed exposition of Egyptian culture and religion. Spencer's approach was eminently historical: in the seventeenth and eighteenth centuries, demonological and allegorical explanations of paganism increasingly gave way to historical ones.[83]

That Warburton followed Spencer in a historical explanation of mentality is evident in his approach to the Mosaic law:

> to form a right idea of that Institution, it will be necessary to know the genius and manners of the HEBREW PEOPLE; though it be, as we conceive, of divine appointment: and still more necessary to understand the character and abilities of their LAWGIVER, if it be, as our adversaries pretend, only of human.[84]

What were Warburton's criteria for understanding what he repeatedly called "Scripture history" or "sacred history"?[85] He tried to balance between the various sources of "sacred and profane history."[86] Although he employed Greek writers as well as scripture, he ascribed

[81] Accommodation would compromise the truth of doctrines. See *Divine Legation*, 6:392.

[82] Ibid., 5:1–2. For other Moderates using accommodation, see Reedy, *The Bible and Reason*, 44; Reventlow, *The Authority of the Bible and the Rise of the Modern World*, 240; and R. S. Crane, "Anglican Apologetics and the Idea of Progress, 1699–1745," in *The Idea of the Humanities and Other Essays Critical and Historical* (Chicago, 1967), 214–87.

[83] Warburton acknowledged John Spencer's *De Legibus Hebraeorum Ritualibus* (1685), at *Divine Legation*, 4:301. For Spencer, see Jan Assmann, *Moses the Egyptian: The Memory of Egypt in Western Monotheism* (Cambridge, MA, 1997), 55–79. For historical approaches, see Funkenstein, *Theology and the Scientific Imagination*, 242–43, and Manuel, *The Eighteenth Century Confronts the Gods*, passim.

[84] *Divine Legation*, 4:79.

[85] Ibid., 4:278, 299, 447, 5:52, 18–19. Warburton used "scripture history" to defend Pope. See *A Critical and Philosophical Commentary on Mr. Pope's Essay on Man*, in *Works*, 11:97–98, 116–17.

[86] *Divine Legation*, 4:116.

uncontested authority to scripture and reason: no discrepancy could arise between the historical account that emerges from scripture and an external source:

> Whatever therefore they [the Greek sources] say of the high antiquity of Egypt, unsupported by the reason of the thing, or the testimony of holy Scripture, shall never be employed in this inquiry; but whatever Reason and Scripture seem to contradict, whether it serve the one or other purpose, I shall always totally reject.[87]

Warburton's use of history came to the fore in his treatment of ancient Egyptian culture. Was Egypt an advanced culture that heavily influenced the Israelites, or was it a relatively primitive one that did not? In Warburton's day so renowned an advocate of revelation as Isaac Newton argued for the primitive state of Egyptian culture and society, and thus against the evidence of the Bible, in order to establish Judaism's antiquity. In contrast, the deists used the Bible to argue for Judaism's derivative nature.[88]

Newton's efforts in general resembled Warburton's: he was determined to uphold the accuracy of the Bible as a source of history. He treated the Bible as the most faithful and accurate guide to events. He tried to supplement that account with scientific evidence: he used astronomy, and in particular the precession of the equinoxes, to determine the chronology of events. To assemble that astronomical information, Newton combed a vast array of arcane ancient texts. For Newton, the two unassailable forms of factual knowledge were the Bible and empirical science.

Yet Newton differed from Warburton by insisting that Judaism was both more ancient than Egyptian and Greek culture and the very font of civilization. He held that conventional accounts made the Greek and Egyptian civilizations too old: Solomon's reign was the first great ancient monarchy and the source of all forms of wisdom and learning. This view was obviously at odds with the Bible itself, which showed Egypt as an advanced kingdom at the time of the Israelite's exodus.[89]

Warburton tried to correct the reversal between believers and deists in order to reestablish scripture as a source of history. Following Spencer's

---

[87] Ibid., 4:86.

[88] Ibid., 4:80. Toland made his argument in *Origines Judaicae* (London, 1709).

[89] Isaac Newton, *The Chronology of Ancient Kingdoms Amended* (London, 1728). See Frank Manuel, *Isaac Newton, Historian* (Cambridge, MA, 1963), 66, 89, 99, 133. On Warburton's criticism of Newton, see 180–81. See also Richard Popkin, "Newton as a Bible Scholar," in *Essays on The Context, Nature and Influence of Isaac Newton's Theology*, ed. James E. Force and Richard H. Popkin, (Dordrecht, 1990), 103–18.

lead, he showed that the Bible was accurate in depicting Egypt as an advanced culture. Using the principle of accommodation, he maintained that the Mosaic legislation represented something radically new, even if many elements derived from Egyptian practices.[90] The principle of accommodation enabled him to confirm both the Bible's credibility as a historical source and the Mosaic law's uniqueness.

Warburton was historical rather than historicist in maintaining the unity between the biblical text's literal and verbal meanings. Outside sources did not represent true history in opposition to the biblical account. Since history was part of scripture rather than independent of it, Warburton was able to recognize historical change without relativizing revelation. This use of history was characteristic of Moderation.[91]

Warburton also expressed his historical stance by opposing the nascent documentary hypothesis, namely, that the various names of God denoted distinct strands of the text that were written at different times. This notion first appeared in the works of Spinoza (1632–77) and Richard Simon (1638–1712). The early Moderates were unable to form a coherent response.[92] Warburton used the principle of accommodation to counter this effort to dissolve the text into its alleged component parts. For example, he asserted that the name Jehovah was introduced at a late point in order to serve the Jewish people, who were saturated with Egyptian prejudices ("This compliance with the *Religion of Names* was a new indulgence to the prejudices of this people"), adding that there was no basis to the claim of separate authors.[93] In response to Spinoza, he argued that "some blind manu-

[90] For Spencer, see Assmann, *Moses the Egyptian*, 65, 71. For Warburton's understanding of Egyptian culture, see ibid., 96–115. Warburton's treatment of hieroglyphs was famous on the Continent, being translated and reprinted numerous times, most recently by Jacques Derrida. Siegmund Jacob Baumgarten, in the preface to Romelyn de Hooghe *Hieroglyphica, oder Denkbilder der Alten Volker* (Amsterdam, 1744), called Warburton's treatment "an extensive, scholarly and fundamental consideration of the Egyptian hieroglyphs." See P. Rossi, *The Dark Abyss of Time* (Chicago, 1984), 236–45, and Assmann, *Moses the Egyptian*, 104ff., 242 n. 45. For criticism of the postmodernist use, see J. Milbank, "William Warburton: An Eighteenth-Century Bishop Fallen among Post-Structuralists," *New Blackfriars* 64 (1983): 315–24, 374–83.

[91] Such Moderates as Edward Stillingfleet (1635–99) and Thomas Burnet (1635–1715) maintained that scriptural history was more reliable than secular history. See Reedy, *The Bible and Reason*, 40–45, and Hans Frei, *The Eclipse of Biblical Narrative: A Study in Eighteenth- and Nineteenth-Century Hermeneutics* (New Haven, 1974).

[92] Hans-Joachim Kraus, *Geschichte der historisch-kritischen Erforschung des Alten Testaments*, 2nd ed. (Neukirchen, 1969), 44–73. Early Moderates knew Simon's books, which were translated in the 1680s. See Reedy, *The Bible and Reason*, 107–13, 146–55.

[93] *Divine Legation*, 4:286. Warburton quoted M. Astruc, *Conjectures sur le livre de la Genèse*, at 4:287.

script is always at hand to support the blinder Criticism," and added, "had more time been employed in the study of the nature of Scripture History and somewhat less in collations of manuscripts, those would have found a nearer way to the wood, who now cannot see wood for trees."[94]

Warburton took issue with the deists' version of biblical history by focusing on Voltaire and Bolingbroke. Warburton thought Voltaire's attack on ancient Judaism was indefensible. Voltaire had contended that "human sacrifices made a part of the Mosaic ritual," seeing it condoned in the case of Jephta's daughter (Judges 11) and in the conquest of the land of Canaan (when women and children were understood to be "devoted" for such sacrifice). Warburton carefully analyzed the relevant biblical passages to show that Voltaire had misconstrued the evidence.[95] Warburton attacked Bolingbroke, the Tory and deist, for his attempt to strip Moses of his divine mission and make him a mere human legislator, or, worse, to make God and Moses "deceivers." Here again, Warburton turned the historical evidence of the Bible against the deists. Other moderates, such as Edmund Gibson, similarly defended scripture against deist attacks.[96]

Warburton proposed an alternative to the deists' anticlerical reading of history: he held that politicians, rather than priests, created political tyranny and corrupted religion. Pharoah, and not the priests, decided to keep the invention of writing secret from the people. Moreover, the greatest imposters in history—"Mahomet, Ignatius Loyola and Oliver Cromwell"—although they began as religious fanatics, became politicians: "the most successful Impostors . . . have set out in all the blaze of Fanaticism, and completed their schemes amidst the cool depth and stillness of politics." True religion played no role in these cases in which "great and powerful empires have been created out of nothing." His examples were significant. Mahommed figured in the deists' histories as propagating true monotheism, as opposed to corrupt Trinitarianism; Loyola represented the worst of popery; Cromwell personified Puritan enthusiasm.[97]

[94] *Divine Legation*, 4:447.

[95] Ibid., 6:356–57ff. Warburton attacked Voltaire's claims about the Jews at 5:7, 10–11.

[96] For Bolingbroke's interpretation of the Bible, see *Divine Legation*, 5:202–45; for "barefaced naturalism," see 2:211–63. Edmund Gibson defended the New Testament's "truth and authority" against Tindal's *Christianity as Old as the Creation* by asserting its inspired composition and mundane transmission. See Gibson, *The Late Bishop of London Dr. Gibson's Five Pastoral Letters to the People of His Diocese*, 248–54.

[97] *Divine Legation*, 4:116, 154, 3:261–64. Champion, *The Pillars of Priestcraft Shaken*, 106–15.

Warburton renewed other inherited exegetical methods. He defended the notion of a "secondary" sense (allegory, types, figures) central to the Christological reading of scripture. He could accept that a humanist such as Grotius (1583–1645) would want to treat the Bible like other ancient texts, but criticized his refusal to admit that the Old Testament prophecies pointed to Jesus.[98] Warburton vehemently attacked the deist Anthony Collins (1676–1729), who had asserted that authoritative exegesis (typological, allegorical, and secondary) demonstrating the fulfillment of Old Testament prophecies in the New Testament was erroneous. Collins examined numerous proofs for Christianity, beginning with the virgin birth, to show that they were "not to be found in the Old [Testament], or not urg'd in the New, according to the literal obvious sense"; that is, they were "apply'd in a secondary, or typical, or mystical, or allegorical, or enigmatical sense, [namely], in a sense different from the obvious and literal sense, which they bear in the Old Testament."[99]

Warburton recognized Collins's work as "one of the most able and plausible books ever written amongst us against our holy Faith." Warburton reiterated the traditional Christian claim that the Old Testament could bear the Christians' "allegorical" or "spiritual" reading as well as the Jews' "literal" or "carnal" one. He read God's command to Abraham to sacrifice Isaac as a "sign" of things to come: "the COMMAND to offer up Isaac was the very revelation of CHRIST's DAY, or the Redemption of mankind, by his death and sufferings." Abraham was thereby made aware of the future "redemption of mankind," even though this knowledge was not available to a "carnal-minded Jew" or even a "System-making Christian" reading the text. The original dispensation to the Jews was merely "preparatory." Similarly, Warburton asserted that the Old Testament prophets' inspiration enabled them to allude simultaneously to the Jewish and Christian dispensations, although these allusions eluded the Jews while their own "extraordinary Providence" was in effect. Furthermore, Warburton criticized those Christian writers who applied the methods of allegory to the

---

[98] *Divine Legation*, 6:92–93. Collins praised Grotius in *A Discourse on the Grounds and Reasons of the Christian Religion* (London, 1724), 244.

[99] Collins, *A Discourse on the Grounds and Reasons*, 39–40. For this work, see Reventlow, *The Authority of the Bible*, 362–69, and Frei, *The Eclipse of Biblical Narrative*, 65–80. On Collins as a "Spinozist," see Jonathan Israel, *Radical Enlightenment: Philosophy and the Making of Modernity, 1650–1750* (Oxford, 2001), 614–19. Collins used accommodation to attack conventional scripture interpretation. See *An Essay Concerning the Use of Reason in Propositions: The Evidence Whereof Depends Upon Human Testimony*, 2nd ed. (London, 1709), 14–15.

New Testament: once Christianity had been revealed, the need for allegory had ceased:

> the Author of Judaism allegorized in order to prepare his followers *for the reception of a more perfect Dispensation*, founded on Judaism, which was preparatory of it; and, at the same time, to *prevent* their *pre-mature rejection* of Judaism, under which they were still to be long exercised.

Warburton thereby further justified his claim of inseparable Jewish and Christian revelations.[100]

Warburton's middle way of history also entailed a vindication of miracles. Following Spinoza, deists such as Toland had denied the necessity of miracles, arguing that natural religion and reason satisfied mankind's needs. In addition, they deemed particular miracles implausible or absurd.[101] In contrast, Warburton asserted the absolute necessity of miracles to establish the veracity of revealed religion:

> in the first propagation of a *new Religion* from Heaven, the will of God must be attested by MIRACLES; since nothing less than this instant Evidence is sufficient to assure us of its divine original.[102]

Moreover, miracles were part of the very nature of the Jewish theocracy: the "civil" and "miraculous" were equally part of a divine economy:

> The Sacred History, besides the many *civil* facts which it contains, has many of a *miraculous* nature . . . for the civil and the miraculous facts, in the Jewish Dispensation, have the same, nay, a nearer relation to each other, than the two hands of the same body.[103]

The miracles that pervaded the early phase of Judaism proved its "extraordinary Providence," such that "the whole Bible is one continued

---

[100] *Divine Legation*, 6:138, 94; 5:8–9, 75, 100–102. See also 6:98. Early Moderates were primarily interested in literal interpretation. See Reedy, *Bible and Reason*, 13.

[101] On Spinoza in England, see Rosalie Colie, "Spinoza and the Early English Deists," *Journal of the History of Ideas* 20 (1959): 23–46, and idem, "Spinoza in England, 1665–1730," *Proceedings of the American Philosophical Society* 107 (1963); and Israel, *Radical Enlightenment*, 212–14, 599–627.

[102] *Divine Legation*, 6:340. Warburton defended miracles in *A Critical and Philosophical Commentary on Mr. Pope's Essay on Man*, in *Works*, 11:138–39, and *Julian, or a Discourse concerning the Earthquake & Fiery Eruption, Which Defeated the Emperor's Attempt to Rebuild the Temple at Jerusalem* (1750). See Robert Ingram, "William Warburton, Divine Action and Enlightened Christianity," in *Religious Identities in Britain, 1660–1832*, ed. William Gibson and Robert G. Ingram (Aldershot, 2005), 97–117.

[103] *Divine Legation*, 5:18–19.

history of it [miracles]." God performed miracles for the state as "tutelary deity," for individuals as "supreme magistrate."[104]

Warburton also defended the New Testament's miracles. He rejected the deists' contention that reason can ascertain the truth of revelation; rather, revelation follows standards that transcend human reason. Miracles were the sole criterion to establish with absolute certainty a doctrine's divine origin:

> in my opinion the REASONABLENESS of a Doctrine pretended to come immediately from God, is, of itself alone, no PROOF, but a PRESUMPTION only of such its divine Original. . . . MIRACLES, and MIRACLES ONLY, demonstrate that the Doctrine, which is seen to be *worthy* of God, did, indeed, COME IMMEDIATELY from him.[105]

Nevertheless, he tempered his affirmation of miracles by arguing that the doctrine had to meet distinct criteria:

> that it be so connected with the system to which it claims relation, as that it be seen to make a part of it, or to be necessary to its completion . . . that cause be so important as to make the *Miracle* necessary to the ends of the DISPENSATION, this is all that can be reasonably required to entitle it to our belief.[106]

In fact, Warburton recognized three possible functions for miracles: that they certify Christ's or His followers' mission, that they be part of or complete the Gospel system, and that they verify divine predictions challenged by the impious. He also categorically denied the possibility of pagan miracles: God would not interpose to support idolatry.[107] As in his treatment of natural religion, in his discussion of miracles Warburton protected both Judaism's and Christianity's divinity.

Warburton's endorsement of miracles was characteristic of the religious Enlightenment in drawing the distinction between truths opposed to reason (*contra rationem*) and truths above reason (*supra rationem*). The Moderates considered the mysteries of Christianity to be truths above reason confirmed by miracles.

Yet miracles had an additional function: they supplied seemingly unassailable proof of scripture's truth. Moderates invoked miracles to prove the integrity of all aspects of scripture—doctrine and law, prophecy and history. Deists criticized the unmistakable circularity of this

[104] Ibid., 5:135.
[105] Ibid., 5:322–23.
[106] Ibid., 6:320.
[107] Ibid., 6:321–22, 339.

argument, namely, that the miracles used to authenticate scripture were only reported in scripture.[108]

ESTABLISHED RELIGION

Warburton provided a historical justification for established religion that complemented the natural rights argument in the *Alliance between Church and State*. Established religion was a universal: "an *established religion* is the voice of nature; and not confined to certain ages, people or religions."[109] The Athenians, Romans, and Egyptians all had an established religion. The citizens of Athens had to take an elaborate oath to defend and "conform to the national religion." Anyone who presided over religious rites also had to swear an oath. In Warburton's eyes, Athens boasted not only an established religion but also a test law. In Rome there was a keen awareness that foreign customs and rites ultimately subverted religion itself, while in Egypt the state made the greatest possible use of religion.[110]

In the pagan world, religion was established, although not in its "due form." Pagan worship rested on "tutelary deities," as was the case in Egypt, and consisted of "conformity in public ceremonies." Religion served numerous purposes, including

> preserving the being of religion; bestowing additional veneration on the person of the Magistrate, and on the laws of the State; giving the Magistrate the right of applying the civil efficacy of religion: and giving Religion a coactive power for the reformation of manners.

Yet religion was imperfectly established in the pagan world. Religion did not constitute a "separate society": it lacked "unity of the object of faith" and "conformity to a formula of dogmatic theology."[111] Its relationship to the state was not a true alliance of separate societies.

Christianity first enabled religion to be a true separate society and church and state to have a proper "alliance." Though a revealed religion, Judaism was incapable of such a relationship since it produced a theocracy. Christianity thus superseded paganism and Judaism not only in doctrine and belief but also in church-state relations.

---

[108] Reedy, *Bible and Reason*, 10, 34, 46–62, 128–31. The deists attacked truths above reason. See John Toland, *Christianity Not Mysterious*, and Collins, *An Essay Concerning the Use of Reason in Propositions*.

[109] This historical vindication addressed contemporary concerns. See *Divine Legation*, 2:265.

[110] Ibid., 2:292–94.

[111] Ibid., 2:297–98.

Warburton similarly understood Christianity to represent a new stage in toleration. Toleration was a "universal practice" in the pagan world that rested on respect for liberty of conscience. In addition, since paganism consisted in "rites and ceremonies" rather than in doctrines, it accommodated virtually infinite variety: one set of worshippers could "admit the other's pretensions." Warburton termed this ability to worship other Gods in common "intercommunity." While he lauded intercommunity's effect, he disparaged its underlying cause: toleration derived from paganism's "egregious falsehood and absurdity." Pagan toleration was the right conclusion drawn from the wrong premise. In contrast, Christianity could offer toleration based on truth. "Intolerance under the Christian religion, proceeded from its truth and perfection; [intolerance was] not the natural consequence . . . of a *false* Principle, but the abuse of a *true* one."[112] Needless to say, for Warburton "an established religion with a test-law is the universal voice of nature" and the best guarantee of toleration.[113]

JUSTIFICATION, PHILOSOPHY, AND SCIENCE

Just as history was integral to Warburton's Moderation by enabling him to reconcile natural and revealed religion, natural law and theocracy, as well as to defend established religion, so a broadly Arminian notion of justification by faith and works allowed him to embrace reason and science alongside scripture.

Warburton understood Moderation's theological triumph as maintaining the proper balance between justification by faith and works. The Puritans' embrace of faith at the expense of works engendered an enthusiastic immorality that undermined the constitution. The Latitudinarians restored the balance to support the constitution. The advent of deism presented a new challenge: Warburton had to navigate between the Scylla of lurking (Puritan and dissenting) enthusiasm (read "faith") and the Charybdis of rampant (deist) unbelief (read "works" or "morality"). In addition, Catholicism ("Popery") remained a threat, and the anti-Catholic sentiment strong and vocal, though it had begun to recede by mid-century.[114]

---

[112] Ibid., 2:302–3.

[113] Ibid., 2:292.

[114] Ibid., 3:387–89. On enthusiasm and moderation, see J.G.A. Pocock, "Enthusiasm: The Antiself of Enlightenment," in *Enthusiasm and Enlightenment in Europe, 1650–1850,*

Warburton's middle way depended on Arminianism and John Locke. Arminianism was to salvation what collegialism was to church-state relations: a fundamental revision of militant Calvinism. In contrast to the Calvinist doctrine of "gratuitous" and "irresistible" grace, which asserted that Jesus had suffered for and redeemed merely the elect, the Arminians were "advocates of universal grace." Grace was available to all mankind through faith and works.[115] Whereas Calvinism stressed the Fall, Arminianism emphasized the role of free will in the economy of salvation. Again in contrast to Calvinist predestination, Arminianism asserted God's freedom to forgive as well as to punish. Arminianism's assertion that faith could affect salvation gave new value to the sacraments, and for that reason Calvinists accused early Arminians of lapsing into Catholicism.

Arminianism had gained ground in England after the Synod of Dort (1618–19), gone underground during the Commonwealth, and reemerged at the heart of religious developments in the Restoration. Opponents saw Arminianism as leading inexorably to deism or Socinianism. Some moderates did become Socinians. The majority, including Warburton, considered Arminianism the best defense against that very danger.[116]

Locke provided not only the philosophical idiom of Moderation but also an influential formulation of Arminianism. In some respects this was an unexpected development, since many theologians saw Locke's rejection of innate ideas as tantamount to the dismantling of Christianity. The deists and skeptics who relied on sensationalist

---

ed. Lawrence E. Klein and Anthony J. La Vopa (San Marino, CA, 1998), 7–28, and Lawrence E. Klein, "Sociability, Solitude and Enthusiasm," in ibid., 153–78. On Catholicism, see Walsh and Taylor, "Introduction: The Church and Anglicanism in the 'Long' Eighteenth Century," 57–58.

[115] The phrase is William Whitaker's (1595). Quoted in Nicholas Tyacke, *Anti-Calvinists: The Rise of English Arminianism, c. 1590–1640* (Oxford, 1987), 30. For Calvinists, Jesus's death was "sufficient" for the salvation of all mankind but "efficient" only for the elect.

[116] See *Divine Legation*, 1:198. For the Arminian notion of justification, see Spellman, *The Latitudinarians and the Church of England*, 89–111. For Arminianism's origins, see A. W. Harrison, *The Beginnings of Arminianism to the Synod of Dort* (London, 1926). For England, see Tyacke, *Anti-Calvinists*. For Pocock on the "Arminian Enlightenment," see "Clergy and Commerce: The Conservative Enlightenment in England," 528–29. H. R. Trevor-Roper made Arminianism central to the Enlightenment. See "The Religious Origins of the Enlightenment," in *The European Witch-Craze of the Sixteenth and Seventeenth Centuries and Other Essays* (New York, 1969), 193–236. See also Cragg, *From Puritanism to the Age of Reason*, 15–31.

epistemology confirmed these suspicions. Nevertheless, other theologians, and especially the Moderates, recognized that the Gospel was not yoked to a particular epistemology. They welcomed the opportunity to use Locke's sensationalism to defend and articulate belief. Indeed, the Moderates probably did more to disseminate Locke's philosophy than the deists.[117]

Many Moderates claimed Locke as a source of authority. Edmund Gibson, Bishop of London at the High Church end of Moderation, quoted Locke extensively on the relationship between reason and revelation (*"Revelation* is natural Reason *Enlarged"*) and deemed his views "the wise and pious Sentiments of an ingenious Writer of our own Time."[118] Warburton called Locke "the true philosopher" and "the honour of this age and the instructor of the future."[119] Yet more than epistemology accounted for Locke's impact.

Locke's *Reasonableness of Christianity* (1695) was an eminently Arminian answer to the deists. Locke had had contact with Arminian circles during his residence in Holland and knew Arminian theology. He advocated justification by faith and works. While he acknowledged the necessity of faith, he circumscribed its scope to two issues: assent to Jesus as messiah and the miracles he performed. Locke emphasized that faith was an indispensable encouragement, but that salvation without works was impossible:

> faith without works, i.e. the works of sincere obedience to the law and will of Christ, is not sufficient for our justification. . . . Thus we see, by the preaching of our Saviour and his apostles, that he required of those who believed him to be the Messiah, and received

[117] On Locke's influence in Germany, see Andrew Brown, "John Locke and the religious 'Aufklärung,'" *Review of Religion* 13 (1949): 126–54. For France, see John Yolton, *Locke and the French Materialists* (Oxford, 1991). For Locke and deism, see S. G. Hefelbower, *The Relation of John Locke to English Deism* (Chicago, 1918). Locke's views are distinct from the uses made of them. See John C. Biddle, "Locke's Critique of Innate Principles and Toland's Deism," *Journal of the History of Ideas* 37 (1976): 411–22; Jacob, *The Newtonians and the English Revolution*, 211–16; and John Marshall, *John Locke: Resistance, Religion and Responsibility* (Cambridge, 1994), 407–9. On the Moderates' use of Locke, see John W. Yolton, *John Locke and the Way of Ideas* (Oxford, 1956), 181–202, and Alan P. F. Sell, *John Locke and the Eighteenth-Century Divines* (Cardiff, 1997).

[118] *The Late Bishop of London Dr. Gibson's Five Pastoral Letters*, 72. Cf. 73–75, 126, 268. Gibson would have persecuted the deists if Walpole had allowed it. He opposed Latitudinarianism because he thought it reduced Christianity to mere morality. He blocked the careers of such Latitudinarians as Samuel Clarke and Benjamin Hoadly. See Sykes, *Edmund Gibson: Bishop of London*, passim.

[119] *Divine Legation*, 1:162, 6:321. Sell would hand Warburton the "prize for eulogy." See *John Locke and the Eighteenth-Century Divines*, 268–69.

him for their Lord and Deliverer, that they should live by his laws.[120]

Jesus' revelation was also required, since unaided reason was incapable of discovering the truths of natural religion and disseminating them among mankind.[121] At the same time, Locke's views of the Trinity, satisfaction, and original sin led some contemporaries to accuse him of Socinianism, a charge he energetically resisted.[122]

Like Locke, Warburton enunciated a decidedly Arminian notion of justification that embraced both works and faith. He treated works not as coequal with faith but as a necessary stage in making man capable of attaining grace:

> This is the true use and value of Works with regard to FAITH; and greater cannot be conceived. Hence it appears, that JUSTIFYING FAITH is so far from excluding GOOD WORKS, that it necessarily requires them. But how? Not as sharing in that JUSTIFICATION; but as procuring for us a title to God's *favour* in general, they become the *qualification* of that inestimable Reward, revealed by the Gospel, to be obtained by FAITH ALONE.[123]

Warburton was adamant that faith was the means to salvation: "FAITH ALONE JUSTIFIETH, or, in other words, is the *sole condition* of recovering the possession of what we lost by ADAM."[124] He perhaps weighted works less than Locke, yet he maintained the balanced position at the heart of Moderation. Moderates needed justification by works, in concert with natural law, to refute the Calvinists and other enthusiasts' claims to justification by faith alone. Moderates needed justification by faith to confute the deists' claims to morality without belief.

Warburton's position resembled Locke's on revealed religion's essential role in establishing morality. Mankind needed revelation to gain its

---

[120] Locke, *The Reasonableness of Christianity as Delivered in the Scriptures*, in *Works*, 7:111, 125. For Locke's understanding of justification and the Latitudinarians, see Dewey D. Wallace, Jr., "Socinianism, Justification by Faith, and the Sources of John Locke's *The Reasonableness of Christianity*," *Journal of the History of Ideas* 45 (1984): 51–63. For Locke as a Latitudinarian, see Reventlow, *The Authority of the Bible*, 243–85. Baumgarten considered Locke an Arminian. See *D. Siegmund Jacob Baumgartens Auslegung des Briefes Pauli an die Roemer* (Halle, 1749), 14. For Locke's Dutch contacts, see Marshall, *John Locke*, 331–33. Warburton included Locke's *Reasonableness of Christianity* in his theology curriculum. See "Directions for the Study of Theology" (1769), in *Works*, 10:363.

[121] *Reasonableness of Christianity*, 7:139, 145.

[122] Marshall, *John Locke*, 342–50, 415–22.

[123] *Divine Legation*, 6:306.

[124] Ibid., 6:305. Justification by faith was central from the outset. See Spellman, *The Latitudinarians and the Church of England*, 27.

primordial understanding of religion and its true obligations, even though these principles, once discovered, seemed so obvious that it was hard to imagine why revelation had been necessary in the first place.[125]

Religion was needed to maintain collective morality as well. While certain exceptional individuals might be able to attain morality, Warburton made the argument common to the religious Enlightenment that "the generality of mankind" needed religion to be moral:

> For though a *rule of right* may direct the Philosopher to a principle of action; and the *point of honour* may keep up the thing called Manners amongst Gentlemen; yet nothing but *Religion* can ever fix a sober standard of behaviour amongst the common People.[126]

Only the sense of obedience to God's will can motivate "the great body of Mankind" to be moral.[127]

Warburton followed Locke in delineating additional ways in which revelation supplemented reason. Revelation was required for those subjects unfathomable to reason. For example, God's way of disseminating knowledge was inscrutable:

> we are not to prescribe to the Almighty his WAY of bringing us to the knowledge of his Will. It is sufficient to justify his goodness, that he hath done it; and whether he chose the way of REVELATION, or of REASON, or of the CIVIL MAGISTRATE, it equally manifests his wisdom.[128]

Likewise, "the whole system of God's moral dispensation" transcends human reason; revelation is needed to convey even the most basic understanding of God's moral attributes. For mankind to attempt to do so comprises "the abusive exercise of our Faculties, employed on objects which those Faculties can neither apprehend nor reach."[129] Warburton particularly confronted the philosophers' pretensions: he wanted them to admit that, whatever the extent of their knowledge, they too had to accept the validity of revelation and miracles:

> For even these Intimados of Nature [philosophers] know no more of Her than what lies just before them, in common with those whom they most affect to despise; And all they know, if not a Miracle, is yet a Mystery.

---

[125] *Divine Legation*, 3:212–15. For a similar passage in Locke, see *Reasonableness of Christianity*, in *Works*, 7:145.
[126] *Divine Legation*, 4:5. Cf. 1:274–75.
[127] Ibid., 1:234–35.
[128] Ibid., 3:224.
[129] Ibid., 2:261, 6:225, 2:227.

Let these her Closet-acquaintance *steal*, as they are able, to her inmost recesses, they *can bring nothing* from thence concerning God's natural and moral Government, as the Poet finely expresses it, BUT UNDECIPHERED CHARACTERS, which only teach us the need we have of a better Decipherer, than that REASON on which these men so proudly rely.[130]

Warburton linked Arminianism to Newton's physics and Locke's philosophy. Locke and Newton put an end to speculation by establishing our knowledge of nature ("the book of nature") on the solid foundation of "facts" and "experiments." "Henceforth, NATURE was set before us unveiled; and her Sacred Mysteries held out to the knowledge and admiration of all men."[131]

Warburton's endorsement of Newton and Locke demonstrated the Moderates' characteristic faith in the new science (and, as we shall see, the entire religious Enlightenment's). Newtonian science was so critical to the Moderates that they were among the first to popularize it. The Boyle lectures of Richard Bentley (1692), who saw Newton's gravity "as the immediate *Fiat* and Finger of God, and the execution of the divine law," and Samuel Clarke (1704), who used Newton's science to attack deism, were some of the first expositions for an educated audience. Moreover, they enjoyed considerable longevity.[132]

It would be wrong, however, to identify Moderation in England with Newtonianism or vice versa. Newton was a nearly omnipresent figure in eighteenth-century intellectual life. Figures across the political and theological spectrum laid claim to his authority. The Moderates can at best be said to have made such early and consistent use of Newton as to turn him into a mainstay of their worldview. Their reliance on science was not surprising, since from its inception Arminianism had been associated with scientific knowledge.[133]

---

[130] Ibid., 6:339–40.

[131] Ibid., 6:227. Warburton cited Newton's *Optics* and *Principia* in *A Critical and Philosophical Commentary on Mr. Pope's Essay on Man*, 4, 14, 21, 48–49.

[132] Richard Bentley, *Eight Sermons Preached at the Hon. Robert Boyle's Lecture in the Year MDCXCII* (Oxford, 1809), 108. Cf. 236. Samuel Clarke, *A Demonstration of the Being and Attributes of God, More Particularly in Answer to Mr. Hobbes, Spinoza and Their Followers, Wherein the Notion of Liberty Is Stated, and the Possibility and Certainty of it Proved, in Opposition to Necessity and Fate* (London, 1705), 164, 229–32. For "theological Newtonianism," see R. E. Schofield, "An Evolutionary Taxonomy of Eighteenth-Century Newtonianisms," *Studies in Eighteenth Century Culture* 7 (1978): 177. On Clarke, see Larry Stewart, "Samuel Clark, Newtonianism, and the Factions of Post-Revolutionary England," *Journal of the History of Ideas* 42 (1981): 53–72. For the continuing use of Bentley and Clarke, see Margaret Jacob, "Newtonianism and the Origins of the Enlightenment: A Reassessment," *Eighteenth Century Studies* 11 (1977–78): 2.

[133] In general, see Gerd Buchdahl, *The Image of Newton and Locke in the Age of Reason* (London, 1961). For science, see Schofield, "Evolutionary Taxonomy." For High Church

Perhaps a more accurate way to understand Warburton and the Moderates' use of science is to see it in the tradition of physico-theology, namely, the argument from design used to prove the existence and define the attributes of God. This argument pervaded early and medieval Christian thought, where it was associated with arguments for the intrinsic teleology of living organisms or of the analogy of God as creator of living organisms. The argument flourished in the seventeenth and eighteenth centuries when the analogy of God as inventor of complex mechanisms, especially the clock, replaced the older conception of design. The argument found expression in the late seventeenth century in the works of Robert Boyle, Robert Hooke, and John Ray. It then gained a new lease on life in the work of Newton and the Boyle lecturers, including Bentley, Clarke, and William Derham (Derham's 1713 lectures were entitled *Physico-theology*).[134] The Moderates made physico-theology a major weapon in their intellectual arsenal. This alliance between theology and science was to go largely unchallenged until the third quarter of the nineteenth century, when Darwin's theories shook theology's foundations.

Warburton thought Locke and Newton's impact on theology was salutary. Theology cannot rely on speculation and imagination; it must depend on "acknowledged facts, as they are recorded in Sacred Scripture."[135] Warburton endorsed "experiments" of the kind that Locke and Newton had performed: "Had *no experiments been made in Nature,* we had still slept in the shade, or been kept entangled in the barren and thorny paths of SCHOOL PHILOSOPHY; and had *no experiments been made in Religion,* we had still kept blundering on in the dark and rugged Wilds of SCHOOL DIVINITY."[136]

Warburton refused to apply scripture to science and politics. Fearing the dangerous consequences of biblical literalism, he argued for strictly distinguished spheres of knowledge. While the Bible is the source of all knowledge needed "unto salvation," "natural" and "civil" knowledge are to be derived from other sources. For example, the Bible cannot be treated as a "Treasury of Science." Those who regard it as such are

---

Tory Newtonians, see Anita Guerrini, "The Tory Newtonians: Gregory, Pitcairne, and Their Circle," *Journal of British Studies* 25 (1986): 288–311. For a Newtonian ideology, see Jacob, *The Newtonians and the English Revolution*; idem, "Newtonianism and the Origins of the Enlightenment: A Reassessment," 1–25, and idem, *The Radical Enlightenment: Pantheists, Freemasons and Republicans* (London, 1981). For Arminianism and science, see Tyacke, *Anti-Calvinists*, 120, and Rosalie L. Colie, *Light and Enlightenment: A Study of the Cambridge Platonists and the Dutch Arminians* (Cambridge, 1957).

[134] Dahm, "Science and Apologetics in the Early Boyle Lectures," *Church History* 39 (1970): 172–186; Gascoigne, *Cambridge in the Age of Enlightenment*, passim.

[135] *Divine Legation*, 6:223.

[136] Ibid., 6:231.

"enthusiasts": to search the first two chapters of Genesis for scientific truth can only lead to abuse. Science must be based not on exegesis, imagination, or speculation but on solid empirical knowledge:[137]

Warburton similarly argued that the Bible cannot be made a source of politics:

> how impiously have the JEWISH LAW and the GOSPEL OF JESUS been abused by Slaves and Sycophants, to find, the DIVINE RIGHT OF KINGS; and, in the other, the SUPREME DOMINION OF THE CHURCH.[138]

In general, Warburton advocated the need to search for truth in nature and divinity.[139]

Warburton's Arminianism enabled him to reconcile a traditional interpretation of scripture with Newtonian science and Lockean philosophy. The Bible could serve as a source of history, but not of science or politics. Science and philosophy could unlock truths of the physical and metaphysical realms while leaving room for revelation.

In pursuing his "heroic moderation," Warburton understood himself to be working in a central Church of England tradition: he located Moderation in a line extending from Richard Hooker to the Cambridge Platonists. Warburton called Hooker the "great master of Reason" and praised his understanding of the "politique use of Religion." He repeatedly quoted "the accurate Cudworth."[140] Warburton named the figures with whom he wanted to be identified when he enumerated those members of the Church of England who were misunderstood and abused: "But this was . . . the fortune of Hooker, Hales, Stillingfleet, Cudworth, Bp Taylor. They were called *Politiques, Sceptics, Erastians, Deists and Atheists*."[141]

SECULAR CULTURE

With the publication of *The Divine Legation*, Warburton's career soared. In 1746 he was elected to the preachership in Lincoln's Inn; in 1752 he

---

[137] "The Nature and Condition of Truth," *The Principles of Natural and Revealed Religion*, in *Works*, 9:10–12.

[138] *Divine Legation*, 6:219. Warburton followed earlier Moderates in renouncing typological arguments for contemporary politics. See Reedy, *The Bible and Reason*, 79–85, and Reventlow, *The Authority of the Bible*, 229–35.

[139] *Divine Legation*, 6:231–32.

[140] For Hooker, see ibid., 6:235, 3:311–12. For Cudworth, 3:152, 168.

[141] Ibid., 4:31. Warburton cited Bishop Taylor at *Alliance*, 7:iv. In his curriculum for theology he deemed these figures indispensable. See "Directions for the Study of Theology" (1769), in *Works*, 10:357–75.

was named a prebendary at Gloucester Cathedral, in 1754 a chaplain to the king, in 1757 to the deanery of Bristol, and in 1760 bishop of Gloucester. At the same time, he became one of the preeminent figures in English literary and intellectual life. Warburton's "heroic moderation" was entirely compatible with engagement in secular culture. In the late 1730s Warburton became friendly with Alexander Pope, and in 1742 he published a defense of Pope's *Essay on Man*. Warburton went on to edit Pope's poems, and after Pope's death served as executor of his published works. Warburton's other literary activities included an edition of Shakespeare (1747), a preface to Richardson's *Clarissa*, and a discussion of the origins of books on chivalry and romance in a translation of *Don Quixote* (1742).[142]

Warburton's literary writing extended his theology. A French author, De Crousaz, had accused Pope of espousing unorthodox ideas in his *Essay on Man*. By treating the poem as a "system of philosophy," Warburton put in the poet's service ("to vindicate our Great Countryman from his Censure") his already well-articulated ideas on fate and free will, individual and civil society, providence and the future life.[143] The main charges he refuted were atheism ("Spinozism" and "Hobbism") and fatalism. He did so by showing either that the translator had misconstrued crucial passages or that the commentator had misunderstood them. Warburton vehemently accused the French author of lack of charity and "excess of zeal," the very vice he consistently attacked in the *Divine Legation* and his sermons:

> I leave it with Mr. De Crousaz to think upon the different Effects which Excess of Zeal in the Service of Religion, hath produced in him . . . he became guilty of a deliberate and repeated Act of the highest Injustice; the attempting to deprive a virtuous Man of his honest Reputation.[144]

Warburton's friendship with Pope propelled his edition of Shakespeare. Warburton roundly criticized two previous editions. He thought Rowe's work "irresponsible" because it did not rest on the collation of manuscripts. Theobald and Hanmer's edition he thought exemplified bad editing and criticism: "they separately possessed those

---

[142] Evans, *Warburton and the Warburtonians*, 116–28, 143–64. Fielding mentioned Warburton in the "Invocation to Learning" in the thirteenth book of *Tom Jones*. See ibid., 126.

[143] *A Critical and Philosophical Commentary on Mr. Pope's Essay on Man*, in *Works*, 11:23. Earlier Warburton had been critical of Pope. See Evans, *Warburton and the Warburtonians*, 71–76.

[144] *A Critical and Philosophical Commentary on Mr. Pope's Essay on Man*, in *Works*, 11:144.

two qualities which, more than any other, have contributed to bring the art of criticism into disrepute, *dulness of apprehension* and *extravagance of conjecture*."[145] He deemed Pope's edition the "best foundation for all further improvements" and built upon it. He thought the critic's job was to teach the public "with reason to admire," which translated into three goals: restoring the genuine text; explaining the author's meaning; and offering a "critical explanation of the author's beauties and defects; but chiefly of his beauties."[146]

He rejected the charge that such an edition diverted him from his "clerical profession." Literature teaches mankind about itself. It was the Renaissance philologists and critics who brought mankind out of the Dark Ages: "had it not been for the deathless labours such as these [Scaliger, Casaubon, Salmasius, Spanheim], the western world, at the revival of letters, had soon fallen back again into a state of ignorance and barbarity, as deplorable as that from which Providence had just redeemed it."[147] The renowned church father Chrysostom, who lived with his copy of Aristophanes, epitomized the symbiosis of faith and literature. Yet for Warburton, Shakespeare was superior to Aristophanes. In showing us "knowledge of our nature," Shakespeare "is confessed to occupy the foremost place," revealing "every hidden spring and wheel of human action."[148]

As is abundantly manifest, Warburton was a bellicose polemicist given to sarcasm, invective, and abusive language. Leslie Stephen spoke of his "everflowing and illimitable pugnacity" and called him "a man possessed of huge brute force, though of no real acuteness." Gibbon said that "he reigned the dictator and tyrant of literature"; another writer called him the "haughty and overbearing Colossus" of English letters. Still another named him the "big stick" of orthodoxy. One writer has called his method "dirt throwing"; some contemporaries accused him of lowering the tone of English letters.[149] There was undeniable truth in these charges. Warburton's moderate ideas were

---

[145] Warburton's preface to *The Plays of William Shakespeare in Twenty-One Volumes* (London, 1803), 1:231. For the opposite view, see Marcus Walsh, *Shakespeare, Milton, and Eighteenth-Century Literary Editing* (Cambridge, 1997), 149–54.

[146] Preface to *The Plays of William Shakespeare*, 1:228–33.

[147] Ibid., 1:244.

[148] Ibid., 1:240–41.

[149] *English Thought in the Eighteenth Century*, 2 vols. (New York, 1949), 1:347, 353; Edward Gibbon quoted in Evans, *Warburton and the Warburtonians*, 1; Mark Pattison, "Life of Bishop Warburton," *National Review* (1863), 143 (reprinted in Henry Nettleship, ed., *Essays by the Late Mark Pattison*, 2 vols. [Oxford, 1889]); Mossner, *Bishop Butler and the Age of Reason*, 67–68. Pattison, "Life of Bishop Warburton," 160.

immoderately held and expressed. As his sympathetic biographer put it, "When his moral feelings were touched, he was apt to be transported into some intemperance of expression, and was not always guarded, or even just, in his censures or commendations."[150] Nonetheless, we should not fall into the scholarly trap of allowing manner to obscure matter.

MODERATION IN DECLINE

In the closing decades of Warburton's life, Moderation began to wane. Political sponsorship had brought Moderation ascendance and triumph; a new political realignment following the accession of George III in 1760 inaugurated its decline. Moderation had flourished when the Whigs used it to promote stability and the status quo. In the last third of the century, with the cessation of the Jacobite threat and the general acceptance of the Glorious Revolution, circumstances had fundamentally changed. George III gradually abandoned the Whig alliance as Tories embraced him and the Hanoverian dynasty. Moreover, the growth of such radical causes as the Wilkites and dissenters, American rebels, and Jacobins meant that many of Moderation's key ideas were associated not with the status quo but with the various reform impulses that threatened it.[151] Dissenters, for example, made consent the foundation of their claims to equal status, while the advocates of reform in liturgy and the thirty-nine oaths (Feathers Tavern) used stock ideas of Moderation.[152] Moreover, the Moderates themselves splintered into various factions, some favoring reform, others rejecting it, and still others sitting on the fence. Moderation "could no longer cope with the new rifts emerging in government and society as they entered the age of revolutions."[153] Thus the alliance with the state came undone. Through patronage, the state expressed its preference for the new supernaturalism and evangelicalism. Whereas in Warburton's generation Moderation had been the high road to preferment, it now became the back road to obscurity.[154]

---

[150] Hurd, "A Discourse by Way of General Preface." Hurd quoted Pope's assessment: "he had a genius equal to his pains, and a taste equal to his learning." Ibid., 99.

[151] Gascoigne, *Cambridge in the Age of Enlightenment*, 188–236; Ian Christie, *Wars and Revolutions: Britain, 1760–1815* (London, 1982), 29ff.; Clark, *English Society, 1688–1832*, 199–348.

[152] For Latitudinarian attacks on the articles, see Barlow, *Citizenship and Conscience*, 147.

[153] Fitzpatrick, "Latitudinarianism at the parting of the ways," 227.

[154] Gascoigne, *Cambridge in the Age of Enlightenment*, 237–70.

CONCLUSION

Warburton's Moderation was representative of the first fully realized version of the religious Enlightenment. Although key elements of the religious Enlightenment were formulated in Holland in the revision of militant Calvinism, those elements first fused into a coherent position that gained state sponsorship in England. The religious Enlightenment represented the migration of Collegialism and Arminianism, toleration and reason, science and natural law from the heterodox periphery to the orthodox center. In consequence, Moderation in the Church of England had a tremendous impact on all subsequent versions of the religious Enlightenment. We now turn to the significant example of Calvinist Geneva.

Opposite: Jacob Vernet. Portrait of Jacob Vernet by Jens Juel (1745–1802). Oil on canvas, 1779. Photograph by permission of Département iconographique, Bibliothèque de Genève.

CHAPTER TWO

Geneva

Jacob Vernet's "Middle Way"

FROM ITS FOUNDATION IN 1536, the Republic of Geneva considered itself a "city set on a hill" that aspired to be "the most perfect school of Christ that ever was on earth since the days of the Apostles." Whether or not the city-state on the upper Rhone achieved its spiritual ambitions in its 262 years of independence, it did acquire the reputation of being "the Protestant Rome," the headquarters of one branch of the Protestant revolution.[1] Yet in the eighteenth century, Geneva's ambitions faced unprecedented challenges of affluence, political conflict, and cultural ferment.

Whereas John Calvin and Theodore Beza had approved of capitalist enterprise, they attempted to restrain its effects through sumptuary laws and an independent clergy. The eighteenth century brought unparalleled prosperity to Geneva. It became the center of various forms of luxury manufacture (watches, jewelry, and painted cloth); a major commercial entrepôt linking the Mediterranean and Atlantic economies; and a hub of European finance, with numerous banks that floated loans for Europe's polities, especially France, and eager investors who bought a disproportionate share of each issue. Despite its modest size—some 15,000 persons at its inception, some 28,000 in the eighteenth century—Geneva's economy almost rivaled that of Europe's leading cities.

The self-governing republic that Calvin and Beza had dominated recognized the sovereignty of all citizens by investing ultimate power in a General Council while according legislative and executive authority to two smaller ones. In the seventeenth century, this arrangement yielded an inefficient, self-serving, and corrupt oligarchy. In the eighteenth century the same elite produced an efficient and honest government justifiably proud of its achievements: a balanced budget, rebuilt fortifications, and subsidized food staples. Yet these paternalistic patricians were deaf to the lower bourgeoisie's demands for sovereignty. In

---

[1] Quotation from John Knox, pastor to the English refugees in Geneva, cited in Wilhelm Oechsli, *History of Switzerland, 1499–1914* (Cambridge, 1922), 165. This account relies on Patrick O'Mara, "Geneva in the Eighteenth Century: A Socio-Economic Study of the Bourgeois City-State During Its Golden Age," Ph.D. thesis, University of California–Berkeley, 1954. For early images, see Alain Dufour, "Le mythe de Genève au temps de Calvin," *Revue suisse d'histoire* 9 (1959): 489–518.

consequence, constitutional squabbles, some resulting in armed confrontation, punctuated the century.[2]

Calvin and Beza had tried to secure the republic of Christian virtue by creating an independent clergy. By the eighteenth century the clergy had become an appendage of the city-state that owned its property and paid its salaries. Once the Venerable Company of Pastors had repudiated scholasticism, what defined Calvinism? What was the meaning of a religiously grounded republic in an age of Enlightenment, declining church attendance, and apparent moral decay? What role could sumptuary laws play in the face of growing affluence? Could Geneva have a theater and remain Calvinist?

Jacob Vernet (1698–1789), Geneva's dominant theologian and the guardian of its Calvinist heritage in the second third of the eighteenth century, responded to these challenges. Vernet represented the second generation of "enlightened orthodoxy," promoting the "middle way" of "reasonable" belief in opposition to such threatening extremes as deism and Catholicism, indifference, and enthusiasm, yet also Calvinist dogmatism. Predicated on the God-given power of human reason yet equally on revelation and miracles, his theology was inspired by Arminianism, Cartesian philosophy, and Anglican moderation.[3]

---

[2] Geneva's crises were characteristic of much of Switzerland. See William Martin, *Switzerland: From Roman Times to the Present*, trans. Jocasta Innes (New York, 1971), 121–32, and Jonathan Steinberg, *Why Switzerland*, 2nd ed. (Cambridge, 1996), 37.

[3] For Vernet's representative status, see, for example, N. Charles Falletti, *Jacob Vernet: Théologien genevois, 1698–1789* (Geneva, 1885), 25–26; James I. Good, *History of the Swiss Reformed Church Since the Reformation* (Philadelphia, 1913), 282; Graham Gargett, "Jacob Vernet: Theologian and Anti-*Philosophe*," *British Journal for Eighteenth-Century Studies* 16, no. 1 (1993): 35–52, esp. 36, and idem, *Jacob Vernet: Geneva and the Philosophes* (Oxford, 1994); Samuel S. B. Taylor, "The Enlightenment in Switzerland," in *The Enlightenment in National Context*, ed. Roy Porter and Mikulás Teich (Cambridge, 1981), 80; and Helena Rosenblatt, *Rousseau and Geneva: From the First Discourse to the Social Contract, 1749–1762* (Cambridge, 1997) 15–17.

For "enlightened Orthodoxy," see Helena Rosenblatt, "The Language of Genevan Calvinism in the Eighteenth Century," in *Reconceptualizing Nature, Science and Aesthetics: Contribution à une nouvelle approche des Lumières helvétiques*, ed. Patrick Coleman, Anne Hoffmann, and Simone Zurbuchen (Geneva, 1998), 69–78; Martin I. Klauber, "The Eclipse of Reformed Scholasticism in Eighteenth-Century Geneva: Natural Theology from Jean-Alphonse Turretin to Jacob Vernet," in *The Identity of Geneva: The Christian Commonwealth, 1564–1864*, ed. John B. Roney and Martin I. Klauber (Westport, CT., 1998), 129–42; Martin Klauber, "Between Calvinist and *Philosophe*: Jacob Vernet's Theological Dilemma," *Westminster Theological Journal* 63 (2001): 377–92; and Jean-Louis Leuba, *Jean-Jacques Rousseau et la crise contemporaine de la conscience* (Paris, 1980), 13–24.

The German is *"vernünftige Orthodoxie."* See Paul Wernle, *Der schweizerische Protestantismus im XVIII. Jahrhundert*, 4 vols. (Tübingen, 1923–28), 1:468–69. Ulrich Im Hof applies the term to Catholicism as well. See *Aufklärung in der Schweiz* (Berne, 1970), 14–17, 57–61.

Like Warburton, Vernet espoused a state-centered politics dedicated to stability. Seeing patrician rule as the true middle way, he enunciated a conservative natural law theory promoting "a just subordination" designed to avert the extremes of tyranny and anarchy. He also used natural law theory to champion religious toleration and freedom of conscience (thereby winning accolades from Rousseau): he endorsed a multiconfessional society and eschewed persecution for beliefs. He was a self-avowed "republican."

Vernet was also a self-styled man of letters connected to the French *philosophes*. He edited Montesquieu's *De l'esprit des lois*, helped to restore Rousseau to Calvinism, and corresponded with and then crossed swords with d'Alembert and Voltaire. In those controversies with the philosophes he refined his notion of the Enlightenment as a "middle way" of reasonable piety and obedience.

Vernet was educated in the theology that emerged from the seventeenth-century controversies over Arminianism and Cartesian philosophy. For Geneva, developments at the Protestant Academy of Saumur, France, were crucial because of the constant traffic of students and teachers. Such figures as Moïse Amyraut (1596–1664), Josue de la Place (1596–1665), and Louis Cappel (1585–1658) had challenged Calvinist orthodoxy by questioning the idea of selective grace for a limited elect ("supralapsarian predestination"), instead suggesting a "hypothetical universalism": God wanted to save all men, yet original sin blocked most from true belief. They similarly softened the idea of original sin by separating its "inherent" from its "hereditary" character. Furthermore, some of them reinterpreted the idea of scripture's inspiration. Cappel, for example, held the masoretic vocalization to be manmade rather than divine, a distinction he thought had no impact on scripture's salvific message. These views were threatening less because of their innate radicalness than because of the theologians' authority and prestige. Although French Protestants convened a number of synods to address these issues, they remained unresolved.[4]

At Geneva, Louis Tronchin (1629–1705) and Jean-Robert Chouet (1642–1731) represented the generation of transition. Tronchin, a professor of theology at the Genevan Academy, taught a form of enlightened Calvinism: he rejected scholasticism and refused to accept ideas on the basis of authority alone, reserving the right to scrutinize them

[4] Maria-Cristina Pitassi, *De l'Orthodoxie aux Lumières: Genève, 1670–1737*, Historie et société 24 (Geneva, 1992), 11–15; Martin I. Klauber, *Between Reformed Scholasticism and Pan-Protestantism: Jean-Alphonse Turretin (1671–1737) and Enlightened Orthodoxy at the Academy of Geneva* (Selinsgrove, 1994); and Philip Benedict, *Christ's Churches Purely Reformed: A Social History of Calvinism* (New Haven, 2002), 316–17, 335–39, 348–52.

according to scripture and Descartes. His sympathies were largely Arminian: he was inclined to "hypothetical universalism" and embraced the idea of natural religion. He had tremendous influence on his students, including Pierre Bayle (1647–1706) and Jean Le Clerc (1657–1736). While a student at the Academy Bayle wrote to his father:

> I do not dissimulate at all in saying that [Tronchin] is the most penetrating and judicious theologian of our communion. He is free from every popular opinion and general sentiment that have no foundation other than that they were believed by our predecessors, though without being supported by the authority of Scripture.[5]

Chouet, later professor of philosophy at Geneva, had been the first to teach Cartesian method at Saumur (from 1646). According to Vernet, "that nascent light opened [Chouet's] eyes" with its "sound principles of reasoning and method." Chouet insisted on philosophy's independence from theology, seeing no tension between them. He embraced the fideist elements in Cartesianism that he felt were consistent with Calvinism prior to its scholastic reformulation. Influencing an entire generation of students at Geneva, where he taught from 1669, he also conducted scientific experiments following Descartes, although cast in scholastic language.[6]

The twin threat of Arminianism and Cartesianism alarmed conservative theologians. Led by François Turrettin (1623–1687), they introduced an oath designed to guarantee purity of belief. The Helvetic or Formula Consensus, which was adopted by the Swiss Confederation in 1675, the Genevan Company of Pastors in 1678, and the Council of Two Hundred in 1679, defended scripture's form and content and endorsed salvation of the elect, a position known as infralapsarianism. It also reasserted original sin's "inherent" and "hereditary" character. Yet the theologians who wrote the Formula neither named names nor condemned Descartes. The Formula Consensus's one obvious casualty was Tronchin's gifted student, Jean Le Clerc, who, outraged that his moderate ideas were now deemed heretical, left Geneva.[7]

---

[5] Pierre Bayle's letter (Sept. 21, 1671) quoted in Pitassi, *De l'Orthodoxie aux Lumières*, 26.

[6] Jacob Vernet, "Eloge historique de Mr. Chouet," in *Bibliothèque Italique ou Histoire littéraire de l'Italie*, vol. 12 (Sept.–Dec. 1731), 108, 114. Chouet's teachers rejected Aristotelian science; he clarified an uncertain situation. See Michael Heyd, *Between Orthodoxy and Enlightenment: Jean-Robert Chouet and the Introduction of Cartesian Science in the Academy of Geneva* (Hague, 1982), 69–72, 80, 86, 114, 134–45.

[7] The Formula was a compromise. See Pitassi, *De l'Orthodoxie aux Lumières*, 17–20; Benedict, *Christ's Churches Purely Reformed*, 348–50; and J. Gaberel, *Histoire de l'Eglise de Genève depuis le commencement de la reformation jusqu'à nos jours*, 3 vols. (Geneva, 1853–62), 3:145–50, 158–68. On Turretin, see James T. Dennison, Jr., "The Twilight of Scholasticism:

The debate over the Formula Consensus was between conservatives and reformers within the patrician elite. The Turretin, Tronchin, and Chouet families were among the wealthiest in Geneva. Moreover, there was considerable intellectual common ground: Turretin accepted Cartesianism, for example, so long as it was confined to physics.[8]

Chouet's life amply illustrates the patricians' cohesion. He left his professorship and embarked on a political career, serving on the Council of 25 from 1686, as secretary of the Council from 1689 to 1698, as Syndic in 1699, and as First Syndic in 1701. During the political crisis of 1707, in which the bourgeoisie demanded the restoration of sovereignty in fiscal matters, Chouet defended the patrician position, and Vernet claimed that "his resoluteness was one of the factors that contributed the most to restore peace."[9] It was this political rebellion, rather than the religious controversy, that exacted the ultimate price: Pierre Fatio (1662–1707), a patrician who led the bourgeoisie's struggle, was executed for sedition.

Chouet's political position enabled him to reform the Academy. In the seventeenth century the Academy had been a seminary for Calvinist ministers. Chouet attracted students who wished to prepare for careers in law, commerce, and the military. Accordingly, he revamped the Academy's curriculum (1704), creating chairs in mathematics and Church history, and the Academy later introduced two chairs in natural law (1722–23), becoming the training ground for Geneva's patrician elite. Cartesian philosophy and enlightened Orthodoxy rapidly became the establishment ideology.[10]

Turrettin's only son, Jean-Alphonse (1671–1737), personified the new era by repudiating the Formula Consensus and propagating an "enlightened Orthodoxy." A student of Tronchin's and Chouet's, Turretin was educated from the outset in Cartesian philosophy. After his

---

Frances Turretin at the Dawn of the Enlightenment," in *Protestant Scholasticism: Essays in Reassessment*, ed. Carl. R. Trueman and R. Scott Clark (Carlisle, Cumbria, UK, 1999), 244–55. On Jean le Clerc, see Maria-Cristina Pitassi, *Entre croire et savoir: Le problème de la méthode critique chez Jean le Clerc* (Leiden, 1987).

[8] For patrician wealth and political divisions, see O'Mara, *Geneva in the Eighteenth Century*, 93, 135. For Turretin's views, see Pitassi, *De l'Orthodoxie aux Lumières*, 25.

[9] Vernet, "Eloge historique de Mr. Chouet," 119. Vernet thought Chouet acted with exemplary "mildness" ("*une grande douceur*"), one of his favorite approbations. See also Rosenblatt, *Rousseau and Geneva*, 102–3.

[10] Pitassi, *De l'Orthodoxie aux Lumières*, 7–8. For the patrician ideology, see Heyd, *Between Orthodoxy and Enlightenment*, 204–35. The contentious issue was whether the Company of Pastors should retain control of the Academy or share it with one of the councils. See Michael Heyd, "The Geneva Academy in the Eighteenth Century: A Calvinist Seminary or a Civic University?" in *The University and the City: From Medieval Origins to the Present*, ed. Thomas Bender (New York, 1988), 79–99.

studies at the Academy, Turretin traveled in Holland, France, and England. He was especially taken with Anglican Moderation—he met Tillotson, Compton, Tennison, and Wake, developing a lifelong friendship with the last—in which he saw, as Vernet wrote, "the excellence of Christianity taken in its purity and centered on practice."[11] Arminianism and Moderation were Turretin's formative influences. Returning to Geneva, he was ordained a minister, appointed professor of ecclesiastical history (nonstipendiary) in 1697 at age twenty-six, and subsequently appointed professor of theology in 1705, succeeding Tronchin.

Turretin's fundamentally apologetic theology—designed to refute deists, enthusiasts and Catholics—affirmed God-given reason. He recognized a range of truths accessible to reason (natural theology) that, while able to gain the deists' and other unbelievers' assent, needed revelation to secure salvation and a common morality. Turretin thought reason supported revelation's external (miracles, fulfilled prophecies, eyewitness testimony) and internal marks (beauty of doctrines, utility, harmony of reason and faith). He used the principle of accommodation to separate scripture's salvific truths from temporally conditioned matters.

Turretin played a major role in dismantling his father's Formula Consensus: the oath was abolished in 1706, the Formula repudiated in 1725. He emphasized the liturgy as a source of confessional unity, which he helped to revise along Arminian lines. Turretin advocated toleration of fellow Protestants, albeit not Catholics, and aimed to reunite the Protestant world, for which he enlisted the English and Prussian monarchs. Writing almost exclusively in Latin, Turretin won his fellow scholars' admiration but did not reach a wider audience. Not surprisingly, he was politically conservative and opposed the revolution of 1734.[12]

Vernet, Turretin's protégé and successor, made Arminianism the public creed of Geneva: "Turretin discretely opened the gates of Geneva

[11] Jacob Vernet, "Eloge historique de Mr. Jean Alphonse Turrettin, pasteur & professeur en théologie & en histoire ecclésiastique à Geneve," in *Bibliothèque raisonnée des Ouvrages des Savans de l'Europe*, vol. 21 (July–Sept., 1738), 8, 15. For "the darkness which the obscure subtlety of the scholastics spread in religion," see *Pièces fugitives sur l'Eucharistie* (Geneva, 1730), iv.

[12] Vernet, "Eloge historique de Mr. Jean Alphonse Turrettin," 463. For liturgical change, see Pitassi, *De l'Orthodoxie aux Lumières*, 59–60, and Gaberel, *Histoire de l'Eglise de Genève*, 3:12–16. For Turretin's thought, see Klauber, *Between Reformed Scholasticism and Pan-Protestantism*, and Maria-Cristina Pitassi, "L'Apologétique raisonnable de Jean-Alphonse Turrettini," in *Apologétique 1680–1740: Sauvetage ou naufrage de la théologie?* ed. Maria-Cristina Pitassi (Geneva, 1991), 99–118.

to [Arminianism], Vernet conferred citizenship upon it."[13] Educated in Geneva, Vernet lived abroad while launching his career. He spent nine years, from 1720 to 1729, as a tutor in Paris, where he met outstanding religious and intellectual figures and also published his first articles and books. He traveled to Italy with his tutee in 1728, meeting Lodovico Muratori and Montesquieu, as well as the economist John Law, and to Holland, where he became acquainted with a number of the Collegialists, as well as with Jean Barbeyrac (1644–1720), the French translator of Pufendorf's natural law theory and Tillotson's sermons, the quintessence of Moderation. In 1730 the first two volumes of his expanded French edition of Turretin's Latin theological theses appeared (*Traité de la vérité de la religion chrétienne*); Vernet would work on this project for the next half-century.

Vernet returned to Geneva in 1730 to a country parish in Jussy. He also tutored Turretin's only son and in 1732 accompanied him to Switzerland, Germany, Holland, England, and France. In Holland, Vernet found a militant Calvinism that relied on formularies of belief. Vernet wrote to Turretin, "The more experience I acquire the more I see that much of the formularies are frequently only instruments of oppression in the hands of the less scrupulous against those who are more honest."[14] He spent four formative months in England, which he came to see as a model of liberty in government and simplicity and moderation in religion.[15] At Marburg he had coffee with the philosopher Christian Wolff, who impressed him as a figure "who inspired moderation in his disciples."[16]

Vernet rapidly settled into his various duties in Geneva: as pastor at St. Pierre and St. Gervais (1734), rector of the Academy (1737), professor of belles lettres (1739), and later professor of theology (1756). He published on a broad range of theological issues and, typically of religious enlighteners, on belles lettres, history, and politics, as well as editing the works of others. Vernet was first Geneva's "pontiff' and later its

---

[13] Falletti, *Jacob Vernet*, 91.

[14] Ibid., 24.

[15] Quoted in Eugene de Budé, *Vie de Jacob Vernet: Théologien genevois, 1698–1789* (Lausanne, 1893), 63–64. On his travels, see Gargett, *Jacob Vernet*, 16–64. For Anglican Moderation's impact on his theology, see Falletti, *Jacob Vernet*, 23–25, 30, 41, 85, and Klauber, *Between Reformed Scholasticism and Pan-Protestantism*, 72–86. In his controversy with d'Alembert, Vernet used the persona of an English clergyman, cited England as a model of toleration, and named six believing philosophers—Descartes, Boyle, Locke, Clark, Newton, and Wolff—of whom four were English. See *Lettres critiques d'un voyageur anglois sur l'article Genève du Dictionnaire encyclopédie, et sur la lettre de Mr. d'Alembert à Mr. Rousseau touchant les spectacles*, 2 vols., 3rd ed. (Copenhagen/Geneva, 1766), 59, 147–50.

[16] Letter to Turretin cited in Budé, *Vie de Jacob Vernet*, 49.

"revered patriarch"; to "study Vernet," N. Charles Falletti wrote, "is to study a chapter in the history of [Geneva's] church."[17]

THEOLOGY

Vernet articulated his theology through the idea of the "middle way" (*juste milieu*) which he defined with two categories, the "reasonable" (*raisonnable*) and "enlightened" (*éclairé*), and the principle of accommodation. In opposition to the inveterate foes of enthusiasm and Catholicism and to incipient deism and indifference, Vernet delineated an ideal of Christianity that was virtually coterminous with Geneva's Calvinism, which he considered to be a "purified, reasonable and tolerant theology."[18] As much of a status quo apologist as Warburton, Vernet understood practice, rather than correct doctrine, as a Christian's primary concern.

The middle way pervaded Vernet's theology from the moment he spoke in his own voice (1730).[19] It became his tacit organizing principle and standard of judgement, structuring his most accomplished work of theology, the five-volume *Christian Instruction* (1751–54), a textbook in the form of a catechism, in which he asserted "the middle way . . . constitutes the true religion."[20]

The middle way first and foremost defined Christianity vis-à-vis natural religion. Like other religious enlighteners, Vernet recognized natural religion as the shared basis of morality that, by affirming

---

[17] Falletti, *Jacob Vernet*, 26.

[18] "Eloge historique de Monsieur Cramer, professeur de philosophie & de mathématiques à Genève," *Nouvelle bibliothèque germanique*, vol. 10 (1752), 368.

[19] *Pièces fugitives sur l'Eucharistie* (Geneva, 1730), 176. In his first work he used fictitious persona. See *Deux lettres à monsieur l'Abbé *** chanoine de Nôtre Dame de Paris, sur le Mandement de Monseigneur le Cardinal de Noailles, du 10. aout 1725, au sujet de la guerison de la dame La Fosse, femme d'un ébeniste du Faux-bourg St. Antoine* (Cologne, 1726). Falletti noticed Vernet's emphasis on the *juste milieu*. See *Jacob Vernet*, 49.

[20] *Instruction chrétienne, divisée en cinq volumes; seconde édition, retouchée par l'auteur & augmentée de quelques piéces*, 5 vols. (Geneva, 1756), 1:177. Vernet aimed at people "who read and reason." See "Avertissement sur cette second édition," I :vi. I have used the augmented second edition of 1756. The work was reprinted in 1771, 1807 (twice), and 1808. One historian called it "the classic manual of religious instruction for two generations." See Baron Hermann Freiherr von der Goltz, *Genève religieuse au dix-neuvième siècle* (Geneva, 1862), 89.

I have concentrated on the *Instruction* because Vernet wrote it at the height of his powers and did not revise after the second edition. Most scholars have focused on the better known *Traité*, but that work poses formidable textual problems, such as distinguishing Vernet's ideas from Turrettin's, as well as the need to sort out multiple editions with innumerable revisions.

mankind's universality, created a platform for dialogue with deists and unbelievers. Morever, the relationship between natural religion and one's own confession was of the utmost importance.[21]

Vernet thought Christianity restored natural religion. Adam and Eve had received natural religion when gaining knowledge of good and evil but lost it with their corruption. The Ten Commandments reiterated its tenets. Judaism did not restore natural religion, however, since it depended on sacrifices, practices "accommodated" to the Israelites' primitive mentality.[22] Jesus first restored natural religion, making Christianity its only sustainable form, though Christianity obviously superceded natural religion as well.[23] Christianity represents a middle way between two omnipresent dangers: impiety or "contempt for religion," including atheism, and superstition that confuses true religion with false, especially the immoral practices of idol worship.[24]

Natural religion was unsustainable since it lacked adequate notions of worship and the world. As the case of Adam and Eve demonstrated, "there is no country in which, without the aid of revelation, natural religion has been able to preserve itself in its primitive purity." Like other religious enlighteners, Vernet averred that philosophy is too abstract and too impersonal to maintain morality. Religion alone impresses the common man with its notions of creation, providence, and divine intervention. It teaches a correct notion of the deity and, through its cult, virtue, piety, and atonement.[25]

The middle way applied to Christianity's origins. Whereas Vernet held a positive view of Judaism—the Old Testament abounded in wisdom and morality, its miracles were "public and indubitable events," and Moses was a true prophet—he was also a supercessionist who used the principle of accommodation. Judaism could not be a universal religion as the Israelites were still in their infancy: the Mosaic law was "proportional to the[ir] condition and needs." Moreover, by Jesus's time, an erroneous notion of morality prevailed. The Pharisees emphasized

---

[21] See *Instruction*, 1:1–57. For Turrettin, see *Traité de la verité de la religion chrétienne*, 3 vols., 2nd ed. (Lausanne, 1772); volume 1 is devoted to natural religion and the utility of revelation. On Turretin, see Michael Heyd, "Un Rôle nouveau pour la science: Jean-Alphonse Turrettini et les débuts de la théologie naturelle à Genève," *Revue de Théologie et de Philosophie* 112 (1980): 25–42.

[22] *Instruction*, 1:62, 269, 288. Cf. *Lettres critiques*, 2:26.

[23] *Instruction*, 1:iv, 1:58–64, 2:146. He reiterated this idea in the *Reflexions sur les mœurs: Sur la religion et le culte* (Geneva, 1769), 17. See Falletti, *Jacob Vernet*, 83.

[24] *Instruction*, 1:77. For idolatry, see 1:11–16, 177, 2:35, 3:70; *Abrégé de l'histoire universelle, pour la direction des jeunes gens*, 2nd ed. (London, 1801), 12; and *Reflexions*, 15, 76–77. For the Reformation, see *Lettres critiques*, 2:124–45.

[25] Quotation at *Instruction*, 1:63. On Adam and Eve, see 1:196. Cf. ibid., 1:59–60, 64, 172, 2:148, 3:277.

outward behavior over true probity, while pagans separated religion from morality. Jesus reconstituted the middle way, reconnecting religion and morality in making love of God man's first duty.[26]

Christian anthropology found a middle way in the covenant of grace. God destined man to pursue the twin goals of happiness and perfection by endowing him with reason and liberty. Yet liberty also enables him to recognize that he is "weak and corrupt": witness Adam, who plagued mankind with a state of enduring corruption.[27] The Gospel teaches man to employ his liberty for a moral life and good works: "nothing is more beautiful than for a reasonable creature to imitate the goodness of his Creator."[28] The Gospel also offers "a middle way between self-esteem and discouragement" that inspires the virtue of humility, which begets all other virtues.[29] Nevertheless, the Gospel recognizes that man will fail. Jesus introduced the covenant of grace, a universal means of expiation through his sacrifice, to solve this quintessentially human problem. No other religion offers an equivalent: "there is only one light and one divine grace that is capable of elevating man above himself." Here is the core of Vernet's Arminian theology. Man's intact faculty of reason makes him free to be moral, while his corruption makes him need Jesus for expiation and grace.

True Christian observance was a middle way from its inception. Pagan cults proffered indecent visual spectacles; the Jews' sacrificial cult was spatially limited. Christianity presented a visual cult aimed at the soul limited neither in time nor space. Through the offer of grace in Jesus's death, Christianity created "a thoroughly simple and reasonable cult." Vernet's own ideal was an unornamented service centered on early Christianity's few ceremonies (baptism, communion): "true piety is one in which there is much reflection and little sensible emotion, much reason and no passion." He thought it imperative to resist the Catholic temptation to multiply observances or enhance existing ones: "It is . . . the penchant of the multitude for the theatrical, for the striking, which so often makes religion degenerate into superstition, crudeness, puerility, and makes it lose that reasonable simplicity, that

---

[26] Quotation at ibid., 1:75. Cf. 1:282–283, 288, 2:5–40, 249, 5:7. For Turrettin's similar views, see *Traité de la verité de la religion chrétienne*, vol. 2.

[27] Quotations at *Instruction*, 1:46, 194, 2:53. For man's happiness and perfection, 1:1–7, 49, 194, 250, 3:229–237; for man's reasonableness, 3:290–94.

[28] Quotation at *Instruction*, 1:163. Cf. 1:194–201. For Adam's hereditary sin, 1:198. He praised Pelagius for finding the "middle way" between Manicheanism's sinful man and Jovinian's sin-free man in *Bibliothèque italique*, vol. 5 (May–August, 1729), 88.

[29] *Instruction*, 2:102–3, 3:68. See also 2:53, 76, 83.

spiritual purity which is its essential character."[30] Such efforts inevitably divagated from the pristine simplicity of the "middle way that was so well marked for us by the Gospel." Lent and Carnival are obvious extremes that diverge from the Protestants' "wise middle."[31]

Christianity's middle way emerged in "a century strongly enlightened in respect to human knowledge"; it offers "an enlightened piety" that is "the root of all virtue." Vernet proclaimed that "the Gospel announces itself as a reasonable doctrine which does not fear to be examined by the rules of common sense." In contrast, atheism and Judaism were neither enlightened nor reasonable: "Nothing is more unreasonable, just as nothing is more dangerous, than atheism." Judaism's corporeal ceremonies were suited to the unenlightened and unreasonable Israelites.[32]

Vernet's enlightened and reasonable middle way was opposed to enthusiasm's false miracles and erroneous practices. His first book, published in 1726, was devoted to a miracle that allegedly occurred while he was in Paris. During the Jansenist controversy's second phase, which turned on access to communion and was punctuated by miracles, an invalid woman claimed to have been healed when the Blessed Sacrament was paraded past her street. Catholics in part directed this miracle at the Protestants who resided there. Vernet wrote a fictitious dialogue questioning the miracle. Above all, he enunciated the idea, typical of Protestant religious enlighteners, that miracles had ceased with Christianity's founding: "It was divine wisdom to employ extraordinary means to confirm revelation and to establish a new law. But once this faith was established, miracles are no longer necessary and God does nothing that is not necessary."[33] Furthermore, the miracles were too partisan to be above suspicion: "Frankly, Sir, these marvels thus multiply at the present moment and always in favor of the same party."[34]

---

[30] Ibid., 2:388, 93; *Reflexions*, 89; *Lettres critiques*, 2:22.

[31] *Instruction*, 3:201, 202:399; *Lettres critiques*, 2:149.

[32] *Instruction*, 2:4, 1:271, 1:110, 2:484, 1:42, and 1:289, 304.

[33] *Deux lettres a monsieur l'Abbé*, 14. See also *Instruction chrétienne*, 3:140. For Church leaders after the Apostles having no claim to supernatural illumination, see ibid., 2:467, 470. For the incidents, see Gargett, *Jacob Vernet*, 8–10; and Falletti, *Jacob Vernet*, 13–14. For Jansenist miracles, see Robert Kreiser, *Miracles, Convulsions, and Ecclesiastical Politics in Early Eighteenth-Century Paris* (Princeton, 1978). For the Jansenist controversies, see Dale Van Kley, *The Religious Origins of the French Revolution: From Calvin to the Civil Constitution, 1560–1791* (New Haven, 1996). For Protestant enthusiasm in Geneva, see Pitassi, *De l'Orthodoxie aux Lumières*, 67–74.

[34] "Lettre à Mons . . . sur la 3e. 4e. & 5e. Lettre d'un Docteur de Sorbonne au sujet du prétendu Miracle du Fauxbourg S. Antoine," *Bibliothèque germanique ou histoire littéraire*

Vernet did not repudiate miracles. He strenuously defended God's ability to intervene in the world, acknowledged the truth of Jesus's miracles, and enumerated criteria for distinguishing between true and false miracles. Rather, the Gospel's supernatural order of grace put an end to miracles. When "the spirit of God" now functions, it does so through Providence and secondary causes: God primarily "acts in a manner in conformity with our reason and our liberty, and by means of the natural faculties he has given us."[35]

By disputing the Catholic interpretation of the Eucharist that informed the Parisian "miracle," Vernet brought his Cartesianism to the fore. How could Jesus be present in the Eucharist "without needlessly overthrowing the laws of nature"? At issue was whether Jesus's presence was literal or symbolic, as understood through such Cartesian ideas as accidents (if they are not real, then the body of Jesus cannot be real in the sacrament) and the extension and impenetrability of material (which would make it impossible for Jesus to exist in more than one place at more than one time). Vernet vehemently argued that the primitive Church had espoused a symbolic interpretation for which the early Church fathers had developed a theory of symbols. The present dilemma comes from "the common people [les Peuples grossiers] and the scholastic doctors [who] have confounded the physical and the moral, the literal sense with the figurative, [and] produced an unintelligible jargon in the Catholic Church." Vernet was in the characteristic Protestant position of trying to "eliminate inappropriate additions or to reduce a confused but sacred language to distinct ideas."[36]

Vernet affirmed the symbolic interpretation. The transformation of the bread and wine into Jesus's body and blood is accomplished "by the benediction and by virtue of the Holy Ghost." The new status is "purely spiritual or moral because it comprises a reconciliation between man and God." It can be conferred by a strictly symbolic process: "receiving its symbol or receiving the literal flesh is for us the same." This symbolic construction in fact represented "the middle way

---

de l'allemagne, vol. 19 (1730), 226. See also Deux lettres a monsieur l'Abbé, 37, where he calls it a "partisan blow."

Vernet also rejected the Jansenists' use of the formal vous to address God, affirming the Protestant practice of using tu. See Lettres sur la coutume moderne d'employer le vous au lieu du tu; et sur cette question: doit-on bannir le tuteyement de nos versions, particulièrement de celles de la Bible? (Hague, 1752), 75–77.

[35] Instruction, 1:165–66, 2:163–66, 347–358.
[36] Pièces fugitives, vi–vii, 161, 163–73, 188, v.

[*juste milieu*] between those who would empty the Sacrament and those who would disfigure it by dint of exalting it."[37]

Vernet's interpretation of the Eucharist was characteristic of religious enlighteners insofar as he adjured truths contrary to reason (*contra rationem*) but not above it (*supra rationem*). The Eucharist is "a means by which God for his part acts faithfully, and gives us an equivalent of the body and the blood of Jesus Christ that enables us to participate in his sacrifice." Vernet thought it unnecessary to ascertain precisely how the sacrament works. Christians should accept the mystery: the Eucharist succeeds "without [humans] penetrating the reasons or the competence of divine conduct." He similarly accepted a number of mysteries as being above reason and explanation (God's design of the world, God's vouchsafing revelation by degrees, the design of Christianity).[38]

Truths above reason did not compromise Christianity's claim to being a reasonable or an enlightened religion. In fact, Vernet insisted on reason as a criterion or method in understanding religion in general and Christianity in particular. He called reason and revelation the "two lights" and used them in tandem. He discussed such truths as God's qualities on the basis of reason, and then employed scriptural quotations to corroborate and elaborate those propositions. He believed in "the perfect accord of the two lights" such that "reason and God's word collaborate on an equal basis in establishing and fortifying our faith."[39]

He employed reason to understand scripture and prophecy, using the same method to interpret the Bible as other books. One has to determine what the author said without appeal to one's own prejudices and preconceptions; to be attentive to the oriental language and its manner of speaking; to know the history that illuminates the author and his time; to be alert to the context in order to find the meaning that best fits what precedes and follows; and to compare passages that are mutually illuminating. Finally, the reader must always prefer the "light of reason" so as not "to attribute to Scripture an unreasonable sense contrary to clearly known truth." Prophecy is also subject to reason insofar as a true prophet's doctrine must be "good in itself, that is,

---

[37] *Ibid.*, 187, 162, 176. For the symbolic understanding, cf. *Instruction*, 2:417–21. For ideas that have a sign or symbol being powerful, cf. *Reflexions*, 86. On Calvin's understanding of the Eucharist, see B. A. Gerrish, *Grace and Gratitude: The Eucharistic Theology of John Calvin* (Minneapolis, 1993), 162.

[38] *Pièces fugitives*, 175; *Instruction* 1:71, 136–38, 253, 2:12, 54. For acceptance of mysteries, see *Lettres critiques*, 1:116, 2:261.

[39] *Instruction*, 1:112. Using reason and then scripture structures all five volumes.

reasonable, useful, important and appropriate for advancing the glory of God and the true welfare of mankind."[40]

How far had Vernet traveled in creating his "enlightened Orthodoxy"? Ever since d'Alembert's famous article ("Geneva") in the *Encyclopédie*, Vernet has repeatedly been accused of "perfect Socinianism." For d'Alembert, Geneva's Calvinism was distinguished from "pure Deism" only by "respect for Jesus Christ and the Scriptures." The ministers believed neither in Jesus's divinity nor in Christianity's mysteries. The ministers collectively disputed this charge, and Vernet attacked it at length.[41] The charge of Socinianism rested on subverting Christian mysteries in two fundamental ways: denying Jesus's divinity and denying the Holy Ghost's role in grace.

On occasion Vernet did use language suggesting Jesus was a mere human with a divine mission. For example, he characterized Jesus as "the most important model and the most holy doctor that ever was;" as "the doctor sent by heaven, who is perfectly instructed in the will of God;" as having "the spirit of God without measure."[42] He also wrote of Jesus as a "mediator" and "envoy" and Christianity as "a very excellent Philosophy."[43] There is no gainsaying Socinian overtones.

At the same time, Vernet recognized Jesus's divinity: "[Jesus] did not hide the divinity of his origin or his mission." "Son of God" can be just a title when applied to Adam, yet in regard to Jesus the appellation designates a relationship unlike any other: "divinity was communicated and united intimately in him." Indeed, the mysteries that Jesus is at once human and divine, "the son is properly God manifested in flesh," and that God is not divided between father and son but still unified, so that to doubt the son is to doubt the father, are scripture truths that defy human comprehension (*supra rationem*).[44] In responding to

[40] Ibid., 1:101, 70.

[41] D'Alembert's article is conveniently reprinted as "Description abrégée du gouvernement de Genève," in *Œuvres de d'Alembert*, 5 vols. (Paris, 1822), 4:411–22. Vernet's refutation is in *Lettres critiques*.

[42] *Instruction*, 2:87, 146; *Abrégé de l'histoire universelle*, 28, 2:271. For similar Socinian language, such as the "divine mission" of Jesus, the purity and saintliness of Jesus and the Apostles, see *Traité de la verité de la religion chrétienne*, 3:135–217, 266–73.

The accusation of Socinianism originated with the article "Genève" in volume 7 of the *Encyclopédie*, reprinted in *Œuvres de d'Alembert*, 4:411–22. Falletti saw Vernet as Socinian in a historical rather than a technical theological sense. See *Jacob Vernet*, 91–93. Gargett's accounts of Vernet's theology are unreliable. See *Jacob Vernet*, passim. Budé denies that Vernet was Socinian. See *Vie de Jacob Vernet*, 184–91.

[43] *Reflexions*, 20–23; *Instruction*, 3:454.

[44] *Instruction*, 2:154, 236–37, 240–41, 243. For Jesus's divinity, cf. 2:172–73, 200, 285, 366. Falletti argues that Vernet was unequivocally Socinian in his Latin thesis of 1777. See *Jacob Vernet*, 70–83.

d'Alembert, Vernet expressly confirmed his adherence to the Christian mysteries.[45] Vernet also left no doubt about Jesus's mediating role in atonement and expiation. In his divine aspect, Jesus is savior, mediator, and judge of the world. Those roles, and the economy of grace, separate Christianity from natural religion and Judaism: "a full rehabilitation in the favor of God and in the law and eternal life. Such scope and such happy results of divine clemency were not at all known before Jesus Christ."[46]

Vernet further distanced himself from Socinianism in acknowledging the Holy Ghost. During Jesus's lifetime it was enough for a Christian to believe in "God the father and Jesus Christ the son"; after his death one had to believe in the Holy Spirit that inspired the Apostles. Belief in the Holy Ghost became a "third principle of Christian faith."[47]

An additional source of confusion is Vernet's extensive use of the exegetical principle of accommodation. By the eighteenth century the Arminian-Remonstrant and Socinian usages had merged. Calvin had used the principle to show that the Bible contained neither errors nor textual contradictions. In contrast, Socinus used it to disqualify problematic biblical passages; he was only concerned that scripture be entirely reliable in matters of doctrine. Turrettin essentially accepted the Socinian use of the principle via Grotius and the Remonstrants: the Old Testament's obscurity derived from God's accommodation to the ancient Israelites. He did not defend the accuracy of Genesis but instead vindicated its doctrinal content. In contrast, he used accommodation to defend the New Testament's integrity and divine inspiration.[48]

Vernet followed Turretin's use of accommodation. He applied it to the Old Testament to explain Judaism's particularity and inferiority.[49] He applied it to the New Testament to confirm Jesus's and the Gospel's truth and genius. The Gospel itself, and God's sacrifice of his son, are a form of "condescendence" to man's weak and sinful nature through grace. The New Testament's genius is grace: on other subjects the

[45] *Lettres critiques*, v.

[46] *Instruction*, 2:53. Cf. 2:245–46.

[47] Ibid., 2:274.

[48] Ford Lewis Battles, "God Was Accommodating Himself to Human Capacity," *Interpretation* 31, no. 1 (1977): 19–38, and Martin I. Klauber and Glenn S. Sunshine, "Jean-Alphonse Turrettini on Biblical Accommodation: Calvinist or Socinian?" *Calvin Theological Journal* 25 (April, 1990): 7–27.

[49] The Israelites were a primitive people in their infancy (*Instruction*, 1:282–83; 1:288); their revelation was "proportional to the[ir] condition and needs" (1:282–83); the "holy writers accommodated themselves to common language of the people" (1:279). The mosaic law was "une excellente Police religieuse" (2:249).

Apostles were men subject to error. Jesus accommodated to his Jewish audience by speaking in a simple, conversational mode, and he and the Apostles quoted the Old Testament, especially prophetic language, to "accommodate" themselves to the Jews. Finally, Vernet used accommodation in regard to the early church. The early councils of Apostles did not make dogmatic judgments or pronouncements of faith but rather regulated matters of discipline as a form of accommodation to the congregation.[50]

Vernet's "reasonable" and "enlightened" Christianity was an Arminianism balanced between liberty and original sin, reason and faith, that rested on revelation and miracles, truths beyond reason, and Jesus's divinity. In keeping, Vernet held that a Christian's true concern is practical. Christianity's aim was not speculation but practice: "the major point of the Christian profession is the purity of morals [*mœurs*]." True religion consists in "true piety" in the "practice of moral virtue." "The most religious man is also the most just."[51]

Vernet's Christian morality was also a middle way. Unlike natural law, Christianity actively shapes the internal characteristics required for virtue and a moral life. A Christian acts with an eye on the future life, striving for interior perfection as well as virtuous action. In regard to emotions, the Gospel offers "a middle way between self-esteem and discouragement" by inspiring the foundational virtue of humility. Humility represents the middle way between the evils of pride and baseness. Pride "is the greatest obstacle which the human heart can oppose to all sentiment of religion," since it keeps one from admitting sin and submitting to God.[52] Baseness, libertinism and sensual excess feed our passions and undermine reason's ability to transcend the physical world to discern the spiritual one: "all that which inflames the passions and undermines the empire of reason is precisely that which is most contrary to the spirit of piety. For piety requires that man reflect and keep a reign on his passions. The peculiar strength of Christian faith is to direct our sight to invisible goods and to convert carnal man to spiritual man."[53]

Such character traits have social consequences. Society depends on the principle of justice.[54] The virtues support justice, the vices destroy it. Justice especially requires charity. Again unlike law, which teaches neither personal nor civic virtues, Christianity inculcates the meaning

[50] *Instruction*, 2:57, 82–83, 1:90, 2:152, 257, 469–70.

[51] Ibid., 1:v, 93, 3:5, 1:270, 1:8, 2:29.

[52] Ibid., 3:26–27, 3:68, 248–49.

[53] Ibid., 3:313.

[54] Ibid., 3:312, 132, 4:17.

and practice of charity, elevating love of one's neighbor to an active pursuit. The Gospel is "a bond of fraternity among men," and "Christian charity is the renewal of the pure law of nature." In contrast, pride and avarice are inimical to charity and civility. "Avarice attaches the heart to lesser interests, and pride meddles and embitters everything, because it takes offence and will not yield." Those vices also rupture social bonds: the proud man refuses to tolerate or honor others, the avaricious one refuses to give alms. In contrast, "the Christian religion institutes order and peace throughout; in reconciling first God with man, it creates harmony with himself, and it makes him live in peace with his fellow men."[55]

Christianity's role in erecting a moral society links Vernet's theology to his politics and figures in his response to the philosophes.

POLITICS

Vernet responded with remarkable consistency to Geneva's key political events: the crisis of 1734, the discussion of the early 1750s, the debates of the 1760s. He formulated a conservative interpretation of natural law theory in the idea of a "just subordination," defining liberty in terms of order and private possessions rather than sovereignty. He subsumed taxes, one of the galvanizing issues for Geneva's bourgeoisie, under a citizen's duties. He rejected the people's right to resist an unjust government, recommending paternalist reform. A government that concerned itself with the people's welfare could mitigate subordination and inequality. He promoted the hallmark Enlightenment idea of the ruler as the servant of his people and used the middle way to delineate his character.

At the same time, Vernet used his natural law theory to advocate freedom of conscience and toleration. The Church's legitimate means are the same as Jesus's—teaching and persuasion. Pastors should be models of moderation and above all should avoid fanatic intolerance. The state must respect liberty of conscience by permitting diversity of opinion and, if necessary, a multiconfessional society.

As we have already seen, Vernet thought natural law emerged as a counterpart to natural religion. The fear of an omnipotent and omniscient God gives rise to both, with natural law consisting first and foremost in an idea of justice: "after the respect which is due to God, [justice] is the first and most necessary of all the virtues. It is one of the great principles of natural law. It is the foundation of all order; it is the

---

[55] Ibid., 4:8–9, 29–44, 69, 234, 137, 211, 19, 252.

base of public tranquility, and the support of human society." God wants man to live in a just society ruled by law.[56]

During paganism's reign, the extremes of "barbarism" and "opulence" subverted the true middle way of natural law. Like natural religion, natural law could not survive without revelation. While Judaism reintroduced law and morality in the decalogue, the Gospel first reestablished a "true system of morality"—"natural law and the law of mankind brought to all their perfection." Gospel law is universal and, unlike civil law, "leads and purifies the interior."[57]

Vernet's conservative understanding of natural law emphasized order and subordination. In discussing the social contract he mentioned not liberty but obedience. Without society, men would live in a state of "war, pillage and plunder." The original contract emerged when families, "the first and most natural of all [societies], the root of all others," joined together to form a people. This collective life guaranteed the peace of each individual: "to be more secure and at liberty for his life, his family, his religion, his honor, and his possessions." It also fostered the advantages that accrue from society: "the sciences, the arts and commerce."[58]

For Vernet society's indubitable purpose was to "introduce order, . . . to make [society] more secure and advantageous for each individual." Unlike Saul and David's monarchies, God does not directly establish most governments; nonetheless, they exercise legitimate power. The ruler's sovereignty is sacred; each time a new ruler takes power the original contract is automatically renewed.[59]

The principle of subordination establishes order: "human society could not exist without subordination." The idea of a just subordination is equally important to Christianity and society. Man's free choice between virtue and vice rests on obedience: the exercise of free will is not about liberty but about subordination or insubordination.[60] Subordination is created in various ways. Not surprisingly, it begins in the family, the social contract's primordial site. Vernet deemed a wife's obedience to her husband "the natural and primitive order of God."[61] Subordination is further established at home: as the fifth commandment prescribes, civil life begins with obedience to parents:

[56] Quotation at ibid., 4:17. Cf. 5:8–9.
[57] *Reflexions*, 14–15, 17–18. On the decalogue and natural law, see *Lettres critiques*, 2:26.
[58] *Instruction*, 4:2, 5:3–4.
[59] Ibid., 4:6, 5:3, 8, 11.
[60] Ibid., 1:223, 3:13.
[61] Ibid., 5:120.

[D]omestic discipline is the first apprenticeship of civil life. Whoever is accustomed to obey in the home, will easily submit to the obedience which is due to the law and the magistrate; in contrast, the independent spirit that young people contract in their families disposes them to show insolence and license outside of it."[62]

Assigning men to a hierarchy of ranks and occupations establishes a subordination that carries God's stamp: "because it is divine providence that established subordination as necessary to society, each person must piously submit to that order, whatever the place accorded him, whether it be that of superior or inferior." Vernet thought this "just subordination" of "inferiors . . . to their superiors . . . must appear in the exterior and the manner of life." Moreover, whereas Vernet thought the extremes of wealth and poverty were detrimental to society, preferring a middle condition, he considered inequality valuable, because "taken only to a certain extent, [it] is useful for maintaining subordination and industry, and for preventing a lack of hands for low and hard occupations."[63]

Inequality challenges society; religion has a fundamental role in making it bearable. Christianity teaches the "natural law that ties us to our fellow men" and also subordination. "True piety demands complete obedience," and "the highest degree of respect consists in that profound veneration, in that complete acquiescence, in that submission of spirit and heart, which is due only to God and his word. This is what we call religious faith."[64] Submission to God fosters submission to all authority:

[P]iety makes men more docile and capable of discipline. It makes them regard the civil order as a divine establishment, and disposes the people to submit to it; it makes them regard the sovereign as the minister of the king of kings, it makes their person and their authority sacred and inviolable. Nothing better establishes the chain of subordination than to relate it back to the natural source of all power and all empire.[65]

Moreover, Christianity inculcates a sense of conscience that supports subordination:

[T]he principle of all subordination consists in that men are first of all subject to God, that the earthly judges fear the celestial judge, that

[62] Ibid., 5:133. Cf. 1:268, 5:161–62.
[63] Ibid., 5:106, 1:223, 3:366, 4:58.
[64] Ibid., 4:12–13, 69, 3:51, and *Lettres critiques*, 138. Cf. *Instruction*, 3:259, and *Lettres critiques*, 255.
[65] *Instruction*, 5:14–15.

oaths are inviolably respected, and that people are directed to do that which is good, not only because of fear of civil punishment, but because of conscience.[66]

Historical Christianity also reinforced social subordination. Jesus and the Apostles were sterling examples of it, while the Reformation's leaders followed St. Paul's dictum to submit to temporal authority. Subordination informs the Church as an institution: as in any society that follows natural law, members submit to the church's leaders.[67]

The ruler's behavior is essential to maintaining subordination. Whereas indolent superiors sharpen social tensions, industrious and well-employed superiors diminish them: "the inequality of conditions is well mitigated when each person shows himself to be usefully occupied, albeit in a different manner." Superiors who command through reason alleviate the sting of subordination, as do those who utilize Vernet's much prized virtue of "gentleness." "For the human heart does not naturally accommodate to dependence; it is necessary to mitigate [dependence] with the mildness of the command." In short, "it is for [public persons] to give an example of obedience to the law, and of a just subordination."[68]

The superiors' maxims are as important as their example. Vernet employed one of enlightened absolutism's hallmark ideas: "The people are not made for the king, but the king is made for the people. The public authority which [he] assumes is not given to [him] to serve his will. It is given to him . . . to watch over the public good."[69] A Christian prince is obligated to observe the law of nations and mankind in order to "procure the public good" and promote well being. He is to institute piety and "all of the Christian virtues" because these benefit the people: "piety and good morals are so necessary for the public good that a Prince cannot dispense with them." These same qualities define a prosperous or happy state:

A state prospers when good harmony reigns in it, when the superiors are equitable and vigilant, when the inferiors are obedient and affectionate, when everyone at his post does that which is rightly expected of him. All goes well, said an ancient, when the people obey the magistrate and the magistrate [obeys] the law.[70]

---

[66] Ibid., 3:134, 4:291.
[67] *Instruction*, 2:309, 329, 324, 464. Cf. *Lettres critiques*, 2:127.
[68] *Instruction*, 3:376, 5:48–49, 5:50.
[69] Ibid., 5:11.
[70] Ibid., 5:12–14, 69.

Vernet explored subordination from the ruler's perspective in a manual he wrote for the prince of Saxe-Gotha (1750), his tutee at Geneva's Academy. He delineated the "middle way" to becoming an enlightened monarch.

Vernet stressed the ethics of friendship. The prince should surround himself with a few people "remarkable for their merit and virtue, their prudence and knowledge, the luster of their example, and the elegance of their demeanor" in which he acts as "a man of quality among his friends" and treats them as "polite company in private life." Such friendships will enable him to "preserve the middle way between inhuman arrogance and degrading familiarity," the extremes that destroy a ruler's character and his ability to act on his subjects' behalf. By keeping good company the prince will learn the sincerity and probity that enable him to know and rule himself, the prerequisite for ruling others. In matters of dress the prince must find the "just medium" between the "Sloven" and the "Fop."[71]

The prince must gain true knowledge and devote himself to reason, "the great master, to whose government and authority everyone seems willingly to submit." Raison d'état is inextricably linked to belief. The prince must strive to achieve true belief in God, because "the knowledge of God is the noblest science that the mind can acquire." God in fact provides the model for correct government: the prince should emulate God by "administer[ing] justice with impartiality and disinterestedness, with equity and wisdom."[72]

Moreover, God teaches how to legitimate subordination. Whereas natural law and the Gospel point to human equality, there is "a certain subordination, that results naturally from the different talents and capacities of men, and that is both just and necessary in Civil Society."[73] What makes subordination acceptable? The ruler should first look to "the just subordination and the perfect harmony which He has established in the world."[74] Subordination is part of the divine order:

> The subordination established in a court is an image of that which is established among men, and of the limits that are prescribed to each rank and condition; limits, which neither Prince nor Subject can

---

[71] *Dialogues on some Important Subjects, drawn up After the Manner of Socrates, For the Use of His Serene Highness the Prince of Saxe-Gotha*, trans. Rev. Archibald Maclaine (London, 1753), 67, 56. Cf. *Instruction*, 5:33–38; *Reflexions*, 26–27.

[72] *Dialogues*, 1:26–39, 144, 57, 167–68, 86, 100, 90. On God as a model for our actions in general, see *Instruction*, 3:106–7.

[73] *Dialogues*, 43–49.

[74] Ibid., 106.

transgress, without breaking in upon the general order, and forming rebellion against the Sovereign of the Universe.[75]

Merit makes subordination acceptable and the ruler a success. The prince must earn his office, "excel[ling] others in virtue and knowledge as far as he surpasses them in rank and dignity." He must augment his "external authority" with the "internal authority" that derives solely from "that natural ascendant that men acquire over others by superior degrees of capacity and merit." The first monarchs, because they were elected, were the best; the prince must be so superlative that, were his subjects able to choose, they would elect him sovereign.[76]

A convinced republican in Geneva, Vernet did not oppose monarchy elsewhere. Vernet thought Christianity politically neutral: Calvin's religion aimed to "sanctify man in all states and under all conditions."[77] Christianity perfects all governments with virtue and moderation:

[Christianity] limits itself to the spiritual without touching the temporal, allowing every established government to subsist. . . . It inspires all of the social virtues, and does not forget to mark the duties of those who govern as well as those who are governed. Without changing the form of government, it tempers everything, it perfects it and restores it to its true goal. With Christianity there can be neither tyranny nor anarchy, which are the two extremes to be feared.[78]

Vernet first formulated his ideas on liberty and the middle way in politics in response to the crisis of 1734, which concerned the right to raise funds: Did that right belong to the patrician-dominated Petit Conseil or the General Council of all citizens? Geneva's foundational edicts (1568) left the issue unresolved. While the Petit Conseil gained power to raise taxes in 1570, it was unclear whether that was a temporary or permanent arrangement, although it appeared permanent when the General Council did not convene throughout the seventeenth century. As a result of the bourgeoisie's protests in 1707, the General Council began to meet every five years. Yet these periodic meetings were suspended in 1712. In 1714 the fortifications were rebuilt and a new tax

---

[75] Dialogues, 112, 33. See Reflexions, 103: "the first link of general subordination is assuredly the respect due to the first and grandest of all masters."

[76] Dialogues, 22, 203, 210–15.

[77] Lettres critiques, 2:160. Vernet was not enamored of France's monarchy. In addressing God in the Bible, he rejected the formal Vous, appropriate to a monarchy addicted to titles and formal address, for the informal Protestant tu. See Lettres sur la coutume moderne.

[78] Instruction, 5:6.

was imposed. The bourgeoisie again demanded representation through the General Council.

Matters came to a head with renewal of the fortifications impost in 1734. The bourgeoisie petitioned to request calling the General Council, claiming that the arrangement of 1570 had been an expedient and the suspension of the General Council in 1712 unconstitutional. In his account, Vernet presented this bourgeois (*representant*) position in three pages. He devoted three times that to the Petit Conseil's rebuttal. The General Council was to be convened only for matters of overwhelming importance, and taxation did not qualify; the arrangement of 1570 was publicly known and permanent; the Petit Conseil acted on behalf of the people. Vernet defended the patrician position as the middle way:

> [I]t is a chimera to believe that liberty consists in exercising sovereignty oneself. A people that governs itself is the least free and the most unhappy of all peoples. The best use that a wise nation can make of its power is to put it in good hands where it will be handled with appropriate confidence. Thereby one maintains at once order and liberty and avoids the two equally dangerous pitfalls, tyranny and anarchy.[79]

Vernet's dyad of order and liberty expressed a classic republican preference for hierarchy over democratic participation: order is synonymous with submission to authority, liberty with nominal sovereignty.[80] The dangerous extremes of tyranny and anarchy are to politics what impiety and superstition are to religion. Patrician rule in a republic is the counterpart to Christianity in religion: each is the respective middle way.

Vernet continued to discuss these issues in the *Instruction chrétienne* (1751–54), published during another installment of the patrician-bourgeois conflict. He asserted that false liberty, construed as "independence," leads to the horrible extreme of rebellion, a form of anarchy.[81] True liberty consists in "useful" rather than "prejudicial dependence" that "depend[s] upon the law and those who execute the law. For if no one were subject to the [laws], no one would be free." In other words, liberty and submission are identical. "Yet when everyone submits to the laws and the courts, all are truly free, that is to say, all truly have the ownership and use of their rights, because each finds in the magistrate a defender against all injustice and violence."

---

[79] *Relation des affaires de Genève* (Geneva, 1734), 15.

[80] For Jean Luzac (1746–1807), a Dutch Huguenot republican of similar views, though two generations younger, see Jeremy Popkin, *News and Politics in the Age of Revolution: Jean Luzac's* Gazette de Leyde (Ithaca, 1989).

[81] *Instruction*, 4:256.

Vernet distinguished liberty from sovereignty. Liberty is either private, meaning material well-being and freedom of conscience, or personal, meaning the enjoyment of public employment and honor derived from the state. In contrast, sovereignty concerns the right to rule:

> Is liberty the same thing as sovereignty? No. Sovereignty consists in governing a state as chief without recognizing a superior. Instead liberty consists in each citizen being neither troubled nor unjustly vexed in regard to his life, his religion, his family, his honor and his possessions; and that he finds the door open to employment and distinctions which are the natural reward of talent and service. Every people who enjoy these advantages are a free people, whatever the form of their government. And every government that procures these advantages for individuals is a good government, whatever name it is called.[82]

The government determines the extent of liberty without the people's consent:

> [L]iberty is mild for all men and is one of the possessions which the government is to preserve for them, which is not to be limited more than is required by the necessity of government itself, which may need at times to disturb individuals in order to preserve public liberty.[83]

The people may not exercise countervailing power. Government serves the people's good; they are not empowered to resist. Subjects must accept their superiors' mistakes in the name of subordination:

> Therefore one must suffer patiently the severity of a sovereign, a father, a master out of respect for divine providence which subjected us to them; out of regard for the public well being which requires that subordination be maintained; and out of gratitude for the obligations that we have towards the same person.[84]

Subjects must follow their ruler's commands "in just matters, and even in all those that are morally indifferent, however difficult and painful." The one exception is a command contrary to divine law. Then a subject may question or even resist, since "this is not actually disobeying the prince, it is obeying God." The law is above the sovereign, and contravening it will lead to "manifestly illegitimate and dangerous consequences."[85]

---

[82] Ibid., 5:5. Cf. 2:92.
[83] Ibid., 5:29–30.
[84] Ibid., 4:227.
[85] Ibid., 5:57.

If the sovereign persists in ordering illegal acts, do subjects have the right to rebel? Vernet followed Calvin's doctrine of nonresistance. "It is not at all permitted to an individual either to rise up or undermine the person or the authority of the sovereign, just as a son may never forget the respect due to his father, even if he is unjustly treated."[86] Vernet cited David's flight from Saul's persecution as well as Jesus's and the Apostles' acceptance of the Pharisees' injustice. He endorsed Jesus's rejection of terrestrial arms in favor of "truth, patience and good works."[87]

Can subjects correct government's abuse or misrule? Vernet asserts a paternalistic republicanism. Most abuse is more apparent than real; the common people are too irascible and generally misunderstand the nature of government; only someone responsible who would be able to rectify abuse should judge the situation. "Even when by his status one is called upon to propose a change in the state, it is necessary to work through regular, mild and legitimate means, and not by violent ways, which disturb order and cause more harm than good." Vernet endorsed reform by elites. Rebellion promotes sedition and anarchy: it is "a crime worse than murder and worse than theft; for one does wrong not just to an individual but one disturbs the general order."[88]

The issues of representation and consent that agitated Geneva are conspicuously absent in Vernet's account of taxation. In the *Instruction chrétienne* he responded to the General Council's vote (1750) not to renew the special taxes first levied to rebuild the city's fortifications.[89] The sovereign has the right to impose taxes that serve the common good so long as they cover necessary costs and are imposed equitably: "that the burden be carried equally in proportion to the abilities of each one; that the taxes be raised in a gentle [*douce*] and imperceptible manner; finally, that there be neither embezzlement nor plundering among those who touch public funds." Paying taxes is a routine duty needed to maintain society; it is equal to obeying the laws and acting for the public good. Failure to pay is a form of theft, as unjustifiable as the poor stealing from the rich; a species of fraud that forces the sovereign to squander resources; a "sin" of disobedience against a "legitimate sovereign." Paying is a Christian duty.[90]

---

[86] Ibid., 5:58. For Calvin's doctrine, see William A. Mueller, *Church and State in Luther and Calvin*, 2nd ed. (Garden City, NJ, 1965).

[87] *Instruction*, 3:205–7.

[88] Ibid., 5:60–61.

[89] O'Mara, *Geneva in the Eighteenth Century*, 287.

[90] *Instruction* 5:31, 55–56, 65, 4:61–62, 5:66–67.

At the same time that Vernet used natural law theory to champion subordination and obedience, he used it to justify toleration through ideas of individual liberty and freedom of conscience that echoed Collegialism. Were these liberal views on toleration in tension with his conservative politics?[91]

Religion required toleration and freedom of conscience. Its legitimate means are "the way of persuasion and gentleness ... the only ones that served Jesus Christ and the Apostles and of which they would have approved. Nothing besides charity and mutual support is recommended in the Gospel." Therefore it is "a sacrilege to use religion to arm one group of people against another."[92] Freedom of conscience or "liberty [of belief] is a natural right" the Reformation enacted. Each person has the right to examine a preacher's sermon or teacher's doctrine according to his own understanding of Scripture.[93]

Religion lies outside the state's purview: "liberty of conscience is one of the possessions or the natural rights of each citizen which the sovereign is required to preserve." Under a wise ruler who respects freedom of conscience, a society can thrive with numerous sects or even a religion different from his own. For Vernet, "diversity of opinion is a misfortune but not a crime." Vernet opposed the fanatical persecution that promotes political instability (read: anarchy): "The diversity of ideas on matters of religion does not break the ties of civil society or of domestic society. Therefore nothing is more odious or unjust than the revolts, the hatred and the persecutions caused by religious zeal."[94] The sovereign must set a good example for his own religion by respecting the distinction between civil and ecclesiastical toleration, correcting his subjects' errors without coercion or infringement of civil status: "Religion, like other forms of knowledge, needs only doctors who can teach, not Judges who deliver verdicts." Vernet upheld the right (*jus emigrandi*) the Peace of Westphalia granted sovereigns to exile a dissident or opposition sect as a "political precaution" against sedition (but with their goods and children, for the time a generous interpretation).[95]

---

[91] Vernet mentions "natural law" twice in the *Instruction*, 2:464 and 471. In his *Lettres critiques* he mentions Locke's *Letters on Toleration* (1:146) and dates the origins of natural law to the sixteenth century (2:123).

[92] *Instruction*, 2:462.

[93] Ibid., 2:471, 4:464, 5:225.

[94] *Instruction* 2:466, 4:212.

[95] Quotations at ibid., 5:16–20. For an application of the law (1731–35) that shocked contemporaries, see Mack Walker, *The Salzburg Transaction: Expulsion and Redemption in Eighteenth-Century Germany* (Ithaca, 1992). For Jews in Geneva, see A Nordmann, "Histoire des Juifs à Genève de 1281 à 1780," *Revue des études juives* 80 (1925): 1–41.

Like Warburton, Vernet admitted the minor and not the major ban. Church membership is entirely voluntary. Members are free to withdraw, and the church may exclude members who embrace hostile doctrines or behave reprehensibly. Such exclusion is reserved for matters of importance; minor religious issues, or issues such as science or politics, do not qualify. Exclusion is permitted only if it does not affect the person's civil status.[96]

The church should concern itself with conformity to discipline and behavior. The sovereign has "power of government for the externals of the church that are necessary for the good of the state." The church should not insist on fine points of dogma or doctrine. A council or synod's decision cannot be "infallible or unreformable"; it is a "consultation of experts" and does not issue a "divine decree." The church should concentrate on piety, practice, and the promotion of good morals.[97]

Vernet's ideal pastor and theologian were to personify toleration by avoiding fanaticism. The pastor's cardinal aim is his flock's spiritual well-being. A pastor should employ only the means of instruction—"he received the key of knowledge and not the sword of justice"—and it should be concrete and practical, arguing according to the "two lights" of "right reason and Scripture." His sermons should contain, "all the purity, the dignity and the vehemence appropriate to inspiring great respect for God." In administering ecclesiastical discipline he must find the middle way that is "neither a misguided rigidity nor a dangerous relaxation." He must "tolerate diversity of opinion on nonfundamental points" and act with "prudence and mildness" to avoid dissension and conflict. He should adopt "the spirit of moderation, tolerance and gentleness. These are the best means to prevent disputes or to dampen them."[98] Theologians should adopt an irenic and practical view of religion. They must be knowledgeable in scripture and civil and ecclesiastical history and exercise sane judgment. A theologian "must remain within his spiritual functions and should never use a religious pretext for temporal goals." In times of trouble he should preach "moderation and concord." Like other

[96] Ibid., 2:452–60. Geneva's Consistory held the power of excommunication (from 1555); in most Protestant countries the secular authorities held that power. See E. William Monter, *Calvin's Geneva* (New York, 1967), 138. The major ban—civil punishment and death for heresy—was abolished in 1632; excommunication was abolished in 1766. See Gaberel, *Histoire de l'Eglise de Genève*, 3:74, 115.

[97] *Instruction*, 5:19, 2:468–69, 469–72.

[98] Ibid., 5:80, 83, 2:474.

"men of letters [*gens de lettres*]," he should serve the state and be honored by it.[99]

Vernet's use of natural law theory appears incongruous. How could he combine a politics of subordination with an Arminian theology of free will, toleration, and liberty of conscience? Did subordination and freedom not conflict? Vernet did not sense this difficulty. He understood subordination to be as essential to Christianity as to society: Christian morality and good citizenship equally required a "just subordination." His views exemplified the extent to which toleration had become compatible with a conservative politics. Other prominent partisans of the patrician cause, especially his close friend Jean-Jacques Burlamaqui, espoused similar views.

Burlamaqui (1694–1748) was appointed the first professor of natural and civil law at the Genevan Academy (1723). He was coopted first to the Council of 200 (1740) and then the Petit Conseil (1743). Despite poor health, he could not refuse the "call of his homeland," showing himself to be, "a magistrate equally humane and enlightened" who possessed "perfect knowledge of the nature of our government and the true interests of our republic." He was "a true man of the state."[100] Vernet prepared Burlamaqui's lectures for publication after his death.

Burlamaqui and Vernet's views on theology and natural law theory were mirror images. Like Vernet, Burlamaqui posited reasonableness and its harmony with revelation: the "happy agreement between natural and revealed light, is equally honorable to both." Just as Vernet grounded Christianity in natural law, Burlamaqui grounded natural law theory in Christianity. He also thought Christianity provided society with the best moral education:

> [N]othing is more conducive to so good an end in states, than to inspire the people in the earlier part of life with the principles of the Christian religion, purged from all human invention. For this religion includes the most perfect scheme of morality, the maxims of which are extremely well adapted for promoting the happiness of society.

Finally, both thought in terms of the middle way. While Vernet sought to steer between impiety and atheism, Burlamaqui pursued the "just medium" in government, which he found in two forms: either a "monarchy, wisely limited" or an "elective aristocracy, tempered with some privileges in favor of the body of the people." He and Vernet tried to

---

[99] Ibid., 5:75, 89, and *Lettres critiques*, 2:141–43.
[100] "Eloges historique de Monsieur Burlamaqui," *Mercure suisse*, April 1748, 325–26.

harmonize Arminian theology and patrician republicanism, embracing sovereignty and subordination and abhorring democracy and liberty.[101]

Vernet identified with the Enlightenment from the start of his literary career. After the mid-century controversies with d'Alembert and Voltaire, however, he distinguished the true Enlightenment of reasonable belief from the philosophes' pernicious extremes of indifference and deism. Vernet became an adversary of the philosophes while remaining a stalwart advocate of the religious Enlightenment, which included his opposition to luxury and the theater.

Vernet announced his cultural loyalties during his travels in Italy. His 1729 article on the peninsula's culture reads like a typical Enlightenment tract. The retrograde forces of prejudice and the Church impede the Enlightenment's dissemination. The common people in Italy do not read and reason as much as they do "among us [in Geneva]," yet while "the Enlightenment is not generally known . . . it is alive where it is found," among writers.[102] The obstacles are numerous: little contact with other countries; a dearth of books; no encouragement from Princes; and the public's indifference to, indeed suspicion of, men of letters. Moreover, the Church raised barriers only the most intrepid could negotiate, such as teaching Copernicus as a hypothesis. This situation testified to scholasticism's iron grip. By asserting theology's right to arbitrate truth in all realms, the scholastic doctors make theology a hollow metaphysics that constrains minds and represses science. Vernet asserted the need for freedom of thought: "There is never progress without a bit more liberty."[103] He was also optimistic that change would prevail, as France's earlier cultural struggle was now replaying in Italy.

There was little to distinguish Vernet's account as that of a religious enlightener until he discussed other signs that scholasticism's reign was coming to an end. Some theologians, asserting the right to draw on scripture and early tradition, had begun to abandon the fine points of Spanish scholasticism for dogmatics and history, as was the case in

---

[101] J. J. Burlamaqui, *The Principles of Natural and Politic Law*, trans. Thomas Nugent, 2 vols., 3rd ed. (London, 1784), 1:312, 2:145, 70, 87–88, 93–96.

[102] "Lettre écrite à un des auteurs de ce Journal par Mr. Vernet, laquelle peut servir de Supplément au leur article du tome second de cette Bibliothèque italique," *Bibliothèque italique*, vol. 4 (1729), 119–36.

[103] Ibid., 122.

France. Preaching was similarly being reformed following the French model.

Vernet early associated with the Enlightenment by editing Montesquieu's *De l'esprit des lois* (1748). Vernet had met Montesquieu in Italy. When Montesquieu started looking for a publisher who would protect his anonymity, he was put in contact with Vernet, who happily agreed to assume responsibility. Montesquieu looked to Geneva as a center of French-language publishing free from France's constraints. For the same reason he had published his earlier works in Holland. It was also common practice in the eighteenth century for a scholar resident in a publishing center to oversee the publication of another scholar's work.[104] In an arrangement typical of the age, Vernet dealt with the publisher, made suggestions for emendations to the text, and oversaw the production process, an achievement of which he was extremely proud. Montesquieu, in contrast, voiced discontent with Vernet's handling of some matters. Whatever his qualities as an editor, Vernet's involvement testified to his commitment to the Enlightenment as a man of letters. Moreover, some of Montesquieu's ideas influenced him profoundly.[105]

Vernet's relationship with other philosophes was fraught. His association with Voltaire was not just acrimonious but adversarial. Vernet had met Voltaire in 1733 in Paris. They corresponded, discussing the possibility of a Geneva edition of Voltaire's works (who initiated that discussion remains a subject of controversy). When Voltaire moved to Geneva in 1754, relations rapidly deteriorated. A many-layered imbroglio unfolded involving polemics and heated correspondence, satire and invective. Vernet and Voltaire had public exchanges over history and religion, including Calvin's character, Servetus's execution, and Geneva's state of belief and practice. Geneva's government became involved when the Syndics rebuked Vernet over one aspect of the public controversy; when he applied to research Servetus's execution, they

---

[104] The Genevan mathematician Cramer edited Wolf and Bernoulli's mathematical works and the Leibnitz-Bernoulli correspondence. See Vernet, "Eloge historique de Monsieur Cramer, professeur de philosophie & de mathématiques à Genève," *Nouvelle bibliothèque germanique*, vol. 10 (1752), 380. For an example in Avignon, see L.W.B. Brockliss, *Calvet's Web: Enlightenment and the Republic of Letters in Eighteenth-Century France* (Oxford, 2002), 323ff.

[105] For an unsympathetic summary, see Gargett, *Jacob Vernet*, 73–87. Vernet edited and wrote a preface to Lévesque de Pouilly, *Théorie des sentimens agréables* (Geneva, 1747). Vernet edited the Latin version of Burlamaqui's *Elements du droit naturel*, for which he wrote an appreciation of his friend's life and work. *Juris naturalis elementa* (Geneva, 1754). See Budé, *Vie de Jacob Vernet*, 149. Vernet published a volume of sermons of Amédée Lullin (1724–56), a much revered pastor. See Budé, ibid., 129–49; Gaberel, *Histoire de l'Eglise de Genève*, 3:93.

refused him access to the archives. There was also a personal dimension: Voltaire accused Vernet of dishonesty and avarice, and when this accusation became public, Vernet twice felt compelled to defend himself in writing to the Syndics. Vernet and Voltaire were also at loggerheads over Voltaire's private theater productions in which patricians participated despite Geneva's ban. The imbroglio gained broader scope and lasting publicity when d'Alembert visited in order to prepare his entry on Geneva for the *Encyclopédie*. D'Alembert resided with Voltaire and consulted with Vernet; in fact, Vernet prepared a long memorandum on Geneva's history and government for him. The famous article (volume seven of the *Encyclopédie*, 1757), as well as the numerous works it elicited, belong to Vernet's continuing relationship with Voltaire.

That entry also involved Rousseau. Repudiating his adolescent conversion to Catholicism, Rousseau had contacted Vernet about being readmitted to the Genevan church (1754), and they maintained a cordial correspondence. Rousseau came to the aid of Geneva's pastors, including Vernet, with his contribution to the controversy over the article on Geneva (*Lettre à M. d'Alembert sur son article Genève*, 1758) in which he opposed the introduction of a theater. The relationship collapsed in the early 1760s when Rousseau endorsed the bourgeois, *representant* position (*Contrat social*, 1762) and renounced revealed religion (*Émile*, 1762). As had the Sorbonne, the Genevan Consistory condemned both these works, and Vernet played a pivotal role in the condemnation.[106]

Vernet articulated his two versions of Enlightenment in response to d'Alembert's article. D'Alembert, it will be remembered, had accused Geneva's pastors of a "perfect Socinianism" distinguished from "pure Deism" only by "respect for Jesus Christ and the Scriptures." They no longer believed in Jesus's divinity or Christianity's mysteries. In their sermons they preached only morality; they avoided dogmas and mysteries for fear of offending reason. Further, the pastors denied eternal punishment and embraced temporary purgatory, a position d'Alembert found paradoxical, since this was a foundation doctrine of Protestantism. D'Alembert also pointed directly at Vernet, although without naming him, when he asserted that the pastors accepted revelation's "utility" but not its "necessity": Vernet had so altered a chapter title between the first and second editions of the *Traité*.[107]

---

[106] For Vernet's relationship with Rousseau, see Gargett, *Jacob Vernet*, 98–100, 151–64, 332–69. Budé, *Vie de Jacob Vernet*, 268–85.

[107] "Description abrégée du gouvernement de Genève," 419–22.

To respond to these charges, Vernet adopted the transparent persona of an Anglican minister in Utrecht. He accused Voltaire and d'Alembert of conspiring to introduce deism to Geneva. They were the leaders of

> a poetic-philosophiste sect which, deluding itself with the agreeable chimera of reducing Christianity to nothing more than a vain name, wanted to pass off this fiction as an idea that had already been realized after a fashion in a celebrated Church and in a city which he [d'Alembert] pretended to glorify as a philosopher.[108]

The sect had attempted to dominate the republic of letters in the past half-century. Its members deployed a false brilliance: Voltaire in particular was a "bel esprit" but not a true philosopher, a poet with a superficial knowledge of philosophy and history who presented his material in an agreeable but inaccurate and often deliberately false manner and showed an appalling ignorance of scripture. The sect denigrated Christianity to promote skepticism. Voltaire and d'Alembert targeted Geneva because it would be a sterling example of philosophy's triumph over Christianity. In Vernet's eyes, the sect had "a fairly complete plan of deism lightly disguised."[109]

Vernet impugned Voltaire and d'Alembert for employing reprehensible means, singling out d'Alembert's shoddy arguments: he argued by imputation without citing evidence, made global assertions rather than addressing specifics, and used an oblique language of "hint[s] and tangled phrases." He also did not do his homework: d'Alembert's assertion about sermons was based on listening to one sermon. The pastors in fact preached all aspects of Christianity—dogmas, mysteries, scripture. D'Alembert's argument about the pastors' attitude to the nature of revelation, that is, "utility" versus "necessity," derived from his reading chapter titles: Vernet had changed the title, the contents remained the same. D'Alembert also used false logic, erecting a syllogism based on misleading terminology. Vernet averred that "it is always by superficiality that [d'Alembert] sins." The philosophes also used the deist Toland's tactic of attempting to undermine belief through a disorienting substitution of terms: "prejudice" for ancient opinion, "credulity" for faith,

---

[108] *Lettres critiques*, iv–v. First edition, 1762; definitive 3rd ed., 1766.

[109] Ibid., 1:7–10, 16–17, 81, 87, 182–85. Quotation at 2:259. The motif of Swiss intellectual independence versus French luxury and morals was central to the Swiss Enlightenment. See Roger Francillon, "The Enlightenment in Switzerland," in *Reconceptualizing Nature, Science and Aesthetics: Contribution à une nouvelle approche des Lumières helvétiques*, ed. Patrick Coleman, Anne Hoffmann, and Simone Zurbuchen (Geneva, 1998), 13–27.

"bigotry" for devotion, "superstition" for religion, "fanaticism" for zeal.[110]

Vernet's most telling criticism was that d'Alembert and Voltaire viewed the world through the extreme lenses of religious indifference and Tridentine Catholicism. Religious indifference was their aim, motivation, and key to their arguments. They opposed the Reformation because it had not abandoned Christianity altogether. They advocated toleration to further indifference: "It is because no principle of toleration is recognized other than indifferentism, and confusing the two things in spirit, they believe in extending and giving credence to the one through the other."[111] In the name of indifference or deism they employed all means of ridicule, satire, and shoddy argumentation.

At the same time, d'Alembert and Voltaire rigidly adhered to the Council of Trent as a standard by which to criticize and subvert whatever faith remained. D'Alembert saw the Reformation's abolition of indulgences as leading to the abolition of the mass; Lutheranism was heresy. He has "sacrificed his reason to everything that was decided by the Council of Trent."[112] He accused Geneva's Calvinists of heresy because they did not adhere to such early Church doctrines as the Athanasian creed. Finally, d'Alembert reiterated the Catholic canard that Protestantism inevitably begets Socinianism or deism.[113]

Vernet thought that d'Alembert oscillated between two extremes that reincarnated the age-old evils of impiety (indifference) and superstition (Catholicism). D'Alembert preached tolerance but then championed the most intolerant church; he advocated liberty and philosophy but then endorsed Catholic superstition. The belief that d'Alembert, Voltaire, and their sect could not kill with indifference's satire, ridicule, and shoddy logic they murdered with Catholicism's unyielding dogma. D'Alembert and his sect thus unfolded a "philosophy [that] does not allow for the middle road."[114]

[110] Quotation in *Lettres critiques*, 1:198. Cf. 1:17, 116–117, 129, 169, 218–19, 261–62; 2:119–20. Vernet also analyzed d'Alembert's vindication of his article.

[111] Ibid., 1:58–60. Quotation at 60.

[112] Ibid. 1:40–42. Here Vernet refers to d'Alembert's "Lettre à J. J. Rousseau," in which he wrote that the heresy "which began by attacking indulgences ended by abolishing the mass." See 1:433.

[113] Ibid., 1:249–61, 268–69. Vernet thought d'Alembert's understanding of Protestantism resembled seventeenth-century polemical works, such as Aubert de Verse, *Nouvelle apologie de la foi catholique contre les sociniens & les calvinistes* (1692). For Voltaire's attitude, see André Delattre, "Voltaire and the Ministers of Geneva," *Church History* 13 (1944); 243–54.

[114] *Lettres critiques*, 1:65, 276. For this point, see Gaberel, *Histoire de l'Eglise de Genève*, 3:192.

The philosophes wished to destroy the middle way of Protestantism in general and Calvinism in particular. In the sixteenth century, Vernet argued, the great Reformers navigated between libertinism and Epicureanism at one extreme and Catholic superstition at the other. Protestant toleration exhibits a "perfect accord" between the law of conscience and the sovereign.[115] Protestant countries like England and Switzerland are models of true Christian toleration, not indifference's sham toleration. Similarly, the Protestant practice that Geneva exemplifies consists of the "wise middle," avoiding such obvious extremes as Lent and Carnival.

Vernet erected a pantheon of reverent philosophers to exemplify the middle way, consisting of "Descartes, Boyle, Locke, Clark, Newton, Wolf." That four of the six are English shows Moderation's abiding influence. He also located Calvin among them. Calvin was not "the Pope of the Protestants," one of Voltaire's well-turned but false phrases, since he offered no bulls, no decrees, no benefices; he merely "taught, wrote and preached." Rather, Calvin was to theology what Descartes was to philosophy and Newton to astronomy: he introduced new truths and corrected errors. Vernet further praised Calvin as a "man of the state [*homme d'État*]," an approbation he had applied to Burlamaqui.[116]

Vernet addressed these themes in his *Reflections on Mores, Religion and the Cult* (1769), which he wrote at the end of a decade of crisis that began with the debate over Rousseau's *Émile* and *Social Contract* (1762). The Small Council issued a condemnation (June 1762) in which Vernet played a critical role: he both negotiated with Rousseau to find ways to preclude the condemnation and wrote the analysis that underpinned it. The next year Rousseau's many supporters among the lower bourgeoisie insisted that only the General Council had the right to take such a step.[117] Rousseau's books reopened Geneva's struggle over sovereignty after almost three decades of peace. This struggle grew in 1766 when the General Council refused to confirm the magistrates and then rejected outside mediation (France, Berne, Zurich) that was likely to favor the patrician party. Finally, in the so-called Conciliation of March 11, 1768 (the "Edict of Pistols"), the General Council effectively put an end to patrician rule by assuming power to elect the Small Council and the Council of Two Hundred. At the same time, Geneva's unparalleled prosperity fueled a debate over labor. The introduction of "life annuities [*rentes viagères*],"

---

[115] Quotation in *Lettres critiques*, 1:65. Cf. 2:124–25.

[116] Ibid., 2:149, 157–58, 154. Vernet compared Calvin to Paolo Sarpi.

[117] On Vernet's and Rousseau's condemnation, see Gargett, *Jacob Vernet*, 332–69. On the condemnation, see O'Mara, *Geneva in the Eighteenth Century*, 287–92. The lower bourgeoisie repudiated the ban during the revolution (December 1792). See ibid., 402.

from floating loans to France, had freed many Genevans, including merchants and artisans, from having to work.[118]

Vernet's book combined general considerations about the relationship of religion and politics with specific observations about Geneva as a small republic. This was at once a clergyman and a committed republican's credo, containing Vernet's fullest response to the philosophes.

Vernet unabashedly treated religion in terms of its utility or "temporal advantages." He spoke of Christianity as a "philosophy" because "[religion is] indispensable in a republic like ours, where individual conduct can have the greatest influence on public well being."[119] In Geneva there was no division between private and public. Each citizen is a "public man"; the electorate and the elected were indistinguishable. Virtue was required of both.

> This character does not consist only in being well-informed about the laws and the true interests of the homeland; it consists above all in being honest and beyond reproach, in conducting oneself without passion, in preferring the general good to individual interest, and in giving a good example in every respect.[120]

That Geneva was a republic dependent on each citizen's virtue made religion vital. Because Geneva was "a natural and primitive fraternity," a small assembly in which all classes and groups convene, it is important that a spirit of piety inspires the whole, injecting a sense of "mutual benevolence." Thus, "piety is the cement of the entire edifice," constituting the middle way.[121] There is no substitute for revealed religion in averting the omnipresent dangers of impiety and superstition: natural religion, philosophy and codes of honor are unequal to the task.[122]

In the contemporary debate over religion's place in the state, Vernet sought to navigate between what he perceived to be Hobbes's and Rousseau's erroneous extremes. Underestimating religion's power, Hobbes vouchsafed too much authority to the state. Recognizing religion but only its natural form, Rousseau mistakenly denied the need for a cult. Vernet found the middle way in a proposal of Louis René de La Chalotais (b. 1701) that had provoked a major discussion in France

---

[118] O'Mara, *Geneva in the Eighteenth Century*, 64, 83.

[119] *Reflexions*, 128, 23, 120–21.

[120] Ibid., 10.

[121] Ibid., 71, 109–11, 121. For the phrase "cement of edifice," see also 115. Cf. *Instruction*, 3:199.

[122] *Reflexions*, 15, 76–77, which echoes *Instruction*, 1:11–16, 177.

in 1763. Chalotais wanted to secularize education by shifting control from Church to state:

> My purpose is to claim for the nation an education which depends only on the State, because it belongs essentially to the State; because every nation has an inalienable and undeniable right to educate its own citizens; because the children of the State should be educated by members of the State.

He proposed replacing the Jesuits' scholastic curriculum with "a civil education" emphasizing practical subjects that "will prepare each succeeding generation to fill successfully the various professions of the State." He understood moral education to be essential: "The teaching of divine laws is the business of the Church; but the teaching of morality is a function of the state and always has been." Chalotais endorsed the natural law tradition (Grotius, Pufendorf, Barbeyrac, Burlamaqui) and its Christian foundations. He also recognized the need for public worship lest the populace lapse into idolatry.[123]

Vernet appreciated Chalotais's state-centered views and followed him in locating revealed religion's efficacy in a proper public cult: "a people without a cult soon becomes an entirely profane people, an impious people, and is consequently delivered to great excess." A cult not only promotes piety but also prevents potential immorality: "the public cult is rather like a good government: it is not a means to stop all disorders but it does stop most."[124] Vernet reiterated the argument of the *Instruction chrétienne*. Christianity teaches man's proper relationship to the true God which then ramifies to all social relationships: "the first link of general subordination is assuredly the respect due to the first and grandest of all masters." For Vernet, "submission to laws and the magistrates" is one of a long list of desirable virtues threatened by the growing unbelief and atheism. His age needs "dependence and obedience."[125]

When Vernet came to the issues of luxury and the theater, his adherence to the patrician cause seemed to waver. The Enlightenment's evaluation of luxury diverged from Christianity's. Christian doctrine regarded luxury as a sign of man's presumption, arrogance,

---

[123] *Essay on National Education or Plan of Studies for the Young*, trans. H. R. Clark (London, 1934), 47–48, 33, 150. Chalotais, an attorney general to the *Parlement* of Brittany (Rennes), achieved fame for his judicial report advocating the dissolution of the Jesuits, an instant best-seller. Ibid., 10–13. On Chalotais, see Harvey Chisick, *The Limits of Reform in the Enlightenment: Attitudes toward the Education of the Lower Classes in Eighteenth-Century France* (Princeton, 1981), 26–27, 89–102. To teach religion, Chalotais recommended either Grotius or Turrettin's *Traité* in Vernet's translation. See *Essay*, 155.

[124] *Reflexions*, 105, also 70–75. Cf. *Instruction*, 3:199.

[125] *Reflexions*, 103, 61.

and sinful nature. In contrast, the Enlightenment doctrine of *"doux commerce"* viewed luxury positively: commerce, by promoting a range of pacific transactions, contributed to society's general progress. Luxury goods significantly stimulated commerce and the economy.

Geneva had adopted elaborate sumptuary laws in the sixteenth century. In the eighteenth century these laws became controversial. Geneva's patricians generally embraced the idea of doux commerce and revalued luxury. They gradually abrogated the sumptuary laws, which in any case distinguished between different income groups. In contrast, the bourgeois or *representant* party rejected luxury and endorsed the sumptuary laws in the name of republicanism.[126]

Vernet straddled this divide. While emphasizing obedience and subordination, he opposed luxury as symbolic of irreligion, impiety and immorality. "[L]ittle or no luxury" is one of the self-evident virtues of any healthy, moral society, yet an absolute necessity to a republic dependent on the virtue of each citizen.[127] Vernet saw luxury as one cause of Athens's downfall and Pericles' disgrace. Pericles corrupted Athens's morals with a "philosophical epicureanism" of luxury, self-interest and personal vanity. In consequence, "[the Athenians] lost the liberty of which they were so jealous."[128] Sparta possessed true civility and morality. Vernet, Montesquieu, Burlamaqui and Chalotais, not to mention Rousseau, idealized Sparta.[129]

Indeed, Vernet discerned an age-old conflict between Christian morality and Epicureanism (luxury). Christianity was born in opposition to an Epicurean and pyrrhonist opulence and luxury. The conflict had frequently recurred: "every century of luxury is a century of Epicureanism."[130] In the papal monarchy of the late Middle Ages (from the thirteenth century), Rome for a second time became the "theater of pride, luxury and avarice"—and of Epicureanism and atheism: "It is in

---

[126] Rosenblatt, *Rousseau and Geneva*, 66. Cf. A. O. Hirschman, *The Passions and the Interests: Political Arguments for Capitalism Before Its Triumph* (Princeton, 1977); Christopher J. Berry, *The Idea of Luxury: A Conceptual and Historical Investigation* (Cambridge, 1994); and Laurence Dickey, *"Doux-Commerce* and Humanitarian Values: Free Trade, Sociability and Universal Benevolence in Eighteenth-Century Thinking," in *Hugo Grotius and the Stoa: Philosophy, Politics and Law*, ed. Hans Blom (Assen, 2004), 271–318.

[127] *Reflexions*, 4–5, 10. Cf. *Instruction*, 3:367.

[128] *Reflexions*, 12. See also *Lettres critiques*, 2:218–19. For luxury sapping courage, see *Instruction*, 3:416.

[129] *Lettres critiques*, 2:214–15. For Montesquieu's image, see Elizabeth Rawson, *The Spartan Tradition in European Thought* (Oxford, 1969), 228–30. Rousseau was the "arch priest of laconism" (231–42). See Burlamaqui, *The Principles of Natural and Politic Law*, 2:94, and on him, Rawson, ibid., 229, 235. For Chalotais, see *Essay*, 37, and Chisick, *The Limits of Reform in the Enlightenment*, 239.

[130] *Reflexions*, 33–34.

the womb of this political hypocrisy that one sees the rebirth of the systems of Epicureanism and atheism, which seemed to have expired with paganism, yet whose pernicious seed Italy carried to the other parts of Europe."[131]

Such Epicureanism rages in the present. Irreligion accompanies luxury in England and other Protestant countries as a virtual "delirium and almost a fanaticism of irreligion," a "scandal" that threatens to become a "contagion." Vernet identified deists and atheists as irreligion's obvious champions, but also saw *"bel esprit"* who pled its cause as disseminating it in often imperceptible ways: "just as a barbarous century furnishes examples of a brutal impiety, a century of luxury furnishes thousands of a refined and subtle impiety." And, of course, "impiety brings in its train the depravation of morals." The result was the combined "abuse of riches with the abuse of the spirit." These two evils destroy private and civil life in any polity but especially a tiny republic. Vernet saw Geneva beset by a formidable alliance of "practical Epicureanism" (a "corrupting luxury") and "speculative Epicureanism" (an "abuse of the spirit"). These resulted from some thirty years of prosperity, especially the "dangerous lure of life annuities," which threatened to undermine the example of "good discipline, laborious industry, charity, modesty and regularity" that Geneva used to exemplify.[132] In sum, "nothing is more inimical to republican liberty than libertinism: that will be the downfall of [Geneva's] happy Constitution."[133]

Vernet also parted company with some patricians over the theater. Geneva's sumptuary laws (1617) prohibited a theater. In the course of the eighteenth century, private performances and then, during the period of disturbances (1734–1738), the opening of a public theater at the request of foreign diplomats tested that prohibition. In both cases some patricians championed the cause. Nonetheless, the Consistory reimposed the ban (1739) after the diplomats left. The issue reappeared when Voltaire began to organize private performances at his residence (from 1755) in which some patricians again participated. Despite resistance from the Council and leading families, a theater opened in Geneva in April 1766 under pressure from the French envoy then in residence. Geneva finally built a theater in 1782, also in response to a resident French envoy.[134]

---

[131] *Lettres critiques*, 2:97. Cf. 2:124.

[132] *Reflexions*, 34, 48, 68, 113. On luxury and morals, cf. *Instruction*, 3:364–73, 4:74–75, 84. On life annuities, see O'Mara, *Geneva in the Eighteenth Century*, 64–67.

[133] *Lettres critiques*, 2:216

[134] Rosenblatt, *Rousseau and Geneva*, 220–21; Gaberel, *Histoire de l'Eglise de Genève* 3:75–77, 80–81. For complaints about the theater, see Linda Kirk, "'Going Soft': Genevan Decadence in the Eighteenth Century," in *The Identity of Geneva*, 146–67.

Vernet defended the prohibition: theater was another threatening manifestation of luxury and unbelief. Vernet echoed many of Rousseau's arguments from his famous antitheatrical *Lettre à d'Alembert* (1758), although aimed toward a different goal. Rousseau aspired to a secular notion of virtue to resist theatricality or "spectacles" in Geneva's life. Vernet wanted to reinforce inherited Calvinist/republican virtue.[135] Vernet agreed with Plato and Thomas More in excluding the theater from an ideal society. D'Alembert had recommended the theater as a "school of customs and virtue" that offered "the natural fruits of morality set in action." Vernet disputed theater's pedagogical utility. The writer is rarely as good a moralist as he is a poet; instruction is usually subordinated to pleasure. D'Alembert argued that tragedies offered a "grand and useful moral lesson more or less developed." For Vernet, the theater is incapable of addressing serious issues. He questioned whether it was necessary for the progress and maintenance of the arts and for the formation of taste.[136] The most effective means of moral instruction is Christianity: "A pure religion is assuredly the best means to give humanity its original nobility and all of its mildness [*douceurs*]. A good Christian is properly a reintegrated and restored man."[137]

Vernet also had serious reservations about the impact of actors on a small republic. Actors are an immoral and debauched group. Their baneful influence did not matter in large cities like Paris that were already "cesspits" of vice. As Rousseau had pointed out, comedy is only good for a corrupt society. Similarly, a monarchy's diversity easily accommodates actors. A small, homogeneous society like Geneva would only suffer. Would the actors be Protestants? Could Geneva attract excellent actors or only mediocre ones? In addition, as Rousseau had argued, maintaining a theater is expensive; who would bear the financial burden?[138]

While Vernet amassed pragmatic arguments against theater, his opposition ran deeper. The theater was a sign of depravity, the very reason d'Alembert wanted to promote it: "the depravity of taste always comes by reason of the depravity of morals [*moeurs*]." Vernet suspected the philosophes wanted "the theater as a school of totally pagan philosophy."[139] D'Alembert thought that a theatre would make it possible for Geneva to "reunite the wisdom of Sparta with the civility of Athens." Vernet

---

[135] For the antitheatrical argument, see Jonas Barish, *The Antitheatrical Prejudice* (Berkeley, 1981), 256–94. For the theatricality argument, see David Marshall, "Rousseau and the State of Theater," *Representations* 13 (1986); 84–114.

[136] *Lettres critiques*, 2:206–11, 220–23, 185.

[137] Ibid., 2:185.

[138] Ibid., 2:225–45.

[139] Ibid., 2:206.

asserted that Athens had an erroneous civility; it was a model of corruption. Sparta had no theater yet had enjoyed true civility. The philosophes' deliberate mistake was to try to purvey Paris's false and corrupt civility. As a republic, Geneva was the "abode of liberty," and "nothing is more inimical to republican liberty than libertinism: that will be the downfall of its happy Constitution."[140]

Vernet raised a clarion call to virtue, requesting an intellectual counteroffensive in which believers would aggressively confront deists on fundamental issues. Irreverent and unbelieving philosophes should not be allowed to live by ridicule and satire. They should be pressed to argue from first principles; it was easier to raise objections than to make sustained points. They should not be allowed to confuse religion with its "abuse" or "accidental accessories"; to attract the young by turning "a pleasantry" into an "argument"; or to let audacity parade as genius. They also should not be permitted to use sloppy arguments or rhetorical sleights of hand.[141] Vernet was the hoary schoolmaster reprimanding the schoolboy philosophes.

Vernet further called for an impassioned commitment to morality and the republic in the form of an "enlightened enthusiasm . . . of reason, of virtue or good sentiments." He envisioned a reverent philosopher defending the republic on the model of Cato or the Reformation's leaders. Finally, he sought to awaken all the well-intentioned through a public display of virtue: the majority's good example would vanquish the minority's bad behavior.[142]

Did Vernet's opposition to the philosophes and his position on theater and luxury affect his patrician alignment? Voltaire actively favored theater and was allied with the patricians who participated in his productions. In contrast, Rousseau allied with the bourgeois or *représentant* party in opposing the theater for the sake of Geneva's civic virtues. The divisions were not clear-cut, however. Burlamaqui was an outspoken opponent of luxury, and there were other patricians, as well as many bourgeoisie, who applauded Rousseau's opposition to the theater in the *Lettre à d'Alembert*. Moreover, Voltaire broke ranks over politics with the patricians who supported his theater productions: he first shifted to the *représentant* position and then embraced the *natifs*.[143]

---

[140] Ibid., 2:214–16. D'Alembert's quotation from "Description abrégée," 4:417.

[141] *Reflexions*, 41–46; *Lettres critiques*, 2:119–43.

[142] *Reflexions*, 55, 118–22. On youth and good morals, see *Instruction*, 4:96–97.

[143] For Burlamaqui, see *Principles of Natural and Public Law*, 2:205–6. For support for Rousseau, see Rosenblatt, *Rousseau and Geneva*, 227–40. Voltaire's involvement in the Covelle affair aroused his sympathies for the representants (1765). See Peter Gay, *Voltaire's Politics: The Poet as Realist*, 3rd ed. (New Haven, 1988), 202–38.

There was no clear correlation, then, between patrician politics and opinion on luxury and the theater. Vernet could oppose both without confusing his loyalties.

Geneva Transformed

Enlightened Orthodoxy held sway in Geneva for the better part of the eighteenth century; Turretin and Vernet succeeded in making it the republic's creed. The ideas that Turretin first broached in Latin works Vernet disseminated in a shelf of French books. To be sure, Vernet was less an original thinker than a highly influential and skillful popularizer who benefitted from clear exposition, boundless energy, and the will to public engagement. He did not rival Warburton's erudition and novel arguments. While somewhat prosaic, Vernet's middle way was also fundamental to an era. Although his death in 1789 could not have more clearly marked that era's endpoint, enlightened Orthodoxy had already begun to crumble as a result of rapidly changing circumstances.

The patrician-bourgeoisie conflict re-erupted in 1781–82 as the bourgeoisie seized control to introduce greater equality. The effort backfired. Foreign troops not only intervened and reimposed patrician rule but in fact erased the bourgeoisie's half-century of gains by returning to the 1738 terms of mediation.[144] The new patrician regime suppressed the bourgeois *cercles* and, against the clergy's opposition, built a theater and reformed the Church. Such reforms had been contemplated in 1777 when the Conseil Général had raised the pastors' salaries and considered reducing the number of sermons. In the name of economy the patrician regime decided to eliminate four and one-half pastors and the third professor of theology at the Academy, as well as to reduce the number of sermons (from 1,077 to 398). It also deprived the clergy of its power over appointments to the Academy. The clergy protested, and in 1785 Vernet was asked to present the case before the Council of 200. Vernet's two-hour protestation had little effect. In 1786 the Council decided to implement the plan, but without so drastically reducing the number of sermons (518).[145]

Before these changes could have a significant impact, events that were "a microcosm of the French Revolution as it was enacted at Paris,

---

[144] O'Mara, *Geneva in the Eighteenth Century*, 308–14.

[145] Wernle, *Der schweizerische Protestantismus*, 2:501–3, 530–31, 562; Gaberel, *Histoire de l'Eglise de Genève*, 3:65, 424.

at Lyon, at any one of the most radical French towns" overtook them.[146] The accelerating chain of events included a repudiation of patrician rule in February 1789; the full triumph of the lower bourgeoisie in the Constitution of March 22, 1791; the moderate rule of Committees of Administration and Security for sixteen months (from December 1792); a Revolutionary Tribunal (July 18, 1794), which introduced a two-month period of "Terror"—executions, confiscations, and capital levies; a Reconciliation of September 21, 1795; and finally the incorporation of Geneva into France in April 1798, which spelled the end of the independent republic.

These events confronted Geneva's church with the gravest challenge of any of the Swiss churches.[147] Athough an overwhelming majority of Geneva's citizens (2,800 vs. 382) voted to maintain the city's Calvinist character (1794), the pastors lost control over education and, during the Terror, were prohibited from performing religious rituals. In addition, facing imminent persecution, many chose to flee. When the Terror ended and a general amnesty was passed, the pastors returned, only to find they had lost control over pastoral appointments as well: in some cases new pastors had been "elected" in their place.

More fundamentally, Calvinism lost its hegemony and the populace lost its confessional homogeneity. From the moment Geneva became part of France's Department of Léman, it gained a large Catholic population. Under French rule, Catholic Masses were again performed (Saint-Germain, October 1803) and a skillful and energetic priest began to press the Catholic cause. Napoleon's Concordat officially recognized Protestantism and designated Geneva's Academy the site to train pastors for all of France: Beza's ambitions for the Academy were ironically realized at the very moment that the city's commitment to Calvinism was most sorely tested.

After 1815, Geneva was restored to the Swiss confederation, although in a thoroughly altered form. No longer an independent republic, it gained new territories from France and Savoy that changed its essential composition: its larger population was 40 percent Catholic.[148] The Calvinist Church now faced competition from without and within. Catholics vigorously campaigned to end Calvinism's hegemony by creating a public presence. A revival within the Calvinist Church championed a new pietism that, ironically, rejected enlightened Orthodoxy as a dangerous deviation from Calvin, Beza, and the early reformers.

---

[146] Quotation in O'Mara, *Geneva in the Eighteenth Century*, 389.

[147] Wernle, *Der schweizerische Protestantismus*, 3:536.

[148] For Geneva and French Protestantism, see Daniel Robert, *Genève et les Églises réformées de France: De la "Réunion" (1798) aux environs de 1830* (Geneva, 1961).

While Vernet's thought developed within the ambit of Descartes's philosophy, the English Moderation that inspired him had arisen within the ambit of Locke's. The next chapter examines a version of religious Enlightenment that emerged in relationship to the rationalism of Christian Wolff, whom Vernet had visited in Marburg.

Opposite: Siegmund Jacob Baumgarten. Frontispiece, Johan Salomon Semler, ed., *Ehrengedächtnis des weiland Hochwürdigen und Hochgelarten herrn Siegmund Jacob Baumgartens* (Halle, 1758). Photograph by permission of the Andover-Harvard Theological Library, Harvard Divinity School.

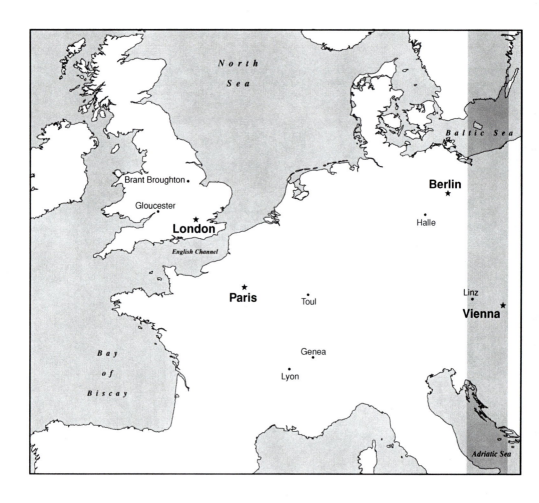

CHAPTER THREE

Halle

SIEGMUND JACOB BAUMGARTEN'S "VITAL KNOWLEDGE"

THE HUNDREDS OF STATESMEN WHO negotiated the Peace of Westphalia (1648), which terminated a century of religious warfare by providing the legal framework for the coexistence of three religions, Catholicism, Lutheranism, and Calvinism, could not, however, negotiate the reform of the militant religions that tumultuous century had produced. The task of redirecting the confessions toward toleration and irenicism fell to theologians and territorial authorities. Nowhere was this challenge greater than in the multireligious territories of Brandenburg-Prussia, whose rulers pioneered the related practices of state sovereignty and toleration.

Dubbed "the jewel in the crown of German scholarship" by Voltaire, and one of the few theologians appointed to the Berlin Royal Academy (1749), Siegmund Jacob Baumgarten (1706–57) was the preeminent representative of "theological Wolffianism," the first full expression of the religious Enlightenment among German Protestants.[1] Drawing on the Lutheran heritage and Pietism, the early Enlightenment and English Moderation, Baumgarten advocated natural law and natural religion, toleration and freedom of conscience, while also staunchly defending revelation and scripture. He called his alternative to an orthodoxy born of confessional strife "the true middle way."[2] A renowned teacher whose students ranged across the spectrum of eighteenth-century Lutheranism, he was also one of the best-known historians of his generation.[3]

The Peace of Westphalia marked the symbolic end of the Holy Roman Empire's era of "confessionalization." The struggle for religious hegemony that unleashed the Thirty Years War had convinced most Catholics, Lutherans, and Calvinists that a stalemate grounded in mutual toleration was preferable to catastrophic despoliation and unprecedented suffering. Thus, Catholics had to renounce the ideal

---

[1] Voltaire reportedly said of Baumgarten that "he who wishes to see the jewel in the crown of German scholarship must travel to Halle." See Martin Schloemann, *Siegmund Jacob Baumgarten: System und Geschichte in der Theologie des Überganges zum Neuprotestantismus* (Göttingen, 1974), 22 n. 38. For the Berlin Academy, see 51. For Voltaire's visit, see *D. Johan Salomo Semlers Lebensbeschreibung von ihm selbst abgefasst*, 2 vols. (Halle, 1781), 1:108.

[2] See *Siegm. Jac. Baumgartens kleine teutsche Schriften* (Halle, 1743), 77, 301, 346. Cf. *D. Siegm Jac. Baumgartens Erläuterung der christlichen Alterthümer,* (Halle, 1768), 11.

[3] Schloemann, *Baumgarten,* 21.

of a universal church, Lutherans were forced to accept two Protestantisms, and Calvinists had to rest content with the substantial if still piecemeal gains of their "second Reformation."[4]

In recognizing the rights of Catholics, Lutherans, and Calvinists, the Peace sounded the death knell for the confessional state (religious uniformity). Even though the Thirty Years War made the empire's territories more religiously homogeneous, with Protestant and Catholic states forming virtual blocs in the north and south, there were still numerous polities with significant religious minorities, polities whose ruler and subjects had different faiths (e.g., Brandenburg, Württemberg, Saxony) or polities with near parity between confessions (e.g., Osnabrück, Augsburg).[5]

After 1648 the principle of sovereignty gradually displaced the confessional state ideal. The Reformation and the era of confessionalization had strengthened sovereignty in multiple ways. By gaining control over religious life, the secular authority had significantly expanded its scope and administrative apparatus. Identification with a particular confession increased state power, while state-led campaigns of conversion or reconversion, as well as the creation of gymnasia and universities to promote confessional education, further amplified it.[6]

The Holy Roman Empire's federative character, which had previously fed the Reformation and the confessional state, now nurtured absolutist aspirations. The Peace of Westphalia had enhanced sovereignty by recognizing the right of the empire's more than three hundred polities to conduct foreign policy independently, a right many had already

[4] Heinz Schilling, ed., *Die reformierte Konfessionalisierung in Deutschland: Das Problem der "Zweiten Reformation," Schriften des Vereins für Reformationsgeschichte*, 195 (Gütersloh, 1986).

[5] Robert Bireley, "Confessional Absolutism in the Habsburg Lands in the Seventeenth Century" in *State and Society in Early Modern Austria*, ed. Charles W. Ingrao (West Lafayette, IN, 1994), 36–53, and Anton Schindling, "Delayed Confessionalization: Retarding Factors and Religious Minorities in the Territories of the Holy Roman Empire, 1555–1648," in *State and Society*, 54–70.

[6] For confessionalization and state building, see Heinz Schilling, "Die Konfessionalisierung im Reich: Religiöser und gesellschaftlicher Wandel in Deutschland zwischen 1555 und 1620," *Historische Zeitschrift* 246 (1988): 1–45 (English translation in Heinz Schilling, *Religion, Political Culture and the Emergence of Early Modern Society* [Leiden, 1992], 205–45). For universities, see Volker Press, *Kriege und Krisen: Deutschland, 1600–1715* (Munich, 1991), 137–49, and Rudolf Vierhaus, *Germany in the Age of Absolutism*, trans. Jonathan Knudsen (Cambridge, 1988), 60–61. Cf. Gerald Strauss, *Luther's House of Learning: Indoctrination of the Young in the German Reformation* (Baltimore, 1978).

exercised during the Thirty Years War.[7] That war had made clear the advantages of a strong military: the Regensburg Diet's ruling (1654) enabled sovereigns to require financing from the estates for standing armies. As a source of prestige, income, and trained personnel, universities increasingly served territorial and dynastic as well as confessional purposes.[8] In addition, the example of Louis XIV's Versailles heightened sovereignty's allure.

The year 1648 marked the end of the confessional state ideal but not the era's religious formations. The three denominations' efforts at dominance had resulted in their institutionalization: the militant theologies that emerged after the Peace of Augsburg persisted.[9] These dogmatic formulations had matured through the seventeenth century's incessant polemics. In particular, Lutherans and Calvinists disputed over the Augsburg confession (1530), developing elaborate dogmatics—in scholastic language, especially Spanish neoscholasticism—marking confessional boundaries. The authorities also enlisted the formal scholastic propositions of confessions and creeds of belief to suppress the proliferating chiliasts and prophets who flouted Church discipline.[10]

The Lutheran orthodoxy that emerged from these controversies canonized Luther's life and works, yet also permitted the scholastic discourses of university theologians and a university educated clergy to marginalize the Bible reading and justification by faith he had deemed central. Orthodox dogmaticians were quick to condemn all their opponents since, by definition, they represented heresy and the devil's work.[11]

---

[7] John Gagliardo, *Germany Under the Old Regime, 1600–1790* (London, 1991), 110; Schilling, "Die Konfessionalisierung im Reich," 40–41.

[8] Press, *Kriege und Krisen*, 333, 301.

[9] Schilling, "Die Konfessionalisierung im Reich."

[10] P. Petersen, *Geschichte der aristotelischen Philosophie im protestantischen Deutschland* (Leipzig, 1921); H. E. Weber, *Der Einfluß der protestantischen Schulphilosophie auf die orthodox-lutherische Dogmatik* (Leipzig, 1908); Lewis White Beck, *Early German Philosophy: Kant and His Predecessors* (Cambridge, MA, 1969), 118–26; *Protestant Scholasticism: Essays in Reassessment*, ed. Carl R. Trueman and R. Scott Clark (Carlisle, Cambria, UK, 1999). For the Thirty Years War and apocalyptic speculation, see Robin Bruce Barnes, *Apocalypticism in the Wake of the Lutheran Reformation: Prophecy and Gnosis* (Stanford, 1988). For a conflicting view, see Johannes Wallmann, "Zwischen Reformation und Pietismus: Reich Gottes und Chiliasmus in der lutherischen Orthodoxie," in *Verifikationen: Festschrift für Gerhard Ebeling zum 70. Geburtstag*, ed. Eberhard von Juengel, Johannes Wallmann, and Wilfried Werbeck (Tübingen, 1982), 187–205.

[11] F. Lau, "Orthodoxie, altprotestantische," in *Religion in Geschichte und Gegenwart*, ed. Kurt Galling 6 vols. (Tübingen, 1957–62), 4:1719–30. The best English accounts are Robert D. Preus, *The Theology of Post-Reformation Lutheranism: A Study of Theological Prolegomena* (St. Louis, 1970), and Bengt Hagglund, *History of Theology* (St. Louis, 1968), 299–324.

Baumgarten was acutely aware of Orthodoxy's problematic nature.

> In our church . . . one had gradually accepted the use of scholastic terminology and the general scholastic method, and even organized textbooks according to that method since, being the Papists' customary form of instruction, it was necessary to use it in order to prevail in the controversies with them, while it was also required for the frequent controversies in our own church. . . . [Its proponents] wanted to improve the correct and sufficient framework for the purpose of the extant controversies, with the result that the derivation from Scripture was neglected.[12]

Baumgarten's criticism of orthodoxy was characteristically sober and specific. More partisan scholars supplied blanket condemnations.[13]

The true nature of Lutheran Orthodoxy is difficult to ascertain. Its proponents were sincere, pious Lutherans, many of whom opposed scholasticism, fearing that it would divert theology from practice.[14] Theology students were constantly reminded of the gravity of the office to which they aspired; once in office, many earnestly discharged their pastoral duties. In particular, they preached on the basis of the Bible rather than dogmatics; the repentance (Bußpredigt) and not the didactic sermon (Lehrpredigt) was representative of the age. Orthodoxy also produced important devotional works and prayer books, religious poetry, and church music, as exemplified by the works of Bach. In addition, Orthodoxy produced reformers of piety, education, and devotion.[15]

---

[12] Evangelische Glaubenslehre, 3 vols. (Halle, 1759), 1:66. Cf. Geschichte der Religionspartheien (Halle, 1766), 1217, 1263.

[13] Robert Preus wrote, "No other era in Lutheran Church history has been depicted by historians, even Lutheran historians, with such a spirit of antagonism, no other era has been described with such lack of sympathy and censured with such lack of justification." The Inspiration of Scripture: A Study of the Theology of the Seventeenth Century Lutheran Dogmaticians (Edinburgh, 1955), vi. For the scholarship see, Hans Leube, "Die altlutherische Orthodoxie: Ein Forschungsbericht" and "Die Theologen und das Kirchenvolk im Zeitalter der lutherischen Orthodoxie," in idem, Orthodoxie und Pietismus: Gesammelte Studien, Arbeiten zur Geschichte des Pietismus 13 (Beilefeld, 1975), 19–35, 36–42; idem, Die Reformideen in der deutschen lutherischen Kirche zur Zeit der Orthodoxie (Leipzig, 1924), 4–33; and Norbert Haag, Predigt und Gesellschaft: Die Lutherische Orthodoxie in Ulm, 1640–1740 (Mainz, 1992), 1–2.

[14] For Orthodoxy's dating (1577–1713), see Preus, The Theology of Post-Reformation Lutheranism, 65. For opposition to scholasticism, see Preus, The Theology of Post-Reformation Lutheranism, 41 and Johannes Wallmann, "Zwischen Reformation und Humanismus: Eigenart und Wirkungen Helmstedter Theologie unter besonderer Berücksichtigung Georg Calixts," Zeitschrift für Theologie und Kirche 74 (1977): 344–70.

[15] Leube, "Die Theologen und das Kirchenvolk im Zeitalter der lutherischen Orthodoxie," 36–74; Haag, Predigt und Gesellschaft: Die Lutherische Orthodoxie in Ulm. For dedicated parish clergy, see Hans-Christoph Rublack, "'Der Wohlgeplagte Priester': Vom

If Orthodoxy was not as sclerotic as its critics contend, neither was it as effective as its apologists claim. Orthodoxy did not successfully address individual spiritual life. It was too closely identified with state authority and the estate system, reinforcing conventional notions of law and respectability, and too closely governed by the nobility through patronage and preferment (testimony to a century of upheaval). The educated clergy and university theologians' near monopoly on knowledge reinforced this relationship to social hierarchy and widened the divide with the unlearned laity, the very divide Luther had hoped to eliminate through "the priesthood of all believers."[16] Indeed, even Orthodoxy's reforms were instituted "from above" by consistorial regulation. Finally, Orthodoxy was intolerant: this held not only for early representatives (Johann Gerhard, 1582–1637; Abraham Calov, 1612–86) but also for later ones (Valentin Ernst Loscher, 1674–1749; Johann Melchior Goeze, 1717–86).[17]

Just as Lutheran Orthodoxy emerged out of the circumstances of the confessional age, so a new formation focused on spirituality, toleration, and freedom of conscience arose in the early eighteenth-century cultural configuration associated with Brandenburg-Prussia and Halle's Friedrichs University.

After 1648, Brandenburg-Prussia led the way in erecting a multireligious estate society: while repopulation and economic development made toleration desirable, politics and the populace's composition made it indispensable. A Calvinist sovereign ruled over a primarily Lutheran populace, yet also over Catholics, Calvinists, and Jews. In

---

Selbstverständis lutherischer Geistlichkeit im Zeitalter der Orthodoxie," *Zeitschrift für historische Forschung* 16 (1989): 1–30. For Valentin Ernst Löscher (1674–1749), see Martin Greschat, *Zwischen Tradition und neuem Anfang: Valentin Ernst Löscher und der Ausgang der lutherischen Orthodoxie* (Witten, 1971), 93, 196. For reform, see Leube, *Die Reformideen*. Against a separate "reforming Orthodoxy," see Johannes Wallmann, "Pietismus und Orthodoxie," in *Geist und Geschichte der Reformation: Festgabe Hanns Rückert zum 65. Geburtstag* (Berlin, 1966), 418–42.

[16] For patronage and preferment in Ulm, see Haag, *Predigt und Gesellschaft*, passim. For the educated clergy, see Rublack, " 'Der Wohlgeplagte Priester,' " 29, and Deppermann, *Der hallesche Pietismus, und der preussische Staat unter Friedrich III* (Göttingen, 1961), 12–21.

[17] For reform "from above" and "from below," see Gawthrop, *Pietism and the Making of Eighteenth-Century Prussia*, 101–3. For toleration in Ulm, see Haag, *Predigt und Gesellschaft*, 412–14; for the reformers, see Leube, *Die Reformideen*, 84–85, 109; for Hamburg's Lutheran clergy, see Joachim Whaley, *Religious Toleration and Social Change in Hamburg, 1529–1819* (Cambridge, 1985). For Löscher, see Greschat, *Zwischen Tradition und neuem Anfang*, 56; for Goeze, see Harald Schultze, "Toleranz und Orthodoxie: Johann Melchior Goeze in seiner Auseinandersetzung mit der Theologie der Aufklärung," *Neue Zeitschrift für systematische Theologie* 3–4 (1961–62): 197–219. For Orthodoxy's problems, see Klaus Deppermann, *Der hallsche Pietismus*, 12–21.

addition, he had to contend with estates allied to Lutheran orthodox consistories. The Hohenzollerns' strategy was to use sovereign power to secure religious toleration. Friedrich Wilhelm, the Great Elector (1640–88), forbade polemical sermons in his tolerance edicts (1662, 1664), dispensed with oaths on the symbolic books, and invited Socinians (1658), Jews (1670), Huguenots (1685), and Waldensians (1688) to settle his thinly populated territories.[18] Friedrich III (1688–1713) forbade oaths on the Formula of Concord, prohibited requiring confession before Communion, and deprived the churches of the right of excommunication. He also attempted, but failed, to reunite Calvinists and Lutherans (1697–1703).[19]

Raison d'état motivated Friedrich III's founding of the University of Halle (1694), which was to offset the two bastions of Lutheran Orthodoxy in neighboring Saxony, Wittenberg and Leipzig, by training pastors to minister in a spirit of confessional harmony to the recently acquired bishoprics of Magdeburg and Halberstadt. The countervailing forces Friedrich promoted at Halle were Pietism and the Enlightenment. These were the formative influences in Baumgarten's life.[20]

Baumgarten grew up in a distinctly Pietist milieu. Pietism was an effort to regenerate the Lutheran church from within. Created by Philip Jacob Spener (1635–1706) and August Hermann Francke (1663–1727), with its heyday from approximately 1675 to 1730, Pietism proposed neither a new theology nor a distinct ecclesiology. Rather, drawing on English Puritanism, reform efforts in Lutheranism, and the mystical tradition, the Pietists contended that the Church had preserved Luther's doctrinal reformation (*Reformation der Lehre*) but had failed to institute a practical one (*Reformation des Lebens*). Pietism replaced Orthodoxy's doctrinal emphasis with edifying preaching, devotion, and Bible reading that, aiming to promote each individual's relationship to God, were to be crowned with a conversionary "rebirth" (*Wiedergeburt*) in faith.

---

[18] Press, *Kriege und Krisen*, 306. Cf. Bodo Nischan, "John Bergius: Irenicism and the Beginning of Official Religious Toleration in Brandenburg-Prussia," *Church History* 51 (1982): 389–404. For "summus episcopus," see Johannes Heckel, "Die Entstehung des brandenburgisch-preussischen Summepiskopats," *Zeitschrift der Savigny-Stiftung für Rechtsgeschichte* 44, Kanonistische Abteilung 13 (1924): 266–83.

[19] Hans Leube, *Kalvinismus und Luthertum im Zeitalter der Orthodoxie* (Leipzig, 1928), 375ff.; Deppermann, *Der hallesche Pietismus*, 24–26, 32; Gawthrop, *Pietism and the Making of Eighteenth-Century Prussia*, 73.

[20] Wilhelm Schrader, *Geschichte der Friedrichs-Universität zu Halle*, 2 vols. (Berlin, 1894), 1:1–8. For aristocratic students, see Charles E. McClelland, *State, Society, and University in Germany, 1700–1914* (Cambridge, 1980), 33–35.

Pietism had sociopolitical ramifications. Since it aimed to form a holy community, Pietism's most characteristic institution was the conventicle (*ecclesia pietatis*), a study and devotional circle that aspired to Luther's ideal of "the priesthood of all believers." Functioning outside the established Church, and having members of different estates associate as equals, conventicles were so offensive that in many instances Orthodoxy's representatives cooperated with the temporal authorities to suppress them. As Pietism matured, especially in Prussia, where it enjoyed state sponsorship, it first marginalized and then renounced the conventicle.[21]

Pietism generated social activism. Especially for Francke, the individual's "rebirth" was to be manifested in moral rigorism and outward confirmation of conversion. These two impulses produced an effort to purify and reform the world. The most striking example was the orphanage and industries (book publishing, pharmaceuticals) Francke established at Halle to realize Pietism at home and disseminate it abroad: the Pietists helped pioneer the Protestant mission in Eastern Europe and Africa.[22]

In shifting emphasis from the visible church of sacraments and doctrine to the invisible church of personal devotion and ethical behavior, Pietism championed freedom of conscience for the individual and, by extension, toleration of other religions. Once Pietism gained state sponsorship, however, its adherents turned intolerant and persecuted rivals.[23]

Baumgarten's father, Jacob (1668–1722), made the transition from Orthodoxy to Pietism: a theology student at the University of Leipzig, he was present during the controversies surrounding A. H. Francke (early 1690s). Then an advanced student and Spener's protégé, Francke gave lectures on the Bible that fomented a virtual rebellion: theology students stopped attending lectures and formed conventicles. The Saxon authorities suppressed the student rebellion and, eventually, Pietism. As a result of his experiences in Leipzig, Jacob Baumgarten became a Pietist. He finished his theological education at Halle, whose Faculty of Theology quickly became a Pietist stronghold; Francke was appointed

[21] Gawthrop, *Pietism and the Making of Eighteenth-Century Prussia*, 123–36.

[22] Mary Fulbrook, *Piety and Politics: Religion and the Rise of Absolutism in England, Württemberg and Prussia* (Cambridge, 1983); F. Ernst Stoeffler, *The Rise of Evangelical Pietism* (Leiden, 1965), and idem, *German Pietism During the 18th Century* (Leiden, 1973); Martin Brecht, ed., *Der Pietismus vom siebzehnten bis zum frühen achtzehnten Jahrhundert* (Göttingen, 1993); Johannes Wallmann, "Pietismus und Orthodoxie," and idem, *Der Pietismus* (Göttingen, 1990); Gawthrop, *Pietism and the Making of Eighteenth-Century Prussia*.

[23] Carl Hinrichs, *Preussentum und Pietismus: Der Pietismus in Brandenburg-Preussen als religiöses-soziale Reformbewegung* (Göttingen, 1971), 352. For the Theology Faculty, see Schrader, *Geschichte der Friedrichs-Universität zu Halle*, 1:123ff.

to teach the Bible in Halle's Faculty of Philosophy, and then (1698) moved to the Faculty of Theology. Jacob studied with Francke and became a lifelong friend. He also held a typical Pietist post, serving as a military chaplain (from 1713). Frederick William I (1718) established a separate military church system to which he appointed largely Pietist pastors.[24]

Siegmund Jacob Baumgarten belonged to the first generation of Lutherans for whom the conflict between Pietism and Orthodoxy was moot. Though he grew up within Pietism and thus at a remove from Orthodoxy, he commanded Orthodoxy's vast literature. In his works he attempted to address all Lutherans.[25]

The oldest of four sons, Siegmund Jacob received an unusually rigorous education from his father. Jacob's Pietism was scholarly and sober, devoid of mysticism and enthusiasm. Jacob taught scripture in the original languages, steering an exegetical course between allegory and literalism. He supplemented scripture with edifying works in German and other languages. General education consisted of classical languages, classical literature, and modern languages, especially French, Italian, and English. Tutors instructed Siegmund Jacob in mathematics and art, while Jacob introduced him to philosophy and logic. In his free time Siegmund Jacob read widely in history. His education especially benefited from two activities. He gained facility as a teacher by instructing his younger brothers. He learned to organize his knowledge by writing a daily essay on his reading in his father's substantial library.[26]

Baumgarten's Pietist background highlights the differing role of "enthusiasm" in the religious Enlightenment. Warburton and the Anglican Moderates abhorred "enthusiasm," especially Puritanism and other "inner light" sects. Turretin and Vernet rejected the chiliasts and prophets who circulated in the early eighteenth-century Huguenot diaspora. In contrast, many Lutheran religious enlighteners either grew up as Pietists or experienced it firsthand. While they rejected Pietism's excesses and separatism, they often appropriated other aspects for enlightened belief.[27]

---

[24] For Leipzig, see Leube, *Orthodoxie und Pietismus*, 170–211. On Halle's theology appointments, see Schrader, *Geschichte der Friedrichs-Universität zu Halle*, 1:47–51, 110.

[25] Emanuel Hirsch, *Geschichte der neuern Evangelischen Theologie*, 5 vols. (Gütersloh, 1951), 2:318, 373; Schloemann, *Baumgarten*, 62.

[26] His father's library contained 10,000 volumes. See Johann Salomon Semler, "Kurzer Entwurf des Lebens des wohlseligen Herrn D. Baumgartens," in *Ehrengedächtnis des weiland Hochwürdigen und Hochgelarten Herrn Seigmund Jacob Baumgartens*, ed. Johann Salomon Semler (Halle, 1758), 74–83.

[27] See Dieter Narr, "Berührung von Aufklärung und Pietismus im Württemberg des 18. Jahrhunderts: Eine Einführung in die Problematik," *Blätter für württembergische*

Baumgarten attended the local gymnasium for two years (1722–24), and then matriculated in theology at Halle (1724). His professors encouraged him to study on his own rather than attend lectures. He devoted himself to patristics and especially the oriental studies—Aramaic, Syriac, and Arabic—in which Halle excelled in this period.[28] He defended his dissertation in 1726.

He taught a few hours a day at the Pietist orphanage in exchange for free meals, a common practice among theology students. At first he taught Greek and Hebrew, later taking responsibility for theology and after 1726 offering philosophy and Latin composition. He also gave sermons in local churches and, after ordination in 1728, preached regularly at the "Market church" as well as holding devotional hours at the orphanage. Baumgarten was an exceptionally effective preacher able to convey his deep devotion through sober exegesis.

Baumgarten enjoyed such success as a teacher that he was encouraged to offer instruction at the university. He began by lecturing in philology and philosophy. He then tried his hand at theology, and in 1732 was appointed to a lectureship in the Faculty of Theology. When a full professorship fell vacant in 1734, he was called to it. Baumgarten relinquished all other duties in order to concentrate on his university teaching and scholarship.[29]

Baumgarten's Halle was also home to the early Enlightenment (*Frühaufklärung*), which scholars usually date to the 1680s and associate with a number of thinkers who, often as a result of contact with the Dutch universities or travel in England and France, began to introduce the new science and philosophy. As a result, they started to depart from Orthodox formulations of faith, but not from Lutheranism.[30] Perhaps the earliest such figures were the political and legal philosopher Samuel von Pufendorf (1632–94), who introduced concepts of natural law independent of theology, and the philosopher, scientist, and mathematician Gottfried Wilhelm Leibniz (1646–1716), who reconciled Cartesianism and scholasticism.

Kirchengeschichte 66/67 (1966–67): 264–77. Johann Lorenz Mosheim had no experience of Pietism. See Hirsch, *Geschichte der neuern evangelischen Theologie*, 2:363–64.

[28] On Baumgarten's studies, see Semler, "Kurzer Entwurf des Lebens des wohlseligen Herrn D. Baumgartens," 88–92. For oriental studies, see Otto Podczeck, "Die Arbeit am Alten Testament in Halle zur Zeit des Pietismus: Das Collegium Orientale theologicum A. H. Franckes," *Wissenschaftliche Zeitschrift der Martin-Luther-Universität Halle-Wittenberg* 7, no. 5 (August 1958): 1059–74.

[29] Semler, "Kurzer Entwurf des Lebens des wohlseligen Herrn D. Baumgartens," 92–99; Schrader, *Geschichte der Friedrichs-Universität zu Halle*, 1:122.

[30] Beck, *Early German Philosophy*, 6–7.

Halle housed the two figures who formulated the early Enlightenment's principal tendencies. Christian Thomasius (1655–1728), who had
studied in the Netherlands, developed empiricism. Thomasius had
been forced to leave the University of Leipzig (1690) and subsequently
taught in the faculties of law and philosophy at Halle. According to
most historians, Thomasius, following Luther, espoused a radical separation between belief and reason in which ultimate salvation as a
Christian depended on faith, while reason was limited to the practical
sphere of individual improvement. On the basis of this "Christian pessimism," Thomasius developed eclectic views intended to impart a
worldly education to would-be diplomats and statesmen, but also to a
new bourgeois ethic. Drawing on the natural law theory of Pufendorf
and Grotius, he made ethics the foundation of law and subsumed philosophy under law rather than theology. In contrast, a recent historian
has asserted that Thomasius embraced a form of enthusiastic, separatist, and anti-intellectualist "religion of the heart" that produced his
skepticism about philosophy and his views of "history, moral philosophy and the interpretation of natural phenomena." In either case, in the
spirit of Prussian policy Thomasius advocated free exegesis of scripture, toleration, and a "territorialism" in which the state exercised control of external church affairs. He considered the state the best guaran-
tor of freedom of conscience. His life exemplified the intimacy of the
early Enlightenment and Pietism. Thomasius supported his colleague
Francke during the unrest at Leipzig and helped bring him and other
Pietists to Halle, but became disenchanted with Pietism once it began
to enforce its version of piety, and Francke started to view its institutions as providential.[31]

Christian Wolff (1679–1754) fashioned the early Enlightenment's
rationalist trend by marrying science to scholasticism. Wolff initially
came to Halle in the chair of mathematics (1707), writing a number of
textbooks that won him the title "praeceptor Germaniae." Beginning in
1712 he published a series of philosophical treaties in which, by system-
atizing the thought of Descartes and Leibniz, he attempted to create an

---

[31] For "Christian pessimism," see Hinrichs, *Preussentum und Pietismus*, 352–87. Max
Wundt, *Die deutsche Schulphilosophie im Zeitalter der Aufklärung*, 2nd ed. (Tübingen, 1964),
19–61; D. A. Tholuck, *Geschichte des Rationalismus: Geschichte des Pietismus und des ersten
Stadiums der Aufklärung* (Berlin, 1865), 107–119; Beck, *Early German Philosophy*, 247–55. For
"religion of the heart," see Thomas Ahnert, *Religion and the Origins of the German Enlight-
enment: Faith and the Reform of Learning in the Thought of Christian Thomasius* (Rochester,
NY, 2006). For the state guaranteeing freedom of conscience, see *Das Recht evangelischer
Fürsten in theologischen Streitigkeiten und wider die papistischen Lehr-sätze eines Theologi zu
Leipzig* (Halle, 1696).

"omnicompetent instrument of public enlightenment." Trying to ground all aspects of philosophy in reason, and fashioning German equivalents of Latin philosophical terms in order to compose his treatises in the vernacular, he made the new scientific-mathematical thinking widely available and gained a reputation throughout German-speaking Central Europe. Yet in continuing the Leibnizian project of reconciling the new thinking with scholasticism, he devised a system of a priori logic and metaphysics rife with the scholastic mania for definition and logical demonstration.[32]

Friedrichs University in Halle was a house divided: Pietists and enlighteners were allies against Orthodoxy, yet rivals for students' hearts and minds. A clash was inevitable. Asserting that his views were inimical to true belief, Pietists had Thomasius prohibited from teaching philosophy (1696), restricting him to law.[33] Pietists also attacked Wolff, and those attacks were to affect Baumgarten.

Baumgarten's relationship to Wolff's thought developed over a decade (1724–34). In 1723 the Prussian king dismissed Wolff: Pietist opponents at Halle had worked to secure his ouster, with a direct petition to the king from a cabal at court clinching it.[34] Wolff was expelled a year before Baumgarten arrived at the university. Baumgarten's original sympathies lay with the Pietists. Though Baumgarten followed his early interest in mathematics at Halle, it does not seem to have affected his attitude toward Wolff, since he used English rather than German texts. The earliest indications of a change were in 1726, when he taught philosophy at the orphanage. For the first time he formed a favorable impression of Wolff's work. His younger brother, Alexander Gottlieb (1714–62), who became famous as one of the founders of aesthetics and has been called "the most competent—and in the long run perhaps the

---

[32] Beck, *Early German Philosophy*, 261. Cf. H. J. de Vleeschauwer, "La genèse de la méthode mathématique de Wolff," *Revue Belge de philologie et d'histoire* 11 (1931): 651–77. The mathematical texts included *Anfangsgründe aller mathematischen Wissenschaften* (1710), *Elementa matheseos universae* (1713–15), and *Lexicon mathemathicum* (1716). See Wundt, *Die deutsche Schulphilosophie im Zeitalter der Aufklärung*, 132. For a glossary of terms, see "Das erste Register, Darinnen einige Kunst-Wörter Lateinisch gegeben warden," in *Vernünftige Gedancken von Gott, der Welt und der Seele des Menschen* (Frankfurt and Leipzig, 1729), 672–78. On his contribution to German, see E. A. Blackall, *The Emergence of German as a Literary Language*, 2nd ed. (Ithaca, 1978), 26–48.

[33] Hinrichs, *Preussentum und Pietismus*, 399–418; Schrader, *Geschichte der Friedrichs-Universität zu Halle*, 1:74, 205–11. Cf. Thomas Albert Howard, *Protestant Theology and the Making of the Modern German University* (New York, 2006), 87–102.

[34] Hinrichs, *Preussentum und Pietismus*, 399–418, 421–22; Schrader, *Geschichte der Friedrichs-Universität zu Halle*, 1:212–19.

only philosophically important—adherent of the Wolffian philosophy," played a role as well. Alexander studied at Halle and was named professor of philosophy in 1738 (he moved to the University of Frankfort on the Oder in 1740). Both brothers appear to have become seriously interested in Wolff's philosophy by about 1730. Alexander organized a Wolffian study circle, and in 1734, after Siegmund was appointed full professor, he lived in Siegmund's home, where the study circle met. The Baumgarten brothers became Wolffians together.[35]

Why the attraction to Wolff? In its first generation, Pietism was driven by its originality. In Leipzig and Halle, Francke awakened students with exegeses of scripture calling for a disciplined Christian life of faith and conversion. Halle's Faculty of Theology, which Pietists dominated from the start, succeeded for over three decades in inspiring large numbers of students. By the late 1720s, however, the novelty had worn off. The faculty lacked either a rigorous intellectual method or a research agenda. G. A. Francke (1696–1769), who succeeded his father, was an undistinguished scholar and teacher. The most productive scholar, J. H. Michaelis (b. 1663), restricted himself to the Old Testament.[36] A high-ranking Berlin Pietist such as Johann Gustav Reinbeck (1683–1741), who understood that Halle Pietism needed intellectual renewal, sought it in Wolff's philosophy. In a series of sermons honoring the Augsburg confession's bicentenary (1733), Reinbeck employed Wolff's method to chart a middle course between the atheist's exclusive reliance on reason and the believer's exclusive reliance on scripture. He demonstrated the complementarity of reason and revelation, natural and revealed religion. Reinbeck also used his considerable influence in Berlin to champion Wolff's return to Halle.[37]

Baumgarten turned to Wolff's philosophy for the same reason as Reinbeck, which quickly resulted in the single most significant event in his

---

[35] Beck, *Early German Philosophy*, 283. For the brothers and Wolff, see Schloemann, *Siegmund Jacob Baumgarten*, 34–35, and G. F. Meier, *Alexander Gottlieb Baumgartens Leben beschrieben* (Halle, 1763), 12–14.

[36] For early appointments, see Schrader, *Geschichte der Friedrichs-Universität zu Halle*, 1:142–49, and for the 1720s and 1730s, see 223–24. For dogmatics, see Hirsch, *Geschichte der neuern Evangelischen Theologie*, 2:186–93. For theological study, see Rudolf Mau, "Programme und Praxis des Theologiestudiums im 17. und 18. Jahrhundert," *Theologische Versuche* 11 (1979): 71–91.

[37] *Betrachtungen über die in der Augsburgischen Confession enthaltene und damit verknüpfte Göttliche Wahrheiten*, 2 vols. (Berlin and Leipzig, 1733). See *Allgemeine Deutsche Biographie*, 56 vols. (Leipzig, 1875–1912), 28:2–5; D. A. Tholuck, *Geschichte des Rationalismus: Geschichte des Pietismus und des ersten Stadiums der Aufklärung*, 142–43. For Berlin, see Hinrichs, *Preussentum und Pietismus*, 415.

professional life.[38] Like Wolff, Baumgarten attracted large numbers of students and the envy of older faculty. Joachim Lange (1670–1744), who had been with Francke in Leipzig and was then a member of Spener's circle in Berlin, had been a key figure in Wolff's 1723 ouster. He and other Pietists in the Theology Faculty had opposed Wolff's philosophy for a host of reasons: limiting God's omnipotence with the laws of nature, offering a determinism in conflict with Pietist voluntarism, advocating a temperate enjoyment of the world at odds with Pietist asceticism, and proposing a new scholasticism that privileged knowledge over belief and practice.[39]

A mediocre teacher whose academic reputation rested on a Latin and Greek grammar, Lange especially disliked Wolff's crowded lecture halls. Lange faced a repetition of that experience with Baumgarten, though the new threat was even greater, since Baumgarten taught Lange's own subject. From the moment Baumgarten began to lecture, Lange's enrollments plummeted. In 1733–34 he brought serious accusations against Baumgarten, including that he used Wolff's forbidden method to teach theology. These accusations remained within the university and were without consequence. In the meantime, the king (1733), without consulting the university, had invited Wolff back to Halle, yet he declined. The rumor of Wolff's possible return roused Lange to write another polemic; he also directed his attention to Baumgarten as a representative of Wolffianism. Two years later Lange made his case against Baumgarten at the Berlin court, while G. A. Francke, who had earlier sponsored Baumgarten, did the same at the university.[40] These accusations were among the Pietists' final efforts to avert Wolff's full rehabilitation.

The Theology Faculty investigated Baumgarten on the grounds that he had not requested its approval to publish a textbook, that he led students away from the Gospel by teaching dogmatics and theological

---

[38] Baumgarten introduced Pietist students to logical rigor. See Paul Knothe, "Siegmund Jakob Baumgarten und seine Stellung in der Aufklärungstheologie," *Zeitschrift für Kirchengeschichte*, 46, n.s. 9 (1928): 510; and Hirsch, *Geschichte der neuern Evangelischen Theologie*, 2:373. For Pietism's anti-intellectualism and Baumgarten's impact, see Semler, *Lebensbeschreibung von ihm selbst abgefasst*, 1:79–81, 90, 95–122.

[39] For Wolff and Pietism, see Hinrichs, *Preussentum und Pietismus*, 388–96. On Wolff's theology, see Mario Casula, "Die Theologia naturalis von Christian Wolff: Vernunft und Offenbarung," in *Christian Wolff: Interpretationen zu seiner Philosophie und deren Wirkung*, ed. Werner Schneiders (Hamburg, 1983), 129–38.

[40] Lange attacked Wolff throughout the 1720s and 1730s. See Hinrichs, *Preussentum und Pietismus*, esp. 426. For the invitation to Wolff, see 433–34. For Lange's visit to the King, see 436–38. On Lange's career, see Schrader, *Geschichte der Friedrichs-Universität zu Halle*, 1:132–35.

morality with Wolff's pernicious mathematical method, and that he used German rather than Latin terms. While the practice of seeking the faculty's imprimatur for books had fallen into desuetude, it could still be invoked for younger faculty, especially when publishing a textbook. Baumgarten defended himself by arguing that he used the Gospel alone for unalloyed revelation (*articuli puri*), philosophy only for truths derived from nature as well as revelation (*articuli mixti*).[41] Michaelis, the faculty's most senior member, found nothing heterodox in Baumgarten's book, although he feared that Wolff's philosophy might become a new scholasticism.[42]

The Prussian government rebuked both parties. It prohibited Lange from attacking Wolff in print, encouraging him to attend to his own scholarship and teaching. It instructed Baumgarten to submit to the faculty's censorship, to desist from using "incomprehensible philosophical" terms, and to teach a "true active Christianity"—as Francke had done.[43] Despite the rebuke, Baumgarten emerged victorious: he remained in office to discharge the faculty's mission. His vindication belonged to the government's rehabilitation of Wolff. In 1739 the government required that theologians study Wolff's philosophy, and in 1740, at the invitation of the new king, Friedrich II, Wolff returned to Halle in triumph as vice-chancellor and privy councilor (*Geheimrat*). From this point Baumgarten's star rose as his energy and erudition made him one of the most respected scholars of his age. His theology can be comprehended through four themes.

"THE UNION WITH GOD"

Baumgarten's success largely rested on his ability to fashion a theology surmounting the divisions among Lutherans. By reconstruing key Pietist notions, he managed to reconcile Wolff's method with a transcendent, supernatural Christianity consistent with Orthodox dogma. While he fully recognized reason and nature, he was thoroughly ani-

---

[41] Baumgarten used this distinction, a commonplace by the mid-seventeenth century. See *Evangelische Glaubenslehre*, 38–39, and Preus, *The Theology of Post-Reformation Lutheranism*, 152–55.

[42] The book was *Unterricht vom rechtmässigen Verhalten eines Christen oder Theologische Moral* (Halle, 1738). For the investigation, see Schloemann, *Baumgarten*, 42–43. For Baumgarten's role in rehabilitating Wolff's philosophy, see Hinrichs, *Preussentum und Pietismus*, 431. For Michaelis, see Schrader, *Geschichte der Friedrichs-Universität zu Halle*, 1:110, 132.

[43] Hinrichs, *Preussentum und Pietismus*, 434. The directive (Sept. 22, 1736) appears in Schrader, *Geschichte der Friedrichs-Universität zu Halle*, 2:462–63.

mated by the mysteries of grace and revelation. These ideas found full expression in two works: his posthumously published *Lutheran Dogmatics* (1759), which, hailed as "the first major dogmatics written in German," introduced vernacular terms that permanently shaped German theology, and his *Instruction on the Proper Behavior of a Christian* (1738), the theological morality that the Faculty of Theology had investigated.[44]

Baumgarten built his theology around the Pietist notion that Christianity's true end was the union of man with God. He defined "theological science" as "deriv[ing] from Scripture and mak[ing] comprehensible and demonstrable the totality of truths pertaining to our union with God."[45] This notion of union (*Vereinigung*) had a central position in Pietism: in the first line of Spener's catechism it denoted the attainment of grace through the indwelling of the divine. Baumgarten's innovation was to give the concept an ethical and supernatural interpretation. He explicitly repudiated the mystical or enthusiastic understanding of union as an instantaneous conversion or "rebirth."[46] Instead, he viewed conversion as a long-term process that required assiduous application through prayer, contemplation, and study of scripture, as well as sanctifying life through the proper use of time. Only such concerted effort made possible the state of grace in which the individual determines all of his behavior according to Christ. Conversion involved both a turn away from sin through recognition and remorse and a turn toward God through a new obedience.

[44] Hagglund, *History of Theology*, 345. Baumgarten outlined his ideas in his inaugural lecture, *Siegmund Jacob Baumgartens öffentliche Anzeige seiner dissmaligen Academischen Arbeit, dabei zugleich von den vornehmsten Vortheilen bei Erlernung der Theologie auf hohen Schulen gehandelt wird* (Halle, 1734), 4–5. The dogmatic theology was based on students' notes of his lectures; the title derives from a volume of Spener's sermons. For the text's reliability, see Schloemann, *Baumgarten*, 99–100. For Baumgarten's coining of terms, see Knothe, "Siegmund Jakob Baumgarten und seine Stellung in der Aufklärungstheologie," 522. For the terms' permanence in German theology, see Hirsch, *Geschichte der neuern evangelischen Theologie*, 2:371.

[45] *Evangelische Glaubenslehre*, 29. Cf. 46. For a similar definition, see *Unterricht vom rechtmässigen Verhalten*, 9–10. For the meaning of "union with God," see *Siegmund Jacob Baumgartens öffentliche Anzeige*, 4–5; *Evangelische Glaubenslehre*, 1:84–95; and *Unterricht von rechtmässigen Verhalten*, 92–93, 115–16, 693–94, 731–66. For Pietist terminology, see August Langen, *Der Wortschatz des deutschen Pietismus* (Tübingen, 1954), 107–300. Baumgarten derived his dogmatics from his Pietist predecessors at Halle, who had relied on Spener. See *Evangelische Glaubenslehre*, 1:97, and Hirsch, *Geschichte der neuern evangelischen Theologie*, 2:186–93.

[46] *Evangelische Glaubenslehre*, 1:85; *Unterricht vom rechtmässigen Verhalten*, 134. See Knothe, "Siegmund Jakob Baumgarten und seine Stellung in der Aufklärungstheologie," 528, and Hirsch, *Geschichte der neuern evangelischen Theologie*, 2:375. For Spener's catechism, see Schloemann, *Baumgarten*, 88.

This union with God required "vital knowledge." Knowledge was vital if it was able to penetrate the will and motivate actions. Vital knowledge depended on the distinction between natural and revealed theology—fundamental to all religious enlighteners—that allowed Baumgarten to answer the deists' and atheists' objections and establish Christianity's efficacy and superiority.[47]

"Natural theology" consists of those truths known "from reason" and "from nature" that agree with revealed theology's truths since they share "one creator and one purpose."[48] In this specific sense, natural theology limited revealed theology but without determining its substance. Nevertheless, a significant difference separates them: natural theology can "improve the soul" but cannot procure salvation. Comprehending God and His will through natural means requires extraordinary efforts, of which only the few are capable. Even so, in respect to salvation natural theology's knowledge is "dead." Baumgarten recapitulated the argument common to Anglican Moderates, the Genevan "enlightened orthodox," and fellow German "theological enlighteners" that natural theology, despite teaching many of the same truths, is inferior and only preparatory to revealed theology.[49]

Revealed theology disseminates the "vital knowledge" that leads to salvation by encompassing a broader range of convincing truths: not only God's nature, perfection, and relationship to mankind but also atonement, reconciliation, and the soul's immortality. Revealed theology provides these with a "certainty" and easy comprehensibility that enable them to affect the will and determine behavior, leading the individual from "sensuality" and "illusory desires" to knowledge of God as "the highest good."[50] These otherwise unknowable supernatural truths are authenticated in three ways: they must not contradict other truths, they must agree with the truths of natural theology, and they must bear the undeniable imprint of God. Re-

---

[47] For "vital" knowledge, see *Evangelische Glaubenslehre*, 77–78, 80–81. For natural versus revealed theology, see introduction, *Unterricht vom rechtmässigen Verhalten*, unpaginated.

[48] *Evangelische Glaubenslehre*, 38, 53.

[49] Knothe, "Siegmund Jakob Baumgarten und seine Stellung in der Aufklärungstheologie," 499. On revealed truth, see introduction, *Unterricht vom rechtmässigen Verhalten*, unpaginated. On natural theology and salvation, see 97. For a similar argument, see Johann Franz Budde, *Erbauliche Gedancken von Predigten, nebst einer kurtzen Anzeige, wie es ferner in den Nachmittags-Predigten des Sonntags in der Collegen-Kirchen soll gehalten werden* (Jena, 1724), 22–24.

[50] *Evangelische Glaubenslehre*, 76–77. See Knothe, "Siegmund Jakob Baumgarten und seine Stellung in der Aufklärungstheologie," 496–98.

vealed theology alone "suffices to mankind's salvation and union with God."[51]

The means to achieve the "union with God" were ultimately supernatural. To be sure, an unstinting natural commitment was necessary: "no one is a born Christian."[52] Baumgarten traced in minute detail the stages an individual was to travel on the road to union. Moreover, those efforts had to continue even after union was achieved: "at all times a Christian becomes either better or worse, grows or diminishes."[53] Yet only by virtue of the supernatural means offered by "God's dwelling in man" through His spirit could those efforts result in the supernatural state in which all senses were transformed by and redirected toward God: "the condition of such union with him is so entirely different from, and in contrast to, the condition of natural being, that an alteration of everything must occur among those who wish to be Christians and attain salvation."[54]

This "conversion," "rebirth," or "union" could not be expected to occur miraculously as an instantaneous divine intervention. Rather, this "incomprehensible" union exceeding reason resulted from the mysterious intersection of the orders of nature and grace.[55] Baumgarten asserted the two realms' harmony:

> The great concord between the realms of nature and grace, in their order and general laws as well as in individual variations, increases the perfection of the overall coherence of contingent things and the revelation of divine wisdom.[56]

"Union" was not a miracle but a mystery.[57] As a typical religious enlightener, Baumgarten considered it a truth above (*supra rationem*) rather than opposed to reason (*contra rationem*).

Through this supernatural, ethical notion of union, Baumgarten was able to appropriate a key element of Pietism, if one stripped of all

---

[51] *Evangelische Glaubenslehre*, 81. Cf. *Unterricht vom rechtmässigen Verhalten*, 97. For supernatural truths, see *Evangelische Glaubenslehre*, 3:76–65, and Knothe, "Siegmund Jakob Baumgarten und seine Stellung in der Aufklärungstheologie," 496, 501–2.

[52] *Unterricht von rechtmässigen Verhalten*, 104. Cf. 694, 263. See also *Siegmund Jacob Baumgartens öffentliche Anzeige*, 9.

[53] *Unterricht von rechtmässigen Verhalten*, 138. Cf. 148–53.

[54] Ibid., 112–13. Cf. 697–706.

[55] *Evangelische Glaubenslehre*, 1:78–79; *Unterricht von rechtmässigen Verhalten*, 697–706, 833–34. On the relationship between nature and grace, see Hirsch, *Geschichte der neuern Evangelischen Theologie*, 2:379–83. For an economy of miracles following Wolff, see *Evangelische Glaubenslehre*, 1:84.

[56] *Unterricht von rechtmässigen Verhalten*, 110.

[57] *Evangelische Glaubenslehre*, 1:40.

mystical or enthusiastic interpretations. His concept of union also repudiated Lutheran Orthodoxy's privileging of speculation.[58] The true purpose of Scripture was practical: "The goal of the entire Holy Scripture, and of God's immediate revelation, consists in the application and observation of the truths it contains, and in producing right conduct."[59]

He defined being a Christian in ethical terms: "Everyone is called a Christian who makes the entire direct revelation of God in Scripture the basis of his behavior."[60] He thought a theological treatise's test was the degree to which readers attained its truths. He also asserted that it was possible for the unlearned and unlettered to achieve union with God without a correct knowledge of theology. Finally, Baumgarten recognized as fundamental only those articles indispensable for salvation.[61]

Baumgarten's appropriation of the notion of a union with God indicates the extent to which Pietism was the fountainhead of religious notions in eighteenth-century German Protestantism. Its elaborated ideas of religious experience and subjectivity were formative for a notion of enlightened piety and, later in the century, for many aspects of secular German culture.[62]

While giving priority to practice, Baumgarten was committed to the highest standards of systematic theology or science (*Wissenschaft*). In opposition to Pietism's emphasis on "edification" (*Erbaulichkeit*), he stressed logical rigor.[63]

For Baumgarten, theology and philosophy were not separated by different criteria of truth but by reliance on scripture: theology must be securely grounded in Scripture. Medieval scholasticism failed by virtue of a naive exegesis; Orthodox theology consistently lacked a scriptural foundation. He set out to substantiate the scriptural grounding of all important truths.[64]

---

[58] For opposition to scholastic speculation, see ibid., 1:30–32.

[59] Ibid., 1:31.

[60] *Unterricht von rechtmässigen Verhalten*, 12.

[61] *Evangelische Glaubenslehre*, 1:68, 82–85. For salvation, 1:41–43.

[62] For Pietism's impact on nationalism, see Koppel Pinson, *Pietism as a Factor in the Rise of German Nationalism* (New York, 1934), and Gerhard Kaiser, *Pietismus und Patriotismus im literarischen Deutschland* (Frankfurt, 1973). For Pietism and autobiography, see Guenter Niggl, *Geschichte der deutschen Autobiographie im 18. Jahrhundert* (Stuttgart, 1977). On Pietism and interest in states of mind, see Hans-Jürgen Schings, *Melancholie und Aufklärung: Melancholiker und ihre Kritiker in Erfahrungsseelenkunde und Literatur des 18. Jahrhunderts* (Stuttgart, 1977), and Fritz Stemme, "Die Säkularisation des Pietismus zur Erfahrungsseelenkunde," *Zeitschrift für Deutsche Philologie* 72 (1953): 144–58.

[63] Knothe, "Siegmund Jakob Baumgarten und seine Stellung in der Aufklärungstheologie," 505.

[64] *Evangelische Glaubenslehre*, 1:9, 64–66. For practical knowledge requiring a different degree of rigor, see introduction, *Unterricht von rechtmässigen Verhalten*.

Baumgarten derived his criteria for systematic theology from Wolff's mathematical method of logical demonstration: truth must be clearly defined and its consequences developed by logical inference. Baumgarten attempted to define every relevant concept. He shared Wolff's assumption that the explanation of the word equaled an explanation of the thing. In consequence, his work exhibits Wolff's definition mania.[65]

Clear definition was preparatory to logical proof. While scripture was the source of truth, the authoritative means to ascertain it was the mathematical method's logical procedure. Baumgarten made extensive use of syllogisms, presenting such central theological truths as providence, the trinity, and God's attributes in that form. The syllogism for the divinity of scripture filled thirteen pages. Baumgarten also used some of Wolff's typical logical arguments. He deployed the principle of noncontradiction to prove God's independence and the possibility of revelation in scripture. He applied the principle of sufficient reason to issues ranging from the cosmological argument and providence to miracles and the immortality of prelapsarian beings.[66]

Another key Wolffian concept Baumgarten used was the coherence (*Zusammenhang*) of knowledge, which consists in the connection of all truths to each other as if in an unbroken chain (he also borrowed Wolff's metaphor). Coherence entailed using logical demonstration to achieve a system of linked propositions in which all inferences are related to each other and first definitions. Baumgarten asserted that theology is a science (*Wissenschaft*) "when the divinity and incontrovertibility of Scripture is demonstrable, and all truths are derived from it in a demonstrable and orderly manner, so that the necessity of the conclusions can be referred back to their causes."[67]

The notion of coherence permeated his work. He criticized orthodox theology for a lack of coherence: its organization according to Aristotelian categories separated truths that belonged together, losing the connection between them.[68] He distinguished between the theologian and

---

[65] Baumgarten defined the central term (God), the predicates (independence, necessity, primordial nature, infinite perfection), and their constituents. See *Evangelische Glaubenslehre*, 1:187ff. See Knothe, "Siegmund Jakob Baumgarten und seine Stellung in der Aufklärungstheologie," 505–6. For Wolff's method and scholastic elements, see Schloemann, *Baumgarten*, 68–72.

[66] *Evangelische Glaubenslehre*, 3:760–73. For Baumgarten's method, see Knothe, "Siegmund Jakob Baumgarten und seine Stellung in der Aufklärungstheologie," 507–9, 512–13.

[67] Quotation at *Evangelische Glaubenslehre*, 1:30. Cf. 1:35–37, 46. Wolff defined reason as "the ability to perceive the coherence [*Zusammenhang*] of truths." See *Vernünftige Gedanken von Gott, der Welt und der Seele des Menschen*, par. 368, p. 224.

[68] *Evangelische Glaubenslehre*, 1:96–97. See also *Unterricht vom rechtmässigen Verhalten*, 22. For such phrases as the "coherence of naturally known truths" or the "coherence and

the common man on that basis: the latter's theological ideas lacked clarity, penetration, completeness, and above all "coherence."[69]

The mathematical method promised to yield "certainty" (*Gewißheit*). If theology could meet the mathematical method's criteria of definition, logical demonstration and coherence, then its claims would have the certainty of science:

> [S]cholarly knowledge consists in sagacious, reasonable knowledge, or the ability not only to comprehend but to judge, in accordance with laws and causes, the articles of belief clearly and fundamentally or with certainty in their true coherence [*Zusammenhang*]; thus to demonstrate irreversibly the intelligibility and demonstrability of [these beliefs] from Holy Scripture . . . to connect properly all individual doctrines of God's revelation, and to comprehend the principle of every doctrine both in the Holy Scripture and in its connection [*Zusammenhang*] and mutual relationship with the other revealed truths.[70]

Baumgarten used Wolffian content as well as method. Wolff's ideas figured prominently whenever Baumgarten dealt with "mixed" truths derived from nature and reason as well as revelation. In these instances the new science's optimism was salient. Baumgarten used distinctly Wolffian categories, for example, in his discussions of creation:

> Creation is accomplished through God's will, meaning for the sake of accomplishing his well founded decrees which aim to realize the best, according to his choice grounded in clear representations.[71]

Wolff's ideas are prominent in God's choice of the best of all possible worlds (*electio optimi*) as well as in His acting on the basis of "clear representations." Yet these notions did not conflict with the Christian conception of creation. Baumgarten asserted that Genesis did not contain a scientific account of creation and was not a textbook of science; it instead promoted the "union of man with God." He also contended that science's claims about creation were not empirically grounded and therefore indemonstrable.[72] Like Warburton, Baumgarten compartmentalized rather than harmonized science and belief.

---

internal connection of all truths and propositions found in Holy Scripture," see *Evangelische Glaubenslehre*, 1:38–39, 46, 54–55, 82–83, and *Siegmund Jacob Baumgartens öffentliche Anzeige*, 4–6, 11.

[69] *Evangelische Glaubenslehre*, 1:82.

[70] Ibid., 1:83. Emphasis in the original.

[71] Ibid., 1:615.

[72] Knothe, "Siegmund Jakob Baumgarten und seine Stellung in der Aufklärungstheologie," 518–19, and Schloemann, *Baumgarten*, 76–78.

Baumgarten's embrace of Wolff's concept of nature is further manifest in the proofs he offered for God's existence. Like other religious enlighteners, he preferred the argument from design that relied on God's relationship to the natural world. Here again Baumgarten's reliance on Wolff's optimism comes to the fore:

[T]he infinite wisdom of God reveals itself more in the works of nature and its variations, which follow the course of nature, than in miracles which are brought forth by the use of omnipotence.[73]

While Baumgarten asserted the possibility of miracles, he relegated them to the periphery in establishing God's existence. Nature was preeminent, and Baumgarten understood it in Wolff's terms of the "coherence" of contingent or natural things.[74]

Baumgarten offered an index to his and the Lutheran theological Enlightenment's intellectual lineage in the annotated bibliographies he provided for students. In dogmatic theology he started with late seventeenth-century nonscholastic works. He singled out the founder of Pietism, Philip Jacob Spener, followed by the Halle theologians who taught or inspired him, "Breithaupt, Lange and Freilinghaus," as well as the less-known if equally influential Johann Jacob Rambach (1693–1735), who was a Wolffian as well as the advocate of a historically oriented scriptural hermeneutics.[75] Among contemporary Lutherans he approved of the Berlin theological Wolffian, Reinbeck.

Baumgarten especially lauded the works of two theologians who, despite significant differences, were widely recognized as his companions in creating the Lutheran theological Enlightenment.[76] Johann Franz Budde (1677–1729) taught at Halle (1693–1705) and Jena (1705–15) before being appointed a Church councillor at Gotha. Influenced by Descartes, Pufendorf, and Locke, he rejected scholasticism in the name of an "eclectic" theology and a praxis inspired by Arndt and Spener that mediated between Pietism and Orthodoxy.[77] Christoph Mattheus

---

[73] *Evangelische Glaubenslehre*, 1:814. See Schloemann, *Baumgarten*, 76, and Knothe, "Siegmund Jakob Baumgarten und seine Stellung in der Aufklärungstheologie," 520.

[74] *Unterricht von rechtmässigen Verhalten*, 110. For Baumgarten as the first Lutheran theologian not to make miracles the basis of belief, see Hirsch, *Geschichte der neuern Evangelischen Theologie*, 2:379–83.

[75] Rambach (Halle, 1727–31) may have inspired both of the Baumgartens. See Schrader, *Geschichte der Friedrichs-Universität zu Halle*, 1:136, 223, and Schloemann, *Baumgarten*, 38, 224–29.

[76] Hirsch saw Baumgarten's, Pfaff's, and Budde's thought as "transitional [*Übergangs*] theology." See *Geschichte der neuern Evangelischen Theologie*, 2:318–19.

[77] A. F. Stolzenburg, *Die Theologie des Joh. Fr. Buddeus und des Chr. Pfaff* (Berlin, 1926); Max Wundt, *Die deutsche Schulphilosophie*, 63–75; Hirsch, *Geschichte der neuern*

Pfaff (1686–1760), who spent the bulk of his career at Tübingen before moving to Giessen, was similarly influenced by the Pietist emphasis on praxis. He upheld the congruence of natural and revealed theology and, while endorsing freedom of conscience, vehemently attacked deists and atheists.[78]

Baumgarten also found important examples of the new theology among Dutch Arminians such as Philip Limborch (1633–1712) who "went to great lengths to avoid all scholastic investigation and derived their determinations from historical and Biblical foundations."[79] Baumgarten commended the Calvinists for embracing a historical method distant from scholasticism, and similarly saw them as excellent sources of moral theology. Among Catholics he thought the Jansenists, unlike the Jesuits, "taught a proper morality."[80]

EXEGESIS

Baumgarten consistently revamped his Lutheran heritage. Just as he reinterpreted the Pietist idea of union in an ethical direction, he took issue with Pietists who drew edification from, and the Orthodox who held God to have dictated, each verse. He argued for a philologically precise and historically accurate reading that would allow access to the Bible's teaching of the "union" with God.

Biblical exegesis provided the foundation for Baumgarten's dogmatic theology. An exacting hermeneutical method designed along Wolffian lines enabled the exegete to derive "vital knowledge" in a two-step grammatical and dogmatic analysis. Baumgarten systematically demonstrated how scripture was to be read to allow it "[to] explain itself."[81]

Evangelischen Theologie, 2:319–35. On Budde and Jena, see Max Steinmetz, ed., *Geschichte der Universität Jena, 1548/58-1958: Festgabe zum vierhundertjährigen Universitätsjubiläum* (Jena, 1958), 194–99. Budde opposed Wolff's philosophy. See *Bedencken über die Wolffianische Philosophie* (Freiburg, 1724).

[78] Stolzenburg, *Die Theologie des Joh. Fr. Buddeus und des Chr. Pfaff*; Hirsch, *Geschichte der neuern Evangelischen Theologie*, 2:336–54; Tholuck, *Geschichte des Rationalismus*, 149–157. His attack on deists and atheists was *Academische Reden über den Entwurff der Theologiae Anti-Deisticae, da die Einwürffe der unglaubigen Geister wider die Christliche Offenbahrung entwickelt werden* (Frankfurt, 1759).

[79] *Evangelische Glaubenslehre*, 1:67–68.

[80] *Unterricht vom rechtmässigen Verhalten*, 18.

[81] Quotations in *Unterricht von Auslegung der heiligen Schrift; ehemals für seine Zuhörer ausgefertigt*, 3rd ed. (Halle, 1759), 2, 12. Cf. 140–41. Semler called this work "the first scientific German outline of hermeneutics." See *Semlers Lebensbeschreibung von ihm selbst abgefasst*, 208. Baumgarten may have been responding to Wolff's 1713 call for a reconstruction of hermeneutics in *Vernünftige Gedanken von den Kräften des menschlichen Ver-*

In grammatical exegesis the interpreter carefully analyzed the biblical text in order to extract truths or propositions. This process began with determining the words themselves. Baumgarten insisted on a thorough knowledge of scripture's original languages (Hebrew, Greek) and a scrupulous examination of parallel passages and older translations.[82] The exegete then connected the words' meanings with historical circumstances by studying the speaker, audience, time, location, and cause. These five criteria had to be addressed in sequence; the cause could be ascertained only on the basis of the other factors. The exegete had to be attentive to the speaker's psychology. For example, Baumgarten required detailed knowledge of an Apostle's life prior to conversion as well as his sphere of activity in the church:

> Their former way of life, the sciences that were pursued, the doctrines that many church fathers absorbed before they became Christians, their way of life and standing in Christian society, the character and customs and civic life of the areas in which they lived, and more of the same, all had a strong influence on their habits, opinions and manner of writing.[83]

The exegete also had to be aware of the books' chronology, authors, and contents, since parts of books often stemmed from different periods and previously existing collections.[84]

In recognizing a work's author and his history, Baumgarten took issue with Orthodox Lutheran "inspiration" theory. The seventeenth-century Orthodox dogmaticians, in defending the doctrine of *sola scriptura* against Catholic and Socinians, held scripture to be literally inspired, since God had dictated every word of it. The prophets and Apostles were

---

standes und ihrem richtigen Gebrauche in Erkenntnis des Wahrheit (*Christian Wolf Gesammelte Werke*, Pt. 1, vol. 1) (Hildesheim, 1965), 228–31 (chap. 12). For "scripture reads itself" among Orthodox theologians, see Robert Preus, *The Inspiration of Scripture*, 21–22. For this two-step process, see "Das hermeneutische system Schleiermachers in der Auseinandersetzung mit der älteren protestantischen Hermeneutik," in *Wilhelm Dilthey: Gesammelte Schriften*, 21 vols. (Göttingen, 1957), 14, 2:624. Francke distinguished between exegetical and dogmatic elements. See E. Peschke, "August Hermann Francke und die Bibel," in *Pietismus und Bibel, Arbeiten zur Geschichte des Pietismus* 9, ed. Kurt Aland (Witten, 1970), 65–66. For Baumgarten's exegetical practice, see *D. Siegmund Jacob Baumgartens Auslegung des Briefes Pauli an die Römer* (Halle, 1749) and *D. Siegmund Jacob Baumgartens Auslegung des Evangelii St. Johannis* (Halle, 1762).

[82] *Unterricht von Auslegung*, 29–54.

[83] "Vorrede" to Gottfried Arnold's *Abbildung der ersten Christen*, in *Siegm. Jac. Baumgartens kleine teutsche Schriften*, vol. 1 (Halle, 1743), 62. Baumgarten applied this method in his study of Paul. See *Baumgartens Auslegung des Briefes Pauli an die Römer*.

[84] *Unterricht von Auslegung*, 55–87. Baumgarten outlined these steps in his comments on exegesis in *Evangelische Glaubenslehre*, 1:51–52.

God's amanuenses. As A. Quenstedt (1617–88), professor at Wittenberg and author of *the* compendium of high Orthodox theology, put it:

> The Holy Spirit not only inspired in the prophets and apostles the content and sense contained in Scripture, or the meaning of the words, so that they might of their own free will clothe and furnish these thoughts with their own style and words, but the Holy Spirit actually supplied, inspired and dictated the very words and each and every term individually.[85]

Baumgarten humanized the Bible's authors. Men in a heightened state wrote the biblical books. In some cases there were multiple authors, each of whom drew on his own knowledge and experience. In other instances authors used pre-existing materials. Understanding the Bible meant grasping the precise meaning of the author's language. Baumgarten averred that just as Jesus was simultaneously human and divine, so was the Bible: its human authors conveyed divine revelation.[86]

To support this humanization of the Bible, Baumgarten used the principle of accommodation. Orthodox inspiration theory had made limited use of accommodation to recognize the impact of the amanuenses' individuality. Baumgarten employed accommodation extensively to account for those aspects of scripture that were of a purely temporal nature or subject to error. He thereby took issue with inspiration theory's doctrine of scriptural inerrancy. For the Orthodox dogmaticians, scripture was infallible, "whether it pertains to doctrine, ethics, history, chronology, typography or onomastics." In contrast, Baumgarten distinguished between passages pertinent to salvation (the union of man with God), which were inerrant, and passages addressing other matters, which were not.[87]

Following the Wolffian method, the final step in grammatical analysis was to examine the work's coherence (*Zusammenhang*) to ascertain the author's intention. The exegete had to identify all the work's com-

[85] Quenstedt, *Theologia Didactico-Polemica sive Systema Theologicum* (Leipzig, 1715), I, 72, cited in Preus, *The Inspiration of Scripture*, 40.

[86] *Evangelische Glaubenslehre*, 3:26–32, 12–13. See Schloemann, *Baumgarten*, 221. For his intentionalist view, see *Unterricht von Auslegung*, 7–8. See Lutz Danneberg, "Siegmund Jacob Baumgartens biblische Hermeneutik," in *Unzeitgemässe Hermeneutik: Verstehen u. Interpretation im Denken der Aufklärung*, ed. Alex Buehler (Frankfurt am Main, 1994), 98–99.

[87] Quotation from Quenstedt, *Theologia Didactico-Polemica sive Systema Theologicum*, I, 77, cited in Preus, *The Inspiration of Scripture*, 77. On Orthodox accommodation theory, see 70. On Orthodox opposition to the Catholic and Socinian distinction between inspired and uninspired passages, see 35–40. Cf. Danneberg, "Siegmund Jacob Baumgartens biblische Hermeneutik," 106–111.

ponents and the connections between them. This was especially important since scripture's verse and chapter divisions had been introduced at a relatively late date.[88]

Here Baumgarten again disputed inspiration theory. The Orthodox dogmaticians held that scripture's text was pure: they defended the masoretic text's authenticity and asserted that providence and the Jewish copyists guaranteed the text remained uncorrupted during the centuries of transmission. In contrast, Baumgarten questioned scripture's form: he doubted, for example, that the masoretic text was divine.[89]

The second half of Baumgarten's method was a "dogmatic" analysis in which the interpreter carefully assessed the propositions that emerged from "grammatical" analysis.[90] The interpreter first established a passage's purpose by utilizing the knowledge gained in the grammatical exegesis to resolve ambiguities and adjudicate between competing interpretations. Next, the interpreter, following the premise that "Holy Scripture explains itself," aimed to ensure that he had achieved "completeness, clarity, and certainty (*Gewißheit*)." Such care was essential since human authors had expressed divine truths. Baumgarten consequently delineated many criteria of analysis and explanation. In weighing ideas, the key methods were similarity and analogy. One also had to analyze metaphors, imagery, and figures of speech, and to take account of literary genres, such as examples, parables, riddles, and epigrams. In treating historical passages, events had to be put in chronological order and compared, and the "natural" distinguished from the "supernatural." In dealing with dogmatic passages one had to compile, compare, and establish "coherence." It was also essential to distinguish between fulfilled and unfulfilled prophecies.[91]

In discussing a verse's "stress" (*Nachdruck*), Baumgarten confronted a central Pietist concept. Although early in his career Francke had been

---

[88] *Unterricht von Auslegung*, 87–114.

[89] See Quenstedt, *Theologia Didactico-Polemica sive Systema Theologicum*, 1:206, cited in Preus, *The Inspiration of Scripture*, 139. Cf. Richard Muller, "The Debate over the Vowel Points and the Crisis of Orthodox Hermeneutics," *Journal of Medieval and Renaissance Studies* 10, no. 1 (1980): 53–72. For Baumgarten, see Schloemann, *Baumgarten*, 218. For Baumgarten's knowledge of Richard Simon's work, see John D. Woodbridge, "German Responses to the Biblical Critic Richard Simon: From Leibniz to J. S. Semler," in *Historische Kritik und biblischer Kanon in der deutschen Aufklärung*, ed. Henning Graf Reventlow, Walter Sparn, and John Woodbridge *Wolfenbütteler Forschungen* 41, ed. (Wiesbaden, 1988), 79–80.

[90] *Unterricht von Auslegung*, 213.

[91] Quotations at ibid., 136, 140–41. Cf. 115–36, 173–90. Baumgarten's aim was "to attribute the most correct and demonstrable, also the most complete and fruitful sense to every passage of scripture." Ibid., 28.

a rigorous biblical exegete employing the highly formalized methods of Lutheran Orthodoxy, he later made exegesis contingent on conversion and rebirth by focusing on the text's emotional affect: the emotion of love that defined conversion and scripture should be a reader's aim. The method was to apply a typology to virtually any word or verse in order to evoke a mystical sense of multiple "stresses." At Halle Lange advocated his own version of this highly subjective method.[92]

Baumgarten pitted history against the Pietists' subjective exegesis. The "stress" must always agree with a passage's actual meaning according to the book's historical situation:

> The more through reading the Psalms one is placed in the outlook and frame of mind that was present for David and other men of God during their [Psalms] composition, and the more [one] considers all the truths contained therein in the same historical lineage in which the authors of the Psalms stood, the clearer and more correct will be the insight into [the Psalms], the more truths will it be possible to discover.[93]

He warned against introducing "arbitrary misinterpretations" or imagined meanings unwarranted by historical circumstances.[94] Moreover, Baumgarten repudiated conversion or devotional impact as a legitimate exegetical criterion: "the devotional quality [*Erbaulichkeit*] of an interpretation cannot be the mark of its hermeneutical

---

[92] For Francke, see Ulrich Barth, "Hallesche Hermeneutik im 18. Jahrhundert: Stationen des Übergangs zwischen Pietismus und Aufklärung," in *Die Hermeneutik im Zeitalter der Aufklärung*, ed. Manfred Beetz and Giuseppe Cacciatore (Cologne, 2000), 70–76; Axel Bühler and Luigi Cataldi Madonna, "Von Thomasius bis Semler: Entwicklungslinien der Hermeneutik in Halle," *Aufklärung* 8, no. 2 (1994): 56–58; and E. Peschke, "August Hermann Francke und die Bibel," *Pietismus und Bibel*, 59–88. For Spener, see Martin Schmidt, "Philipp Jakob Spener und die Bibel," in *Pietismus and Bibel*, 9–58. For Lange, see Bühler and Madonna, "Von Thomasius bis Semler," 58–60. For "stress," see Dilthey, "Das hermeneutische system Schleiermachers," 618–20; Jonathan Sheehan, *The Enlightenment Bible: Translation, Scholarship, Culture* (Princeton, 2005), 54–92; and Langen, *Der Wortschatz des deutschen Pietismus*, 64–65. For piety and learning in Pietism, see Chi-Won Kang, *Frömmigkeit und Gelehrsamkeit: Die Reform des Theologiestudiums im lutherischen Pietismus des 17. und frühen 18. Jahrhunderts* (Gießen, 2001). For Pietist anti-intellectualism, see Wolfgang Martens, "Hallescher Pietismus und Gelehrsamkeit oder vom 'allzu großen Mißtrauen in die Wissenschaften,'" in *Res Publica Litteraria: Die Institutionen der Gelehrsamkeit in der frühen Neuzeit*, ed. Sebastian Neumeister and Conrad Wiedemann, 2 vols. (Wiesbaden, 1987), 2:497–523.

[93] *Christian Richters genaue Übersetzung der Psalmen mit einer Vorrede Hrn. Siegmund Jacob Baumgarten* (Halle, 1736), 27. In general, *Unterricht von Auslegung*, 202. See Danneberg, "Siegmund Jacob Baumgartens biblische Hermeneutik," 140–42.

[94] *Unterricht von Auslegung*, 208.

correctness; similarly, the conviction of the correct sense of a writer cannot be based on the inner feeling and sensation of salvific effects."[95] Whereas the Pietists made the exegete's spiritual condition the principal criterion of exegesis, Baumgarten reduced it to a mere aid. Indeed, he went further, proposing societies dedicated to biblical exegesis to replace the Pietist conventicles that encouraged inspired exegesis.[96]

Finally, Baumgarten took exception to Orthodoxy's unmediated extraction of dogma by distinguishing between various kinds of passages. Those in which central doctrines (*Lehren*) were the immediate content readily yielded "edificatory truths" (*erbauliche Wahrheiten*) that could be reduced to propositions and compared. Elsewhere a more laborious process was required. Inferences (*Folgerungen*) could be derived either from the passage's content or its form. The exegete had to be careful to choose only those passages given to such inferences and those truths in keeping with scripture and a particular author's purpose. "Edificatory comments" (*erbauliche Anmerkungen*) were discovered by comparing truths from distant passages to bring out new understanding. Here the exegete connected particular cases with general truths. The exegete also had to exert extreme care in addressing scripture's mysterious meanings: "the exegete cannot either set the mediate or secret sense of the Holy Scripture entirely aside nor can he determine it arbitrarily."[97]

Baumgarten's hermeneutic represented a middle path between Pietism's subjective exegesis and Orthodoxy's inspiration theory. He recognized the Bible's human authorship and fallibile contents that did not bear on the "union" of man with God. By advocating an exacting philological and historical method, Baumgarten shifted the focus to revelation. He brought scripture's salvific content, rather than its form or emotional effect, to the fore.

Baumgarten's approach was characteristic of the theological Enlightenment. Christoph Mattheus Pfaff had dismissed Orthodox inspiration theory as untenable, rejecting scripture's infallibility in regard to history, geography and chronology. Johann Lorenz Mosheim (1694–1755) similarly reconstrued Orthodox inspiration theory by returning to Luther.[98]

---

[95] Ibid., 26. See also 10, 226–27, 229. For Baumgarten's definition of edification, see *Unterricht vom rechtmässigen Verhalten*, 691.

[96] *Unterricht von Auslegung*, 260.

[97] Ibid., 216–29. For orthodox dogmaticians on Scripture's materials and content being equally inspired see Preus, *The Inspiration of Scripture*, 39–48, 139–40.

[98] Hirsch, *Geschichte der neuern Evangelischen Theologie*, 2:345–47, 362–63.

HISTORY, SACRED AND SECULAR

In studying history, Baumgarten sought a "middle way" between the deists' assault on Christianity and the Pietists' attempt to find inspirational models and justify separatism. He insisted on a rigorous historical method that, according to Wolff's criteria, would yield "certain" knowledge. Baumgarten understood historical scholarship to be unitary: the same methods were to be applied to sacred and secular subjects. Baumgarten made the transition to studying history in the 1730s despite its tensions with Wolffianism. Wolff had deprecated history as the study of facts without certainty. Baumgarten wanted history to offer certainty and redefined it using Wolff's criteria.[99] Baumgarten revised Wolff's system in regard to history as well as theology.

Baumgarten defined the study of history through Wolff's concept of coherence: history was not a recitation of facts or events but rather a "comprehensible and lively presentation" informed by an "appropriate narrative coherence." Such a "coherent [account] of events" was innately pleasurable because it was "in accord with the wise purposes of the creator of human nature": "God himself used this mode of teaching in his revelation, which consists mainly of stories."[100] Baumgarten thought the advantage of biography was that the individual's life, rather than abstract concepts, provided coherence. He characterized Church history as "a credible and coherent report of the remarkable events of the divine worship society of Christians."[101]

History's coherence required authenticated evidence; it had to be "a reliable report of events that have occurred." The "narrated events" had to be credible, showing "possibility as well as probability." Baumgarten employed Wolffian categories to delineate the limits of natural and supernatural events. In particular, supernatural events could not contradict themselves, the laws of nature, or divine attributes. By the same token, not all claims to supernatural events were admissible:

> Just as little as the indispensability of the almighty and the unmediated impact of God make the truth of an otherwise impossible event

---

[99] Schloemann, *Baumgarten*, 144–45, 155–56. Peter Reill dismisses him in *The German Enlightenment and the Rise of Historicism* (Berkeley and Los Angeles, 1975), 43.

[100] *Algemeinen Welthistorie*, 8–9, 24.

[101] Vorrede, *Samlung von merkwüridgen Lebensbeschreibungen grösten Theils aus der britannischen Biographie* (Halle, 1754); *Auszug der Kirchengeschichte*, 1.

objectionable, equally as little does every claim to a miracle or pretence to it suffice to make the same believable and to invalidate the [need for] an investigation of internal credibility.[102]

Credibility rested on sources. Eyewitness accounts had to be scrutinized for reliability. Later reports had to be compared with earlier ones. The "character and number of witnesses" had to be tested for ability and accuracy. The historian had to be erudite and industrious to exercise the good judgment required to show "the true coherence of past events and essential circumstances." Baumgarten readily admitted that of all the branches of historical inquiry, church history suffered most from unreliable sources.[103]

If the historian ably discharged his duty and demonstrated an "intelligible relationship . . . toward the events he narrates and the requisite knowledge of them," he could then claim a form of "certainty." Well aware that the alleged lack of certainty drove the criticism of historical writing, he insisted that "there is a true and demonstrable certainty of history" that differs from "mathematical certainty and the demonstrability of general truths." Using Wolffian categories, he argued that a "contingent entity" can be true, provable, and certain and therefore have "outward" necessity even though it by definition lacked "inner" necessity. It was a profound mistake for philosophers not to recognize this species of certainty. Certainty was always dependent on the sources: while most major events could be proven with certainty and many more with likelihood, many remain doubtful and uncertain.[104]

> The greater the importance of the content, the greater is the obligation of exact and nonpartisan scrutiny of all the events therein, in order to bring them to the point of moral certainty, an obligation that carries with it overwhelming approval.[105]

With this category of certainty Baumgarten integrated history into theology as the mediator between human experience and divine truth. He thereby responded to the deists' and Pietist enthusiasts' extreme uses of history.[106]

---

[102] *Algemeinen Welthistorie*, 7, 10.

[103] Ibid., 10–13.

[104] Ibid., 9–20. For Wolff on contingency and necessity, see *Vernünftige Gedanken von Gott, der Welt und der Seele des Menschen*, pars. 575–80, pp. 353–58. Baumgarten's logic of history anticipated Johann Martin Chladenius, Johann Christoph Gatterer, and Jacob Wegelin. See Reill, *The German Enlightenment and the Rise of Historicism*, 100–26.

[105] *Auszug aus der Kirchengeschichte; von der Geburt Jesu an* (Halle, 1743), 1.

[106] Walter Sparn, "Auf dem Wege zur theologischen Aufklärung in Halle: Von Johann Franz Budde zu Siegmund Jakob Baumgarten," *Wolfenbütteler Studien zur Aufklärung*

Aware of intellectual developments across Europe, Baumgarten knew that deists and freethinkers had made history their most effective weapon against Christianity. His concern gained urgency as he became persuaded that freethinking had now made its headquarters in the German states (in the fifteenth and sixteenth centuries it had resided in France and Italy, in the seventeenth century in England) and that its threat was underestimated.[107]

He catalogued the varieties of contemporary freethinking, at first mentioning four predictable types: the skeptical, the atheistic, the deistic, and the "naturalistic" or "indifferentist." Yet he also included an unexpected fifth: the "enthusiastic" or "fanatic" variety, in which revelation is arbitrarily determined by "inner light" reason or feeling.[108] Baumgarten thought deism and enthusiasm so substantially similar as to be subsumed under one rubric. This classification obviously reinforced his search for a middle way.

While his concern with freethinking was mounting, Baumgarten was impressed by the Anglican apologetics based on history, to which Warburton had contributed. He reviewed much of this literature in his journals (*Nachrichten von einer hallischen Bibliothek*, 1748–51; *Nachrichten von merkwürdigen Büchern*, 1752–58) and strove to make it available through translations.[109] He was convinced that freethinking and

---

15 (1989): 84. Baumgarten treated freethinking and enthusiasm together ("Schwermerey sowohl as Freigeisterey"). See Vorrede, *Auszug aus der Kirchengeschichte*. For students needing to study more history, see Schloemann, *Baumgarten*, 127–28.

[107] *Auszug aus der Kirchengeschichte*, 10. Cf. introduction to *D. Nathanael Lardners Glaubwürdigkeit der evangelischen Geschichte*, trans. David Bruhn (Berlin and Leipzig, 1750). For freethinking, see *Siegm. Jac. Baumgartens kleine teutsche Schriften*, (Halle, 1743), 1:209. For recent scholarship, see Winfried Schroeder, *Ursprünge des Atheismus: Untersuchungen zur Metaphysik- und Religionskritk des 17. und 18. Jahrhunderts* (Stuttgart, 1998); Jonathan Israel, *Radical Enlightenment: Philosophy and the Making of Modernity, 1650–1750* (Oxford, 2001); and Martin Muslow, *Moderne aus dem Untergrund: Radikale Frühaufklärung in Deutschland, 1680–1720* (Hamburg, 2002).

[108] *Auszug aus der Kirchengeschichte*, 205–6.

[109] The *Nachrichten von einer hallischen Bibliothek*, 1748–51, contained lengthy reviews of English deists and apologists: Thomas Woolston (1:479–540) and Spinoza's *Tractatus* (1:47–74); Anthony Collins (2:133–70, 268–84, 354–82, 441–76); John Toland (3:299–330); Matthew Tindal (4:448–56); William Whiston (4:237–62, 350–60, 420–40); Samuel Clarke (4:334–51); and Thomas Chubb (5:52–62, 125–74, 193–212). To refute recent attacks on religion the journal summarized "errant books which . . . are proscribed" ("*Vorbericht*," n. p.; between 1:84–85).

Students and friends translated, he wrote the introductions. *Kleine teutsche Schriften* (vol. 1) contains these introductions. See *D. Nathanael Lardners Glaubwürdigkeit der evangelischen Geschichte*, trans. David Bruhn (Berlin and Leipzig, 1750); *Auszug der von Rob. Boyle gestifteten Reden* (Halle, 1738); *Abhandlung von der Beschaffenheit und den Quellen der Freigeisterei* (Halle, 1741); *Jerem. Burroughs Übel aller Übel* (Halle, 1735); *Samlung von Pre-*

atheism resulted from an ignorance that systematic historical knowledge could dispel. He was equally convinced that the incorrect application of historical knowledge permitted freethinking to triumph.[110] Baumgarten epitomized the Enlightenment's optimism in the irresistible power of knowledge, yet knowledge correctly derived and applied.

Baumgarten formulated his ideas about history's ability to correct Pietist excesses in relationship to Gottfried Arnold (1666–1714), the symbol of separatist Pietism. In a famous book, *Nonpartisan Church and Heretic History from the Beginning of the New Testament to 1688* (1699), Arnold had identified the bearers of true Christianity with the reborn and mystical believers who, as the heretics of every age, constituted the invisible church. That church was in principled opposition to the visible church, which had everywhere fallen into irremediable corruption. For Arnold, "nonpartisan" denoted both a method, insofar as his history transcended confessional conflict, and an epistemological principle, in the sense that his identification of true belief with heresy was his interpretive key. Arnold had broken with the institutional Church by resigning his professorship (Giessen, 1698), although he was later to change course by accepting a pastorate.[111]

Baumgarten wrote introductions to new editions of two of Arnold's earliest historical works. Introducing an anthology of two mystical

---

digten Cudworth, Wallis, Barrows (Halle, 1737); and Is. Watts Reden von der Liebe Gottes (Halle, 1739).

Historical works to which he wrote introductions include: *Herrn Bakers vollständige Historie der Inquisition*, trans. M. Christian Tieffensee (Copenhagen, 1741); *Herrn Abts Houtteville Erwiesene Wahrheit der Christlichen Religion durch die Geschichte* (Frankfurt and Leipzig, 1745); *Joh. Salom. Semlers Erleuterung der egyptischen Altertümer durch Übersetzung der Schrift Plutarchs von der Isis und dem Osiris und der Nachricht von Egypten aus Herodots* (Breslau and Leipzig, 1748); and *Johan Legers algemeine Geschichte der Waldenser oder der Evangelischen Kirchen in den Thälern von Piemont*, trans. Hans von Schweinitz (Breslau, 1750).

Baumgarten called Warburton's *Divine Legation* "an extensive, scholarly and fundamental consideration of the Egyptian hieroglyphs." See his preface to Romelyn de Hooghe, *Hieroglyphica, oder Denkbilder der Alten Volker* (Amsterdam, 1744).

Mosheim, also influenced by the English scene, wrote a Latin refutation of Toland (*Vindiciae antiquae Christianorum disciplinae adversus . . . Jo. Tolandi Hiberni Nazarenum*, 1720) and translated the Cambridge Platonist Ralph Cudworth's refutation of atheism (*Radulphi Cudworthi Systema intellectuale huius universi*, Jena, 1733). See Hirsch, *Geschichte der neuern Evangelischen Theologie*, 2:359–60.

[110] *Kleine teutsche Schriften*, 219–21, 241. See Schloemann, *Baumgarten*, 184–85.

[111] *Unpartheiische Kirchen- und Ketzerhistorie von Anfang des NT bis 1688*, 2 vols. (Frankfurt, 1699–1700). See Erich Seeberg, *Gottfried Arnold: Die Wissenschaft und die Mystik seiner Zeit* (Meerane, 1923) (photomechanical reproduction, Darmstadt, 1964), and Hermann Dörries, *Geist und Geschichte bei Gottfried Arnold* (Göttingen, 1963).

Church fathers with whom Arnold closely identified, Baumgarten questioned Arnold's scholarship.[112] In some cases Arnold translated inaccurately or followed Latin translations of the Greek texts too closely. In other cases he disputed Arnold's biographical accounts. Baumgarten then addressed Arnold's tendentiousness: his notes were more polemical than scholarly. He was also critical of Arnold's separatist preference for the inner light and the invisible church.[113]

Baumgarten's other introduction was to the *Image of the First Christians* (1696), Arnold's first major work in church history. Arnold had arranged citations from the Church fathers thematically to draw a collective portrait emphasizing the early Church's purity and subsequent decline.[114] In his introduction (edition of 1740), Baumgarten called for scrupulousness in both the "investigation" and "application" of the first Christians' characteristics, advocating that the historian approach the first Christians "without prejudice and with a true passion for knowledge." Exploiting his detailed knowledge of the English deists, Baumgarten reminded readers that Woolston and Tindal had observed that every church and sect claims to be based on the early Church.[115] Regrettably, Arnold confused the ideal with the real:

> [The *Image of the First Christians* is a work] in which the author treats more the virtues and characteristics than the practices of the first Christians, and which is not always of reliable credibility, insofar as he often reports how things ought to have been instead of providing evidence that they were in fact so constituted.[116]

Both introductions became occasions for Baumgarten to offer lengthy considerations of sacred history. In the 1739 introduction, Baumgarten prescribed four legitimate uses of the Church fathers. The Church Fathers reconfirm scripture's divinity through constant reference. By providing evidence about the history of Christian teachings,

---

[112] The original was *Denkmal des alten Christentums, bestehend in des Heil. Macarii und anderer hocherleuchteter Männer . . . Schriften* (Goslar, 1699). Arnold's translation of Macarius was *Des h. Marcarius Homilien, verdeutscht* (Leipzig, 1696). Baumgarten's introduction to the edition of 1739 was reprinted in *Kleine teutsche Schriften*, vol. 1, 3–48. See Dörries, *Geist und Geschichte*, 154–65.

[113] *Kleine teutsche Schriften*, 38–39, 45, 47. Dörries makes the same point. See *Geist und Geschichte*, 160–64.

[114] *Die erste Liebe der Gemeinen Jesu Christi, das ist wahre Abbildung der ersten Christen* (Frankfurt, 1696). For Arnold the decline commenced after the Apostles' death and reached a turning point with Constantine. See Dörries, *Geist und Geschichte*, 29–32, 149–51.

[115] *Abbildung*, 86–87.

[116] *D Siegm. Jac. Baumgartens Erläuterung der christlichen Alterthümer*, ed. M. Joachim Christoph Bertram (Halle, 1768), 21.

these sources refute false claims about early Christianity. By the same token, many aspects of the early Church were only available in these sources. Finally, the sources offer many "examples of a pious cast of mind" and thus indicate paths to God. Nonetheless, he warned that Protestants must be critical of these works; they cannot be used directly or unqualifiedly for edification.[117]

Baumgarten went further in introducing the *Image of the First Christians*, aiming to define the method that would yield knowledge of the real Church Fathers rather than Arnold's ideal. Such knowledge presumed a critical use of sources ("precise and regular judgment of their correctness") which, combined with detailed knowledge of the language(s) and historical situation of the author, would lead to a "correct and demonstrable interpretation of documents." The historian had to distinguish between an individual's and accepted views and between earlier and later thinkers, and also had to take into account variations over time and space. Above all, one could not understand the great thinkers ahistorically. The historian further had to make critical use of sources to distinguish between mere opinions and "true reports and stories," and to strive for a rounded view of individuals. The aim was a thorough study of the early Church that separated the essential from the inessential.[118]

> The supreme obligation for the exact scrutiny of the certainty of church history rests on the precise connection of Christian doctrine and worship with past events; and this [obligation] has been greatly increased by the unfortunate productivity of earlier periods in [creating] inauthentic and forged writings and fabrications. It is imperative to investigate not only the credibility of the evidence but also the correctness of our understanding of it according to the general rules of interpretation; and in both endeavors all partisanship and prejudice, including the edificatory quality of a narrative, must be painstakingly avoided. If these things are done regularly, then there is no danger that a sceptical uncertainty will need to be addressed.[119]

In Baumgarten's middle way, history was an essential medium of faith. Baumgarten invoked historical precedent to authenticate practice: the early Christians' use of Psalms for edification (*Erbauung*) legitimated the present use.[120] He pointed to the importance of ancient

---

[117] Vorrede, *Denkmal des alten Christentums*, in *Kleine teutsche Schriften*, 4–13, 45.

[118] Vorrede, *Abbildung der ersten Christen*, 58, 62–70. For lack of "certainty" about early Christianity, see ibid., 90.

[119] *Auszug der Kirchengeschichte*, 5.

[120] Introduction, *Richters genaue Übersetzung der Psalmen*, 20–21.

Egyptian worship for correct belief: since it was the most influential source of ancient religion, knowledge of it would show Christianity's superiority, but also that "true divine worship . . . rests upon ancient events and writings."[121]

History also served a cautionary function by revealing the Catholic Church's iniquity, the inescapable fact that, "its reigning coercion of conscience and persecutorial spirit differentiate it from all other confessional parties of Christianity."[122] The papacy's lust for power, aggravated by ignorance, increased its persecutorial appetite: "The greater the number of errors that are introduced as the result of prejudice, the greater and more frequent is the need to resort to force, and to employ coercion in order to stem or counter contradiction." By showing Church practices to be consistently opposed to "Scripture and healthy reason," history undermined the papacy's claims to infallibility.[123]

> An awareness of history is imperative to understand the Reformation and Protestantism. . . . thus it is a necessary duty of those confessional societies which enjoy the great benefit of free use of Holy Scripture and the unobstructed practice of the worship found within it, to keep fresh in memory a clear picture of the former deficiences [of the Roman Church], and diligently to renew [that picture] with the aid of historical knowledge.

Baumgarten expressly rejected misusing history to fabricate a Protestant heritage consisting of an unbroken sectarian lineage starting with the earliest heretics. He severely criticized Count Nicolaus Ludwig Zinzendorf (1700–60) and his followers, the Herrnhutter or Moravian Brethren, who asserted a direct link to the Waldensians.[124]

Baumgarten did not make history a literal arbiter of faith, however. Just as he rejected an unmediated effort to draw inspiration from scripture, so he repudiated Church history as an unmediated source of practice and belief. The historian approaches the sources critically to discover the "true middle way."[125] The historian had to measure everything according to God's word in scripture, which is the yardstick of critical method. The Church Fathers, for example, may have made mistakes. The historian had to differentiate the "apologetics and vindica-

---

[121] Introduction, *Semlers erleuterung der egyptischen Altertümer.*

[122] Introduction, *Johan Legers algemeine Geschichte der Waldenser,* 2.

[123] Quotations at Introduction, *Herrn Bakers vollständige Historie der Inquisition,* unpaginated, 4.

[124] Introduction, *Johan Legers algemeine Geschichte der Waldenser,* 13. For Zinzendorf, 14–15.

[125] *Abbildung der ersten Christen,* 77; *Baumgartens Erläuterung der christlichen Alterthumer,* 11–12.

tions of the ancients from what is binding on successors." One could not judge individuals and societies according to their apparent "agreement with Christian antiquity" since external differences may conceal internal similarities. The historian was neither to distance himself from public Christian life, in the manner of Arnold and the Pietist separatists, nor rue living now rather than in antiquity: "Christ is yesterday and today the same in eternity." Finally, as Christians are not born but made, it was necessary to imitate the "sense and spirit" rather than the details of antiquity.[126]

Through the critical method history promoted moderation. History could illuminate the truth of Christian doctrine, counteract freethinking and teach caution in relationship to other religions. It helped to determine whether practices were truly ancient or had a "papist" origin.[127] It promoted nonpartisanship and modesty, helping polemicists to avoid the extremes of "apathy and coercion of conscience." In general it could temper the "fanatical enthusiasm" that turns the history of "apostolic Christianity" into the "most dangerous excesses and possessions." History's task was

in part to safeguard everyone against the equally incorrect ways of disorderly and exaggerated dissatisfaction as well as complacency with the present state of the church; to set limits to complaints about the decline of Christianity; to check the impulse for renewal; and to guard against headstrong partisanship and devotion.[128]

Critical history was foundational for true Protestant belief.

Baumgarten utilized the same critical methods for secular as for sacred history; he was persuaded that secular history also served faith. He edited seventeen volumes of a multivolume world history, originally published in English, for which he wrote extensive commentaries and notes. His commentaries gained such acclaim that they were later translated into English and published as a supplement.[129]

---

[126] *Abbildung der ersten Christen*, 72–85.

[127] *Auszug aus der Kirchengeschichte*, 113; *Baumgartens Erläuterung der christlichen Alterthumer*, 11–12.

[128] Quotation in *Auszug aus der Kirchengeschichte*, 11. Cf. 7–8.

[129] The English original was *An Universal History from the Earliest Account of Time to the Present*, 7 vols. in 9 (London, 1736–44). See Herbert Butterfield, *Man on His Past: The Study of the History of Historical Scholarship* (Boston, 1960), 47. Baumgarten used the commentary to the Dutch edition. The German edition was *Übersetzung der Algemeinen Welthistorie die in England durch eine Geselschaft von Gelehrten ausgefertiget worden. Nebst den Anmerkungen der holländischen Übersetzung. Auch vielen neuen Kupfern und Karten. Genau durchgesehen und mit häufigen Anmerkungen vermeret von S.J. Baumgarten*, 30 vols. (Halle, 1744–67). The last volume on which Baumgarten worked, 17, appeared in 1758. J. S. Semler, among others,

Baumgarten justified the study of secular history in a work that appeared a year (1743) before the first volume of the world history. Through its contribution to knowledge and experience, secular history confirmed faith in providence with "certain" knowledge. The study of history enabled one,

> in part to gain knowledge of past times and distant places; and to be capable of understanding many scholarly writings and discussions; to broaden the boundaries of experience for the increase of wisdom and peace of mind; in part to understand better and make correct use of God's wise and beneficient providence and to be convinced of its certainty as well as to be acquainted better with its nature and establishment; in part to be induced to piety and virtue through the vivid and fruitful portrayl of virtue and vice and their mutual consequences."[130]

Some of Baumgarten's Halle colleagues criticized him for devoting himself to history rather than theology. Baumgarten asserted the work's exemplarity: it was a "coherent" history of the ancient and modern worlds that offered a "thorough understanding of a coherent range of useful truths." It was based on original sources and contained accurate information on language, geography, and calendrification; correlated newer with older travel accounts; provided abundant information on the practices, customs, sciences, and agriculture of diverse peoples; and, last but not least, gave a full account of biblical history that, by virtue of being integrated with general history, answered the freethinkers' criticisms.[131]

Yet history's role was even more profound: it was both inherent to society and socially necessary. After arguing that reading a "coherent account of events" is innately pleasurable and that God himself used history in revelation, Baumgarten added, "Man is of a social nature; he is made and obligated to social life." Society is comprised of, and functions through, "events [*Begebenheiten*]," and its welfare also depends on knowledge of "events."[132]

The knowledge of history that is absolutely essential to society fulfills a number of functions. It was imperative for individuals: "The more knowledgeable a person is of people and societies . . . the easier

---

continued the work. The translation of Baumgarten's notes was *A Supplement to the English Universal history, lately published in London . . . designed as an improvement and illustration of that work . . . The whole carefully translated from the original German of the eminent Dr. Baumgarten*, 2 vols. (London, 1760).

[130] *Auszug aus der Kirchengeschichte*, 5–6.

[131] Vorrede, *Algemeinen Welthistorie*, 36, 46–47.

[132] Ibid., 25–26.

will he be able advantageously to arrange his behavior, the less will he have to cope with the confusion of unexpected things, with the loss of needed presence of mind."[133]

Concrete example taught virtue more effectively than abstract doctrine: it was the most "fruitful and attractive instruction in correct and virtuous behavior." Knowledge of history was salutary to belief, providing proof of revelation and Providence: "the greatest use of history consists in the undeniable promotion of the knowledge and service of God, whereby people are brought to true virtue and happiness in the enjoyment of the highest goodness."[134] Echoing his case for the moderating influence of sacred history, Baumgarten claimed that knowledge of secular history, by contravening false assumptions, protects against "superstition" and "fanaticism," on the one side, and "ungodliness and freethinking" on the other. Knowledge of history thus spared society the terrible consequences that flowed from an "active contradiction of history."[135]

Under the influence of Anglican Moderates like Warburton, Baumgarten strove to reclaim history from freethinkers, Pietists, and other adversaries of true belief, weaving it into the fabric of his theology. Yet it is worth identifying Baumgarten's exact use of history. He did not belong to the so-called eclectic school that compartmentalized history and dogma. Johann Budde, for example, utilized history solely to illuminate the sources of belief; dogma retained its metaphysical grounding. The same held for Johann Lorenz Mosheim. A founder of the discipline of church history, his celebrated works showed history's impact on the shape of belief, but he kept it distinct from dogma by deriving the latter directly from scripture.[136] In contrast, Baumgarten contributed to a "critical" history that defined dogma through historical exegesis. By 1720 Christoph Mattheus Pfaff had advocated the development of a historical dogmatics. From the late 1730s Baumgarten recognized history as an alternative form of authority capable of raising questions about dogma or, for that matter, the received interpretation of scripture. In short, Baumgarten dismantled the barrier between history and dogma to fashion a moderate

---

[133] Ibid., 27.

[134] Quotations at ibid., 27, 31.

[135] Ibid., 32.

[136] For Budde's eclecticism, see Sparn, "Auf dem Wege zur theologischen Aufklärung in Halle," 71–76. For Mosheim's statutes drafted for Theology at Göttingen, making history essential to practical theology, see "J.L. v. Mosheims Entwurf der Statuten der Theologischen Facultät" (Juli 1735), in *Die Gründung der Universität Göttingen*, ed. Emil F. Rössler (Göttingen, 1855), 281–83. For the historical origins of ecclesiastical laws, see *Allgemeines Kirchenrecht der Protestanten* (Helmstedt, 1760), 36, 48–50, 215–32, 502–6.

version of critical history that relativized neither revelation nor belief.[137]

NATURAL RIGHT AND TOLERATION

Baumgarten advocated toleration and freedom of conscience on the basis of the natural rights theory that shaped his understanding of society and church-state relations. Yet unlike Warburton, Baumgarten did not make his reputation with a treatise on church-state relations; unlike Vernet, he did not intervene in contemporary political events; and unlike Mosheim and Pfaff, he did not write a textbook of ecclesiastical law.[138] Instead, Baumgarten expressed his ideas in "theological responsa [*theologische Gutachten*]" he wrote for ecclesiastical law cases, particularly those involving the status of Jews.

In the German states, Collegialism represented an effort to reassert the Church and the individual's freedom against state absolutism. In the Reformation's aftermath, the theory of episcopalism had justified transferring the Catholic bishops' powers to Protestant sovereigns. In the late seventeenth century, some thinkers (Thomasius) had proposed ideas of natural rights to end sectarian and confessional conflict by devising a theory of "territorialism" that gave rulers authority over the Church.[139] Yet some churchmen felt the territorialists had mistakenly embraced Erastianism. In response, they devised the theory of Collegialism (ca. 1670–1720) that aimed to restore a measure of the Church's independence by recognizing individual members' innate freedom.[140] Territorialism and Collegialism had so much in common that it was often difficult to distinguish them in practice. Both drew on the ecclesiastical natural rights theory derived from Pufendorf. Both viewed the state as a secular institution whose sole religious concern was conformity with the natural religion that guaranteed morality. And both rejected coercion in a

[137] For Pfaff, see *Academische Reden über das so wohl allgemeine als auch teutsche Protestantische Kirchen-Recht* (Tübingen, 1742), 229–43. Cf. Hirsch, *Geschichte der neuern Evangelischen Theologie*, 2:349–50. Sparn groups Baumgarten with Jerusalem and Spalding in "Auf dem Wege zur theologischen Aufklärung in Halle," 35–36. Schloemann argues that Baumgarten excluded history from dogmatics. See *Baumgarten*, 211.

[138] See Pfaff, *Academische Reden*, and Mosheim, *Allgemeines Kirchenrecht*.

[139] For Thomasius's views, see D. Christian Thomasen and Enno Rudolph Brenneysen, *Das Recht evangelischer Fürsten in Theologischen Streitigkeiten und wider die papistischen Lehr-sätze eines Theologi zu Leipzig*.

[140] Klaus Schlaich, *Kollegialtheorie: Kirche, Recht und Staat in der Aufklärung*, Jus ecclesiasticum 8 (Munich, 1969).

Church consisting of auditors and teachers, instead advocating toleration and freedom of conscience.[141] The two differed over the state's powers. Collegialists beginning with Pfaff made individual freedom of conscience the Church's fundamental principle: Pfaff asked the state to grant a thoroughgoing toleration. Mosheim went further, arguing that because believers delegated the state its authority over the Church, it was revocable.[142] In practice the two parted ways over the adiaphora (practices on which scripture was silent): territorialists assigned control to the state, Collegialists to the Church.[143]

In keeping with Prussia's official doctrine, Baumgarten was a territorialist. He argued that individuals were the churches' building blocks: "divine worship societies emerge from the connection of individual persons to a common divine service." Church power was limited to those means that respected freedom of conscience: "The Church as a church can in reality neither decree laws nor utilise external punishments." The Church was permitted the minor ban to exclude dissidents from worship; by not impinging on "the privileges of civil society" [bürgerliche Gesellschaft], the minor ban did not constitute persecution. Similarly, the state had no power over an individual's beliefs: "Governmental authority does not extend to the conscience of subjects."[144] The state's power extended to beliefs only insofar as they disrupted civil society: the state could punish "heretics" and "those who hold false beliefs" as "disturbers of public tranquility." Similarly, the state could restrict polemics between churches.[145]

Baumgarten endorsed toleration as indispensable to the state. "The government cannot force anyone to accept or renounce a religious

---

[141] Schlaich, Kollegialtheorie, 52, 76–80, 121–23. Thomasius recognized Pufendorf's importance in Das Recht evangelischer Fürsten in theologischen Streitigkeiten, 43–44. For Pfaff's view of Pufendorf, see Academische Reden, 21, 270ff.; for Thomasius's territorialism as "Caesaropopia," see 21, 99. For Mosheim's view of Pufendorf, see Allgemeines Kirchenrecht, 7. For criticism of Thomasius, see 189–99, 576–79, 591–98.

[142] Pfaff, Academische Reden, 43–78. On this point, see Schlaich, Kollegialtheorie, 154–57, and Hirsch, Geschichte der neuern Evangelischen Theologie, 2:339, 342–44. Mosheim also defended toleration. See Allgemeines Kirchenrecht, 260–64, 339–45, 395–417. For the jus retrahendi, see 586. Pfaff defended the right of rebellion, especially against the pope. See Academische Reden, 155–59.

[143] Pfaff, Academische Reden, 159–68; Mosheim, Allgemeines Kirchenrecht, 506–41; Schlaich, Kollegialtheorie, 179–80.

[144] Quotations at introduction, Herrn Bakers vollständige Historie der Inquisition, 3, and Unterricht vom rechtmässigen Verhalten, 477, 437. Other Collegialists permitted the minor ban. See Pfaff, Academische Reden, 267. Mosheim recognized the ban's legitimacy but not its use. See Allgemeines Kirchenrecht, 395–417, 478. Thomasius endorsed the minor ban. See Das Recht evangelischer Fürsten in Theologischen Streitigkeiten, 150–67.

[145] Introduction, Herrn Bakers vollständige Historie der Inquisition, 3.

confession." However, a religion's adherents may be forbidden their worship if they are free to emigrate—a noncoercive version of the Peace of Westphalia's *jus emigrandi* that collegialists and territorialists alike accepted.[146]

Citizenship did not require a particular confession. Members of different confessions could be upstanding and productive citizens:

> Accordingly, one cannot be a Christian without being an honorable man and a good citizen or a true subject; nevertheless, the latter is possible without the former, so that someone can be honorable and a good citizen without being a Christian, especially where knowledge of the immediate revelation of God is absent.[147]

Nonetheless, Christianity enhances citizenship: "every good citizen would be a still better one when he is also a Christian, indeed he is that much better a member of society the better a Christian he is."[148]

Protestantism enshrined freedom of conscience, whereas Catholicism was the fount of persecution.

> The principles according to which and from which my expert opinions derive concern the general freedom of conscience of different religious parties, and they are especially indispensable to the vindication of the Protestants' just accusations and grievances against the brutal persecution resulting from papist coercion of conscience.[149]

Baumgarten applied his principles in theological responsa he wrote concerning the Jews' status. The Halle Faculty of Theology often received requests from the king, the Prussian government, or individuals to render an expert opinion on matters governed by ecclesiastical law. As a prominent member of the faculty, Baumgarten gained a reputation as a champion of toleration and therefore received numerous requests to offer a verdict. Next to oral instruction, he saw these theological responsa as his most important contribution

---

[146] *Unterricht vom rechtmässigen Verhalten*, 438. For the same argument, see Pfaff, *Academische Reden*, 49.

[147] *Unterricht vom rechtmässigen Verhalten*, 112. Other Collegialists pointed to Holland as a model multiconfessional society. See Pfaff, *Academische Reden*, 41–42, 73, 127, 144.

[148] *Unterricht vom rechtmässigen Verhalten*, 424.

[149] Preface, *Siegm. Jac. Baumgartens Theologische Gutachten: Erste Samlung* (Halle, 1753). For a similar sentiment, see ibid., 419. For Catholic persecution, see introduction, *Herrn Bakers vollständige Historie der Inquisition*; and *Baumgartens Erlauterung der christlichen Alterthumer*, 12–13. For Mosheim, see *Vollkommene Emigrations-Geschichte von denen aus dem Erss-Bistum Salzburg vertriebenen, und Grossentheils nach Preussen gegangenen* (Frankfurt, 1734).

to teaching. He published those that had wider application or pedagogical value, and they were considered to be exemplary.[150]

Baumgarten's first major responsum on matters Jewish dealt with an incident in the Margrave of Ansbach. A Jewish convert to Christianity had denounced the Jewish liturgy, particularly one prayer, for blaspheming Jesus and Christianity. In September 1744 the authorities confiscated 303 Hebrew books from the synagogues at Ansbach, Fürth, and Schwabach and declared them to contain thirty-eight offensive passages. The authorities then prohibited the Jews from using the liturgy. The incident became a public controversy.[151]

Baumgarten joined the controversy in 1745, asserting that Protestant doctrine prohibited "coercion of conscience": freedom of conscience was the correct middle way between "freethinking and indifference," at one extreme, and "compulsion of conscience and irresponsible partisanship" at the other. He rejected confiscating the Jews' books and proscribing their liturgy as unacceptable partisan acts. Protestants must reject all compulsion of conscience. A Christian sovereign should not forbid the Jews' liturgy or require that they accept the christological interpretation of the Bible. Indeed, the worst transgression of freedom of conscience was to force a particular interpretation of scripture or to forbid someone his own interpretation. For the same reason, Jewish books should neither be censored nor Jews prohibited from selling them to fellow Jews even if they defame Christianity. Uniformity of belief may be advantageous, but not at the cost of compulsion.[152]

Baumgarten delineated acceptable relations between Christians and Jews. The authorities, who in exercising "supervision and authority over all religious associations and parties" were to respect "natural" as well as "revealed" law, were to tolerate the Jews within the limits of the common good. They were to see that Christianity was not

[150] For the responsa, see Udo Arnoldi, *Pro Judaeis: Die Gutachten der hallischen Theologen im 18. Jahrhundert zu Fragen der Judentoleranz, Studien zur Kirche und Israel* 14, ed. Peter von der Osten-Sacken (Berlin, 1993). For their exemplarity, see 14–16. See also Semler, "Kurzer Entwurf des Lebens des wohlseligen Herrn D. Baumgartens," 101–2. The Halle faculty issued twenty-two responsa pertaining to the Jews (1702–67). They originated in two ways. If the king or another official brought an issue to the university faculty, the dean and another faculty member drafted a responsum and then sought the full faculty's approval. In this case the faculty received the fee. If private parties approached an individual faculty member he collected the fee.

[151] Arnoldi, *Pro Judaeis,* 107–35.

[152] *Theologisches Bedenken von gewissenhafter Duldung der Juden und ihres Gottesdienstes unter den Christen und über Christian Wilhelm Christliebs kurzen Auszug aus den Selichoth oder jüdischen Busgebeten* (Halle, 1745), 6, 9, 18, 66–67, 26, 14. See Arnoldi, *Pro Judaeis,* 136–56.

defamed orally or in writing, or at least that books which do so were not sold to Christians. The authorities were to certify teachers and worship services and ensure that no itinerant preachers delivered sermons without permission. Commerce on Christian holidays was to be forbidden, and as far as possible Jews were to be under the jurisdiction of Christian courts. The Jews must be given the freedom to organize their worship services. Similarly, they were to adjudicate their own internal conflicts. On the other side, the authorities were to keep the Christian populace from defaming Judaism or interfering in its worship, and Christian preachers were to refrain from polemical and inflammatory sermons. Baumgarten justified this wide range of civil liberties by using the inherited Christian distinction between the sinner and his sin: the Jew as a person was to be tolerated, whereas Judaism was not.[153] Baumgarten's plea for toleration did not exclude inherited Christian aims: he repeatedly affirmed the ultimate goal of converting the Jews.

Baumgarten's responsum displayed deep sympathy for the Jews' plight. He regretted the Crusades and the Inquisition—though responsibility for these obviously fell on Catholics.[154] In general, Jews had suffered from excessive Christian zeal:

> [A]fter careful consideration before God I find myself in the end obligated to the opinion, in part from compassionate love and heartfelt sympathy for this unfortunate people, with whose suffering above other nonbelieving peoples we Christians are obligated to sympathize by so many aspects of our revealed doctrine, and whose improvement is more hindered than helped by all efforts at forceful conversion.

He added empathy to his natural rights argument on behalf of the Jews: how would Christians in Muslim lands feel were they denied their liturgy?[155]

In 1752–53 Baumgarten wrote two opinions on one case that further demonstrated his adamantine adherence to natural rights and freedom of conscience. A Jewish father of four children had converted to Christianity. Did his conversion require that he divorce his wife? If so, who

---

[153] *Theologisches Bedenken*, 7–26. Gotthilf Francke endorsed curtailing the Jews' worship. See Arnoldi, *Pro Judaeis*, 149.

[154] *Theologisches Bedenken*, 11. The expulsion of Prague's Jews (1745) may have influenced Baumgarten.

[155] Ibid., 5. Cf. 67. For reactions to Baumgarten's opinion see Arnoldi, *Pro Judaeis*, 152–56.

should have custody of the children? In which religion should the children be raised?[156]

Baumgarten asserted that the husband should divorce his wife, respecting her rights by neither infringing on her property nor prohibiting her remarriage (by granting a proper writ of divorce). In implementing these procedures the civil authority must be careful to avoid "coercion of conscience."[157]

Baumgarten argued against taking the children from the mother and raising them as Christians. Instead, the father should raise them in both religions so that, when they reached maturity, they could choose a religion. This arrangement alone respected the children's natural rights.[158] In offering this solution Baumgarten recognized the privileges of the majority faith: "a tolerated religion does not enjoy equal privileges with the ruling religion." Yet he was also sensitive to the minority religion's precarious position. The oppressive laws governing Protestants in France, for example, dictated that in a cross-confessional marriage with a Catholic father the children were automatically raised Catholic. Mindful of Christians under Muslim rule as well as Protestants in Catholic countries, he asserted the rule of natural law: "All restrictions on the freedom of tolerated religious parties must be arranged according to the general principles of natural law so that arbitrary determinations may not infringe on the natural privileges of individuals as well as of simple societies."[159] Surprisingly, he admitted that Jewish education might be more effective than Christian in teaching morality and God's way. Nevertheless, he also recognized the state's right to promote the ruling religion so long as it respected freedom of conscience:

> The toleration of a religion is a privilege given to the residents of a country to profess [that religion] and to live according to its laws, as long as one believes oneself obligated to it by conscience. But the obligation never to leave it, without the loss of one's natural rights, even when one discerns its mistakenness, would be a case

---

[156] "Von eines zum Christentum getretenen Juden Scheidung von seiner jüdischen Frau, und der Erziehung ihrer gemeinschaftlichen Kinder, auch nötigem Verhalten desselben gegen seine Eltern" (November 1752), in *Siegm. Jac. Baumgartens Theologische Gutachten; erste Samlung* (Halle, 1753), 287–336, and "Prüfung der Schrift, vom Recht eines bekehrten Juden über seine im Judentum erzeugte Kinder," ibid., 337–420. The wife's supporters approached Baumgarten. See Arnoldi, *Pro Judaeis*, 173.

[157] "Von eines zum Christentum getretenen Juden Scheidung . . . ," 289–309.

[158] "Prüfung der Schrift, vom Recht eines bekehrten Juden . . . ," 356.

[159] Ibid., 329. Cf. 315.

of coercion of conscience. The sovereign cannot deem any such contracts beneficial which stipulate such strict obligation. Least of all can the sovereign approve [of such a contract] when it prevents someone from accepting the religion which the sovereign himself professes and which [the sovereign] is obligated to spread in so far as this can occur without coercion. For that would mean that the sovereign would sacrifice his own conscience and religious freedom for the sake of the religious toleration of his subjects.[160]

In other words, toleration of one religion could not be at the expense of another, especially the sovereign's or the majority's:

[N]o religious toleration is to extend to the point that it damages the rights of a third. [Religious toleration] consists in the freedom granted to the residents of a country to serve God according to their own views. But this divine service is everywhere subject to the qualification that it cannot impair the rights and freedom of conscience of other religious groups, either those the sovereign likewise tolerates or in fact the ruling religion, the faith the sovereign himself professes.[161]

Based on a natural rights theory of church-state relations, Baumgarten's middle way made him a prominent advocate of freedom of conscience and toleration. In eighteenth-century Prussia the Jews' toleration was the most contested. Baumgarten was thus asked to help define the meaning of toleration and freedom of conscience in highly controversial cases. His "expert opinions" were remarkable for combining an unfailing commitment to natural rights and freedom of conscience with inherited Christian views (Judaism's errancy) and aims (the Jews' conversion).

NEOLOGY AND THE STATE

During Baumgarten's lifetime the theological Enlightenment gained recognition and began to win institutional support, especially at the new University of Göttingen. In the decades after his death in 1757, a version of the theological Enlightenment known as neology secured state sponsorship in Prussia. Neology's success gave rise to a varied opposition that culminated in Wöllner's infamous "Edict of

---

[160] Ibid., 347–48. Cf. 311.
[161] Ibid., 353.

religion" (1788). Baumgarten's students played a prominent role in these developments.[162]

Toward the end of Baumgarten's career the theological Enlightenment found a home at the new Hanoverian University of Göttingen (1737). The university's founders, who in general aspired to make it a training ground for the state-sponsored professions, hoped to overshadow Halle by creating a theology faculty that would be doctrinally impeccable and, by luring the best scholars with guaranteed freedom of conscience and high salaries, academically preeminent. The university began to realize these ambitions when Mosheim, who drafted the faculty's statutes, accepted the premiere professorship in 1747, and, a decade later, Christian Walch (1726–84) became professor of church history. By the 1770s the faculty was fully identified with the theological Enlightenment and helped develop its next phase, neology.[163]

Neology consisted of an enlightened piety and practice guided by a critical-historical method of scriptural interpretation. The neologs set out to create an enlightened piety commensurate with the more autonomous individual that Wolffian philosophy, eclectic history and Collegial theory envisaged. Baumgarten had shown the way by recasting Pietist concepts. The neologs described their ideal with the idea of "edification" (*Erbauung*), a medieval mystical term the Pietists had used to denote the re-creation of the individual in and through conversion. For the neologs, edification addressed the "whole man," the heart as well as the head, to create a moral, tolerant, and socially useful Christian. It was the means to salvation ("felicity"; *Glückseligkeit*). The neologs especially devoted their sermons, the premiere instrument of religious education, to edification.[164]

[162] Prominent neologs among Baumgarten's students were Anton Friedrich Busching (1724–93), Friedrich Germanus Lüdke (1730–92), Johann August Nösselt (1734–1807), and Johann Gottlieb Töllner (1724–1774).

[163] The university's founder, Gerlach Adolph Freiherr von Münchhausen (1688–1770), wanted a middle way between "atheism and naturalism" and a "Lutheran papacy." See "Nachträgliches Votum Münchhausens über die Einrichtung der Universität in der Sitzung des geheimen Raths-Collegium" (16 Apr. 1733), in *Die Gründung der Universität Göttingen*, 33–34. On the faculty, see Johannes Meyer, "Geschichte der Göttinger theologischen Fakultät," *Zeitschrift der Gesellschaft für niedersächsische Kirchengeschichte* 42 (1937): 17–102. Mosheim rejected Orthodoxy's emphasis on precise beliefs, stressing "living faith and active piety" plus historical study. See "J.L. v. Mosheims Entwurf der Statuten der Theologischen Facultät" (July 1735), in *Die Gründung der Universität Göttingen*, 281.

[164] On neology, see Sparn, "Auf dem Wege zur theologischen Aufklärung in Halle," 71–89; Hans Erich Boedeker, "Die Religiosität der Gebildeten," in *Religionskritik und Religiosität in der deutschen Aufklärung*, ed. Karlfried Gründer and Karl Heinrich Rengstorf,

The neologs forged a new relationship to Wolff's philosophy. Baumgarten had adopted the mathematical method with the full panoply of interminable definitions organized according to numbered paragraphs, syllogisms, and proofs. The neologs appropriated some of Wolff's key ideas but without his method. Some of their works were such models of clear exposition that they reached a popular audience.[165]

The neologs followed Baumgarten in seeking an alternative to the dangerous fanaticisms of deism and Pietist enthusiasm: if deism represented reason without revelation, then enthusiasm represented revelation without reason. They treated Augustine's doctrines of original sin and the eternal damnation of heathens as negations of morality.[166] The Peace of Westphalia had put to rest the idea of the confessional state; neology now tried to do the same for dogmatic confessionalism.

In response to the debate between deists and Anglican moderates Baumgarten had laid the foundations of a critical-historical method that scrutinized the contents of revelation and scripture while main-

---

Wolfenbütteler Studien zur Aufklärung 11 (Heidelberg, 1989): 145–195; and Karl Aner, *Die Theologie der Lessingzeit* (Halle, 1924). Neology and its central categories were often misinterpreted, scholars assuming that "felicity [*Glückseligkeit*]" spelt eudaemonism rather than salvation. See Werner Schutz, "Die Kanzel als Katheder der Aufklärung," *Wolfenbütteler Studien zur Aufklärung* 1 (1974): 151ff.

Mosheim's sermons made him the "German Tillotson." See Johann Lorenz von Mosheim, ed., Christian Ernst von Windheim, *Anweisung, erbaulich zu predigen*, 2nd ed. (Erlangen, 1771). Mosheim drew on two models, the Pietist's address to the will and the Latitudinarian treatment of ideas. See ibid., 29–30, 189. A famous neolog preacher, Johann Joachim Spalding (1714–1804), influenced by Wolff and the Anglican Moderates, considered the sermon a vehicle for the "edification" of the "enlightened Christian." See *Über die Nutzbarkeit des Predigtamtes und deren Beförderung* (Berlin, 1771), 89. On Spalding, see Joseph Schollmeier, *Johann Joachim Spalding; Ein Beitrag zur Theologie der Aufklärung* (Gütersloh, 1967).

[165] Friedrich Wilhelm Jerusalem (1709–1789), who had studied in Holland and England, made "benevolence" central to a book that enjoyed multiple editions. See *Betrachtungen über die vornehmsten Wahrheiten der Religion*, 3rd ed. (Braunschweig, 1770–1776). Johann August Eberhard (1739–1809), a pofessor at Halle, used Wolff's notion of perfection. See *Neue Apologie des Sokrates, oder Untersuchung der Lehre von der Seligkeit der Heiden* (Berlin, 1772).

[166] Jerusalem's middle ground was the revealed religion that enabled man to realize his "benevolence": it "is that which most successfully develops all of our abilities according to the determination of our nature." *Betrachtungen über die vornehmsten Wahrheiten der Religion*, 1:341, 359. Echoing Baumgarten, Eberhard attacked Pietist enthusiasm as the fundamentally mistaken idea that virtue can be achieved by "inspiration" or "instantaneous conversion." He affirmed natural religion by rejecting the eternal damnation of heathens: "God cannot reject the virtuous souls of the heathens; even less [can he] reject them eternally. The most we can justifiably say about them is that they err." *Neue Apologie des Sokrates*, 181–95, 434.

taining belief. The neologs went further in formulating a Christian apologetics that could defend scripture's content without sacrificing reason's autonomy. Johann Salomo Semler (1725–91), Baumgarten's most gifted student and his successor at Halle, drew on the humanist tradition to advocate the free application of reason to all of scripture, including the New Testament.[167]

Neology quickly allied with the Prussian state. The neologs were appointed to the state offices that enabled them to control patronage and preferment, aiming to usurp Pietism's state sponsorship as well as religious practice. Why this alliance? After the Seven Years War, Frederick and his bureaucrats realized that religion could play a key role in their efforts to transform the state into a more homogeneous political and administrative entity. They therefore attempted to integrate religion into the state mechanism. After 1763 the theological Enlightenment's moderate religious doctrine served absolutist reform from above.[168]

The first neologs were appointed to professorships just after mid-century. Frederician Prussia had centralized the supervision of religious affairs in a Supreme Church Council (1750) that in 1764 took responsibility for Lutheranism. By 1770 this council had become a bastion of theological Enlightenment. Neologs received the professorships and benefices in the council's gift, and reformed the hymnal, the liturgy and religious education.[169]

[167] For Semler's historical method, see "Einleitung in die dogmatische Gottesgelersamekit" in Baumgarten, *Unterricht von Auslegung der heiligen Schrift* (Halle, 1759), and *Abhandlung von freier Untersuchung des Canon; nebst Antwort auf die Tübingische Vertheidigung der Apocalypsis*, 2nd ed. (Halle, 1776). For Semler's historical thought, see Gottfried Hornig, *Die Anfänge der historisch-kritischen Theologie: Johann Salomo Semlers Schriftverständnis und seine Stellung zu Luther* (Göttingen, 1961), and Eric Carlsson, "Johann Salomo Semler, the German Enlightenment and Protestant Theology's Historical Turn," Ph.D. dissertation (University of Wisconsin–Madison, 2006).

[168] On recruitment, see Anthony J. La Vopa, *Grace, Talent and Merit: Poor Students, Clerical Careers, and Professional Ideology in Eighteenth-Century Germany* (Cambridge, 1988). For Prussian policies, see Walther Schneider, "Die Kirchenpolitik Friedrich des Grossen," *Historische Vierteljahrschrift* 31 (1937): 275–92, and Walther Hubatsch, *Friedrich der Grosse und die preussische Verwaltung* (Köln, 1973). For the clergy and the state, see Henri Brunschwig, *Enlightenment and Romanticism in Eighteenth Century Prussia* (Chicago, 1974), 22–26. For Frederick's attitudes, see Paul Schwartz, *Der erste Kulturkampf in Preussen um Kirche und Schule (1788–1798)*, Monumenta Germaniae Paedagogica 58 (Berlin, 1925), 19–20. Dilthey claimed Frederick's attitudes shifted after the Seven Years War. See "Friedrich der Grosse und die deutsche Aufklärung," *Gesammelte Schriften*, 3:128ff.

[169] The first academic appointments were Johann Gottlieb Töllner (1724–74), a Baumgarten student, at Frankfurt an der Oder (1756), and Wilhelm Abraham Teller (1734–1804) at Helmstedt in 1761. See Aner, *Die Theologie der Lessingzeit*, 83–89, 111–12. On the new "Ministry of Religion [*Geistliche Departements*]," see Hubatsch, *Friedrich der*

The state's alliance with the theological Enlightenment aroused adversaries at both ends of the spectrum. The continuing growth of a public sphere of journals and reading societies in the 1770s, and especially the 1780s, gave adversaries great scope for public opposition. Johann Georg Hamann (1730–88) and Johann Gottfried Herder (1744–1803), for example, questioned the Enlightenment's fundamental assumptions. Other figures pushed beyond the theological Enlightenment toward unalloyed reason. Hermann Samuel Reimarus (1694–1768) moved in the direction of deism, and when Gotthold Ephraim Lessing, who opposed both neology and orthodoxy, published Reimarus's works posthumously in the 1770s, he became embroiled in a famous polemic with Johann Melchior Goeze (1717–86), the proponent of intolerant Lutheran Orthodoxy who was Baumgarten's former student. Karl Friedrich Bahrdt (1741–92) also represented the radical rationalist turn and politicization of the late Enlightenment. Many of these views resounded in the posthumous debate over Lessing's beliefs (1784–86), the so-called pantheism controversy, which began as an exchange between Friedrich Heinrich Jacobi (1743–1819) and Moses Mendelssohn (1729–86) over Lessing's relationship to Spinoza and quickly became the decade's intellectual cause célèbre.[170]

Opposition to the alliance arose in the state as well: an indigenous counterattack preceded the French Revolution. Frederick William II's minister of ecclesiastical affairs, Johann Christoph Wöllner (1732–1800), another Baumgarten student, attempted to undo the alliance. He thought the neologs were extirpating Christianity from Prussia, and tried to expel them from the universities and schools, church and army. His Religionsedikt (1788) prepared the way by investing the symbolic books with normative authority. He prohibited all innovation; officeholders were to conform or face dismissal. In short, Wöllner tried to assert the sovereign's right to dictate belief, in opposition to natural rights and the Hohenzollern tradition of freedom of conscience.[171]

Grosse und die preussische Verwaltung, 190–212. On the Oberkonsistorium, see Schwartz, *Der erste Kulturkampf*, 19–32. The neolog appointees were J.J. Spalding (1764), Teller and A. F. Büsching (1767), the last a Baumgarten student, and J. S. Diterich (1770). See Martin Bollacher, "William Abraham Teller: Ein Aufklärer der Theologie," in *Über den Prozess der Aufklärung in Deutschland im 18. Jahrhundert. Personen, Institutionen u. Medien*, ed. Hans Erich Boedeker and Ulrich Hermann (Göttingen, 1987).

[170] The public largely remained loyal to the state. See James J. Sheehan, *German History, 1770–1866* (New York, 1989), 190–206. For Barth, see Günter Mühlpfordt, "Karl Friedrich Bahrdt und die radikale Aufklärung," *Jahrbuch des Instituts für deutsche Geschichte* 5 (1976): 49–100. For the pantheism debate, see Alexander Altmann, *Moses Mendelssohn: A Biographical Study* (Alabama, 1973), 638–711, and Frederick Beiser, *The Fate of Reason: German Philosophy from Kant to Fichte* (Cambridge, MA, 1987), 44–164.

[171] For opposition before 1789, see Fritz Valjavec, "Das Wollnersche Religionsedikt und seine geschichtliche Bedeutung," *Historisches Jahrbuch* 72 (1953): 386–400, and

Baumgarten was representative of the first fully articulated version of the religious Enlightenment that enjoyed state sponsorship in the German lands. While it had an enormous impact on German Lutherans, it also exerted significant influence among other confessions. The Protestant theological Enlightenment played a decisive role as Jews and Catholics in the German states created their own versions of religious Enlightenment.

Martin Phillipson, *Geschichte des preussischen Staatswesens vom Tode Friedrich des Großen bis zu den Freiheitskriegen*, 2 vols. (Leipzig, 1880–82), 1:198. For Wöllner's views, see Schwartz, *Der erste Kulturkampf*, 73–86. Wöllner attempted to destroy the neologs' power base (Oberkonsistorium, Halle Theology Faculty) and introduce strict censorship, an approved catechism, and belief tests for candidates for pastorates and teaching posts.

Opposite: Moses Mendelssohn. Frontispiece, G. B. Mendelssohn, ed., *Moses Mendelssohn's gesammelte Schriften*, 7 vols. (Leipzig, 1843). Courtesy of Memorial Library, University of Wisconsin–Madison.

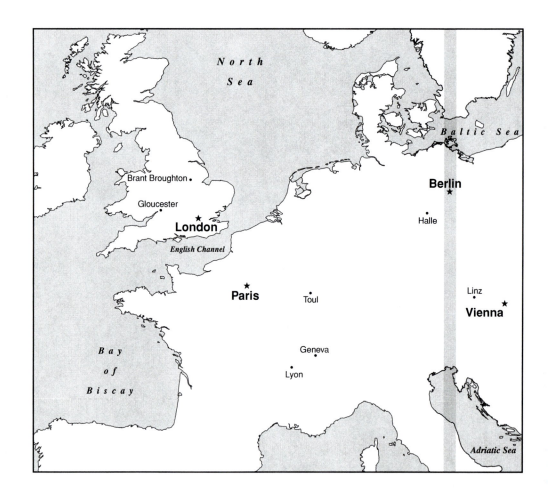

CHAPTER FOUR

Berlin

Moses Mendelssohn's "Vital Script"

THROUGHOUT THE MIDDLE AGES, AND especially during periods of heightened creativity, Jews interacted intensively with the surrounding culture. In the post-Reformation period, in contrast, Ashkenazi Jewry of Central and Eastern Europe increasingly isolated itself in a world of Talmudic casuistry and mysticism, losing touch with large portions of its textual heritage as well as with Europe's intellectual revolutions. This cultural isolation peaked after the Peace of Westphalia (1648), when, paradoxically, Europe's religious stalemate and incipient toleration promised an amelioration of the Jews' political and social position. That the advocates of amelioration judged the Jews on the basis of their cultural attainments only magnified the paradox.

The Haskalah ("Enlightenment") originated as an indigenous effort to correct the historical anomaly of a Judaism out of touch with central aspects of its textual heritage and the larger culture. The Haskalah tried to reclaim the Bible, Jewish philosophy, and the Hebrew language, as well as to absorb Enlightenment science and philosophy, in order to fashion a reasonable understanding of Judaism. In a later stage, in the 1770s and 1780s, it became a movement that engaged the Jews' political and social position, aiming to alter Jewish society and attain increased privileges and equal rights.[1]

Moses Mendelssohn (1729–86) was the foremost representative of the Haskalah ("from Moses unto Moses there was none like Moses"), known for his translation of the Pentateuch into German (1779–83) and his combined defense of Judaism and plea for emancipation (*Jerusalem*, 1783). He was also a leading figure of the Berlin Enlightenment. He

---

[1] For early modern Ashkenazi Judaism, see Haim Hillel Ben-Sasson, *Hagut ve-Hanhagah* (Jerusalem, 1959); Isadore Twersky, "Talmudists, Philosophers, Kabbalists: The Quest for Spirituality in the Sixteenth Century," in *Jewish Thought in the Sixteenth Century*, ed. Bernard Dov Cooperman (Cambridge, MA, 1983), 431–59; Jacob Elbaum, *Petihut ve-Histagrut: Ha-Yetsira ha-Ruhanit-Sifrutit be-Polin ube-Artsot Ashkenaz be-Shalhei ha-Meah ha-Sheish Esrei* (Jerusalem, 1990); Joseph M. Davis, "The Cultural and Intellectual History of Ashkenazic Jews, 1500–1750. A Selective Bibliography and Essay," *Leo Baeck Institute Yearbook* 38 (1993), 343–90, and idem, *Yom-Tov Lipmann Heller: Portrait of a Seventeenth-Century Rabbi* (Oxford, 2004); and Elhanan Reiner, "Changes in the Yeshivot of Poland and Germany in the 16th and 17th Centuries and the Debate on Pilpul" (Hebrew), in *Ke-Minhag Ashkenaz u-Folin: Sefer Yovel le-Chone Shmeruk*, ed. Israel Bartal (Jerusalem, 1993), 9–80.

wrote widely on literature, aesthetics, and philosophy, won a major prize from the Berlin Academy of Sciences in 1763, and published a European best-seller in 1767 that gained him the sobriquet "the Socrates of Berlin." Having standing in two realms was characteristic of the religious Enlightenment, yet his preeminence was remarkable. Mendelssohn was a legend in his lifetime, and the best known of this book's six figures.

Mendelssohn's sources were as varied as his attainments. Within Judaism he drew on the medieval Andalusian tradition of practical philosophy and piety (Nahmanides, 1194–1270; Judah Ha-Levi, 1085?–1140?), yet also on Maimonides (1135–1204). In European philosophy he was an independent disciple of Christian Wolff; he read Locke, first in Latin, and translated Rousseau and Shaftesbury. He was well versed in the Protestant religious Enlightenment—Dutch Arminianism, English Moderation, German theological Enlightenment, and neology. He sought to renew Judaism intellectually while avoiding monolithic Talmudism at one extreme and Maimonidean speculative rationalism at the other. Not only was Mendelssohn the Haskalah's most prominent figure, he was among its few members to make the transition from intellectual renewal to politics.[2]

Like other versions of religious Enlightenment, the Haskalah initially concerned intellectual renewal: it aimed to promote a reasonable understanding of Judaism by reforming the Hebrew textual curriculum. A practice-oriented interpretation of the Talmud was to replace casuistry. Medieval Hebrew philosophy was to displace Kabbalah as the major supporting discipline. The Bible was to be studied independently using the tradition of plain (*peshat*) or literalist exegesis. Systematic study of Hebrew language and grammar was to ground these pursuits. Finally, knowledge of science and vernacular languages would infuse all inquiry with current ideas. Jewish authorities largely welcomed rather than resisted these efforts; in

[2] The scholarship on Mendelssohn is vast. Excellent bibliographies are Hermann Meyer, *Moses Mendelssohn Bibliographie* (Berlin, 1965); Michael Albrecht, "Moses Mendelssohn: Ein Forschungsbericht 1965–1980," *Deutsche Vierteljahresschrift für Literaturwissenschaft und Geistesgeschichte* 57 (1983): 64–166; and Willi Goetschel, "Neue Literatur zu Moses Mendelssohn," *Lessing Yearbook* 29 (1997): 199–208. Biographies are Alexander Altmann, *Moses Mendelssohn: A Biographical Study* (Tuscaloosa, AL, 1973), and Dominique Bourel, *Moses Mendelssohn: La Naissance du judaïsme moderne* (Paris, 2004). Recent studies are Allan Arkush, *Moses Mendelssohn and the European Enlightenment* (Albany, NY, 1994), David Sorkin, *Moses Mendelssohn and the Religious Enlightenment* (Berkeley, 1996), and idem, "The Mendelssohn Myth and Its Method," *New German Critique* 77 (Winter, 1999): 7–28.

the early Haskalah rabbis were prominent as supporters and participants.[3]

The early Haskalah's effort to broaden the curriculum drew on Judah ben Bezalel Loew of Prague's (1525–1609; acronym: the Maharal) century-old critique of Ashkenazi education. The leading scholar and rabbi of his day, the Maharal opposed Ashkenazi Jewry's exclusive concentration on Talmud study and especially the casuistic method (*pilpul*), fearing that its shocking ethical indifference would compromise the legal tradition. He wanted the curriculum to include independent study of the Bible and Mishnah, formal study of Hebrew language and grammar, and science. His disciples repeated these criticisms. An ideal of Sephardi education complemented this pedagogical critique. Sephardic schools in cities such as Amsterdam and Bordeaux taught the subjects and employed the methods the pedagogical critics advocated. It became commonplace for Ashkenazi critics to counterpoise Sephardi schools to their own.[4]

The early Haskalah (1720–70) emerged against the backdrop of the Jews' position as a quasi-estate on the margins of estate society. They suffered from disabilities and discrimination that ranged from occupational and residential restrictions to higher taxation and special levies, collective responsibility for debt, and the transit tax otherwise applied to cattle. Nevertheless, they were better off than most members of the

[3] David Sorkin, *The Berlin Haskalah and German Religious Thought* (London, 2000), 38–62. Shmuel Feiner cites only one opponent, Jacob Emden. See *The Jewish Enlightenment* (Philadelphia, 2004), 74–75.

[4] Ben Zion Bokser, *From the World of the Cabalah: The Philosophy of Rabbi Judah Loew of Prague* (New York, 1954), 133–45; A. F. Kleinberger, *Ha-Mahshava ha-Pedagogit shel ha-MaHaRaL mi-Prag* (Jerusalem, 1962), 136–42; André Neher, *La Puits de l'exil: La Théologie dialectique du Maharal de Prague (1512–1609)* (Paris, 1966); O. D. Kulka, "The Historical Background of the National and Educational Teaching of the Maharal of Prague" (Hebrew), *Zion* 50 (1985): 277–320; David Ruderman, *Jewish Thought and Scientific Discovery in Early Modern Europe* (New Haven, 1995), 76–81. Disciples were Ephraim Luntshitz (1550–1619), Yom Tov Lipman Heller (1579–1654), and Sheftel Horowitz (1590?–1660?).

On *pilpul*, see M. Breuer, "The Rise of Pilpul and Disputes in the Ashkenazi Yeshivot" (Hebrew), in *Sefer ha-Zikaron le-Moreinu Y. Y. Weinberg*, ed. Azriel Hildesheimer (Jerusalem, 1969), 241–55; Zalman Dimitrovsky, "The Method of Pilpul" (Hebrew), in *Salo Wittmayer Baron Jubilee Volume* (Hebrew section), 3 vols. (Jerusalem, 1974–75), 3:111–81; and Reiner, "Changes in the Yeshivot of Poland and Germany."

Prague criticism and the Sephardi ideal converged in Shabbetai Bass (1641–1718). See *Sefer Siftei Yesheinim* (Amsterdam, 1680) and Shimeon Brisman, *A History and Guide to Judaic Bibliography* (Cincinnati, 1977), 9–13. Zvi Ashkenazi (1660–1718) wished to reform Polish schools using the Sephardi model. See Jacob Emden, *Megilat Sefer*, ed. Bick (Jerusalem, 1979), 29, 35–36, 67–68, 71–72. See Ismar Schorsch, "The Myth of Sephardic Supremacy," *Leo Baeck Institute Yearbook* 34 (1989): 47–53.

larger society. They exercised internal autonomy, governing themselves according to Jewish law (*halakha*) in their own courts and maintaining their own schools, hospitals, and charitable institutions. Yet that autonomy was always contingent on negotiation with the Christian authorities.[5]

In the eighteenth century a concatenation of external (mercantilism, state absolutism) and internal developments (court Jews) was undermining this communal formation. The Reformation and post-Reformation expulsions had virtually emptied the Germanies of Jews. The absolutist states' mercantilist policies enabled Jews to resettle Central Europe during and after the Thirty Years War. The Jews either repopulated existing settlements, or reestablished former settlements, or created entirely new ones, often centered around a court Jew. These settlements were often either more vulnerable or from their inception subject to increasing state interference.[6]

As the creation of a religious minority, the Haskalah was separated from other instances of religious Enlightenment. The Jews lacked a state's infrastructure (universities, academies, benefices, a civil service) and a public sphere (journals, newspapers, coffeehouses, voluntary associations). The Haskalah depended on the sponsorship of state surrogates, namely, the mercantile elite and court Jews, who had fewer resources than a state and dispensed them capriciously.[7]

---

[5] Salo Baron, "Ghetto and Emancipation," *Menorah Journal* 14, no. 6 (1928): 515–26.

[6] On Jews in the German states, see Mordechai Breuer, "The Early Modern Period," in *German-Jewish History in Modern Times: Tradition and Enlightenment, 1600–1780*, ed. Michael Meyer (New York, 1996), 79–260, and David Sorkin, *The Transformation of German Jewry, 1780–1840* (New York, 1987), 41–50. On resettlement, see Jonathan Israel, "Central European Jewry during the Thirty Years War," *Central European History* 16 (1983): 3–30; idem, *European Jewry in the Age of Mercantilism, 1550–1750* (Oxford, 1985); and Steven M. Lowenstein. "The Social Dynamics of Jewish Responses to Moses Mendelssohn," in *Moses Mendelssohn und die Kreise seiner Wirksamkeit*, ed. Michael Albrecht, Eva J. Engel, and Norbert Hinske (Tübingen, 1994), 342.

[7] David Sorkin, "The Problem of Patronage and Institutionalization: Some Reflections on the Haskalah and Some Remarks on the Armenians," in *Enlightenment and Diaspora: The Armenian and Jewish Cases*, ed. Richard G. Hovannisian and David N. Myers (Atlanta, 1999), 131–43. For the state in the Enlightenment, see Robert Wuthnow, *Communities of Discourse: Ideology and Social Structure in the Reformation, the Enlightenment and European Socialism* (Cambridge, 1989), 157–349.

Another minority version of religious Enlightenment is the Anglo-Catholic Cisalpines. See Joseph Chinnici, *The English Catholic Enlightenment: John Lingard and the Cisalpine Movement, 1780–1850* (Shepherdstown, WV, 1980). For a comparison, see David Sorkin, "Enlightenment and Emancipation: German Jewry's Formative Age in Comparative Perspective," in *Comparing Jewish Societies*, ed. Todd Endelman (Ann Arbor, MI, 1997), 96–99.

The early Haskalah (1720–70) began among individuals who turned a profound sense of inferiority at their ignorance of European culture and the Hebrew textual tradition into a "quasi-erotic" passion for knowledge. The early maskilim usually started their pursuit of ideas as isolated "orphans of knowledge."[8] They became aware of like-minded brethren first and foremost through books. In the course of the eighteenth century an early Haskalah "library" emerged, consisting of works of grammar, science, and philosophy, that came off the same presses as casuistic and mystical works. A separate Haskalah press did not exist.[9] A watershed in creating the Haskalah library was the republication by the Wolffian press of two of Maimonides' major works. His *Mishneh Torah*, the first systematic presentation of Jewish law, appeared in 1739 (it had last been reprinted in Amsterdam in 1702–3). Three years later came the first reissue in almost two centuries of his *Guide of the Perplexed*, a central text of medieval Jewish philosophy notable for its systematic effort to reconcile Judaism with Aristotle. David Fränkel (1707–62), the rabbi of Dessau and Moses Mendelssohn's teacher, tacitly approved these publications.

The early maskilim also overcame their isolation by publishing a book. A would-be author had to guarantee the publisher his costs if not a modest profit. If the author was not independently wealthy or did not have a rich sponsor, he had to travel to sign up advance subscribers (the subscription list then adorned the front of the book). In addition, the author had to reside near the publisher for an extended period to see the manuscript through the press (the task Vernet discharged for Montesquieu). In an age when travel was expensive and difficult, these were rare opportunities for early maskilim to meet as well as seek patrons. In addition, there was correspondence among the early maskilim. Although not enough letters survive to ascertain whether there was an actual "republic of letters," the rudiments certainly existed.[10]

---

[8] Feiner, *The Jewish Enlightenment*, 23–27, 37–50. For "orphans of knowledge," see Isaac Euchel, *Toldot Rabeinu he-Hakham Moshe ben Menahem* (Berlin, 1788), 7.

[9] Menahem Schmelzer, "Hebrew Printing and Publishing in Germany, 1650–1750: On Jewish Book Culture and the Emergence of Modern Jewry," *Leo Baeck Institute Yearbook* 33 (1988), esp. 371–72; Moritz Steinschneider, "Hebräische Drücke in Deutschland," *Zeitschrift für die Geschichte der Juden in Deutschland"* (1892): 154–86, esp. 168; Gershon Hundert, "The Library of the Study Hall in Volozhin, 1762: Some Notes on the Basis of a Newly Discovered Manuscript," *Jewish History* 14 (2000): 225–44. On the proliferation of halakhic works in the eighteenth century, see Zeev Gries, *The Book in the Jewish World* (Oxford, 2007), 37–39.

[10] Feiner, *The Jewish Enlightenment*, 44, 77–79. For *Hameasef*'s alternative means to enlist presubscribers, see 229.

There were three groups of early maskilim: autodidacts, physicians, and rabbis. Israel Zamosc (1700–72), an autodidact who came to Berlin from Galicia, wrote one book in which he attempted to displace casuistry by showing that mathematics and astronomy were indispensable to studying the Talmud, and a second in which he tried to renew the discipline of Hebrew philosophy by updating a medieval philosophical commentary.[11] Naphtali Herz Wessely (1725–1805), an autodidact who was born to a court Jewish family in Copenhagen and belonged to Amsterdam's maskilic circles, wrote a two-volume study of selected biblical synonyms that aimed to revive the discipline of plain exegesis (peshat) and restore bible study to the Ashkenazi curriculum.[12] As for occupations, Zamosc tutored the children of Berlin's mercantile elite, as well as an aspiring maskil like Mendelssohn; Wessely was a wealthy merchant who, after losing his fortune, sought sponsorship in Berlin.[13]

Physicians trained at German universities (Prussia admitted Jews to medical faculties in the 1670s) tried to convey to coreligionists their knowledge of contemporary science and philosophy by writing popular works or aiding the autodidacts. Tobias Cohen (1652–1729), one of the first Jews to study medicine at Frankfurt on the Oder (1678–79), wrote a medical and scientific textbook in Hebrew that included Harvey's theory of blood circulation.[14] Asher Anshel Worms (1695–1769), also educated at Frankfurt on the Oder, wrote an algebra textbook in Hebrew (1722), and forty years later defended the masoretic text's

---

[11] *Netzah Yisrael* (1741) and *Sefer Ru'ah Hen* (1744). See Sorkin, *The Berlin Haskalah*, 50–52, and Ruderman, *Jewish Thought and Scientific Discovery in Early Modern Europe*, 332–34, 341–43.

[12] *Levanon*, 2 vols. (Amsterdam, 1765–66). See Sorkin, *The Berlin Haskalah*, 99–101; Edward Breuer, "Naphtali Herz Wessely and the Cultural Dislocations of an Eighteenth-Century Maskil," in *New Perspectives on the Haskalah*, ed. Shmuel Feiner and David Sorkin (Oxford, 2001), 27–47.

[13] Isaac Wetzlar (1680–1751) combined the Prague School and the Sephardi ideal. See *The Libes Briv of Isaac Wetzlar*, ed. and trans. Morris M. Faierstein, *Brown Judaic Studies* 308. (Atlanta, GA, 1996). On Wetzlar, see Azriel Shohat, *Im Hilufei Tekufot* (Jerusalem, 1960), 131–33, 201–7, and Sorkin, *The Berlin Haskalah*, 48–50.

On patronage, see Monika Richarz, *Der Eintritt der Juden in die akademischen Berufe* (Tübingen, 1974), 67–82; M. Bodian, "The Jewish Entrepreneurs in Berlin and the Civil Improvement of the Jews in the 1780s and 1790s" (Hebrew), *Zion* 49 (1983): 159–84; and Sorkin, "The Problem of Patronage and Institutionalization," 131–43.

[14] *Ma'aseh Tuvyah* (Venice, 1707), reprinted Jessnitz, 1721. See Ruderman, *Jewish Thought and Scientific Discovery*, 229ff. On Jews at German universities, see Richarz, *Der Eintritt der Juden*, 23–42. On Jewish doctors, see John M. Efron, *Medicine and the German Jews: A History* (New Haven, 2001), 64–104.

authenticity and the need for plain exegesis.[15] Aaron Solomon Gumpertz (1723–69), scion of a family of scholars and court Jews who received a medical degree, wrote an intellectual autobiography in which he tried to revive plain (peshat) Bible interpretation and vindicate the study of science using the experimental method.[16] The university-educated doctors were children or relatives of court Jews and the mercantile elite.

Finally, rabbis such as David Fränkel in Dessau and later Berlin and Hirschel Lewin (1721–1800) of Berlin studied science and philosophy, Hebrew, and vernacular languages. The early maskilim were dedicated to renewing established Jewish disciplines of study.[17]

Mendelssohn numbered among the early Haskalah's autodidacts. Born in 1729 to a poor family of distinguished lineage in Dessau, a community that developed around the court Jew Moses Wulff (d. 1729), he studied with David Fränkel, who taught him noncasuistic methods of Talmud study. He also studied Maimonides' works recently republished at the local press (which Moses Wulff founded). He went to Berlin in 1743 to continue his studies at the new Yeshiva with Fränkel, who had been appointed the city's rabbi.[18] Israel Zamosc tutored him in Jewish philosophy. He acquired a secular education with the help of two medical students, including Gumpertz, but largely through personal exertion; for example, he read Locke in Latin. By the time Mendelssohn met the aspiring playwright and intellectual Gotthold Ephraim Lessing (1729–81), in 1754—and their friendship became an important symbol of the Enlightenment's ability to surmount religious differences—he was already well oriented in Wolff's philosophy.

[15] *Mafteah ha-Algebra Hadasha* (Offenbach, 1722) and *Seyag le-Torah* (Frankfurt am Main, 1766). See Edward Breuer, *The Limits of Enlightenment: Jews, Germans, and the Eighteenth-Century Study of Scripture* (Cambridge, 1996), 112–15.

[16] *Megaleh Sod* (1765). See Sorkin, *The Berlin Haskalah*, 56–62; Ruderman, *Jewish Thought and Scientific Discovery*, 334–35, 343–44; Gad Freudenthal, "New Light on the Physician Aaron Salomon Gumpertz: Medicine, Science and Early Haskalah in Berlin," *Zutot* (2003): 66–77; idem, "Aaron Salomon Gumpertz, Gotthold Ephraim Lessing, and the First Call for an Improvement of the Civil Rights of Jews in Germany (1753)," *Association for Jewish Studies Review* 29, no. 2 (2005): 299–353.

[17] Isaac Einstein Barzilay, "The Background of the Berlin Haskalah," in *Essays on Jewish Life and Thought*, ed. Joseph Blau (New York, 1957); J. Eschelbacher, "Die Anfänge allgemeiner Bildung unter den deutschen Juden vor Mendelssohn," in *Festschrift Martin Philippsons* (Leipzig, 1916); Feiner, *The Jewish Enlightenment*, 24–25.

[18] Max Freudenthal, "R. David Fränckel," in *Gedenkbuch zur Erinnerung an David Kaufmann*, ed. M. Brann and F. Rosenthal (Breslau, 1900), 575–89. Moritz Stern, "Das Vereinsbuch der Berliner Beth Hamidrasch," *Beiträge zur Geschichte der jüdischen Gemeinde zu Berlin* 4 (1931).

Mendelssohn arrived in Berlin when Wolff's influence was at its apogee and Wolffians such as Siegmund Jacob Baumgarten were altering the system. Mendelssohn did for Judaism what Baumgarten had done for Lutheranism: he was the Jewish theological Wolffian, rearticulating belief in Wolffian categories. Much as Baumgarten had done in regard to history, Mendelssohn used Wolff's categories to revise the master. Wolff had identified "practical" with "theoretical" conviction. He thought persuasive *a priori* and *a posteriori* theoretical arguments yielded conviction and thus constituted "vital knowledge." Mendelssohn separated the practical from the theoretical. Mere theoretical argumentation did not necessarily constitute "vital knowledge." In metaphysics, the most demonstrably certain proofs of God's existence were not always the most persuasive. Less certain arguments were often more effective in guiding people's lives, thus comprising "vital efficacious knowledge."[19] Mendelssohn opted for practical over abstract knowledge. He also diverged from Wolff in another respect: like his contemporaries, the Protestant neologues, he eschewed Wolff's encyclopedic method and definition mania for the more accessible exposition that characterized "popular philosophy."[20]

The distinction between the practical and the theoretical informed Mendelssohn's view of Judaism—indeed, it might have derived from it. Mendelssohn aimed to produce a reasonable understanding of Judaism by reviving the tradition of medieval practical rationalism in the cognate disciplines of philosophy and biblical exegesis. He did not aspire to a systematic religious philosophy. Rather, he sought practical knowledge: in biblical exegesis access to revelation and commandment

---

[19] Leo Strauss, "Einleitung," in *Gesammelte Schriften. Jubiläumsausgabe*, 22 vols. in 29 (Stuttgart, 1971–), 2:l–liii (henceforth *JubA*); and Anton Bissinger, "Zur metaphysischen Begründung der Wolffschen Ethik," in *Christian Wolff, 1679–1754: Interpretationen zu seiner Philosophie und deren Wirkung*, ed. Werner Schneiders (Hamburg, 1983), 151. For Mendelssohn, see "Abhandlung," in *JubA*, 2:311–12, 328–29; "Rhapsodie," in *JubA*, 1:413–423. Mendelssohn used the term "vital knowledge" to describe God's knowledge. See "Morgenstunden," in *JubA*, 3,2:101–2.

[20] See the philosophical curriculum (1774), "Anweisung zur spekulativen Philosophie, für einen jungen Menschen von 15–20 Jahren," in *JubA*, 3,1:307, and his letter of Sept. 22, 1777, in *Moses Mendelssohn: Gesammelte Schriften*, 7 vols. (Leipzig, 1843–45), 5:544 (henceforth *GS*).

For "popular philosophy," see Rudolf Vierhaus, "Moses Mendelssohn und die Popularphilosophie," in *Moses Mendelssohn und die Kreise seiner Wirksamkeit*, 25–42; Johann van der Zande, "Popular Philosophy and the History of Mankind in Eighteenth-Century Germany," *Storia della Storiografia* 22 (1992): 37–56; and Doris Bachmann-Medick, *Die ästhetische Ordnung des Handelns: Moralphilosophie und Ästhetik in der Popularphilosophie des 18. Jahrhunderts* (Stuttgart, 1989).

through plain meaning (peshat), in philosophy the logical formulation of key issues.

As the Enlightenment of a religious minority without a state's infrastructure, the Haskalah lacked the division between lay and religious enlighteners that, despite considerable overlap, existed elsewhere: Anglican England had Locke and Hume as well as Warburton; Lutheran Prussia had Wolff, Lessing, and Kant as well as Baumgarten. The Haskalah's personnel was minuscule; the same individuals shouldered the tasks of both lay and religious enlighteners. Yet a distinction emerged over time. The early maskilim, including Mendelssohn, resembled religious enlighteners: they were primarily concerned with Judaism's intellectual renewal. Mendelssohn adhered to the early Haskalah agenda throughout his career. By comparison, the generation of maskilim born after 1750 resembled lay enlighteners in their growing political commitment to reforming the Jews.[21]

While the early Haskalah was a European-wide movement, extending from Lithuania to London, it was concentrated in the cities Ashkenazi Jews had recently settled (Berlin, Königsberg, Breslau, Copenhagen, and to a lesser extent Amsterdam). Why so? These cities had sizable Jewish communities, including court Jews or members of the mercantile elite, to provide them with a livelihood (tutors, bookkeepers) and a patron. Some possessed a Hebrew printing press that offered jobs (proofreaders) and the potential for publishing books. Some had a university or a medical school. Others were a recognized center of Enlightenment. Berlin boasted all of these features, with the exception of a university. In the second half of the eighteenth century it was a court and garrison boomtown, the 1747 population of 100,000, increasing to 172,000 by 1800, with a large Jewish community of 3,500 in 1780. It symbolized the Haskalah, and Mendelssohn was its landmark.[22]

---

[21] Scholars use the criteria of language (Hebrew versus German), generation (those born before and after 1750), and stance (radical versus moderate): the early maskilim wrote in Hebrew and were moderate, whereas the younger wrote in German and were radical. For language, see Isaac Eisenstein-Barzilay, "The Ideology of the Berlin Haskalah," *Proceedings of the American Academy of Jewish Research* 25 (1956): 1–38, and idem, "The Treatment of Jewish Religion in the Literature of the Berlin Haskalah," *Proceedings of the American Academy of Jewish Research* 24 (1955): 39–68. For radical versus conservative, see Moshe Pelli, *The Age of Haskalah* (Leiden, 1979); for generational shifts, see Michael Meyer, *The Origins of the Modern Jew* (Detroit, 1967); for multiple voices, see Christoph Schulte, *Die jüdische Aufklärung* (Munich, 2002); for political engagement, degree of secularity and institutional development, see Feiner, *The Jewish Enlightenment*.

[22] Steven M. Lowenstein, *The Berlin Jewish Community: Enlightenment, Family, Crisis, 1770–1830* (New York, 1994); Hans-Jürgen Krüger, *Die Judenschaft von Königsberg in*

INTELLECTUAL RENEWAL: PHILOSOPHY

The Hebrew works Mendelssohn wrote throughout his career were his main contribution to the Haskalah. He first aimed to renew the tradition of philosophy in Hebrew. In the "Preacher of Morals" (*Kohelet Musar*, published in the late 1750s), Mendelssohn used an unconventional medium to show Judaism and Wolffian philosophy's compatibility in a range of texts. In a commentary to Maimonides' "Logical Terms" (1760–61) he endeavored to update Hebrew philosophy.

In the "Preacher of Morals" Mendelssohn made the "moral weekly" a vehicle of early Haskalah (modeled on the *Tatler* and the *Spectator*, the German moral weekly discussed ethical and cultural issues). Mendelssohn used his journal, the first in Hebrew, to shape a moral outlook for Talmud students and other cognoscenti through commentary on Hebrew texts.[23] He used Wolff's categories to address practical subjects, such as nature as a source of enjoyment or belief (physico-theology), evil and misfortune in daily life (theodicy), and man's relationship to his fellow man and God. Mendelssohn's method was to define the issue in Wolff's categories, apply those categories to an example drawn from Hebrew texts, quote passages of rabbinic or Hebrew philosophical literature that confirmed the analysis, and end with a peroration of Wolffian conclusions. Mendelssohn introduced Hebrew equivalents for Wolff's key philosophical terms.

For the ethical nature of friendship, for example, Mendelssohn used Wolff's definition of love as taking pleasure in another's increased perfection. His illustration was David and Jonathan's friendship, which the rabbinic sages had seen as "unconditional love." Mendelssohn asserted that whereas in human love pleasure arises from the other's increased perfection, in the love of God, since He embodies all perfection, pleasure arises from obeying His law. To confirm the point, Mendelssohn cited the Talmud.[24]

Preussen, 1700–1812 (Marburg, 1966); David Ruderman, *Jewish Enlightenment in an English Key: Anglo-Jewry's Construction of Modern Jewish Thought* (Princeton, 2000).

[23] Wolfgang Martens, *Die Botschaft der Tugend: Die Aufklärung im Spiegel der deutschen Moralischen Wochenschriften* (Stuttgart, 1968), 15–99, 141–60. Mendelssohn and Lessing contributed to a moral weekly in the mid-1750s. For the issues of dating and a collaborator, see Jacob Toury, "Problems of Kohelet Musar" (Hebrew), *Kiryat Sefer* 43 (1968): 279–84; Meir Gilon, *Kohelet Musar le-Mendelssohn al Reka Tekufato* (Jerusalem, 1979), 5–21; and Altmann, *Moses Mendelssohn*, 83–91.

[24] Cited according to Gilon's critical edition (essay number, line numbers, page number). *Kohelet Musar*, 4:109–112, p. 172. For these views, see "Rhapsodie," in *JubA*, 1:406–7.

Mendelssohn also addressed the ideal personality. He contrasted the fool who trusts in God for the sake of material gain, only to think himself abandoned when his fortunes decline, with the wise man who trusts in God at all times. Mendelssohn thought this comparison confirmed Wolff's notion of theodicy and cited a number of concurring rabbinic sources.[25]

Mendelssohn asserted the importance of studying Hebrew language and the Bible. He averred that, contrary to a mistaken interpretation, the exegete Rashi (1040–1105) endorsed Bible study (provided it followed rabbinic tradition). Mendelssohn quoted Maimonides and Jehuda Ha-Levi in praise of Hebrew, argued that it is a disgrace to neglect the language, pointed to the attention other nations lavished on their vernacular, and concluded that Hebrew was a living medium suitable for all occasions and purposes. He translated into Hebrew passages from a well-known contemporary poem to demonstrate Hebrew's abilities.[26]

The *Kohelet Musar* was an unconventional commentary that dealt with diverse issues in Hebrew texts from many periods. Mendelssohn reshaped the "moral weekly" to realize the early Haskalah's agenda of deploying the textual heritage to present a reasonable Judaism. He also offered a rudimentary maskilic view of the textual tradition. By consistently using the medieval Sephardi school—Judah Ha-Levi, Maimonides—as the source of a reasonable Judaism, he made it the main stratum of Hebraica after rabbinics.[27]

Mendelssohn's second Hebrew work was a commentary on Maimonides' succinct twelfth-century primer of logic and philosophy. To revive Hebrew philosophy, Mendelssohn republished the "Logical

---

For a translation, see Edward Breuer and David Sorkin, eds., "Moses Mendelssohn's First Hebrew Publication: An Annotated Translation of the *Kohelet Musar*," *Leo Baeck Institute Yearbook* 48 (2003): 3–23.

[25] *Kohelet Musar*, essay 2, pp. 162–64. For a similar discussion (1757), see "Dankpredigt über den Sieg bei Leuthen," in *JubA*, 10,1:279–288. For the moral weeklies, see Martens, *Die Botschaft der Tugend*, 231–46, 302–21.

[26] For Rashi on Berkahot 28b, see *Kohelet Musar*, 2:25–37, pp.160–61. On this passage, see Mordechai Breuer, "Minu Beneihem min ha-Higayon," in *Mikhtam le-David: Sefer Zihron ha-Rav David Oks*, ed. Y. D. Gilat and E. Stern (Ramat Gan, 1977), 242–61. For Hebrew, see *Kohelet Musar*, 2:3–24, 38–50, pp. 160–61. The poem was Edward Young's "Night Thoughts." Ibid., 6:34–72, pp. 178–80. See Jeremy Dauber, "New Thoughts on *Night Thoughts*: Mendelssohn and Translation," *Journal of Modern Jewish Studies* 2, no. 2 (2003): 132–47.

[27] For Kohelet Musar as an alternative to *pilpul*, see Euchel, *Toledot Rabeinu*, 13, 115. Mendelssohn cited Maimonides for theodicy at *Kohelet Musar*, 1:52–53, pp. 159; Judah Ha-Levi for the perfection of Hebrew at 2:7, p. 160, 5:52, p.175; Ibn Tibbon for translation at 6:17, p. 177.

Terms" with an introduction and commentary. In the introduction he defended logic as an entirely pious pursuit necessary to correct belief. Without logic one can neither fathom God's creation nor distinguish right from wrong. To think without knowing logic is the same as using language without knowing grammar. Anticipating the charge that logic was a foreign (Greek) invention, Mendelssohn claimed that Maimonides had neutralized it: "he swallowed the seed but spat out the shell."[28]

Mendelssohn affirmed the revealed truth that surpassed philosophy (*supra rationem*). Without Torah and tradition we are "like a blind man in the dark." True knowledge derives from Torah and logic combined. Man comprehends divine truth only through the application of God-given reason to Torah and tradition. Only the prophet who has direct revelation can dispense with logic (following Judah Ha-Levi). Mendelssohn recommended that students spend an hour or two per week on logic to support their text studies.[29]

Mendelssohn's commentary provided a bridge between medieval and eighteenth-century philosophy. Maimonides gave a list of terms at the end of each of his chapters. Mendelssohn used these to renew philosophy in Hebrew by giving the Wolffian equivalent in German and Latin (in Hebrew characters) to each Hebrew term. Mendessohn did for Hebrew what Wolff and Baumgarten had done by inventing German equivalents for Latin philosophical and theological terms.[30]

Mendelssohn also introduced the substance of eighteenth-century philosophy. He replaced Maimonides' Aristotelian or Platonic notions, such as that God had created form from an existing primordial matter, with the eighteenth-century Leibnizian-Wolffian view, such as that God had created both matter and form, which better accorded with Jewish

---

[28] "Biur Milot ha-Higayon," in *JubA*, 14:28–29, 52. Mendelssohn borrowed this image from Maimonides (*Guide of the Perplexed*, I:71); it appears in bTalmud Hagiga 15b. For Maimonides' treatise, see Israel Efros, "Maimonides' Treatise on Logic," *Proceedings of the American Academy for Jewish Research* (1937–38): 3–65, and Raymond L. Weiss, "On the Scope of Maimonides' *Logic* or What Joseph Knew," in *A Straight Path: Studies in Medieval Philosophy and Culture. Essays in Honor of Arthur Hyman*, ed. Ruth Link-Salinger (Washington, DC, 1988), 255–65.

[29] "Biur Milot ha-Higayon," in *JubA*, 14:28, 30, 48–49, 51. For Ha-Levi, see *Kusari*, I: 95ff. See Harry Wolfson, "Hallevi and Maimonides on Prophecy," *Studies in the History of Philosophy and Religion* ed. Isadore Twersky and George H. Williams, 2 vols. (Cambridge, MA, 1973–77), 2:60–119. For God-given reason, see *JubA*, 10,1:287.

[30] "Das erste Register, Darinnen einige Kunstwörter Lateinisch gegeben werden," in *Vernünftige Gedanken*, 672–78. For Baumgarten, see Emanuel Hirsch, *Geschichte der neuern Evangelischen Theologie*, 5 vols. (Gütersloh, 1951), 2:371, and Paul Knothe, "Siegmund Jakob Baumgarten und seine Stellung in der Aufklärungstheologie," *Zeitschrift für Kirchengeschichte* 46, n.s. 9 (1928): 522.

belief. In addition, he introduced Wolffian categories, as in the *Kohelet Musar*. In response to Maimonides' mention of external causality, Mendelssohn expounded Wolff's concept of theodicy, quoted a rabbinic source and Maimonides' own *Guide of the Perplexed* that there is no arbitrary evil, and concluded with a peroration of Wolff's concepts.[31]

Mendelssohn's commentary was characteristic of the early Haskalah. Israel Zamosc had published a commentary on the philosophical terms in Maimonides' *Guide of the Perplexed* and later wrote commentaries on two other central medieval philosophical texts. Zamosc's example and tutelage were indispensable for Mendelssohn.[32]

Mendelssohn's commentary showed his affinity to theological Wolffianism. One of the first books Mendelssohn read in German was Johann Gustav Reinbeck's *Considerations on the Augsburg Confession* (1733), which we encountered in relationship to Halle Pietism. Besides charting a middle course encompassing both reason and scripture, Reinbeck vindicated philosophy's role in theology. As the "science of the possible," philosophy is an indispensable aid in achieving correct belief. It teaches reason to scrutinize nature, then leads to the truths of scripture (as do physics and mathematics) and, finally, shows that nature and scripture agree. Moreover, Reinbeck limited philosophy's scope: it not only presupposes and confirms revelation, it also accepts miracles and respects mysteries. Reinbeck made the argument common to religious enlighteners that ultimate theological issues were not contrary to but beyond reason.[33]

Mendelssohn's introduction agreed with Reinbeck's, with the significant difference that he commented on a medieval text. Mendelssohn's approach differed from that of Protestant theologians, who dismissed medieval philosophy, yet resembled that of early reform Catholics, who, as we shall see in the next chapter, combined medieval philosophers (Aquinas) with Wolff (1720–60).[34]

In the *Kohelet Musar* and "Logical Terms," Mendelssohn, as an early maskil and theological Wolffian, used novel means for conservative ends.

---

[31] "Biur Milot ha-Higayon," in *JubA*, 14:80, 99. Mendelssohn addressed theodicy in "Morgenstunden," in *JubA*, 3,2:89–94.

[32] The other texts were Judah Ha-Levi's *Kusari* and Bahya ibn Pakuda's *Duties of the Heart*. See Altmann, *Moses Mendelssohn*, 21–22.

[33] *Betrachtungen über die in der Augsburgischen Confession enthaltene und damit verknüpfte Göttliche Wahrheiten*, 2 vols. (Berlin and Leipzig, 1733), 2:vi–ix, xl–xlv, xxxv–xxxvii, liii. Altmann, *Moses Mendelssohn*, 25–26.

[34] For medieval philosophy among Jews and Protestants, see Amos Funkenstein, "Das Verhältnis der jüdischen Aufklärung zur mittelalterlichen jüdischen Philosophie," *Wolfenbütteler Studien zur Aufklärung* 14 (1990): 13–21.

INTELLECTUAL RENEWAL: EXEGESIS

Mendelssohn's enduring achievement was a monumental Pentateuch translation and commentary that shined the spotlight on the Bible. Mendelssohn understood the Bible as the fount of practical knowledge; his commentaries were designed to aid its intensive study. His efforts to revive Biblical exegesis and Hebrew philosophy were mutually reinforcing.

Mendelssohn inaugurated his exegetical enterprise with a commentary on *Ecclesiastes* (1769–70). In trying to revive the medieval Jewish exegetical tradition devoted to plain meaning, Mendelssohn confronted a major obstacle: the seventeenth-century scholars such as Spinoza and Richard Simon who had developed a new critical approach to the Bible had derided inherited theological interpretations, including the rabbis'. Before Mendelssohn could urge the revival of Jewish exegesis he had to defend its very nature, in particular the four simultaneous modes of interpretation—plain, homiletical, allegorical, and esoteric.[35]

Mendelssohn introduced his commentary with a "natural" defense of Jewish interpretation based on language: multiple meanings are inherent in language's use. Mendelssohn explained this with Maimonides' categories of "primary" and "secondary" intention. The primary intention (*peshat*) arises from the "context and connectedness of discussion." The speaker and listener concentrate on the words' sense rather than on the words themselves. Mendelssohn cited the medieval exegete Ibn Ezra, who famously asserted, in regard to the decalogue's two versions (Exodus 20), that "the meanings are inviolable, the words are not." In contrast, the secondary intention or "homiletical" meaning (*derash*) does not emerge from the context of discussion—in fact, the two must not agree—but from the "close scrutiny of each and every word, each and every letter, each and every jot." Here Mendelssohn quoted Rashi.[36]

Mendelssohn averred that multiple meanings are entirely in keeping with reason as well as God's "superior wisdom": in creation, "one act served many ends." Mendelssohn corroborated this natural argument

---

[35] On reviving Jewish Biblical exegesis, see Gilon, *Kohelet Musar*, 2:25–37, pp. 160–61. For seventeenth-century criticism, see Hans-Joachim Kraus, *Geschichte der historisch-kritischen Erforschung des Alten Testaments*, 3rd ed. (Neukirchen, 1982), 44–79; Emil G. Kraeling, *The Old Testament Since the Reformation* (London, 1955), 43–58; and Breuer, *The Limits of Enlightenment*.

[36] "Biur Megilat Kohelet," in *JubA*, 14:150. See Maimonides, *Guide of the Perplexed*, III: 27, 32, and Ibn Ezra, *Perush ha-Torah Abraham Ibn Ezra*, ed. Asher Weiser, 3 vols. (Jerusalem, 1976), 2:129.

with quotations from rabbinic and mystical literature. This argument "from design" pervaded medieval Jewish rationalism as well as the Enlightenment's physico-theology, such as found in Warburton's use of Newton.[37] Mendelssohn used a central Enlightenment argument to defend rabbinic exegesis.

Mendelssohn maintained that all forms of rabbinic exegesis agreed with the plain meaning. Nevertheless, in the case of Ecclesiastes, "all of the commentators who have preceded me have not fulfilled the obligation of establishing the plain meaning." While the rabbis and exegetes had studied individual words, they had not adequately studied the continuous text as units of meaning. In consequence, Ecclesiastes' import remained in dispute.[38]

Mendelssohn thus addressed Ecclesiastes' controversial inclusion in the Bible. It was alleged to contain contradictions, to be comprised of mere sayings, and to include opinions that bred skepticism or, worse, heresy. Mendelssohn read Ecclesiastes as a philosophical dialogue, attributing contradictory, skeptical, or heretical opinions to notional interlocutors whom Solomon quoted in a process of argument and counterargument.[39]

Mendelssohn treated Ecclesiastes as a dialogue about the soul's immortality and providence. Superior wisdom was to be found in the "fundamental tenets of the true religion": God has not created intelligent beings only to condemn them to witness insufferable injustice without hope of redress. Providence and immortality constitute "genuine superior truth," enabling man to pursue his God-given vocation, perfection.[40]

[37] "Biur Megilat Kohelet," in *JubA*, 14:148, 151. "There are four methods of interpreting our holy Torah—the plain, homiletical, allegorical and esoteric—as is well known. All of them are the words of the living God and are in agreement. This does not contradict the laws of reason or inference, nor is it alien and disturbing to human reason." For Ibn Ezra, see Weiser, *Perush ha-Torah*, 1:7. For physico-theology, see Wolfgang Philipp, *Das Werden der Aufklärung in theologiegeschichtlicher Sicht* (Göttingen, 1957).

[38] "Biur Megilat Kohelet," in *JubA*, 14:150–51.

[39] Mendelssohn may have systematized the insights of earlier plain exegetes. Saadia Gaon had pointed to one passage in *Ecclesiastes*, and Ibn Ezra to a number, in which they thought Solomon presented other people's opinions. "Biur Megilat Kohelet," in *JubA*, 14:153–34, 14:169 (3:12–14). Saadia Gaon, *The Book of Beliefs and Opinions*, trans. Samuel Rosenblatt (New Haven, 1948), 275 (to Ecclesiastes 9:4–6). Ibn Ezra to 3:19–20, 9:4, 9:7, 9:8. Maimonides treated Job as a "parable" on providence. See *Guide of the Perplexed*, III:22–23. In *De sacra poesi Hebraeorum*, Lowth had discussed whether Job could be treated as a drama. For Mendelssohn, see *JubA*, 4:53ff.

[40] "Biur Megilat Kohelet," in *JubA*, 14:154–55, 187 (8:1). See also 14:185 (7:24) and 14:194 (9:12). The *Phaedon's* success encouraged him to bring its ideas to a Jewish audience. See

However innovative his interpretations, Mendelssohn dealt with inherited Jewish concerns. He noted that he derived much from previous exegetes, especially Ibn Ezra and Rashi. In the many instances in which he agreed with them, he reiterated their interpretations without alteration.[41]

Mendelssohn's preoccupation with accepted Jewish concerns accompanied his effort to demonstrate the harmony of Judaism and Enlightenment. Presuming truth to be universal, he had no reservations learning from non-Jewish exegetes. As with his appropriation of logic for sacred study, he confidently tried to harness the best of contemporary culture for pious ends.[42] Moreover, he used a venerable trope to stamp science with the imprimatur of tradition. Mendelssohn imputed to Solomon, as the author of Ecclesiastes, an understanding of the circulation of the blood that accorded with Harvey's theory of blood circulation, enunciated in 1628:

> It is apparent from this that the circulation of the blood or the circulation of the spiritual humors from the brain to the sinews that I have recalled was known to King Solomon, may he rest in peace. Whether he knew it by the powers of his great intelligence, or it was made known to him by divine inspiration, the fact is that this theory was hidden to the sages of all the ancient nations and was not made known until a century ago by experiments.[43]

Mendelssohn's Pentateuch (1779–83), entitled *The Book of the Paths of Peace* (financed by presubscriptions), crowned his efforts to renew the medieval tradition of Jewish exegesis and philosophy. Although the work is generally referred to as the "Biur" or "commentary," it was tripartite. The translation, which was entirely Mendelssohn's work and paramount, aimed to convey the text's plain meaning in a fluent German

---

Hayim Sheli, *Mehkar ha-Mikra be-Sifrut ha-Haskalah* (Jerusalem, 1942), 3–4. A curious example of religious Enlightenment intertextuality is Theodore Preston's assertion that Warburton's *Divine Legation of Moses Demonstrated* would have benefited from Mendelssohn's Ecclesiastes commentary. See *Kohelet: The Hebrew Text and a Latin Version. The Book of Solomon, called Ecclesiastes; with Original Notes, Philological and Exegetical, and a Translation of the Commentary of Mendelssohn from the Rabbinic Hebrew* (London, 1845), 25–29.

[41] "Biur Megilat Kohelet," in *JubA*, 14:160.

[42] Ibid., See also "Biur Milot ha-Higayon," in *JubA* 14:29. For Maimonides, see *Guide of the Perplexed*, I:71.

[43] "Biur Megilat Kohelet," in *JubA*, 14:205 (12:6). Judah Ha-Levi made Solomon the source of all sciences. *Kusari* 2:66. See N. Shapiro, "Natural Sciences and Mathematics as Pathfinders for the Haskalah Movement" (Hebrew), *Koroth* 2 (1958): 326, 331.

translation (in Hebrew letters), thereby replacing two kinds of unacceptable Bible translations—imprecise word-by-word Yiddish translations, and Christian translations (beginning with Luther's) that contained Christological interpretations and amended the masoretic text.[44]

The commentary was designed to support Mendelssohn's choices in translation in relationship to the leading medieval exegetes. It was a guide to the medieval plain tradition. The commentary was also a collective effort. Mendelssohn wrote on Genesis 1–5 and Exodus, enlisting others for the rest. That other maskilim were available attested to the Haskalah's development. When Mendelssohn arrived in Berlin in the 1740s, he found a few like-minded early maskilim, among them Zamosc and Gumpertz. In the 1770s he was surrounded by a new group composed mostly of younger men born after mid-century, for whom Berlin symbolized *Aufklärung* and Haskalah.[45]

Finally, Mendelssohn supported the translation with a preamble ("Light for the Path") that was "the first modern Jewish introduction to the Bible."[46]

Practical Knowledge

Mendelssohn regarded the Pentateuch as teaching practical knowledge through law. In Genesis and Exodus, Mendelssohn understood key terms, such as trust and faith, to have practical definitions. He explicated God's "testing" of Abraham (Genesis 22:1), as illustrating the need to translate convictions into actions.[47]

Such a definition underpinned Mendelssohn's understanding of Exodus as the story first of Moses's and then the people of Israel's growing trust in God and their readiness to act on faith. Truth, trust, and faith are forms of practical knowledge that yield actions. God's miraculous

[44] "Or la-Netivah," in *JubA*, 14:242–44. See Werner Weinberg's discussion, "Einleitung," in *JubA*, 15,1:xx–xxii.

[45] The medieval exegetes were Ibn Ezra, Rashi, Ramban, Kimhi, and Rashbam. "Or la-Netivah," in *JubA*, 14:243–44. The collaborators were Solomon Dubno (Genesis), Naphtali Herz Wesseley (Leviticus), Herz Homberg (Numbers), and Aaron Jaroslav (Deuteronomy). Dubno prepared the notes on the masoretic text (*Tikkun Soferim*) and wrote an introduction Mendelssohn did not publish. See Altmann, *Moses Mendelssohn*, 398–405, and Weinberg, "Einleitung," in *JubA*, 15,1:xxxiii–xxxiv.

[46] Bourel, *Moses Mendelssohn*, 370.

[47] "Biur," in *JubA*, 15,2:206. Cf. *JubA*, 7:75, 95. See R. J. Zwi Werblowski, "Faith, Hope and Trust: A Study in the Concept of Bittahon," *Papers of the Institute of Jewish Studies London*, ed. J. G. Weiss (Jerusalem, 1964), 95–139.

liberation of Israel inspires trust, first climaxing after the parting of the sea, when "the people feared the Lord; and they believed in the Lord and his servant Moses" (Exodus 14:31). The second climax came with the Golden Calf: the Israelites who descended into idolatry lacked trust. Once Moses had been recalled from the mountain, the calf destroyed, and the guilty put to the sword, God created a new covenant of "trust."[48]

This "trust" results in Israel's obedience through the commandments, the preeminent form of practical knowledge. They teach Israel that it was a "chosen people" who had accepted "the yoke of His Kingdom and His government." The God who brought Israel out of Egypt "gave the Torah, commandments, laws and injunctions" to Israel "alone."[49] Moreover, Mendelssohn followed Judah Ha-Levi in stressing that the commandments are heteronomous: the reasons for them are known to the divine legislator but not the human recipients. In his discussion of the dietary laws (Exodus 23:19), for example, Mendelssohn emphasized heteronomy and practice:

> It is not to be inquired why the Holy One blessed be He forbade us meat and milk, since He obligated us to many commandments whose explanation He did not reveal. It must suffice for us that we know that they are commanded by Him, may He be blessed. Since we have accepted for ourselves the yoke of his kingdom, we are required to perform His will. The purpose [of the commandments] is in their performance, not in the knowledge of their explanation.[50]

Mendelssohn complemented his emphasis on practical knowledge by limiting theoretical knowledge in the form of Aristotelian naturalism.[51] The introduction of Aristotelianism into Judaism in the Middle Ages had exacerbated the tension between philosophy and revelation: its naturalism cast doubt on divine omnipotence (pre-existent matter vs. creatio ex nihilo), and its idealization of the contemplative ideal challenged the status of ritual and commandment. Mendelssohn's

---

[48] For the liberation, see "Biur," in *JubA*, 16:57 (Exodus 7:9). For additional examples, see Exodus 12:40–41, *JubA*, 16:103; Exodus 14:13, *JubA*, 16:119; Exodus 14:15, *JubA*, 16:120. For the golden Calf, see *JubA*, 16:125 (Exodus 14:31), 16:352 (Exodus 34:10).

[49] *JubA*, 16:186–87.

[50] Quotation at *JubA*, 16:226. For the same argument, see Genesis 26:5, *JubA*, 15,2:270–71, and "Logical Terms," in *JubA*, 14:95. For heteronomy, see Isaac Heinemann, *Ta'amei ha-Mitsvot bi-Sifrut Yisrael*, 2 vols. (Jerusalem, 1956).

[51] For early passages against philosophical arrogance, see "Philosophische Gespräche," in *JubA*, 1:22–25; "Abhandlung über die Evidenz," in *JubA*, 2:296–97; and "Nacherrinnerung," in *JubA*, 7:47.

opposition to these Aristotelian elements frequently pitted him against Maimonides. This was especially evident in respect to creation.

Mendelssohn stressed creatio ex nihilo. In the "Logical Terms" he had taken issue with the Aristotelian conception of creation, and Maimonides' treatment of it, as the imposition of form on pre-existent matter (see chapter 2). In his Pentateuch commentary he followed Nahmanides in repeatedly stressing the creation miracle: in natural creation, unlike in artificial or artisanal versions, form permeates matter. For Mendelssohn, neither nature nor Aristotle's first cause but God alone is capable of this fundamental miracle.[52]

Mendelssohn's opposition to theoretical knowledge figured prominently in his commentary. Even though he discussed scientific ideas pertinent to specific passages, he asserted that a general disquisition on "science" had no place in a commentary on the creation, "for this does not belong to the issue of Torah or of belief."[53] Mendelssohn's commentary contained no esoteric speculations on creation and the significance of the altar (unlike Maimonides, Ibn Ezra, and Nahmanides). Instead, "for us this Torah is a possession . . . to know the commandments which God has enjoined us to learn and to teach, to observe and to fulfill."[54]

Plain Meaning

The translator's and exegete's task was to make practical knowledge available by explicating the Bible's plain meaning. The notion of plain meaning remained fluid in Judaism even though it had designated the

---

[52] For the "logical terms," see *JubA*, 14:80. "Biur," in *JubA*, 15,2:4 (Genesis 1:2). On creatio ex nihilo, see *JubA*, 15,2:49; 16:66, 150. On creation's cessation, see 15,2:17 (Genesis 2:2); for divine intervention, see 16:47–48 (Exodus 6:2). An earlier argument for miracles is "Sefer ha-Nefesh," in *JubA*, 14:127 (paragraphs 19–21). See Harry Wolfson, "The Platonic, Aristotelian and Stoic Theories of Creation in Hallevi and Maimonides," in *Studies in the History of Philosophy and Religion* 1:234–49. For Nahmanides, see David Berger, "Miracles and the Natural Order in Nahmanides," in *Rabbi Moses Nahmanides (Ramban): Explorations in His Religious and Literary Virtuosity*, ed. Isadore Twersky (Cambridge, MA, 1983), 107–28. For Mendelssohn and Nahmanides, see Weinberg, "Einleitung," in *JubA*, 15,1:lxiii–liv.

[53] "Biur," in *JubA*, 15,2:4 (Genesis 1:2). For the geography of rivers, see *JubA*, 15,2:24 (Genesis 2:11); *JubA*, 16:85 (Exodus 10:19), on the Mediterranean ocean; *JubA*, 16:91 (Exodus 12:2), on the lunar calendar; *JubA*, 230 (Exodus 23:28), on wasps; *JubA*, 16:336 (Exodus 32:20), on chemistry.

[54] "Biur," in *JubA*, 14:243. For creation, see "Biur," in *JubA*, 15,2:7 (Genesis 1:6); for the Garden of Eden (where he mentions that "Ibn Ezra recalled the various opinions of the philosophisers among our brethren") see *JubA*, 15,2:30 (Genesis 3:1); for the altar, see *JubA*, 16:405, in his peroration to Exodus.

"authoritative teaching" or the generally accepted meaning since the rabbinic period.[55] Mendelssohn used the phrase the "profundity of plain meaning" to designate the Bible's unique oral quality as the most effective means to transmit practical knowledge. The Bible had been composed according to a set of principles: the singular qualities of the Hebrew language, including accents and grammar, and the "connectedness" of words, phrases, and the genres of genealogy, legislation, narrative, and poetry. Mendelssohn considered the Jewish exegetes who knew these principles "our eyes in the interpretation of Scripture."[56] On the basis of the concepts of "primary" and "secondary" intention, Mendelssohn used the homiletical interpretation when it agreed with or enhanced the plain one, or when rabbinic tradition deemed it authoritative.

Mendelssohn thought that because the Bible is essentially oral it transmitted practical knowledge most effectively. Hebrew is not only the divine and primordial language: as a result of the masoretic accents it has the singular ability to preserve oral expression. The oral expressions the masoretic accents recorded were divine: God had vouchsafed them to Moses at Sinai, whence they were transmitted orally until recorded. The spoken word's advantage is immediate understanding: the speaker's voice makes the words comprehensible so that it "enters the listener's heart to arouse and to instruct him." Spoken language is the medium for the "vital" and "efficacious" knowledge of practice. In the Bible word and thought agree so perfectly that meaning transfers directly from the "speaker's" to the "auditor's heart."[57]

---

[55] Raphael Loewe, "The 'Plain' Meaning of Scripture in Early Jewish Exegesis," *Institute of Jewish Studies* I (1964): 140–85. For Rashi, Ibn Ezra, and Nahmanides, see Amos Funkenstein, *Signonot be-Parshanut ha-Mikra be-Yemai ha-Beinayim* (Tel Aviv, 1990), 18–56.

[56] "Or la-Netivah," in *JubA*, 14:244. His commentary was a digest from the eleventh (Rashi) to the sixteenth centuries (Obadiah Seforno).

The phrase is *omek peshuto shel mikra*. Samuel ben Meir (Rashbam, 1085–1174) first used the phrase. See Genesis 37:2 in A. I. Bromberg, ed., *Perush ha-Torah la-Rashbam* (Tel Aviv, 1964), 47.

For Mendelssohn's understanding of "plain" meaning, see "Or la-Netivah," in *JubA*, 14:244; his letter to Avigdor Levi (1779), in *JubA*, 19:252; and his comments in "Biur Megilat Kohelet," in *JubA*, 14:150. For examples in the commentary, see *JubA*, 16:221 (Exodus 23:2), *JubA*, 16:184 (Exodus 19:24), and *JubA*, 16:347 (Exodus 33:18). For a passage in which Mendelssohn used the accents to determine his translation and Dubno used the phrase in his comment, see *JubA*, 15,2:368 (Genesis 32:18). See Levenson, *Moses Mendelssohn's Understanding*, 54–55.

[57] "Or la-Netivah," in *JubA*, 14:213, 217–18. Mendelssohn amplified Ha-Levi's argument that Hebrew was a divine language distinguished by its orality. See *Kusari* 2:67–68, 72, 4:25. See Raphael Jospe, "The Superiority of Oral over Written Communication: Judah Halevi's Kusari and Modern Jewish Thought," in *From Ancient Israel to Modern Juda-*

Mendelssohn understood the long history of Jewish Pentateuch translation (Aramaic, Greek, Arabic, Spanish, Yiddish) through Maimonides' categories of "primary" and "secondary" intention. The translator aims to convey the text's practical effect by capturing the "speaker's" meaning. Mendelssohn's model was Onkelos's Aramaic translation that rabbinic tradition deemed authoritative: "Onkelos in particular did not deviate from the primary plain intention, except for those passages where he was forced to do so for the sake of the true meaning, or in those passages where it was necessary to remove obstacles to correct understanding."[58] Following Onkelos, Mendelssohn translated to preserve the Torah's oral character and practical knowledge, conveying both the primary and secondary intention.

Mendelssohn made the masoretic accents a chief guide to plain meaning, using them more systematically than his medieval predecessors. He employed them to establish the meaning of words, the connection between words, the positioning of clauses, and the meaning of entire passages. By taking account of the emotions and inflections the accents conveyed, he highlighted the text's oral quality.[59]

In the last section of his introduction, Mendelssohn outlined the grammatical and logical principles that informed his translation and commentary. Without a knowledge of grammar, God's word, both literal and homiletical, remained incomprehensible. Translation in particular requires a thorough knowledge of both languages. Mendelssohn delineated the singular nature of Hebrew vis-à-vis German. Aiming to teach the skills that would reveal the practical knowledge of the Torah, he recommended that students spend an hour per day studying grammar (he had recommended an hour per week for logic) for two years to understand the Bible and its commentators.[60]

---

ism: Intellect in Quest of Understanding. Essays in Honor of Marvin Fox, 3 vols. (Missoula, 1989), 3:127–36.

[58] Ibid., JubA, 14:235. There is a similar passage in "Alim le-Terufah," JubA, 14:327–29.

[59] "Or la-Netivah," in JubA, 14:235. Ibn Ezra had made extensive use of the accents; others had written treatises about them. See Levenson, Moses Mendelssohn's Understanding, 14. He introduced exclamation points to capture emotions, while elsewhere he tried to render pictorial or mimetic qualities. See ibid., 48–64.

Mendelssohn was convinced that the primary and secondary intentions alternate. He gave precedence to the plain meaning, yet bowed to tradition's verdict. "Or la-Netivah," in JubA, 14:245.

[60] "Mi-Helkei ha-Dibur ve-Shimusheihem bi-Lashon," in JubA, 14:243. In general, JubA, 14:249–67. A recurring phrase is "such is the case in all the vernaculars known to me, but in the holy language." See "Or la-Netivah," JubA, 14:234. Cf. 14:255–56, 259, 266.

Mendelssohn's commitment to grammar is evident in his treatment of anthropomorphisms. How one reconciled corporeal images with divine incorporeality was a litmus test of exegesis. Mendelssohn employed a grammatical version of the principle of accommodation, arguing that the verb "and I have *come down* to deliver them out of the hand of the Egyptians" (Exodus 3:8) indicated not God's physical descent but his condescension. He asserted that Maimonides' philosophical treatment of anthropomorphisms in *Guide of the Perplexed* was mistaken.[61]

In his Ecclesiastes commentary, Mendelssohn had tried to correct the earlier exegetes' failure to study the connectedness that defines units of meaning. He now systematically studied connectedness. A basic problem in translating the Bible was paratactic syntax: most clauses and sentences were connected with "and." Mendelssohn introduced various conjunctions to clarify the relationship between clauses (*or, if*) and adverbs to clarify the relationships of subordination, causality and sequence in time (*beforehand, subsequently, so, thus*). In keeping with his pronouncements and Onkelos's translation, Mendelssohn rearranged the order of clauses and sometimes introduced interpolations, for which he relied on the accents and earlier exegetes.[62]

Connectedness also applied to narrative structure. The principle of "general and particular" was

> an essential and central principle for understanding the Bible. Using it allows us to comprehend several passages in the Bible that otherwise would entirely elude comprehension. In some instances all the exegetes wearied and these mighty men did not succeed in finding the plain meaning of the Bible.[63]

Mendelssohn saw this narrative principle at work in the opening verses of Genesis: the first is the "general" statement, the rest of the Bible the "particular" which explains it, although only one part. Mendelssohn asserted that the conjunction that begins the second verse, "And the earth," "resumes the narrative"—a reading the accents support. The phrase thus means, "But as for the earth which I

---

[61] "Biur," in *JubA*, 16:24.

[62] For Ecclesiastes, see "Biur Megilat Kohelet," in *JubA*, 14:150. For "connection," see *JubA*, 15,2:50 (Genesis 5:3); for "continuity," *JubA*, 16:57 (Exodus 7:9), and 16:111 (Exodus 13:17); for "division," 16:98 (Exodus 12:21); for a "conditional" 16:174 (Exodus 18:23) and 16:248 (Exodus 25:22). See Levenson, *Moses Mendelssohn's Understanding*, 68–80, 105–15.

[63] The Hebrew is *kelal u-ferat* or *perat u-kelal*. Mendelssohn cites the source, Rabbi Eliezer's hermeneutic principles, at Genesis 2:5. See *JubA*, 15,2:18–19. See Levenson, *Moses Mendelssohn's Understanding*, 23–34, 93–104, and Sandler, *Ha-Biur le-Torah*, 107–110.

mentioned," in "God created the heavens and the earth." The heavens are not discussed. The entire Bible is devoted to the "earth," meaning "the world of existence and corruption that is subject to man."[64]

Mendelssohn used this principle to solve other difficult cases. The chronology of Moses's ascent at Mount Sinai to receive the tablets of the law (Exodus 24:13–19) was problematic: were the six days that the cloud covered the mountain included in the forty days or prior to them? Mendelssohn asserted that Ibn Ezra's solution

> did not suffice to elucidate appropriately the connectedness of the text and the duplication of statements. If, however, we explain the text as a "general statement" followed by a "particular" . . . the connectedness and order of the verses are explained without any strain whatsoever.[65]

Mendelssohn attempted to discover the compositional principles of diverse forms of exposition. He adopted Ibn Ezra and Rashbam's insight that genealogy followed the vertical line. He relied on Ibn Ezra and Nahmanides to discern a parallel pattern of descent and ascent in legislation. In the decalogue, for example, the gravity of sin descends from the first commandment: not believing in God is the gravest offence. The ability of man to resist sin ascends from the last commandment (not "coveting"). The first and last are the laws' two pillars.[66]

Mendelssohn devoted special attention to poetry's structure as the most concentrated and effective medium of practical knowledge. Greek, Latin, and contemporary Hebrew poetry are intended "for the ear alone": when set to music they must be altered and their meanings changed. In contrast, biblical poetry is intended

> not for the ear of the auditor alone, but for his heart. [The words] will remain inscribed on the tablets [of his heart], in order to produce in him joy and sorrow, timidity or trust, fear or hope, love or hate, as is appropriate to the intention, and to install in him the honorable attributes and the elevated characteristics as stakes and nails that are implanted, as a peg that cannot be moved.[67]

[64] JubA, 15,2:3. See Levenson, *Moses Mendelsssohn's Understanding*, 25–26.

[65] JubA, 16:239 (Exodus 24:13–18). See Levenson, *Moses Mendelssohn's Understanding*, 93–96.

[66] JubA 16:50–52, 194. See Levenson, *Moses Mendelssohn's Understanding*, 209–12.

[67] JubA, 16:126. Mendelssohn uses the same image ("stakes and nails") for practical knowledge as in "Light for the Path" (JubA, 14:217–18).

Biblical poetry not only fit its music, but the two cooperated to affect the auditor's soul: "its goal was to penetrate the powers of the soul, to rule its capacities and to alter its characteristics."

Biblical poetry and music were able to transmit practical knowledge because "its entire aim was to preserve the meaning, to arouse it." Music enhanced the poetry's comprehensibility: set to music, its short, balanced lines are readily understood and remembered, thus forming the core of practical knowledge. Moreover, as a poetry of meaning it is translatable: even if its form is lost, its meaning can be preserved and still have the desired effect on "the auditor's soul."[68]

Mendelssohn's commentary devoted to the "profundity of plain meaning" was a digest of plain exegesis and rabbinic tradition. Mendelssohn "had grasped the torch of the great medieval commentators and rekindled it."[69]

History

Mendelssohn established his beliefs and the Bible's authenticity through history. In his early pronouncements on exegesis and in his Ecclesiastes commentary he had recognized history as situation and custom.[70] He now grounded "certainty" of belief in the historical facts of the Exodus, the public revelation at Sinai, and Israel's chosenness. Moreover, history guaranteed the biblical text's purity: Hebrew's singular oral nature defined the Bible's nature from its origins and during the transmission process. The historical-critical school, exemplified by Eichhorn and Michaelis, challenged such an interpretation by treating history as corrupting the biblical text. Mendelssohn offered an innovative defense of the traditional Jewish view.[71] Whereas in his introduction to Ecclesiastes he had provided a natural explanation for the

---

[68] Ibid., *JubA*, 16:127. See "Phaedon" *JubA*, 3,1:81, 119.

[69] Franz Rosenzweig, "Der Ewige," in *Die Schrift*, ed. Karl Thieme (Frankfurt, 1964), 34.

[70] For the "genius of various peoples," *JubA*, 4:20–21; for "morals, customs and knowledge" of the age, *GS*, 5:184–85; for "knowledge of man in his particular circumstances," see "*Gegenbetrachtungen*," in *JubA*, 7:95; for "author, times and circumstances," *JubA*, 12,2:22.

For history: Ecclesiastes: "cast your bread upon the waters" (11:1) represented the King's advice to shipping merchants. *JubA*, 14:199; Moses approached Pharoah during his spring visit to the Nile. *JubA*, 16:58–59 (Exodus 7:15).

[71] Mendelssohn opposed "criticism" and emendations: "I do not know in fact when we will get to the end of this audacity. In the meantime, so long as the fashion has the charm of novelty, one must allow it to take its course. In time people will lose their taste for it; and then it will be time to redirect them to the path of healthy reason." *JubA*, 12,2:33 (no. 384; Feb. 16, 1773). See also *JubA*, 12,2:41–3 (no. 391; Feb. 8 1774).

multiple modes of rabbinic interpretation, here he offered a natural explanation for the Bible's authenticity.

Mendelssohn defended the tradition of scriptural transmission and notation. The peculiar endowments that made biblical Hebrew "oral" also prevented the text's corruption. Mendelssohn propounded the inherited Jewish argument that God spoke every word of the Torah to Moses, who duly noted and then transmitted that knowledge to his successors, who preserved it orally. This preserved knowledge precluded the text's corruption. Even the first exile did not affect that oral knowledge. Only a declining knowledge of Hebrew during the Second Temple forced the masoretes to begin transcribing the notations.[72] While the higher critics (such as Eichhorn) asserted that the masoretes invented the notations, Mendelssohn saw them merely committing pre-existing oral traditions to writing. The higher critics asserted that the biblical text had suffered corruption and required emendation. For Mendelssohn it was a sacred book that had escaped corruption through a singular oral tradition; emendation was unthinkable. Hebrew's singular oral tradition also accounted for the richness of plain meaning. This was the advantage of "scribes" over mere "books."[73]

Mendelssohn used the historical idea of direct witness to support Israel's special status of chosenness. On the giving of the tablets (Exodus 19), Mendelssohn commented:

> They will actually hear with their own ears and not according to the word of a spokesman; and not on the basis of signs and wonders alone, rather with the auditory power of the ear since I am sending you to them to offer my Torah. For this reason they will also believe in you forever . . . your embassy to them has been validated by a proof which brooks no doubt or retort, that is, the evidence of the senses publicly known.[74]

Chosenness was manifest in Israel directly witnessing revelation yet also the Exodus: "I am the Lord your God who brought you forth from the land of Egypt from the House of bondage" (Exodus 20:2). The first

---

[72] "Or la-Netivah," in JubA, 14:211–18, 224–28.

[73] "Or la-Netivah," in JubA, 14:243 (this is a pun: "sofrim" vs. "sefarim"). For Johann Gottfried Eichhorn, see Einleitung ins Alte Testament, 2nd ed., 3 vols. (Reutlingen, 1790), 1:297.

[74] JubA, 16:176–78. For an earlier passage, see "Gegenbetrachtungen," JubA, 7:86–88. "Matter of history" is "Geschichtssache," which he used in Jerusalem in regard to Christianity. See JubA, 8:156.

two commandments proclaimed Israel's historical attachment to God's commandments through the Exodus:

> We are His people since He brought us out of Egypt from the House of bondage and performed all of these miracles; [we are] to be His chosen and treasured people among all the nations. He will rule us with His own glory, without the intermediary of an angel, official or star. Behold, we are His servants and are obligated to assume the yoke of His kingdom and His government, and to uphold His laws, and He commanded us not to worship any other besides Him. . . . The exodus from Egypt, from slavery to freedom, is the reason [that we are obligated to perform His commandments]. . . . To us alone did God, may He be exalted, give His Torah, commandments and laws and injunctions, for He is our king and our legislator, and it is incumbent upon us to observe His laws and precepts.[75]

Mendelssohn argued that direct witness and chosenness combine in God's unmediated delivery of the first two commandments to make Israel a nation of "prophets in the belief in God and the interdiction of idolatry."[76] Here was the historical foundation of Mendelssohn's faith.

Mendelssohn was historical without being historicist: he acknowledged history in the Pentateuch rather than the Pentateuch as a product of history. His approach to the Bible showed a remarkable affinity to Siegmund Jacob Baumgarten's historical hermeneutic. By recognizing history in the Bible they were both able to find the "certainty" Wolff's philosophy demanded and to garner the practical truth they thought was the Bible's divine message.

Mendelssohn's *Book of the Paths of Peace* realized the early Haskalah's agenda of reintroducing the independent study of the Bible into a curriculum hitherto dominated by Talmud study and Kabbalah. As a form of religious Enlightenment intellectual renewal, the recovery of Bible study had a direct parallel among Catholics. As we shall see in the next chapter, Habsburg Reform Catholics attempted to replace Baroque piety and scholasticism with a curriculum of the Bible, patristics, and Church history.

Mendelssohn's *Book of the Paths of Peace* initially met with acclaim.[77] It became controversial because of Naphtali Herz Wessely, who, in

[75] *JubA*, 16:187–88.
[76] *JubA*, 16:191.
[77] Hirschel Lewin (1720–1800), rabbi of Berlin, provided an approbation. See "Or le-Netiva," n.p., and Altmann, *Moses Mendelssohn*, 379–80. Lewin wrote approbations for other maskilic works. See M. Freudenthal, "R. Wolf Dessau," in *Festschrift Martin Phillip-*

response to Joseph II's Edict of Toleration, wrote a pamphlet titled *Divrei Shalom ve-Emet* (*Words of Peace and Truth*; 1782) in which, in the course of exhorting his fellow Jews to embrace the new occupational and educational opportunities, he proposed the *Book of the Paths of Peace* as the main textbook of a new curriculum. Wessely's pamphlet aroused a major controversy that for the first time publicly pitted rabbis against maskilim, although the Berlin mercantile elite's truculent response seriously aggravated the situation. This controversy has long obscured the book's abiding success: reprinted in numerous editions, it was *the* nineteenth-century Jewish study Bible.[78]

"Civic Acceptance" and "Divine Legislation"

The autonomous community required an individual to act as an intercessor with the authorities. Mendelssohn's prominence made him a prime candidate for this role. Similarly, Mendelssohn was forced to defend his faith publicly. Mendelssohn eventually exploited these two roles to begin advocating rights.

---

sons (Leipzig, 1911), 190. Ezekiel Landau (1713–93) of Prague defended Mendelssohn's reputation and his son subscribed to the translation. See Altmann, *Moses Mendelssohn*, 383. Feiner emhasizes Landau's misgivings. See *The Jewish Enlightenment*, 130–31. Altona's chief rabbi, Raphael Cohen (1722–1803), was notoriously quick to issue bans. Mendelssohn enlisted the king of Denmark and the Royal Library as subscribers (Altona was then under Danish rule) to preempt him. See Moshe Samet, "Mendelssohn, Wessley ve-Rababei Doram," in A. Gilboa, ed., *Mehkarim be-Toldot Am-Yisrael ve-Eretz Yisrael*, 1 (1970): 236–39, and Altmann, *Moses Mendelssohn*, 383–88, 392–93, 397. On Cohen, see Jacob Katz, "R. Raphael Cohen, Mendelssohn's Adversary" (Hebrew), *Tarbiz* 56 (1987): 2, 243–64, and Peter Freimark, "Die Entwicklung des Rabbinates nach dem Tode von Jonathan Eibenschütz (1764) bis zur Auflösung der Dreigemeinde AHU (1812)," in *Die Hamburger Juden in der Emanzipationsphase, 1780–1870*, ed. P. Freimark and A. Herzig (Hamburg, 1989), 9–12.

[78] Pinhas Horowitz (Frankfurt am Main) attacked the *Book of the Paths of Peace* as nonsense, and Ezekiel Landau criticized its use as a textbook, although not as a work for scholars. On the Wessely controversy, see Altmann, *Moses Mendelssohn*, 474–89; Moshe Samet, "Mendelssohn, Wessley ve-Rabanei Doram"; and Feiner, *The Jewish Enlightenment*, 87–104. For Rabbi David Tevele's sermon, see L. Lewin, "Aus dem jüdischen Kulturkampfe," *Jahrbuch der Jüdischen-literarischen Gesellschaft* 12 (1918): 182–94. For Ezekiel Landau's sermon, see *Jewish Preaching, 1200–1800: An Anthology*, ed. Marc Saperstein (New Haven, 1989), 361–73.

On *The Book of the Paths of Peace* as a study Bible, see Meir Hildesheimer, "Moses Mendelssohn in Nineteenth-Century Rabbinic Literature," *Proceedings of the American Academy for Jewish Research* 55 (1988): 79–133, and Steven M. Lowenstein, "The Readership of Mendelssohn's Bible Translation," in idem., *The Mechanics of Change: Essays in the Social History of German Jewry* (Atlanta, 1992), 29–64.

German Enlightenment political thinking balanced between individual rights and the absolutist state. Mendelssohn was painfully aware that the Jews' "civic oppression" deprived them of their natural rights.[79] In his early acts of intercession (1769–72) Mendelssohn stressed obedience to the state; by the end of the 1770s he had shifted emphasis to natural and individual rights. When his faith was first challenged publicly, in 1770, he defended toleration; the next time, in 1783, he enunciated his understanding of Judaism and made a plea for equal rights. These shifts, characteristic of the late Enlightenment's politicization (*Spätaufklärung*; 1770s–1780s), signaled his leap from the early Haskalah's concern with intellectual renewal to the full Haskalah's political engagement.

Mendelssohn's roles of intercessor and defender of the faith emerged concomitantly. In 1769 the community of Altona asked Mendelssohn to intercede against a charge that the community calendar had defamed Christianity, and he did so successfully.[80] That same year Johann Caspar Lavater (1741–1801), a chiliastic Swiss pastor, offered Mendelssohn a "golden bridge" to Christianity in the form of a dedication to a partial translation of a French-language apology for Christianity. Lavater invited Mendelssohn to repudiate this apology publicly or to "do what Socrates would have done, had he read this work and found it irrefutable," namely, convert.[81]

Mendelssohn answered with a multifaceted defense of toleration. Wolff's philosophy promoted toleration through natural religion and natural law. Theological dispute was out of place: he had chosen "to avoid all religious controversies, and in public writing to discuss only those truths of equal importance to all religions." He rejected Lavater's

---

[79] See "Über Freiwilligkeit und Freiheit," in *JubA*, 3,1:271, and *JubA*, 11:338 (to Isaak Iselin, May 30, 1762). Enlightenment thinkers saw the states guaranteeing freedom against the Holy Roman Empire's imperial pretensions, yet state rule had to accommodate individual rights. See Leonard Krieger, *The German Idea of Freedom: History of a Political Tradition* (Chicago, 1957), 1–85.

[80] Altmann, *Moses Mendelssohn*, 287–88.

[81] Lavater acted on the strength of conversations (1763–64) in which Mendelssohn expressed a "philosophical respect" for Jesus, and a later wishful report that the "philosophical Jews" of Berlin were ripe for conversion. See *JubA*, 7:3, and *JubA*, 7:327. For "golden bridge," see *JubA*, 7:329. Lavater thought Mendelssohn's conversion would trigger the messianic process. See Barukh Mevorah, "The Background of Lavater's Appeal to Mendelssohn" (Hebrew), *Zion* 30 (1965): 158–70; Simon Rawidowicz, "Einleitung," in *JubA*, 7:xiii–xvii; Altmann, *Moses Mendelssohn* 207ff. The apology, Charles Bonnet's *Palingenesie*, had taken issue with Mendelssohn's *Phaedon*, arguing that only revelation proved the soul's immortality. On Bonnet, see Jacques Marx, *Charles Bonnet contre les Lumiéres, Studies on Voltaire and the Eighteenth Century*, vol. 156–7 (Oxford, 1976), esp. 559–81.

claim that one religion had a monopoly on salvation: "he who in this life leads men to virtue cannot be damned in the next." He also attacked all presumptions to absolute truth:

> [The philosopher] must never lose sight of the fact that this is only his conviction, and that other reasonable beings who begin from another point of departure, and follow a different guide, could reach entirely contradictory opinions.[82]

He invoked his distinction between practical and theoretical knowledge. There was no need to correct erroneous ideas that "were too far removed from practical life to be directly deleterious" or, on the contrary, produced virtue—and here Mendelssohn clearly had Christianity in mind. Finally, he argued that Judaism was a tolerant religion: lacking a missionary impulse, the Mosaic law bound only those born to it. The rest of mankind was enjoined to "abide by the law of nature and the religion of the patriarchs," that is, the seven Noahide laws.[83]

In private he vindicated Judaism, making the argument that would be central to his Pentateuch commentary (which we have already encountered): the public revelation of law to the entire nation provided certainty for faith and practice:

> Although witnesses contradict one another so often, they are all agreed that once a "certain" Moses was ordered directly by God to free a "certain" people from slavery; that this ambassador of God realized his project before the eyes and against the will of a great and powerful nation, and thereby performed miracles which transcend all human concepts; that the legislator of nature appeared to this entire people, which was assembled in one location, in His full majesty and gave them laws. Many thousands of witnesses saw this divine manifestation with their eyes and related it to their children. . . .
>
> Here I have a matter of history on which I can rely with certainty.[84]

Under pressure for having violated Enlightenment norms of toleration, Lavater withdrew his challenge, but not his intention of converting Mendelssohn.[85]

Mendelssohn received appeals for aid throughout the 1770s. The community of Mecklenburg-Schwerin in 1772 asked him to intercede with

---

[82] "Mendelssohns Nacherinnerung," in *JubA*, 7:47. For the earlier quotation, see "Schreiben," in *JubA*, 7:10, 12–13. Cf. *JubA*, 7:15, 99.

[83] "Schreiben," in *JubA*, 7:11, 13.

[84] "Gegenbetrachtungen," in *JubA*, 7:86–88. See note 136 above.

[85] Altmann, *Moses Mendelssohn*, 223–34.

the duke to rescind his ban on early or same-day burial (contemporary medical practice dictated a three-day waiting period to prevent premature interment). Mendelssohn proposed the compromise that Jews continue their practice but first obtain a physician's certification, which the duke accepted (Mendelssohn conducted a private correspondence with the rabbi of Mecklenburg-Schwerin and Jacob Emden, which became public in the 1780s).[86] In 1775 Mendelssohn enlisted Lavater's aid to get a ban on procreation lifted for the Jews of Switzerland. The year 1777 saw him successfully resolve a controversy in Königsberg as to whether a central prayer in the liturgy defamed Christianity. Mendelssohn argued historically: the prayer predated Christianity, aiming at idolatry.[87]

That same year Mendelssohn began to transcend intercession by pointing to the Jews' natural rights. Almost half the Jews of Dresden had been expelled for failing to pay an exorbitant annual tax. Again successful in his appeal, Mendelssohn highlighted the human right of domicile:

> Expulsion is for a Jew the harshest punishment: more than mere banishment, it is virtual extirpation from God's earth, for prejudice turns him away at every border with an iron fist. Must fellow human beings who are free of guilt and trespass suffer this harshest of punishments simply because they adhere to different principles of belief and through misfortune are reduced to poverty?[88]

Mendelssohn had also started to address the Jews' rights in a book on property laws he produced at the Prussian authorities' behest (under the supervision of Berlin's rabbi, Hirschel Lewin). The Prussian government wanted to usurp the Jewish courts' jurisdiction (promulgated in the 1750 Jewry Law) by adjudicating property cases in its own courts through consultation of a Jewish law code. Lewin and Mendelssohn wanted rabbis present as consultants. Mendelssohn provided the Prussian government with the requested code yet explicitly argued that it was insufficient for adjudication: a judge had to consult the Talmud in the original to understand diverging opinions and the law's proper application.[89]

---

[86] See Sorkin, *Moses Mendelssohn*, 97–101; Altmann, *Moses Mendelssohn*, 289–95; and Michael Edward Panitz, *Modernity and Mortality: The Transformation of Central European Jewish Responses to Death*, Ph.D. diss, Jewish Theological Seminary (1989), 92–118.

[87] For Switzerland, see *GS* 3:106–7 and Altmann, *Moses Mendelssohn*, 426–27. For Königsberg, see *Moses Mendelssohns und Georg David Kypke Aufsätze über jüdische Gebete und Festfeiern*, ed. Ludwig Ernst Borowski (Königsberg, 1791), and *JubA*, 10,1:307–9.

[88] *JubA*, 12,2:102–3.

[89] Ismar Freund, *Die Emanzipation der Juden in Preussen*, 2 vols. (Berlin, 1912), 2:52–54; Selma Stern, *Der preussische Staat und die Juden*, 4 vols. (Tübingen, 1962–75), 3,1:111–33; and Rawidowicz, "Einleitung," in *JubA*, 7:cviii–cix.

A request from Alsace's Jews propelled Mendelssohn to plead for rights and pronounce publicly on Judaism. Heavily concentrated in money lending and other intermediary occupations, Alsace's Jews were constantly at odd with the surrounding populace. At the peak of tensions, in 1779–80, Mendelssohn received a request to defend the community.[90] Then writing his commentary on Exodus, he enlisted a prolific political journalist and Prussian civil servant, Christian Wilhelm Dohm (1751–1820), to help him draft a memorandum. They emphasized easing restrictive commercial regulations, arguing that increased commerce could improve the relations between Jews and their neighbors in Alsace.

Mendelssohn then boldly asked Dohm to write a treatise advocating the Jews' admission to citizenship. The result was *On the Civic Amelioration of the Jews* (1781), a tract that made the Jews' rights a public issue.[91] Arguing in a framework of raison d'état, Dohm included the Jews among mankind ("The Jew is more a man than a Jew") and attributed their degraded state to oppression: "When the oppression [the Jew] experienced for centuries has made him morally corrupt, then a more equitable treatment will again restore him." He advocated equal rights yet maintained the Enlightenment's political balance by having the state guarantee them.[92] A month after Dohm's tract appeared, in October 1781, Joseph II issued an edict for the Jews of Bohemia, and in January 1782 another for the Jews of Austria, in which he granted freedom of residence and commerce and admission to schools, while leaving in place numerous restrictions.

Mendelssohn aimed to reinforce the impact of Dohm's tract and Joseph's legislation by publishing a German translation of one of the pamphlets Manasseh ben Israel (1604–57) had written to gain the Jews readmission to England a century earlier. In his preface Mendelssohn

---

[90] Arthur Hertzberg, *The French Enlightenment and the Jews* (New York, 1968), 120–21, 287–89.

[91] See Franz Reuss, *Christian Wilhelm Dohms Schrift, "Über die bürgerliche Verbesserung der Juden," und deren Einwirkung auf die gebildeten Stände Deutschlands* (Kaiserslautern, 1891); Horst Moeller, "Aufklärung, Judentum und Staat: Ursprung und Wirkung von Dohms Schrift über die bürgerliche Verbesserung der Juden," in *Deutsche Aufklärung und Judenemanzipation*, ed. Walter Grab *Tel Aviver Jahrbuch für deutsche Geschichte*; 3 (1980), 119–49; Robert Liberles, "Dohm's Treatise on the Jews: A Defense of the Enlightenment," *Leo Baeck Institute Yearbook* 33 (1988): 29–42; and Hans Erich Bödeker, "'Aber ich strebe nach einer weitren Sphäre als bloß litterarischer Thätigkeit': Intentionen, Haltungen und Wirkungsfelder Christian Wilhelm von Dohms," *Zeitschrift für Religions- und Geistesgeschichte* 54, no. 4 (2002): 305–25.

[92] *Über die bürgerliche Verbesserung der Juden*, 2 vols. (Berlin, 1781–83), 1:28, 87.

for the first time publicly advocated "civic acceptance."[93] He argued against the secular prejudice that had supplanted the old religious bias:

> We are excluded from all arts, sciences and useful occupations and activities of mankind; all the means to useful improvement are closed to us, and our lack of applied knowledge is made the cause of our continued oppression. Our hands are tied and we are rebuked for not using them.[94]

Pointing to Holland's example, he argued for economic freedom. Finally, Mendelssohn took issue with Dohm over the relationship between civic freedom and communal autonomy. Dohm had argued that the Jews should continue to adjudicate civil matters such as property in Jewish courts. Mendelssohn argued for integration into the state's legal mechanism.[95] Dohm had asserted that the Jewish community should have the power to issue the minor ban of excommunication. Mendelssohn argued that the ban was inimical to religion's very goals: no religion should have power over its adherents, since opinions and beliefs were not subject to external authority.[96]

Mendelssohn's preface elicited a more serious challenge to his faith than Lavater's. In September 1782 a pamphlet appeared that, masquerading as the work of a famous Austrian statesman, though actually that of a journalist, August Cranz (1737–1801), who favored rights for Jews, seemed to revive Lavater's public challenge. Cranz

[93] Mendelssohn's term was *bürgerliche Aufnahme*. See Vorrede, in *JubA*, 8:4, and Altmann, "Einleitung," in *JubA*, 8:xv. "Emancipation" came into use later. See Jacob Katz, "The Term 'Jewish Emancipation': Its Origin and Historical Impact," in *Studies in Nineteenth-Century Jewish Intellectual History*, ed. Alexander Altmann (Cambridge, 1964), 1–25, and David Sorkin, "Emancipation and Assimilation: Two Concepts and Their Application to German-Jewish History," *Leo Baeck Institute Yearbook* 35 (1990): 17–22. Mendelssohn used "civic incorporation" (*bürgerliche Vereinigung*) to describe the larger social and political process. See "Jerusalem," in *JubA*, 8:200.

[94] "Vorrede," in *JubA*, 8:6. I have translated *Kultur* as "applied knowledge," following Mendelssohn's definition in "Über die Frage: Was heißt Aufklären?" in *JubA*, 6,1:115–19.

[95] For Holland, see "Vorrede," in *JubA*, 8:11. For the courts, see "Vorrede," in *JubA*, 8:17. For Dohm's position, see *Über die bürgerliche Verbesserung der Juden*, 1:124–27.

[96] For Dohm's position, see *Über die bürgerliche Verbesserung der Juden*, 1:124. For Mendelssohn's rejoinder, see "Vorrede," in *JubA*, 8:23. Mendelssohn saw this insight as his contribution to natural rights theory. See "Jerusalem," in *JubA*, 8:151, and Altmann, "Einleitung," in *JubA*, 8:xxxiv. He first developed the idea in his notebook essay of 1781, "Von Vollkommenen und Unvollkommenen Rechten und Pflichten," in *JubA*, 3,1:280–82. See also "Über die Grundsätze der Regierung," in *JubA*, 6,1:131–32. Ibid., *JubA*, 8:21.

asked Mendelssohn for a full account of his belief: in calling for abrogation of the ban, had Mendelssohn not repudiated Judaism? Cranz saw Mendelssohn on the horns of a dilemma: either he realized that Christianity was the true religion and was prepared to convert, or he thought Judaism required fundamental reform. In either case, Mendelssohn should air his views, since these affected his hopes for rights. How would Mendelssohn resolve the conflict between Sabbath observance and army service? How would he reconcile civil marriage with Judaism's prohibition on intermarriage?[97] A postscript accompanied Cranz's pamphlet in which an obscure chaplain, wondering whether Mendelssohn had renounced revelation altogether, requested clarification: "I am a Jew, I am a Christian, I am neither."[98]

In *Jerusalem, or on Religious Power and Judaism,* published in 1783, Mendelssohn elaborated the arguments he had broached in his preface to Manasseh ben Israel. He first provided a general theory of church-state relations based on natural law and the distinction between actions and convictions. He criticized Hobbes for sacrificing liberty for the sake of security and Locke for guaranteeing liberty of conscience at the cost of separating temporal and eternal welfare.[99] He instead developed Wolff's natural law theory of man's innate need for benevolence (Protestant neologues had stressed this same idea).

Mendelssohn argued that the social contract, beginning with marriage and offspring, removes individuals from the state of nature by imposing obligations. Fulfilling the innate human need for benevolence by voluntarily promising to transfer a possession, a person legitimates a claim that can be enforced with compulsion (converting an "imperfect" into a "perfect" right).[100] The first contract, marriage, includes the obligation to educate children. The need for benevolence is thus transformed into the basis of society.

Religion and church, in contrast, do not involve contracts. God and church have no claim on benevolence; there is no "imperfect" right to be converted into a "perfect" one. "The right to our convictions is

---

[97] *Das Forschen nach Licht und Recht in einem Schreiben an Herrn Moses Mendelssohn, auf Veranlassung seiner merkwürdigen Vorrede zu Manasseh ben Israel* (Berlin, 1782), *JubA,* 8:80, 81, 83–84, 85. See J. Katz, "To whom did Mendelssohn reply in his Jerusalem," *Scripta Hierosolymitana* 23 (1972): 214–43; Altmann, *Moses Mendelssohn,* 502–13; and Edward Breuer, "Politics, Tradition, History: Rabbinic Judaism and the Eighteenth-Century Struggle for Civil Equality," *Harvard Theological Review* 85:3 (1992): 369–76.

[98] "Nachscript," in *JubA,* 8:91–92.

[99] "Jerusalem," in *JubA,* 8:103–9.

[100] Ibid., in *JubA,* 8:118, 122–25.

inalienable," the use of compulsion inapplicable. "The church's only rights are admonition, instruction, reassurance and consolation; and the citizens' duties towards the church are an attentive ear and a willing heart."[101]

Since contracts do not apply to convictions, the state does not have the right to coerce or influence them through privilege or prerogative, let alone to administer oaths about them, since oaths "do not create new duties." The best state is one whose members govern themselves through "education." Religion is the sole institution capable of this: its "collective edification" makes even the most abstract concepts practical.[102]

Mendelssohn's uncompromising defense of liberty of conscience, balanced between the individual and the state, was located at the conservative end of late eighteenth-century German natural law theory. Throughout the century, natural law theorists had justified state absolutism, positing that through the social contract the individual embraced a "civil liberty" of unquestioning obedience. In contrast, in the 1770s some thinkers began to argue that the state's duty was to secure the individual's inviolable "natural rights." Mendelssohn generally espoused the older theory. He established an inviolable individual right beyond the state only for liberty of conscience.[103]

To make this argument, Mendelssohn used ecclesiastical natural law theory, especially Collegialism, the religious Enlightenment's common property, yet gave it a radical turn. In the German states both territorialists and Collegialists had granted the church the minor ban that did not impinge on civil status. Dohm had followed the Collegialists. While Mendelssohn recognized that the church or synagogue was a voluntary religious society and "a moral person," he denied that it was based on a contract vouchsafing the right of coercion.[104]

---

[101] Ibid., in *JubA*, 8:128–29.

[102] Ibid., in *JubA*, 8:132, 141.

[103] See his fragment of 1769 in *JubA*, 3,1:271. For German political thought, see Diethelm Klippel, "The True Concept of Liberty: Political Theory in Germany in the Second Half of the Eighteenth Century," in *The Transformation of Political Culture: England and Germany in the Late Eighteenth Century*, ed. Eckhart Hellmuth, (Oxford, 1990), 452–58.

[104] "Jerusalem," in *JubA*, 8:140. See Altmann, "Moses Mendelssohn on Excommunication: The Ecclesiastical Law Background," in *Essays in Jewish Intellectual History* (Hanover, 1981), 182–4. For major exponents of collegialism, see Christoph Matthaeus Pfaff, *Academische Reden über das so wohl allgemeine als auch Teutsche Protestantische Kirchen-Recht* (Tübingen, 1742), and Johann Lorenz Mosheim, *Allgemeines Kirchenrecht der Protestanten* (Helmstädt, 1760), who endorsed the ban at 395ff. See Klaus Schlaich, *Kollegialtheorie: Kirche, Recht und Staat in der Aufklärung* (Munich, 1969).

Having articulated a theory of church-state relations, Mendelssohn turned to the nature of Judaism. A "divine legislation," it is the nonpareil religion of practical knowledge:

I believe that Judaism knows of no revealed religion in the sense in which Christians understand this term. The Israelites possess a divine legislation—laws, commandments, ordinances, rules of life, instruction in the will of God as to how they should conduct themselves in order to attain temporal and eternal felicity. Propositions and prescriptions of this kind were revealed to them by Moses in a miraculous and supernatural manner, but no doctrinal opinions, no saving truths, no universal propositions of reason.[105]

Judaism consists of a set of acts aimed at the "will" rather than a set of beliefs. At the same time, the Pentateuch is "an inexhaustible treasure of rational truths and religious doctrines that are so intimately connected with the laws that they form but one entity."[106] These truths are either "eternal" or "historical." The divinely established eternal truths are of two kinds. The truths of pure mathematics and logic, that are "necessary" since God's "infinite reason" has made them so, are immutable for God as well as man. The truths of nature (physics, psychology) are "contingent" since God chose them as the best (Wolff's "best of all possible worlds"); He could and on occasion does alter them (miracles). "Historical" truths, in contrast, are those that "occurred once and may never occur again; propositions which have become true at one point in time and space through a confluence of causes and effects, and which, therefore can only be conceived as true in respect to that point in time and space."[107] As Mendelssohn argued in his Pentateuch commentary, Judaism was grounded in historical truth.

The God at Sinai was the God of the exodus:

"I am the Eternal, your God, who brought you out of the land of Mizrayim, who delivered you from bondage, etc." A historical truth, on which this people's legislation was to be founded, as well as laws, was to be revealed here, commandments and ordinances, not eternal religious truths. ". . . I am your Redeemer, your Sovereign and King;

---

[105] JubA, 8:157. Emphasis in the original.

[106] Ibid., in JubA, 8:165–66.

[107] "Jerusalem," in JubA, 8:157–58. Mendelssohn reworked Leibniz's categories. See Arnold Berney, "The Historical and Political Conceptions of Moses Mendelssohn" (Hebrew), Zion 5 (1940): 251, and Altmann, "Moses Mendelssohn's Concept of Judaism Reexamined," in Von der mittelalterlichen zur modernen Aufklärung: Studien zur jüdischen Geistesgeschichte (Tübingen, 1987), 234–35.

I also make a covenant with you, and give you laws by which you are to live and become a happy nation in the land that I shall give you." All these are historical truths.[108]

For Mendelssohn, Judaism was tripartite. Its foundation was natural religion: the "eternal truths about God, and his government and providence, without which man cannot be enlightened and happy." God had endowed man with a faculty of reason and knowledge of all truths needed for his temporal and eternal felicity. Here was the basis for toleration in a universally accessible morality and means to salvation.[109] Judaism also contained historical truths about the genesis of the nation and its relationship to God that are "the foundation for national cohesion." Finally, Judaism was comprised of the "laws, precepts, commandments and rules of life" that were "peculiar to this nation" and were designed to bestow "national . . . as well as personal felicity."

The laws bridge between the historical truths of Judaism and the eternal truths. They

> guide the inquiring intelligence to divine truths, partly to eternal and partly to historical truths. . . . The ceremonial law was the bond which was to connect action with contemplation, law with theory.
>
> All laws refer to, or are based upon, eternal truths of reason, or remind us of them, and rouse us to ponder them. Hence, our rabbis rightly say: the laws and doctrines are related to each other like body and soul.[110]

Moreover, these laws and actions impart practical knowledge. Judaism's essential difference was its "divine legislation" or "ceremonial law" in which "religious and moral teachings were to be connected with men's everyday activities." The law addressed man's will, never forcing his belief.[111] Israel's adherence to these laws was the basis of its election and fulfillment of its divine mission as a "priestly nation": the law did not merely indicate the virtuous path, it was the path:

---

[108] "Jerusalem," in *JubA* 8:165. Emphasis in the original. For Mendelssohn's proximity to Jehuda Ha-Levi, see *Kusari* I. 25. On Ha-levi, see Harry Wolfson, "The Double Faith Theory in Saadia, Averroes, and St. Thomas," in *Studies in the History of Philosophy and Religion*, 1:583–84, 597.

[109] "Jerusalem," in *JubA*, 8:191, 160–61. Mendelssohn was unwilling to concede to Maimonides that, to achieve eternal life, non-Jews must recognize the Noahide laws as divine. See *JubA*, 19:178. See Altmann, "Moses Mendelssohn's Concept of Judaism Reexamined," 239–40.

[110] "Jerusalem," in *JubA*, 8:192–3, 166. On the relationship between the acts and the doctrines they recall, see Michael Morgan, "History and Modern Jewish Thought: Spinoza and Mendelssohn on the Ritual Law," *Judaism* 30 (1981): 467–78.

[111] "Jerusalem," in *JubA*, 8:161–62, 184, 166.

[The patriarch's] descendants were chosen by Providence to be a priestly nation; that is, a nation which, through its establishment and constitution, its laws, actions, vicissitudes, and changes was continually to call attention to sound and unadulterated ideas of God and his attributes. It was incessantly to teach, proclaim, and endeavor to preserve these ideas among the nations, by means of its mere existence.[112]

The law's means of transmission also made the Jews a priestly people. Oral transmission made the Bible so readily comprehensible that it immediately penetrated an auditor's heart; preserved the text from corruption; and made the law "vital" knowledge –an effective instrument of individual and collective life.

Mendelssohn asserted that each category of truth has an appropriate form of transmission. The "eternal" truths are communicated by universal nature ("nature and thing"). Apprehending the "necessary" truths (mathematics, logic) requires reason, while the "contingent" truths (physics, psychology) call for observation as well. In contrast, historical truths have a human form of communication, namely, "word and script" intended for a specific people at a specific time. Here Mendelssohn used the principle of accommodation. Moreover, historical truths are dependent on the "authority and credibility" of the narrator: miracles are a means to confirm the veracity of historical truths.[113]

"Truths of reason," in contrast, cannot be attested by miracles.

Miracles and extraordinary signs are, according to Judaism, no proofs for or against eternal truths of reason. . . . For miracles can only verify testimonies, support authorities, and confirm the credibility of witnesses and those who transmit tradition. But no testimonies and authorities can upset any established truth of reason, or place a doubtful one beyond doubt and suspicion.[114]

Mendelssohn made striking apologetic use of religious Enlightenment ideas. Warburton had deflected the deists' criticisms by understanding Judaism as a "republication of natural religion." Mendelssohn saw Judaism as being in accord with natural religion, adding only historical

---

[112] Ibid., in *JubA*, 8:183. Emphasis in original. See his commentary to Exodus 19:5–6, in *JubA*, 16:177.

[113] "Jerusalem," in *JubA*, 8:160. See Edward Breuer,"Of Miracles and Events Past: Mendelssohn on History," *Jewish History* 9,2 (1995): 27–52.

[114] "Jerusalem," in *JubA*, 8:165. For similar passages, see "Über Wunder u[nd] wunderbar," in *JubA*, 6,1:4–5, and his commentary to Exodus 19:9, in *JubA*, 16:178. On this issue, see Alexander Altmann, "Moses Mendelssohn on Miracles," in *Die Trostvolle Aufklärung*, 152–63.

truths and the law, whereas Christianity compromised natural religion with revealed truths. Like Baumgarten, Mendelssohn derived "certainty" from history, but it was the certainty of Judaism's veracity.

An inappropriate form of transmission could have grave consequences. Putting divine truths in human form ("words and script") risked idolatry. Judaism stands as a bulwark against idolatry: it employs oral tradition to transmit the historical truths of laws and ordinances, while "entrust[ing]" doctrines and convictions to "vital, spiritual instruction." The law itself was "a kind of vital script," "rousing the mind and heart, full of meaning, never ceasing to inspire contemplation and to provide the occasion and opportunity for oral instruction." The very means of transmission made the law "vital," practical knowledge.[115]

The law and its oral transmission created a unity of "life and doctrine" so complete that in ancient Judaism "state and religion were not conjoined, but one; not connected, but identical." Ancient Judaism constituted the premiere example of a state whose members were able to govern themselves through education because of its identity of religion and politics: "in this nation civil matters acquired a sacred and religious aspect, and every civil service was at the same time a true service of God. The community was a community of God, its affairs were God's; the public taxes were an offering to God; and everything down to the least police measure was part of the divine service."[116] Ancient Judaism represented an ideal in which every act was benevolent and individual interest accorded with the commonweal.[117] Mendelssohn's portrait of ancient Judaism countered Cranz's contention that in abjuring the ban he had undermined Judaism. All ancient Judaism's punishments were civil infractions; they did not concern beliefs. God has no need for our benevolence since He embodies "infinite benevolence." All divine punishment was benevolently didactic, aiming at the individual's "moral improvement."[118]

---

[115] "Jerusalem," in *JubA*, 8:168. The terms ("Leben und Lehre") appear in a number of key passages. See *JubA*, 8:170, 185, 193. For "living script," see Arnold Eisen, "Divine Legislation as 'Ceremonial Script': Mendelssohn on the Commandments," *Association for Jewish Studies Review* 15 (1990): 239–67.

[116] "Jerusalem," in *JubA*, 8:193–94. See Julius Guttman, "Mendelssohn's *Jerusalem* and Spinoza's *Theological-Political Treatise*," in Alfred Jospe, ed., *Studies in Jewish Thought: An Anthology of German Jewish Scholarship*, 361–86.

[117] "Rhapsodie," in *JubA*, 1:407.

[118] For punishment, see "Jerusalem," in *JubA*, 8:194–95, 188–89. For earlier passages, see "Book of the Soul," in *JubA*, 14:143; "Gegenbetrachtungen," in *JubA*, 7:96; and his commentary on Genesis 3:19 in *JubA*, 15,2:37. For God's "infinite benevolence," see "Biur," in *JubA*, 16:348, and "Jerusalem," in *JubA*, 8:190.

Mendelssohn was quick to acknowledge that this pristine ancient Judaism was singular and short-lived. After the Temple's destruction and the nation's exile, the laws pertaining to land and Temple fell into abeyance, leaving the "ceremonial law." Having argued for Judaism as the nonpareil religion of practical knowledge made "vital" by oral transmission, Mendelssohn made his characteristic argument for heteronomy: he rejected all explanations for the law, especially historical ones ("time, place, and circumstance"), as mere "surmises."[119]

The law also transcended the debate on rights. Mendelssohn claimed unconditional rights on the basis of natural right, arguing that rights should not be made contingent on changes in, or observance of, the "divine legislation". The Jews were duty bound to observe the immutable law. They could join the surrounding society only if allowed to abide by the law: "no wiser advice than this can be given to the House of Jacob. Adapt yourselves to the morals and the constitution of the land to which you have been removed; but hold fast to the religion of your fathers, too. Bear both burdens as well as you can!" Should this not suffice to gain rights, then there is no choice but to forgo them: "We cannot in good conscience depart from the law, and what good will it do you to have fellow citizens without conscience?"[120]

Mendelssohn boldly argued that the state and the Jews had to accord with natural rights. The state must declare itself indifferent to belief beyond natural religion in order to tolerate all religions (including Judaism) and emancipate their members (including Jews). Such a state did not yet exist. The Jews must become a voluntary society without coercive powers, the appropriate form for all religions, in order to become members of the state that would emancipate them ("civil union").

Mendelssohn thus used the novel means of renouncing religious coercion in conformity with natural law to the conservative end of preserving the Jews' religious freedom. Yet he went one step further: the novel means of natural law would also vouchsafe the Jews political

---

[119] "Jerusalem," in *JubA*, 8:198–200. He also used the phrase "personal commandments." See 8:199.

[120] Ibid., in *JubA*, 8:198, 200. For the contract and the ideology of emancipation, see Sorkin, *The Transformation of German Jewry*, 79–104.

Mendelssohn rejected unification of the faiths as a threat to liberty of conscience. See Michah Gottlieb, "Mendelssohn's metaphysical defense of religious pluralism," *Journal of Religion* 86,2 (2006): 205–25, and Christopher Spehr, *Aufklärung und Ökumene: Reunionsversuche zwischen Katholiken und Protestanten im deutschsprachigen Raum des späteren 18. Jahrhunderts* (Tübingen, 2005).

equality. Mendelssohn transcended the inherited roles of intercessor and public apologist by advocating emancipation.[121]

"THE SOCRATES OF BERLIN"

Mendelssohn wrote about Jewish subjects exclusively in Hebrew until the preface to Manasseh Ben Israel and *Jerusalem*. Throughout those decades, the 1750s to the 1780s, he addressed secular subjects in German, gaining a European reputation as an outstanding figure of the Berlin Enlightenment.

All Mendelssohn's philosophical works were grounded in Wolffian metaphysics, yet his early works were at the border of metaphysics and aesthetics. While Wolff had treated aesthetics as a lesser form of knowledge, the next generation of Wolffians, including Alexander Baumgarten, elaborated a theory of aesthetic cognition.[122]

In his first work, *Philosophical Dialogues* (1755), for which Lessing arranged publication, Mendelssohn established his adherence to the Leibnizian-Wolffian notion of a preestablished harmony as well as to the idea of the "best of all possible worlds." Mendelssohn attempted to rehabilitate Spinoza's thought, seeing him as a "sacrifice for human reason" who prefigured many of Leibniz's key ideas.[123]

In the *Letters on the Sensations* and other essays, Mendelssohn, influenced by Shaftesbury, liberated aesthetics from metaphysics through a psychological turn: "every rule of beauty is simultaneously a discovery in psychology." He argued that beauty derives not from the perfection of the object being represented but from the representations' thorough harmony ("a perfect sensuous representation"). Art introduced a beauty not present in nature and, in consequence, possessed its own laws: "the stage has its own morality."[124]

---

[121] "Jerusalem," in *JubA*, 8:198–99. Emphasis in the original. See Sorkin, *The Transformation of German Jewry*, 70–71.

[122] Beck, *Early German Philosophy*, 276–96. Joachim Krüger, *Christian Wolff und die Ästhetik* (Berlin, 1980), 72–80; Ernst Cassirer, *The Philosophy of the Enlightenment* (Princeton, 1951), 332.

[123] "Philosophische Gespräche," in *JubA*, 1:1–39; quotation at 1:14.

[124] The suicide morally reprehensible in life is aesthetically commendable on stage. "Über die Hauptgrundsätze der schönen Künste und Wissenschaften" (1771), in *JubA*, 1:427, 431, 433–34, 443. Cf. "Rhapsodie," in *JubA*, 1:421, and "Über die Empfindungen" in *JubA*, 1:246. See Frederic Will, Jr., "Cognition through Beauty in Moses Mendelssohn's Early Aesthetics," *Journal of Aesthetics and Art Criticism* 14 (1955): 97–105; Werner Segreff, *Moses Mendelssohn und die Aufklärungsästhetik im 18. Jahrhundert* (Bonn, 1984), 62–67; and Liselotte Richter, *Philosophie der Dichtkunst: Moses Mendelssohns Ästhetik zwischen Aufklärung und Sturm und Drang* (Berlin, 1948), 14–17.

In his essays, reviews, and conversations he influenced many of the major strands of German aesthetic thinking: Lessing's notions of drama and poetry's relationship to the plastic arts, Schiller's ideas on art's role in human development, and Kant's conceptions of the disinterestedness of beauty and a third faculty of aesthetic judgment.[125]

Two major metaphysical works secured Mendelssohn's reputation. In *Treatise on Evidence in the Metaphysical Sciences* (1763), which won first prize in Berlin's Royal Academy of the Sciences' competition (Kant won second prize), he asserted that philosophy provided the same level of certainty as mathematics but with less "perspicuity" (*Faßlichkeit*): philosophy dealt with qualities (mathematics with quantities) and also had to be applied to reality. For the existence of God he offered a priori proofs as well as the argument from design (physico-theology). He formulated an ethical principle grounded in the individual's free choice of perfection: "make your internal and external condition and that of your fellow human being, in the proper proportion, as perfect as you can."[126]

His *Phaedon* (1767), a translation and reworking of Plato's dialogue, appeared in numerous languages and won European renown. Mendelssohn argued that the soul, as a simple created substance, is imperishable; only God can destroy it. Because of man's divinely ordained

---

On Mendelssohn's role in aesthetics see Armand Nivelle, *Kunst- und Dichtungstheorien zwischen Aufklärung und Klassik* (Berlin, 1960), 1–3; and Klaus Berghahn, "From Classicist to Classical Literary Criticism, 1730–1806," in *A History of German Literary Criticism, 1730–1980*, ed. Peter Uwe Hohendahl (Lincoln, 1988), 13–99, esp. 55–56, 59–64.

[125] Mendelssohn published reviews in the *Allgemeine deutsche Bibliothek* (1757–58) and from 1759 was involved in the *Literaturbriefe* with Nicolai and Lessing. For the basic facts, see Altmann, *Moses Mendelssohn*, 69–71. For Mendelssohn the literary critic, see Eva Engel: "The Emergence of Mendelssohn as Literary Critic," *Leo Baeck Institute Yearbook* 24 (1979); "Die Bedeutung Moses Mendelssohns für die Literatur des 18. Jahrhunderts," *Mendelssohn-Studien* 4 (1979): 111–59; and "Moses Mendelssohn: His Importance as a Literary Critic," in Ehrhard Bahr, Edward P. Harris, and Laurence G. Lyon, eds., *Humanität und Dialog: Lessing und Mendelssohn in neuer Sicht* (Detroit, 1982), 259–73. On journals in the German Enlightenment, see Klaus Berghahn, "Das schwierige Geschäft der Aufklärung: Zur Bedeutung der Zeitschriften im literarischen Leben des 18. Jahrhunderts," in *Aufklärung: Ein literatur-wissenschaftliches Studienbuch*, ed. Hans-Freidrich Wessels (Königstein, 1984), 32–65.

Most writers stress one aspect of Mendelssohn's influence. Richter, the *Sturm und Drang* and sentimentalism, see *Philosophie der Dichtkunst*; Nivelle, the influence on Lessing and Kant, see *Kunst- und Dichtungstheorien*, 63–64; Segreff, the impact on Schiller, see *Moses Mendelssohn und die Aufklärungsästhetik im 18. Jahrhundert*, 111–114. For drama, see Jochen Schulte-Sasse, ed., *G. E. Lessing, M. Mendelssohn, F. Nicolai: Briefwechsel über das Trauerspiel* (Munich, 1972), 168–98. See also Beck, *Early German Philosophy*, 326–29.

[126] "Abhandlung über die Evidenz in Metaphysischen Wissenschaften," in *JubA*, 2:267–330. Alexander Altmann, *Moses Mendelssohns Frühschriften zur Metaphysik untersucht und erläutert* (Tübingen, 1969), 252–391; Daniel O. Dahlstrom, *Moses Mendelssohn: Philosophical Writings* (Cambridge, 1997), 251–306.

vocation to pursue perfection, the soul is immortal, retaining consciousness and memory.[127]

Mendelssohn was a Berlin landmark; he received numerous visitors at his open salon and the silk factory (where he rose from bookkeeper to manager and then to partner; he was also a recognized expert on silk production, writing memoranda for the Prussian government) and carried on a European-wide correspondence.[128] In 1771 he was elected to the Berlin Academy of Sciences, although the king exercised a pocket veto, dashing Mendelssohn's hopes of a stipend that would free him from the factory. Lessing immortalized him as the character of Nathan in *Nathan the Wise* (1779).

As a result of Friedrich Heinrich Jacobi's claim that Lessing had professed Spinozism, Mendelssohn became involved in the so-called pantheism debate: he defended Lessing's reputation and his relationship to his lifelong friend. While the controversy involved miscommunications, blunders, and acts of bad faith, it turned on whether Lessing subscribed to a fatalistic pantheism or, as Mendelssohn claimed, the sort of "refined pantheism" he had discussed in his *Philosophical Dialogues*. Mendelssohn devoted his last work, *Morgenstunden*, published in 1785, to defending Lessing, offering an extended proof for God's existence, including the ontological argument, and reiterating his understanding of Spinoza.[129]

Mendelssohn was one of the most original of the Wolffian philosophers. His reputation has ebbed and flowed with that of eighteenth-century philosophy prior to the "all-destroying Kant," in Mendelssohn's words.

HASKALAH AND BEYOND

Mendelssohn's authority had largely ensured the Haskalah's moderate course; Frederick the Great's disdain for Jews, including Mendelssohn, precluded improvements to their legal status. The deaths of Mendelssohn and Frederick in 1786 opened a new era in which the Haskalah achieved political maturity. The maskilim deployed the early Haskalah's ideas in a radical manner, enlisting its prescriptions of intellectual

---

[127] "Phaedon, oder über die Unsterblichkeit der Seele in drei Gesprächen," in *JubA*, 3,1:5–128. Altmann, *Moses Mendelssohn*, 140–58; Bourel, *Moses Mendelssohn*, 181–223.

[128] Max Birnbaum, "Moses Mendelssohn, der Seidenfabrikant," *Gemeindeblatt der jüdischen Gemeinde zu Berlin* 19 (1929): 452–54, and Erika Herzfeld, "Moses Mendelssohn als Seidenmanufakturunternehmer," in *Juden in Brandenburg-Preussen: Beiträge zu ihrer Geschichte im 17. und 18. Jahrhundert* (Berlin, 2001), 177–89.

[129] Altmann, *Moses Mendelssohn*, 638–712; Bourel, *Moses Mendelssohn*, 391–450; Frederick C. Beiser, *The Fate of Reason: German Philosophy from Kant to Fichte* (Cambridge, 1987), 44–108.

renewal for political engagement. Younger maskilim born after mid-century made this shift. The younger men's experience differed in two ways. The older group, largely born in the 1720s and 1730s, had pursued their ideas in relative isolation. The younger maskilim formed groups and founded institutions modeled on the Enlightenment's. In addition, they were heavily influenced by the mercantile elite, whose patronage shaped their careers and political outlook.

A key figure in the Haskalah's politicization was Isaac Euchel (1756–1804). He attempted to rally support for educational reform (Königsberg) by turning the stock-in-trade views of the early Haskalah into a manifesto. He advocated erecting a community school that would employ "enlightened men [maskilim] who have languages and substantial knowledge."[130] In 1782, with the financial support of an elite family, the Friedländers, whom he served as a tutor, Euchel organized a reading society, "The Society for the Exponents of the Hebrew Language (*Hevrat Dorshei Lashon Ever*)," whose members were recruited from the city's maskilim, including university students. The society's goal was to publish a journal in Hebrew, *The Assembler (Ha-Measef)*, which began to appear in 1784. The editors, Isaac Euchel and Mendel Breslau (1760–1827), were both in their twenties.[131]

The journal's avowed aim, to "gather from all branches of science and ethics [*musar*] articles and essays whose words benefit and delight the soul that yearns to sit in wisdom's shade," in large part fulfilled the early Haskalah's vision of intellectual renewal. In its first six volumes (until 1790), the journal largely adhered to its stated program. Essays in early issues (Königsberg, 1784–86) concentrated on the textual curriculum and Hebrew, as well as on the vernacular and the sciences. The issues published in Berlin (1788–90) devoted more space to science.[132]

While largely realizing the early Haskalah's program, the *Measef* also began to transcend it through a threefold politicization. For some maskilim the idea of utility to the state gradually displaced the ideal of renewing Jewish culture. These maskilim may be said to have

---

[130] *Sefat Emet* (Königsberg, 1782), 9–10. Like Wessely, Euchel turned the stock-in-trade views of the early Haskalah into an educational manifesto. See Pelli, "The Age of Haskalah," 190–230, and Shmuel Feiner, "Isaac Euchel: 'Entrepreneur' of the Haskalah Movement in Germany" (Hebrew), *Zion* 52 (1987): 427–69.

[131] "Die Gesellschaft der Hebräischen Literaturfreunde." Euchel studied at the University of Königsberg with Friedlander's support. His application for a teaching position was rejected. See Feiner, "Isaac Euchel," 430–443; idem., *The Jewish Enlightenment*, 186–199; and H. Jolowicz, *Geschichte der Juden in Königsberg* (Posen, 1867), 96–100. For the journal's editors and other personnel, see Tsemah Tsamriyon, *Ha-Meassef: Ktav ha-Eit ha-Moderni ha-Rishon be-Ivrit* (Haifa, 1988), 40–41, 56–57.

[132] *Nahal ha-Besor* (Königsberg, 1784), 1–5. Tsamriyon, *Ha-Measef*, 147.

approached if not adopted the mercantile elite's utilitarian outlook. The Berlin Free School (*Freischule*), founded in 1778 by the wealthy merchants Isaac Daniel Itzig and David Friedländer, embodied this idea of utility. The school aimed to make poor children productive by preparing them to serve as clerks and bookkeepers in the mercantile elite's factories and counting houses.[133]

The maskilim also gave evidence of a sharper tone. They now harshly satirized problems and issues that exponents of the early Haskalah had identified. The maskilim frequently questioned the rabbis' authority by criticizing their knowledge and methods of study.[134]

Finally, the maskilim began to propose themselves as an élite capable of leading the Jews. They exhibited incipient group consciousness: some maskilim advocated improved treatment of teachers, others proposed themselves as community leaders. Mendel Breslau, for example, issued a call for an assembly of "the heads of the House of Jacob" to rethink minor aspects of observance.[135] Isaac Euchel created a public

---

[133] For the mercantile elite's notion of utility, see Bodian, "The Jewish Entrepreneurs in Berlin," 159–84. It is conventional to see the Haskalah creating the school, with Mendelssohn playing a pivotal role. See Mordechai Eliav, *Ha-Hinukh ha-Yehudi be-Germanya be-Yemai ha-Haskalah veha-Emanzipaziya* (Jerusalem, 1960), 71–80. For Mendelssohn's role, see Joseph Mendelssohn,"Moses Mendelssohn's Lebensgeschichte," *Gesammelte Schriften*, 1:45. For a reassessment, see Shmuel Feiner, "Educational Programs and Social Ideals: The School 'Hinukh Nearim' (Freischule) in Berlin, 1778–1825" (Hebrew), *Zion* 60 (1996): 393–424. For Mendelssohn as the "intellectual mentor," see Britta L. Behm, *Moses Mendelssohn und die Transformation der jüdischen Erziehung in Berlin* (Münster, 2002), 189–210. For documents, see Ingrid Lohmann, ed., *Chevrat Chinuch Nearim: Die jüdische Freischule in Berlin, 1778–1825 im Umfeld preußischer Bildungspolitik und jüdischer Kultusreform. Eine Quellensammlung*, 2 vols. (Münster, 2001). Tsamriyon fails to distinguish between the idea of utility and the later ideology of emancipation. See *Ha-Measef*, 59, 240–44.

The press, the "Orientalische Buchdruckerei" or Hinukh Nearim, contributed to the early Haskalah ideal of cultural revival. See Feiner, *The Jewish Enlightenment*, 243–51, 324–27.

[134] For satire as a tool of the Haskalah, see Meir Gilon, "Hebrew Satire in the Age of the German Haskalah: An Anatomy of Research" (Hebrew), *Zion* 52 (1987): 211. For a literary-aesthetic approach, see Y. Friedlander, *Perakim be-Satira ha-Ivrit be-Shalhei ha-Meah ha-YH* (Tel Aviv, 1980). An example is Aaron Wolfsohn-Halle's "Sicha be-eretz ha-Hayim" (Conversation in the Hereafter), *Ha-Measef* 7 (1794–96): 67–93, 120–58, 203–28, 279–98. See Moshe Pelli, "On the Genre of 'A Dialogue in the Hereafter' in Hebrew Haskalah Literature" (Hebrew), in *Proceedings of the Eighth World Congress of Jewish Studies* (Jerusalem, 1982), 209–15, and Jutta Strauss, "Aaron Halle-Wolfssohn: Ein Leben in drei Sprachen," *Wolfenbütteler Studien zur Aufklärung* 25 (1999): 57–75.

[135] In general, see Tsamriyon, *Ha-Measef*, 169. Mendel Breslau, "El rodfei Tsedek," 310, wanted to "lighten the burden" of minor customs (*minhagim*). See Tsamriyon, ibid., 146–47, and Moshe Pelli, "First Call of a Hebrew Maskil to Convene a Rabbinic Assembly for Religious Reforms" (Hebrew), *Tarbiz* 42 (1974): 484–91. For the Haskalah and reform, see

controversy on the subject of early burial by publishing (*Measef*;1785) Mendelssohn's correspondence with rabbi Jacob Emden and the Rabbi of Schwerin (from 1772). Euchel's disputatious introduction turned a private scholarly exchange into a public polemic. Euchel institutionalized the controversy by organizing a mutual aid association of bachelors (the Berlin Gesellschaft der Freunde, 1792) that Prussia subsequently chartered (1798) to implement delayed burial.[136]

The Haskalah's ambitions peaked in Euchel's 1787 attempt to turn the local Society for the Exponents of the Hebrew language into a supralocal federation with administrative procedures and centralized control (Society for the Promotion of Goodness and Justice). Its immediate goal was to maintain the *Measef*; its larger aim was to found new schools, establish alternative institutions to finance the maskilim, and use the Berlin Free School press to publish additional maskilic works. This grand vision of an institutionalized Haskalah enjoyed only fleeting success (especially in 1788–90). It quickly succumbed to financial problems: the journal and society closed in 1797. The journal's enduring significance was its attempt to develop a Hebrew-language public sphere.[137]

In the late 1780s and early 1790s, the alliance of masklim and mercantile elite effectively ended. The *Measef* version of Haskalah became one cultural alternative among others, and one progressively more difficult to fund. New figures repudiated the early Haskalah vision of cultural renewal, replacing it with secular knowledge, especially the ideal of *Bildung* (self-cultivation). They advocated reforming the Jews and Judaism to gain emancipation, exceeding the mercantilist criterion of utility to formulate a contract of regeneration for rights.[138]

With the accession of Frederick William II in 1786, David Friedländer, Mendelssohn's disciple and self-appointed successor, began to petition (May 1787) the Prussian government for a fundamental improvement in the Jews' condition. He linked reform to rights in the direct manner that Mendelssohn, but even radical maskilim, had avoided,

---

Michael Meyer, *Response to Modernity: A History of the Reform Movement in Judaism* (New York, 1988), 13–25.

[136] Euchel failed to make this an issue in 1784. See the German appendix to *Measef* (1784), 15. See Samet, "Burying the Dead: On the Controversy over Determining the Time of Death," 423–25; Falk Wiesemann, "Jewish Burials in Germany: Between Tradition, the Enlightenment and the Authorities," *Leo Baeck Institute Yearbook* 37 (1992): 17–31; and Efron, *Medicine and the German Jews*, 95–104.

[137] Tsamriyon, *Ha-Measef*, 48. For the public sphere, see Jürgen Habermas, *The Structural Transformation of the Public Sphere* (Cambridge, MA, 1989).

[138] For the Haskalah's demise, see Feiner, *The Jewish Enlightenment*, 293–363. For the ideology of emancipation in a German-language public sphere see Sorkin, *The Transformation of German Jewry*, 79–104.

while reducing the early Haskalah ideal of cultural renewal to a ves-
tige and emphasizing the Jews' utility to the state.[139]

Similarly, the continuing public controversy over early burial increasingly pitted secular knowledge against Jewish law. Marcus Herz
(1747–1803), a doctor, disseminator of Kantian philosophy, and the first
Jew in Prussia to hold the title of professor of philosophy (1791),
thought medical knowledge took precedence over religious practice
and belief. Early burial "has superstition to thank for its origins and
prejudice for its continuation" and is an obstacle to emancipation. In
the Habsburg lands such practices militated against Joseph II's "divine
work to turn his Jewish subjects into fully formed moral [*gebildeten*]
citizens." Such customs prevented the Jews from gaining the respect
of their "educated" and "moral" neighbors, who should be a model for
emulation.[140]

Finally, mercantile elite families began to request, and one family received, equality, thereby abandoning the community.[141] In contrast,
Mendelssohn's own family was forced to apply to remain in Berlin after his death. His privilege of residence, granted in 1763, was personal
and not transferrable. The family succeeded in receiving a residence
privilege the next year.[142]

Conclusion

Whereas the early Haskalah came to fruition in significant works,
especially Mendelssohn's *Book of the Paths of Peace*, the later Haskalah

---

[139] For Friedländer's memoranda, see *Akten-Stücke, die Reform der Jüdischen Kolonien in
den Preussischen Staaten betreffend* (Berlin, 1793). For his rejection of incremental reform,
28; for textual study, 21; for *Bildung*, 14. For a comparison of his political ideas with Mendelssohn's, see Sorkin, *The Transformation of German Jewry*, 73–78.

[140] *Über die frühe Beerdigung der Juden: An die Herausgeber des hebräischen Sammlers*, 2nd
ed.(Berlin, 1788), 40, 42, 48–49. Herz called his conception "philosophical medicine." See
Martin Davies, *Identity or History? Marcus Herz and the End of the Enlightenment* (Detroit,
1995), 93–117.

[141] Individual Jews gained the "general privilege" of residence from 1760 to 1790. The
Itzigs were the only family to receive the right of hereditary citizenship (1791). See Lowenstein, "Jewish Upper Crust," 185, and idem, *The Berlin Jewish Community*, 69–147. The
daughters of the elite began to experience a startling social integration in salons, which
attracted Berlin's cultural leaders. See Deborah Hertz, *Jewish High Society in Old Regime
Berlin* (New Haven, 1988).

[142] Jacob Jacobson, ed., *Jüdische Trauungen in Berlin, 1759–1813: Mit Ergänzungen für die
Jahre von 1723 bis 1759* (Berlin, 1968), 96. To recognize "the well-known services of her
deceased husband," Fromet Mendelssohn received on March 21, 1787, a General Privilege that carried the rights of a Christian merchant.

failed because it could not retain the mercantile elites' sponsorship. The next chapter examines Habsburg Reform Catholicism, a movement that had some similarities to the Haskalah in renewing neglected intellectual traditions, functioning in Wolff's ambit, and achieving power with the reforming state's sponsorship.

Opposite: Joseph Valentin Eybel (1741–1805). Johann Ernst Mansfeld's engraving of the painting by Andreas Massinger. By permission of the Bildarchiv der Österreichischen Nationalbibliothek.

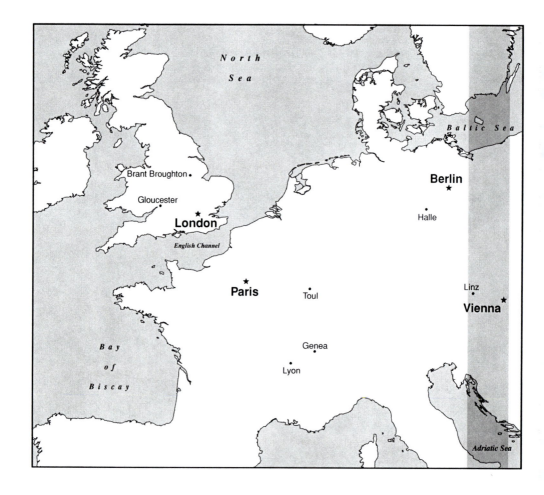

CHAPTER FIVE

Vienna-Linz

Joseph Eybel's "Reasonable Doctrine"

RECONSTITUTING THE HABSBURG MONARCHY AS a centralized, politically defined state was a daunting, indeed, perhaps an insuperable task, but an urgent one after Prussia seized one of the monarchy's wealthiest and most populous territories, Silesia, in 1740. The monarchy was a "a mildly centripetal agglutination of bewilderingly heterogeneous elements," ranging from the southern Netherlands to northern Italy, the Balkans to the Austrian-Bohemian heartland, and consisting of states and provinces, bishoprics and free cities that, ruled by a baffling array of laws, exercised varying degrees of sovereignty.[1] The Austrian and Bohemian lands also belonged to the Holy Roman Empire, whose ruler, by common accord (since 1452), was a Habsburg, except when Maria Theresa (1740–80), by virtue of her sex, was denied the crown—which further safeguarded their independence. The monarchy's subjects prayed at numerous altars—Catholic, Lutheran, Calvinist, Jewish, Greek Orthodox, Uniate—and spoke a staggering number of languages, including German, Italian, Czech, Magyar, Croat, Serbian, Polish, and Yiddish.

Since the sixteenth century, successive Habsburgs had sustained the monarchy with a "confessional absolutism" built on magnate support and Catholic orthodoxy.[2] A militant ideology of imposing visual ceremony and Jesuit education, *Pietas Austriaca*, embodied the Habsburgs' self-understanding as the "Catholic dynasty par excellence," and in the seventeenth century it yielded, at least in Austria and Bohemia, a "record of conversion without parallel in the history of the Counter-Reformation."[3] The process of transforming the monarchy from confessional absolutism to state absolutism and a "state church" vouchsafed Catholicism's reforming currents a crucial role.

Joseph Valentin Eybel (1741–1805), born the same year as Joseph II, has been hailed as the "most important Josephist," and his pamphlet,

---

[1] R.J.W. Evans, *The Making of the Habsburg Monarchy, 1550–1700: An Interpretation* (Oxford, 1970), 447. Cf. T.C.W. Blanning, *Joseph II* (London, 1994), 35.

[2] Charles Ingrao, *The Habsburg Monarchy, 1618–1815*, 2nd ed. (Cambridge, 2000), 101. Cf. P.G.M. Dickson, *Finance and Government under Maria Theresa, 1740–1780*, 2 vols. (Oxford, 1987), 1:297–98. For "confessional absolutism," see Eduard Winter, *Frühaufklärung: Der Kampf gegen den Konfessionalismus in Mittel- und Osteuropa and die deutsch-slawische Begegnung* (Berlin, 1966), 107–49.

[3] Anna Coreth, *Pietas Austriaca*, trans. William D. Bowman and Anna Maria Leitgeb (West Lafayette, 2004), 13; Ingrao, *The Habsburg Monarchy*, 39.

What Is the Pope (1782), has been called "the most famous and typical of all journalistic publications of the Josephist decade."[4] First a professor of canon law and then a civil servant, Eybel used natural law theory to fashion a radical version of reform Catholicism that drew on Gallicanism, Muratori, neo-Jansenism and the ideal of the early church. In the 1780s he played a major role in publicizing issues of church-state reform, implementing Joseph II's policies, and devising a new devotional literature.[5] By all accounts arrogant, inconsiderate, and even brutal, he personified the state's alliance with reform Catholics. Eybel "reflect[ed] the entire spectrum of intellectual conflict of the day" because he endeavored to define and put into practice the prior generation's theoretical reconciliation of Enlightenment and Catholicism.[6]

When Eybel was born, Reform Catholicism was a generation or more old. An effort at a second humanist reform or a "counter-Counter-Reformation," it aimed to alter the post-Tridentine Catholicism that, identified with the Jesuits, consisted of scholasticism in theology, the monarchical papacy in ecclesiology, and in practice the visually impressive Baroque culture of brotherhoods, cults, pilgrimages, and processions.[7] Reform Catholicism offered the intellectual alternatives of Enlightenment science (Copernicus, Newton), philosophy (Leibniz-Wolff, Locke, and eventually Kant), and historical study (scripture, patristics, Church history); the ecclesiology of episcopalism or conciliarism and the idea of toleration; and a new pastoral

---

[4] Manfred Brandl, *Der Kanonist Joseph Valentin Eybel (1741–1805): Sein Beitrag zur Aufklärung in Österreich; Eine Studie in Ideologie* (Steyr, 1976), 146.

[5] Joseph II referred all ecclesiastical matters in Upper Austria to Eybel. See Rudolf Hittmair, *Der Josefinische Klostersturm im Land ob der Enns* (Freiburg im Breisgau, 1907), 57, and Heinrich Ferihumer, *Die kirchliche Gliederung des Landes ob der Enns im Zeitalter Kaiser Josef II.: Haus Österreich und Hochstift Passau in der Zeitspanne von 1771–1792* (Linz, 1952), 70.

[6] Brandl, *Der Kanonist Joseph Valentin Eybel*, 5, 185. Hans Sturmberger, "Zwischen Barock und Romantik: Skizzen zur Geschichte der Aufklärung in Oberösterreich," *Jahrbuch des Oberösterreichischen Musealvereins* 93 (1948): 148–49, 170. Cf. Grete Klingenstein, *Staatsverwaltung und kirchliche Autorität im 18. Jahrhundert: Das Problem der Zensur in der theresianischen Reform* (Vienna, 1970), 97. See also Heinrich Koller, "Joseph Valentin Eybel als Historiker," *Historisches Jahrbuch der Stadt Linz* (1958), 249–64, and Knut Walf, "Der Begriff 'Bischofsamt' bei Joseph Valentin Eybel: Ein Beitrag zur Würdigung der josephinischen Kanonistik," in *Ius Sacrum: Klaus Mörsdorf zum 60. Geburtstag*, ed. Audomar Scheuermann and Georg May (Vienna, 1969), 295–302.

[7] Sebastian Merkle, "Die katholische Beurteilung des Aufklärungszeitalters," in *Sebastian Merkle: Ausgewählte Reden und Aufsätze*, ed. Theobald Freudenberg (Würzburg, 1965), 373; Evans, *Making of the Habsburg Monarchy*, 449; and Richard van Dülmen, *Propst Franziskus Töpsl (1711–1796) und das Augustiner-Chorherrenstift Polling: Ein Beitrag zur Geschichte der katholischen Aufklärung in Bayern* (Kallmünz, 1967), 7.

ideal of reasonable devotion grounded in literacy (vernacular liturgy, Bible reading).[8]

Reform Catholicism's origins were almost exclusively monastic, belonging to that "most spectacular efflorescence of the monasteries" in the south German states and Austria in the late seventeenth and early eighteenth centuries, which included monumental rebuilding and the revival of music and intellectual life.[9] In the Benedictine and Augustinian monasteries large enough to have libraries and scholarly aspirations, some monks began to assimilate aspects of Enlightenment science and philosophy. The results became visible in the 1720s and 1730s in the work of the influential Eusebius Amort (1692–1777), abbot of Pollingen, who discussed Copernicus, only to reject him on scientific grounds; or at a monastery like Saint Emmeram (Regensburg), which adopted a curriculum of science, philosophy, and historical theology; or in Bavaria's first German-language scholarly journal, *Parnassus Boicus*, which appeared in 1722.[10]

Reform Catholics sought intellectual renewal by revising the method of expounding belief rather than belief itself, endeavoring to update early modern scholasticism through contact with the new science

---

[8] Eduard Hegel, *Die katholische Kirche Deutschlands unter dem Einfluß der Aufklärung des 18. Jahrhunderts, Rheinisch-westfälische Akademie der Wissenschaften, Geisteswissenschaften Vorträge* 206 (Opladen, 1975); Bernard Plongeron, "Was ist katholische Aufklärung?" in *Katholische Aufklärung und Josephinismus*, ed. Elisabeth Kovacs (Munich, 1979), 11–56; T.C.W. Blanning, "The Enlightenment in Catholic Germany," in *The Enlightenment in National Context*, ed. Roy Porter and Mikulás Teich (Cambridge, 1981), 118–26; James Van Horn Melton, *Absolutism and the Eighteenth-century Origins of Compulsory Schooling in Prussia and Austria* (Cambridge, 1988), 76–84; W.R. Ward, "Late Jansenism and the Habsburgs," in *Religion and Politics in Enlightenment Europe*, ed. James E. Bradley and Dale K. Van Kley (Notre Dame, IN, 2001), 154–86.

[9] Derek Beales, *Prosperity and Plunder: European Catholic Monasteries in the Age of Revolution, 1650–1815* (Cambridge, 2003), 39–83, quotation at 39.

[10] van Dülmen, *Propst Franziskus Töpsl*, 7, 23–33; J.A. Endres, *Korrespondenz der Mauriner mit den Emmeramern, und Beziehungen der letzteren zu den wissenschaftlichen Bewegungen des 18. Jahrhunderts* (Stuttgart, 1899), 3–11; Georg Heilingsetzer, "Die Benediktiner im 18. Jahrhundert: Wissenschaft und Gelehrsamkeit im süddeutsch-österreichischen Raum," in *Katholische Aufklärung-Aufklärung in Katholischen Deutschland*, ed. Harm Klueting, Norbert Hinske and Karl Hengst (Hamburg, 1993) 208–24. Scholars since the 1970s have emphasized Reform Catholicism's indigeneousness. See Klingenstein, *Staatsverwaltung und kirchliche Autorität*, 99–129, and Blanning, *Joseph II*, 44. For historiographical reviews, see Peter Hersche, "Neue Literatur zur katholischen Aufklärung," *Internationale kirchliche Zeitschrift* 62 (1972): 115–28; Harm Klueting, " 'Der Genius der Zeit hat sie unbrauchbar gemacht': Zum Thema Katholische Aufklärung, oder, Aufklärung und Katholizismus im Deutschland des 18. Jahrhunderts. Eine Einleitung," in Klueting, ed., *Katholische Aufklärung*, 1–35; and Hans Maier, "Die Katholiken und die Aufklärung: Ein Gang durch die Forschungsgeschichte," in ibid., 40–53.

(Franziskus Töpsl, 1711–96) or historical study (Martin Gerbert, 1723–93).[11] Addressing a narrow audience in Latin, Reform Catholics were unified by opposition to the Jesuits, whose curriculum (*ratio Studiorum*, 1599), virtual monopoly on education, and promotion of Baroque piety incarnated the Counter-Reformation. Until the order's abolition (1773), anti-Jesuitism was reform Catholics' rallying cry and link to lay Catholic enlighteners.[12]

A number of intellectual developments within the Church inspired Reform Catholicism. Jansenism, the Augustinian revival that promoted ideas of grace, free will, and morality at odds with the Jesuits' and entered the German-speaking lands through numerous routes (personal correspondence, translation, the Collegium Germanicum in Rome—the training ground for the German clerical elite) had a better reception here than in France. Whereas the Bourbons endeavored to suppress it (we will explore the consequences vis-à-vis Adrien Lamourette), the Habsburg monarchy unofficially adopted it.[13] The French Benedictines of Saint Maur devoted themselves to historical scholarship, with Dom Jean Mabillon (1632–1707), its paragon, showing how monastic life could serve it. Maurist historical scholarship provided German Benedictines with a means to renew, or displace, scholasticism.[14]

[11] For Töpsl ("theology without experimental science is blind; and science's most intimate sister is mathematics") see van Dülmen, *Propst Franziskus Töpsl*, 169. For the distinction between belief (*Lehrsätze*) and method (*Lehrmethode*), see Merkle, "Die katholische Beurteilung," 361–62. On late scholasticism, especially Francisco Suarez (1548–1617), see Karl Eschweiler, "Die Philosophie der spanischen Spätscholastik auf den deutschen Universitäten der siebzehnten Jahrhunderts," in *Gesammelte Aufsätze zur kulturgeschichte Spaniens*, vol. 1, *Spanische Forschungen der Görresgesellschaft* (1928), 251–325; Bernard Jansen, "Die Pflege der Philosophie im Jesuitenorden während des 17./18. Jahrhunderts," *Philosophisches Jahrbuch* 51 (1938): 172–215. On renewing scholasticism, see Karl Werner, *Geschichte der katholischen Theologie: Seit dem Trienter Concil bis zur Gegenwart* (Munich, 1866), 179ff.

[12] Heribert Raab, "Die 'katholische Ideenrevolution' des 18. Jahrhunderts: Der Einbruch der Geschichte in die Kanonistik und Auswirkungen in Kirche und Reich bis zum Emser Kongress," in *Katholische Aufklärung*, 104–18; Richard van Dülmen, "Anti-Jesuitismus und katholische Aufklärung in Deutschland," *Historisches Jahrbuch* 89 (1969): 52–80.

[13] Peter Hersche, *Der Spätjansenismus in Österreich* (Vienna, 1977), and Blanning, "The Enlightenment in Catholic Germany," 120.

[14] David Knowles, "Great Historical Enterprises: The Maurists," *Transactions of the Royal Historical Society*, 5th series, vol. 9 (1959), 169–87; Mme. Laurain-Portemer, "Les travaux d'erudition des Mauristes: Origine et évolution," *Revue d'Histoire de l'Eglise de France* (1957): 231–72; Manfred Weitlauff, "Die Mauriner und ihr historisches Werk," in *Historische Kritik in der Theologie: Beiträge zu ihrer Geschichte*, ed. George Schwaiger (Göttingen, 1980), 153–209. On Mabillon, see David Knowles, "Jean Mabillon," *Journal of Ecclesiastical History* 10 (1959): 153–73. For examples, see Ildefons Stegmann, *Anselm Desing, Abt von Ensdorf (1699–1772): Ein Beitrag zur Geschichte der Aufklärung in Bayern,*

Lodovico-Antonio Muratori (1672–1750), also under Maurist influence, provided another example of imposing historical scholarship, as well as alternative models of charity, church governance, and devotion (emphasizing literacy, liturgy, and pastoral care).[15] Finally, the Gallican Articles(1682) offered a recipe for a state church in a Rome, governed by a general council (the conciliarist ideal), that respected the French Church's liberties.[16]

At the time of Eybel's birth, reform Catholicism was starting to reshape institutions. At Salzburg, the sole Benedictine university, a small yet highly influential group founded a Muratori study circle (1739–42). Their efforts encouraged other Reform Catholics to introduce a new university curriculum (1741; Thomism, Church fathers, and Church history à la the Maurists, science and mathematics à la Wolff), which, by mid-century, after a decade of interruptions and reversals, made Salzburg the premier university in German-speaking Catholic Europe.[17] At Innsbruck, a similar private circle, the Academia Taxiana, studied Muratori's historical works and the exegetical means to reconcile Copernicus with scripture. The circle included Paul Joseph Riegger (1705–75), the first professor to teach natural law at a Habsburg university (1733), and Christoph Anton Migazzi (1714–1803), the future cardinal of Vienna. At Olmütz, Moravia, the monarchy's first royally chartered academy (1747) dedicated itself to promoting the German

---

Studien und Mitteilungen zur Geschichte der Benediktiner-Ordens und seiner Zweige, Ergänzungsheft 4 (Munich, 1929), 177–78, 231; and Ludwig Hammermayer, "Zum 'deutschen Maurinismus' des frühen 18. Jahrhunderts," *Zeitschrift für bayerische Landesgeschichte* 40, nos. 2–3 (1977): 391–444.

[15] Eleonore Zlabinger, *Lodovico Antonio Muratori und Österreich, Veröffentlichungen der Universität Innsbruck* 53 (Innsbruck, 1970); Adam Wandruszka, "Der Reformkatholizismus des 18. Jahrhunderts in Italien und in Österreich," in *Festschrift Hermann Wiesflecker zum sechzigsten Geburtstag,* ed. Alexander Novotny and Othmar Pickl (Graz, 1973), 231–40; Elisabeth Garms-Cornides, "Zwischen Giannone, Muratori und Metastasio: Die Italiener im geistigen Leben Wiens," in *Formen der europäischen Aufklärung: Untersuchungen zur Situation von Christentum, Bildung und Wissenschaft im 18. Jahrhundert,* ed. Friedrich Engel-Janosi, Grete Klingenstein, and Heinrich Lutz (Vienna, 1976), 224–50. A critical study of Muratori in English is a desideratum.

[16] Dale Van Kley, *The Religious Origins of the French Revolution: From Calvin to the Civil Constitution, 1560–1791* (New Haven, 1996), 191–248; Jotham Parsons, *The Church in the Republic: Gallicanism and Political Ideology in Renaissance France* (Washington, DC, 2004).

[17] See Zlabinger, *Lodovico Antonio Muratori,* 25–39; Hersche, *Der Spätjansenismus,* 50–58; Stegmann, *Anselm Desing,* 200–203, 239; and Ludwig Hammermayer, "Die Aufklärung in Salzburg," in *Geschichte Salzburgs,* ed. Heinz Dopsch (Salzburg, 1988), 2(pt. 1):385–91. Frobenius Forster taught scholasticism and Wolff at Salzburg (1745–47). See Joseph Anton Endres, *Frobenius Forster, Fürstabt von St. Emmeram in Regensburg: Ein Beitrag zur Litteratur- und Ordensgeschichte des 18. Jhr, Strassburger Theologische Studien* 4 (Freiburg im Breisgau, 1900), 10–18.

language and historical research. Muratori was a corresponding member.[18]

At the same time, Maria Theresa, impelled by Prussia's conquest of Silesia, initiated a sweeping overhaul of the monarchy that eventually employed Reform Catholicism. The monarchy's enlistment of this indigenous religious movement, which lasted half a century and shaped Eybel's career, was not opportunistic. Maria Theresa and many of her highest officials, lay and clerical, genuinely adhered to versions of Reform Catholicism. In fact, "in Maria Theresa the convergence of Reform Catholicism and the [drive for a] state church reached their high point."[19]

Maria Theresa began the first wave of reforms (1742–56), "recasting the central administration" and undertaking the "most dramatic fiscal reform in Austrian history" to guarantee the funds to wage war to recapture Silesia.[20] She initiated cultural reforms in the 1750s to strengthen the monarchy by drawing on Reform Catholic ideas and personnel.[21] She established a new secondary school, the Theresianum, in Vienna, to train the nobility for state service (1746) as well as Military (Wiener Neustadt, 1751) and Engineering Academies (Savoyard Ritterakademie, Vienna).

Maria Theresa's restructuring of censorship in the years 1751–59 epitomized her emerging alliance with Reform Catholicism. She subjected censorship to more direct state control by shifting authority among competing religious entities. By abolishing the University of Vienna's corporate privilege over censorship, she effectively excluded the Jesuits. By restoring the episcopal prerogative to oversee theological works, she handed that function to the reforming archbishop of Vienna, Johann Josef Graf Trautson (1704–57; in office 1751–57). To censor works in history and politics, she created a mixed board comprising four lay and three clerical members and assigned belles lettres,

[18] Zlabinger, *Lodovico Antonio Muratori*, 40–61. On Innsbruck, see Eckhart Seifert, *Paul Joseph Riegger (1705–1775): Ein Beitrag zur theoretischen Grundlegung des josephinischen Staatskirchenrechts* (Berlin, 1973), 114–19.

[19] Hersche, *Der Spätjansenismus* 388; cf. 148–62. Zlabinger, *Lodovico Antonio Muratori*, 105–10. On Maria Theresa and Joseph II, see Derek Beales, *Joseph II: In the Shadow of Maria Theresa, 1741–1780*, vol. 1 (Cambridge, 1987). For van Swieten, see Erna Lesky and Adam Wandruszka, eds., *Gerard Van Swieten und seine Zeit* (Vienna, 1973). For Migazzi, see Peter Hersche, "Erzbischof Migazzi und die Anfänge der jansenistischen Bewegung in Wien," *Mitteilungen des Österreichischen Staatsarchivs* 24 (1971): 280–309. For Kaunitz, see Franz A. J. Szabo, *Kaunitz and Enlightened Absolutism, 1753–80* (Cambridge, 1994).

[20] Charles Ingrao, *The Habsburg Monarchy, 1618–1815*, 2nd ed. (Cambridge, 2000), 160–61.

[21] Klingenstein, *Staatsverwaltung und kirchliche Autorität*, 85. For economic reforms see Ingrao, *The Habsburg Monarchy, 1618–1815*, 167–68.

philosophy, and medicine to her advisor and personal physician, Gerard van Swieten (1700–1772), in his capacity as prefect of the Court Library. Van Swieten directed this carefully calibrated policy to empower like-minded lay and Reform Catholic figures.[22]

University reform, during the years 1749–60, accompanied reform of censorship. Van Swieten led, beginning with the medical faculty, where he was a professor: he wanted to expel the faculty whose obsolete knowledge and teaching methods were driving students abroad. On January 17, 1749, he had the empress rather than the Consistory name professors, ended the faculty's corporate status, and appointed himself director.[23]

Abrogating corporate status was used to bring other faculties under state administration. The Philosophical Faculty's reform on June 21, 1752, ended the reliance on Aristotelian philosophy and proofs from scripture, thus making way for Wolff's philosophy. The Law Faculty, reformed in April–May 1753, placed natural law at the center: Riegger was appointed to teach van Espen and other Gallican theorists. The reform shifted authority to a Reform Catholic, in this case the archbishop of Vienna, Trautson, who in June 1752 became Protector of the Philosophical and Theology Faculties, and then of the entire university in November 1752.

After Trautson's death in 1757, the office of protector lapsed and was replaced by a Royal Academic Commission (Studienhofcommission, 1760), co-chaired by van Swieten and Archbishop Migazzi, from the Innsbruck study circle, and staffed with reformers. The monarchy ended the university's corporate status and assumed control of its finances, thereby making it a state organ free from Church influence. The commission deposed the Jesuit directors of the Theology and Philosophy Faculties in 1759, prohibited the teaching of Jesuit moral theology ("probabilism"), and put its own members in charge. Thomists and Augustinians were appointed to teach dogmatics alongside Jesuits.[24]

Religious reforms were also integral to Maria Theresa's agenda. The immediate impetus, the continuing existence of crypto-Protestants in the hereditary lands, highlighted the Counter-Reformation's failed mission and the need for improved pastoral care. Maria Theresa's ministers developed plans for a "fundamental and comprehensive reordering of pastoral organization and a new division of church income in the Austrian hereditary lands" that Joseph II's reforms

---

[22] Klingenstein, *Staatsverwaltung und kirchliche Autorität*, 158–202.

[23] Rudolf Kink, *Geschichte der kaiserlichen Universität zu Wien*, 3 vols. (Vienna, 1854) (photomechanical reproduction, Frankfurt, 1969), 1:443–57.

[24] Ibid., 1:458–96.

would largely realize, since, following Kaunitz's counsel, Maria Theresa was committed to securing papal approval for reforms and opened negotiations with Pope Benedict XIV.[25] Himself a reformer, Benedict inspired a figure such as Cardinal Migazzi, who, in Rome during Benedict's heyday, felt he was promoting papal policy in advocating reforms (1757). The pope's reforms were, however, highly circumscribed. Maria Theresa's negotiations yielded concessions on minor issues, such as a reduction in holy days in 1751, guaranteeing the right of asylum in 1752, and approving processions in 1756, but left unresolved major issues, such as control of Church property, taxation, and admission to monastic orders. Her famous marginal note captured the situation: "The matter is to be tabled for now but not forever."[26]

Eybel passed his childhood and adolescence during Maria Theresa's first wave of reform. Born into a bourgeois family in Vienna, he received a humanist education and decided to enter the priesthood. He studied with the Jesuits, concentrating on philosophy, Greek, and Hebrew; like many other Reform Catholics, he later turned on his teachers. He apparently received no systematic training in theology. He then changed his mind and secured a release from his vows. In 1765 he accepted an entry-level post in the state bureaucracy in Graz but soon returned to Vienna to study at the university. Here he benefited from the earlier curriculum reform. He came under the influence of Joseph von Sonnenfels' cameralist theories and Karl Anton von Martini's natural law doctrines.[27] After unsuccessfully applying for chairs in Politics and Economics (Polizei und Kameralwissenschaft) at the University of Graz and the University of Klagenfurt, Eybel turned to law. He studied with Paul Joseph von Riegger, a member of the Innsbruck circle and the first exponent of natural law at an Austrian university, who was called to Vienna in 1749 to a post at the Savoyard Ritterakademie and appointed professor of Church law in the reconstituted Law Faculty at the university in 1753, marking the permanent

[25] Rudolf Reinhardt, "Zur Kirchenreform in Österreich unter Maria Theresa," Zeitschrift für Kirchengeschichte 77 (1966): 105.

[26] Klingenstein, Staatsverwaltung und kirchliche Autorität, 118–21; Hersche, "Erzbischof Migazzi"; Szabo, Kaunitz and Enlightened Absolutism, 216, cf. 209–47. In contrast to Kaunitz, Haugwitz wished to implement the reforms unilaterally. Cf. Ernst Tomek, Kirchengeschichte Österreichs, 3 vols. (Innsbruck, 1959), 3:220–31, 285–303, and C. A. Macartney, Maria Theresa and the House of Austria (London, 1969), 76–77.

[27] Martini, a student of Riegger's, has been called the "prophet of the German natural law school in Austria." See Hans von Voltelini, "Die naturrechtlichen Lehren und die Reformen des 18. Jahrhunderts," Historische Zeitschrift 105 (1910): 70.

transfer of canon law from Theology to Law. As Riegger's protégé and designated successor, Eybel began to teach in 1772, enjoying considerable success. After an adept dissertation defense on April 30, 1773, and Riegger's retirement the next day, May 1, Eybel was named an extraordinary professor of Church law. In 1778 he was promoted to ordinary professor of Church law.[28] He became a prominent representative of Reform Catholicism during Maria Theresa's second wave of reforms.

Maria Theresa's second wave of reforms—once again driven by wartime failures, in particular the Seven Years War, from 1756 to 1763, became characteristic of the co-regency when, following her husband's death in 1765, she elevated Joseph to fellow ruler. For the next fifteen years Joseph joined her and Kaunitz in a triumvirate. Kaunitz produced a wave of reforms, aimed at centralizing governance and increasing revenue, that built on the earlier wave, yet with a difference. The first wave of reforms were manifestations of "traditional Habsburg aristocratic absolutism." The second reforms were more bureaucratic, drawing on the better trained and more numerous personnel issuing from first wave institutions.[29]

Eybel belonged among the radical Reform Catholics who appeared during the second reform wave. They were more radical in part because of the Gallican ideal. The liberties that the Gallican Church had won from Rome in the previous century represented the great prize of a "state church."[30] This ideal permeated Habsburg Reform Catholicism in consequence of Kaunitz's diplomatic revolution of aligning with France in 1756. While the claim to these liberties was not peculiar to France, the Gallican Articles of 1682 were a compelling formulation supported by substantial scholarship (Bossuet, de Marca, Fleury).

There were two additional radicalizing factors. A conservative pope (Clement XIII; 1758–69) who sympathized with the Jesuits and opposed Reform Catholicism's mounting "Gallicanism" aroused anticurialism. Under the pseudonym of Febronius, Johann Nikolaus von Hontheim (1701–90; suffragan bishop of Trier) published a tract that came to symbolize episcopalist opposition to a monarchical papacy, or "Febronianism". The book incited a storm of protest and in 1764 was placed on the Index. In addition, the Jesuits' abrogation in 1773 ended the Reform

[28] Brandl, *Der Kanonist Joseph Valentin Eybel*, 19–21, 40.

[29] Ingrao, *The Habsburg Monarchy*, 184–92.

[30] Klingenstein, *Staatsverwaltung und kirchliche Autorität*, 65–66; Brandl, *Der Kanonist Joseph Valentin Eybel*, 93, 177.

Catholics' and lay reformers' united front, revealing the deep fissure separating moderates from radicals.[31]

Radicalization entailed polarization. Cardinal Migazzi, a "philo-Jansenist," followed Pope Clement XIII and became increasingly conservative in the 1760s, which was evident, for example, in the Censorship Board. After van Swieten's death in 1772, Maria Theresa and bureaucrats under Migazzi's sway increasingly ran the board, and Vienna's Index became thicker than Rome's.[32]

Religious reform also picked up in the 1770s. Kaunitz's policy of negotiated reform held for some fifteen years, from 1753 to 1768, resulting in the cooperation with Rome and reform-minded clergy that marked moderate Reform Catholicism's palmy days. In the face of Pope Clement XIII's intransigence and the success of Milan's reforms, Kaunitz embraced unilateralism (1768).[33] A newly created commission to regulate ecclesiastical matters (Consessus in publico-ecclesiasticis, 1769), which represented a high point of cameralism and philo-Jansenism, revived and extended (1770–71) Haugwitz's reforms. The commission restricted pilgrimages and processions (1769) but notably the monastic orders, raising the age of initial oaths to twenty-one, that of final vows to 24, and capping donations on entrance to a monastery— all of which occurred in October 1770 to January 1771. The co-regency also participated in abolishing the Jesuits, insisting, in keeping with a "state church," that Jesuit property revert to the state and not the papacy.[34]

Another important development was Stephan Rautenstrauch's (1734–85) reform of seminary education (1774), demoting scholastic speculation. He introduced a curriculum of Bible, Church history, patristics, and theological literature as preparation for theoretical or systematic theology, which in turn served as the basis for pastoral care (Seelsorge). Rautenstrauch's acknowledged aim of educating "not only good Christians but good citizens for the state" expressed

[31] On the state of the Church and the lawful power of the Pope, written to reunite Christians who differ in Religion (1763). On Febronius, see Raab, "Die 'katholische Ideenrevolution' des 18. Jahrhunderts," 111–18. On splintering among anti-Jesuits, see van Dülmen, "Anti-Jesuitismus und katholische Aufklärung in Deutschland," 66–80.

[32] Hersche, "Erzbischof Migazzi," T. J. Hochstrasser, "Cardinal Migazzi and Reform Catholicism in the Eighteenth-Century Habsburg Monarchy," in Catholicism and Austrian Culture, Austrian Studies 10, ed. Ritchie Robertson and Judith Beniston (Edinburgh, 1999), 16–31. On censorship, see Klingenstein, Staatsverwaltung und kirchliche Autorität, 196–202.

[33] Szabo, Kaunitz and Enlightened Absolutism, 222–23; Blanning, Joseph II, 46.

[34] Ingrao, The Habsburg Monarchy, 188.

his twin commitments to Reform Catholicism and enlightened absolutism.[35]

These reforms aroused conflict in the ruling triumvirate. Maria Theresa grew increasingly conservative and hesitant after about 1773; Kaunitz and Joseph often forced through reforms against her will.[36]

Energetically promoting views at the radical end of the second reform wave, Eybel quickly provoked Archbishop Migazzi's ire. While Eybel's first years of teaching and publication (1773–75) passed without notice, two subsequent incidents did not. One of Eybel's students, a priest, presented two theses on the Church's power over marriage law drawn from Van Espen, which Eybel then submitted to the university (1775–77). Migazzi strenuously objected to the ideas as heretical and Protestant. Maria Theresa reproached the student and ordered Eybel to "put his teaching in order and make it correct."[37] The priest then audaciously delivered a sermon summarizing his theses. His superior required a public retraction and suspended him from preaching and hearing confession.

Eybel boldly wrote to Maria Theresa that he was disappointed by the lack of freedom to examine ideas in the Church:

I had every cause to be fully consoled and to hope that, whereas some people no longer give to the Church and its pronouncements the honor and submission they deserve, nonetheless your Majesty's highest esteem and most enviable justice would more than suffice to provide adequate restraints for the unfettered freedom to think and in general to examine erroneous and inauthentic doctrines. Unfortunately it is now clear and only too true that the obedience and submission due to the sovereign are themselves in danger as soon as one once defies the Church.[38]

Pressing his case, Eybel republished the work of another priest holding similar views on marriage law. Migazzi now denounced Eybel to Maria Theresa for espousing radical ideas that threatened "dogmas of belief and morality."[39]

[35] Josef Müller, "Zu den theologiegeschichtlichen Grundlagen der Studienreform Rautenstrauches," *Tübinger Theologische Quartalschrift* 146 (1966): 62–97.

[36] Macartney, *Maria Theresa*, 148.

[37] Cölestin Wolfsgruber, *Christoph Anton Kardinal Migazzi: Fürsterzbischof von Wien. Eine Monographie und zugleich ein Beitrag zur Geschichte des Josephinismus*, 2nd ed. (Ravensburg, 1897), 349. The student was Father Dionys Kaltner. For Eybel's early publications, see Koller, "Joseph Valentin Eybel als Historiker," 251.

[38] Quoted in Wolfsgruber, *Christoph Anton Kardinal Migazzi*, 353.

[39] Ibid., 353–55.

At the same time, the state had to decide whether to reapprove Riegger's church law textbook for the university and schools. The situation swiftly grew complicated. Maria Theresa commissioned a rewrite, another group at court opposed this revised edition, and Eybel pushed for official approval of his own book.

On the grounds that Riegger's book was out of print, Eybel assigned students his own textbook (*Introductio*). Eybel had incensed Migazzi by restoring passages that the cardinal, in his capacity as censor, had asked him to delete. Migazzi attacked Eybel's volumes in a letter to Maria Theresa; she now had second thoughts. While persuaded to allow him to use the books for the rest of the academic year, she appointed a commission to evaluate them (October 1778–February 1789). The commission divided: Migazzi attacked the book for advocating excessive state control of the Church, while the civil servant in charge of ecclesiastical affairs, Franz Joseph von Heinke, vehemently defended such control. Migazzi implored Maria Theresa to release Eybel from his professorship.

In March 1779, Maria Theresa finally decided to endorse Riegger's unrevised textbook. Sensitive to royal displeasure, Eybel asked to be relieved of his teaching post and appointed to a civil service position, choosing Linz. Had Eybel managed to remain in his professorship until Joseph came to power, in December 1780, he may have found the wind at his back.[40]

Church Law

Eybel's understanding of Church law typified Reform Catholic radicalism during Maria Theresa's second reform wave. The translator of Eybel's multivolume synthesis, *Introduction to Catholic Ecclesiastical Law*, claimed that whereas Riegger introduced the "true principles of church law," Eybel was "founder of a new epoch."[41] The inflated rhetoric aside, the translator pinpointed a fundamental difference between teacher and student.

Riegger, who studied in Freiburg and Leiden (the Dutch connection), pioneered natural law theory in the Habsburg monarchy. While he has

[40] Ibid., 337–84; Seifert, *Paul Joseph Riegger*, 173–83; Brandl, *Der Kanonist Joseph Valentin Eybel*, 22–23, 52–53; Sturmberger, "Zwischen Barock und Romantik," 166. For Heinke see Hersche, *Der Spätjansenismus*, 224–25; Szabo, *Kaunitz and Enlightened Absolutism*, 226.

[41] Joseph Valentin Eybel, *Einleitung in das katholische Kirchenrecht: Aus dem lateinischen des Herrn Verfassers übersetzt*, 4 vols. (Frankfurt and Leipzig, 1779–82), 1:ix–xi. Latin: *Introductio in Jus ecclesiasticum Catholicorum*, 4 vols. (Vienna, 1777).

been characterized as "the father of Josephism," he was in fact Maria Theresa's favorite canon lawyer, sharing her public moderation.[42] Riegger derived his ideas from the Gallican tradition (van Espen, de Marca, Fleury) and the Protestant theological Enlightenment (Pfaff, Budde), his methods from the natural law theory of Christian Wolff (whom he understood to be "confessionally neutral"). In ecclesiology he was an advocate of state power, a regalist, in natural law theory a moderate territorialist who recognized the Church's independent standing and authority. He used natural law to affirm the status quo: with the one exception of marriage law, he formulated static categories.[43] In the confidential memoranda he wrote for Maria Theresa, in contrast, he explicitly advocated reforms.[44]

Eybel was the quintessential public reformer: he treated natural law doctrines as warrants for change. In Joseph II's spirit he boldly envisioned the creation of a "state church" that would renounce its corporate characteristics and wield authority on the basis of revelation, natural law, and the commonweal. In addition, Eybel was rhetorically aggressive, writing in a *parti pris* spirit critical of the Papacy. This belligerence separated him from Riegger and cost him Maria Theresa's goodwill.[45]

Eybel blurred the fundamental difference between himself and his teacher, writing that Riegger's disclosure of Isidore's "false decretals" (ninth century, justifying the extension of papal power) made him a "hero who banned deceitful fallacies from Church law" in order "to restore the golden age of original and pure teachings":

[H]e did not hesitate to present us with a multitude of purified teachings of church law, to penetrate at great risk through prejudices that are frequently repeated and have stood for hundreds of years, and to

[42] Seifert, *Paul Joseph Riegger*, 23. Cf. 195, 218–21. Seifert relied on published works whereas Ferdinand Maass utilized confidential memoranda to Maria Theresa. See *Der Frühjosephinismus* (Vienna, 1969), 79–87.

[43] For Riegger and Wolff, see Seifert, *Paul Joseph Riegger*, 244–45, 279, 318–19, 326. For Wolff's confessional neutrality, 320. For Pfaff, 317. For Riegger's public commitment to the status quo, 333, 340. For Riegger and natural law theory, see Schlaich, *Kollegialtheorie*, 115, and Voltelini, "Die naturrechtlichen Lehren und die Reformen des 18. Jahrhunderts," 70. For regalism and territorialism, see Isnard W. Frank, "Zum spätmittelalterlichen und josephinischen Kirchenverständnis," in *Katholische Aufklärung und Josephinismus*, ed. Elisabeth Kovács (Munich, 1979), 165.

[44] Maass, *Der Frühjosephinismus*, 83–87.

[45] *Einleitung*, 3:41, 46, 329, 4:8. For criticism of the papacy, see 4:41: "the roman court style that shuts the various parties' mouths and so binds the hands of lower judges." For a state church, see Engelbert Plassmann, *Staatskirchenrechtliche Grundgedanken der deutschen Kanonisten an der Wende vom 18. zum 19. Jahrhundert* (Freiburg, 1968), 9–16.

bring to light genuine teachings, free and impartial, from the ancient monuments of the early Church.

Riegger was therefore able to "clarify the dividing lines between the spiritual and temporal powers." In all this Riegger demonstrated "outstanding piety" and a "burning passion" to "assert the necessity of revelation, defend the full scope of our entirely pure religion, recommend the retention of later yet salutary customs, prove a church discipline and defend its prerogative and venerableness."[46]

Eybel similarly portrayed himself as "an old-style Canonist" who was returning to the church law of the early centuries: "See then how far I have departed from the new doctrine of Church law, by which the flagrant sinner Isidore largely forsook age-old Church law, even more, interpolated and invented in regard to this freedom." Eybel aimed to reverse the papacy's usurpations by restoring rightful power to sovereigns and bishops: "All aspects of our church law must necessarily have the stamp of antiquity, in that each one must rest on the ancient fundament, namely, the precise distinction between the powers without dependence." Finally, he portrayed his program as a "reasonable" and fully pious doctrine:

> This reconciles a reasonable doctrine with true piety; this unites the internal salvation of believers with the external welfare of citizens; this has already brought about, and in future will realize, that from day to day a greater harmony will reign between a holy priesthood and a holy state government.[47]

In his *Introduction to Catholic Ecclesiastical Law*, Eybel constantly referred to Riegger, whom he deemed authoritative, and Riegger's student, Karl Anton von Martini. Eybel followed Riegger in relying on Gallican thinkers, such as van Espen, de Marca, Fleury, and Bossuet, as well as Muratori.[48] Between 1774 and 1778 he published translations of

---

[46] *Joseph Valentin Eybels Gesammelte Kleine Schriften*, trans. Wenzel Sigmund Heinze, 2 vols. (Frankfurt & Leipzig, 1781), 1:8, 18, 29.

[47] Ibid., 39–40, 44, 48. For "a reasonable and well-instructed Christian," see *Was ist der Pabst* (Vienna, 1782), 6,; *Was enthalten die Urkunden des christlichen Alterthums von der Ohrenbeichte?* (Vienna, 1784), 13, "every reasonable person"; *Die Heiligen nach den Volksbegriffen*, vol. 1 (Leipzig, 1791), 1:12, a "reasonable person."

[48] For Riegger and Martini, *Einleitung*, 1:108, 154. For Muratori, 1:57, 109; Rautenstrauch, 1:57, 109; van Espen, 1:83, 85, 87, 89, 92, 108, 154; Fleury, 1:108, 144; Petrus de Marca, 123. At 1:124–25 Eybel listed influential ecclesiastical law scholars: van Espen, Böhmer, Barthel, Zallwein, Riegger, Rautenstrauch, Oberhauser, Schrodts, Ickstätt; the Bavarians Lochstein, Pichler, Neuberger; and Febronius. On the Gallican model, see especially 3:90, 141, 151, 264, 276.

sixteen natural law and Gallican sources (van Espen; Fleury; Benedikt Oberhauser, 1719–28; Antonio Pereira, 1725–97). He also published Reform Catholic pastoral letters (1776–79).[49] In general, Eybel relied on French Catholic and German Protestant scholarship.[50]

In keeping with natural law theory, Eybel presumed reason's autonomy. He posited that laws are derived from nature by means of, and in accord with, reason, and thus it is "the laws of reason [that] teach us about the nature of every society." The study of natural law is thus prior to, and the foundation of, church law, for which its methods of explanation and application are indispensable. Eybel identified Wolff and Montesquieu as exemplars of natural law.[51]

Eybel attached to natural law a typical religious Enlightenment account of belief. He emphasized the "necessity of revelation" because of human nature: "in our state of corruption we can dispense neither with revelation nor the natural light [of reason]." Whatever its powers, reason can neither fathom sin nor achieve atonement and reconciliation with God. Revelation, which "derives its origin from the first and oldest point of human depravity," exceeds reason in teaching the need for grace and the requirements for eternal salvation (*supra rationem*), yet offers nothing contrary to reason or unworthy of God (*contra rationem*). Whereas Judaism gave the Israelites revelation, Christ has given a law for all mankind.[52]

As a "society of men," Christ's church must be consistent with natural law. Eybel asserts "that Christ, aside from what pertains to belief and the sacraments, made no ordinances which are not grounded in natural right"; similarly, revelation confirms man's unchanging natural obligations. In consequence, "in respect to age the first main source of spiritual laws is the law of nature." Yet even those ecclesiastical laws that govern issues that do not derive from nature and reason may not violate them.[53] As God's creations, revealed and natural law cannot conflict.

Riegger had used Wolff's idea that government must promote its subjects' well-being. Eybel similarly argued that Christianity recognizes a sovereign's and state's duty to serve the "well-being of citizens." Eybel's criteria for defining the Church and its relationship to the state

---

[49] For the sixteen books, see Brandl, *Der Kanonist Joseph Valentin Eybel*, 41–44; for the pastoral letters, see 47–48.

[50] *Einleitung*, 1:123–24, 3:90, 141, 151.

[51] Quotation at ibid., 1:59. Cf. 1:109–10, 4:21.

[52] Ibid., 1:5–17.

[53] Ibid., 1:1, 30–31, 57–58.

were, first and foremost, the "well-being of citizens" ("the best of the state"); anything that does not accord with it are "accidental accretions" and subject to abolition. Moreover, not only must laws derived from scripture agree with natural law, but scholars must apply "natural law scholarship" standards to canon law. In examining papal and other Church decrees, one must distinguish historically between actual church law and the "accretion" of a particular time. The same standards define the proper boundary between "civic state power" and "spiritual authority."[54]

Eybel focused on the Isidorean decrees as a tissue of "lies that destroy the common welfare," which resulted in "seven long centuries of continuous, horrible ignorance." The "poison of these principles" was to justify the papacy's unprecedented growth.[55] For the first twelve centuries the Church had "no other court of belief . . . than the bishops"; till the twelfth century, the sources refer to the Roman "Church" but never a "court." At that point Rome, through a series of usurpations, commenced creating multiple institutions to control all important Church business: "finally, after coerced limitation of provincial church councils and dreadful attenuation of episcopal power, almost all difficult matters and decisions of dispensations were brought to the Roman seat."[56] The monarchical papacy's presumptions led to views that "find no hearing outside Italy" and often "contradict the correct sense of the Church council's decrees" so that, "our rights have often been severely damaged." Eybel endorsed the Gallican model by contrasting such "ultramontane" decisions with the "genuine principles of the French Church."[57]

Eybel built his theory of church-state relations on Riegger's distinction between the institutions' respective purposes. The Church aims to realize man's internal happiness or salvation while the state pursues man's external happiness or well-being. Using Riegger's formulation, Eybel deemed the institutions "mutually independent" (recalling Warburton's "alliance").[58]

The church's authority and means are entirely spiritual; it neither needs nor should use other forms of power. It can "instruct, request,

---

[54] Ibid., 1: 54–61. Riegger and Eybel rejected the mathematical model. For Eybel, see ibid., 1:161–62. Eybel did mention "mathematical certainty" in deriving conclusions from basic principles. See 2:106, 251. For Riegger, see Seifert, *Paul Joseph Riegger*, 302, 326.

[55] *Einleitung*, 1:72–73, 115.

[56] Ibid., 1:96–97.

[57] Ibid., 1:86, 88, 94. Cf. 2:93, 153.

[58] Ibid., 2:16. For Riegger, see Seifert, *Paul Joseph Riegger*, 246–50.

admonish;" it can offer "holy love, steadfast patience, and insurmountable trust in God." The church cannot conflict with the state's pursuit of "external happiness": "The superiors of the church cannot enact ordinances contrary to the natural and revealed divine laws and thus also contrary to the well-being of states." The church's exercise of spiritual power should never have "civil consequences": in keeping with the collegiants, Eybel renounced the major ban. "Christ gave his Church power over sins, oaths and all other types of actions only for the court of conscience, but not for the public court with civil consequences and results."[59]

Riegger had attacked Bellarmine's ultramontane contention that, since temporal power derives from the Church, the Pope can depose a sovereign. Eybel reiterated that attack, asserting that the Church's only authority is spiritual: should a Catholic sovereign err, the Church's only recourse is to treat him as a "pagan" and a "publican." He also invoked history: Pope Hildebrand's wielding the sword against temporal powers and Pope Gregory VII's treatment of Henry IV at Canossa in 1077 were equally reprehensible. The Church's claim to power over rulers is "a chimera of the newer canonists."[60]

Eybel's account of the state's powers brought his reform Catholic agenda to the fore. In pursuit of "external happiness" the sovereign should promote belief and reinforce spiritual laws. Councils are the best means: provincial Church councils, by virtue of "gather[ing] the dispersed voices of bishops," effectively prevent "the introduction of teachings that disturb the peace and the best of the state under the false pretense of religion." The ruler can also end theological controversies, especially pointless scholastic ones. He lauded Maria Theresa and Stephan Rautenstrauch: "The ruler has the right and the duty to extirpate empty academic questions—which are without any utility for religion, true scholarship and the state—and continue to occupy the majority of scholastics; just as our most eminent Monarch has exercised this very right, to her immortal honor, by acting according to the theological curriculum proposed by the most esteemed Abbot Stephan Rautenstrauch." In addition, the ruler can prohibit pernicious books, either those that express "contempt for and criticism of our religion" or those that disseminate false ideas dangerous for the soul. He deemed anticlerical, "heterodox" works worse than heretical ones.[61]

[59] Einleitung, 2:98, 25, 104, 194, 95–104.
[60] Ibid., 2:34–53, 90–95. For Riegger, see Seifert, Paul Joseph Riegger, 251–52.
[61] Einleitung, 2:111–12, 129–30, 134–36.

A ruler's most extreme measure is to refuse toleration. Toleration, derived from state law, is in the state's best interest since it prevents the loss of valuable subjects. The Church cannot keep the sovereign from granting free practice to dissenting religions. In support of toleration, Eybel cited Protestant thinkers such as Budde and Wolff. The Jews, for example, must convert willingly, without coercion. Like other religious enlighteners, Eybel limited toleration. He desired religious uniformity: "The best means to realize uniformity is to invite those in error to unification through the sight of the good shepherd and his flock." Moreover, the ruler should deny toleration to those who, by contesting the true religion, disturb both religion and state. Indeed, punishing such individuals does not violate freedom of conscience, which does not include the right to mislead others. In accord with the Peace of Westphalia, Eybel affirms the ruler's right to exile, relocate, or expel pernicious individuals and groups and to institute a hierarchy of religious practice (public, private, domestic).[62]

Eybel's mandate for reform emerges in explaining the sovereign's absolute duty to abolish any "accidental" practices, "accretions and devotional trivialities" that are "injurious to the state." The ruler is to exercise discretion to abolish "irritating retailing and selling of spiritual objects, church ordinances or even loans, unreasonable denials of reasonable dispensations or useful permissions, as well as other abuses" and in addition "to set limits to arbitrary devotions and excessive holidays," including "processions, pilgrimages, brotherhoods." Both Church councils and popes (Urban VIII, 1642) had recognized that excessive holy days and pilgrimages injure the economy. Eybel also expressed reform Catholics' characteristic sense of inferiority vis-à-vis Protestants: with fewer holy days, Protestants have more income, take better care of their families, and donate more to charity.[63]

Eybel's conception of Church government complemented his view of the sovereign's enhanced power. He was an Episcopalist and a conciliarist. He founded Church government on the principle of the bishops' independent authority that had its supreme expression in a general council. While he recognized the Pope's priority and special preroga-

---

[62] Ibid., 2:84–85; 131–33, 187–90. Riegger's natural law theory laid the groundwork for freedom of conscience and toleration. See Charles O'Brien, *Ideas of Religious Toleration at the Time of Joseph II: A Study of the Enlightenment among Catholics in Austria, Transactions of the American Philosophical Society* n.s. 59, 7. (Philadelphia, 1969), 16.

[63] *Einleitung,* 2:104, 113–15. Cf. 2:97. Riegger also assigned the state the *"res mixtae"* (number of holy days, pilgrimages, processions, monastic orders). See Seifert, *Paul Joseph Riegger,* 259–60.

tives, he opposed papal monarchy. The desire to limit papal power, shared by Febronius, neo-Jansenists, and Gallicans, was integral to creating a state church.[64]

Eybel believed bishops and priests had their authority directly from God.[65] The bishops are the "supreme shepherds" of their diocese and are to use all required means to rule it. In fact, "no human freedom can infringe on the authority of a bishop's rights which God not just gave him but in fact imposed as an obligation."[66] Bishops, who must also be priests, "have at all times . . . the sole power to grant ordination," and to choose able subordinates to administer the diocese.[67] Monasteries should be under the bishop's jurisdiction; there are no legitimate grounds for placing them under direct papal control. Bishops should know their diocese through constant visitation and must prohibit "pluralities" (a priest holding multiple benefices), which leave some priests destitute and impair the cure of souls.[68]

That recent popes have severely encroached on episcopal power does not legitimate papal monarchy: practice does not establish rights.[69] Rather, the pope is endowed with the prerogatives of "priority in dignity and power" and "priority in care of the entire Church"—that is, maintaining unity. However, "such priority is not incompatible with the other bishops' equality of power." The pope is neither an "independent judge" nor a "self-ruler."[70]

Maintaining Church unity, the sole justification of papal authority, vouchsafes numerous legitimate powers. The pope can defer existing laws, for example, so long as "other extant laws and episcopal privileges are not violated." In recent centuries, popes have overreached their authority by usurping such powers as confirming new bishops (fourteenth century); creating new sees, combining old ones, and transferring bishops (an eleventh-century "Isidorean invention"); accepting

[64] For conciliarism, see Francis Oakley, *The Conciliarist Tradition: Constitutionalism in the Catholic Church, 1300–1870* (Oxford, 2003), and Brian Tierney, *Foundations of the Conciliar Theory: The Contributions of the Medieval Canonists from Gratian to the Great Schism* (Cambridge, 1955). For papal power, see Plassmann, *Staatskirchenrechtliche Grundgedanken*, 14–15, and Hersche, *Der Spätjansenismus*.

[65] *Einleitung*, 3:40. Cf. 3:34, 47–8, 255. On Eybel's conciliarism and episcopalism, see Walf, "Der Begriff 'Bischofsamt' bei Joseph Valentin Eybel."

[66] *Einleitung*, 3:254–57.

[67] Ibid., 3:174. Cf. 3:265, 278–79, 315.

[68] Ibid., 3:258–60; 265–66, 300–302.

[69] Ibid., 3:223.

[70] Ibid., 3:32–33, 41, 47–48, 124, 143.

appeals (ninth century); and distributing benefices (previously in the bishops' gift, yet routinely ascribed to the pope).[71]

Ultimate authority rests with "a general council, consisting of bishops from all of Christendom, [that] represents the complete Church of God." Infallibility adheres to the collective Church as embodied in a council: "a general church council is infallible in regard to doctrines of belief and morality necessary to eternal salvation."[72] Moreover, "church councils are the most powerful means to deal with mistaken teachings and the corruptions of Christian discipline."[73] According to scripture and tradition, "a general Church council represents the entire Church . . . receives its authority directly from God . . . all Christians are to obey its pronouncements." Significantly, a General Council can depose a Pope.[74]

In addition to relying on Gallican sources (van Espen, de Marca) and the Gallican model for his Episcopalist, conciliarist views, Eybel defended Febronius by arguing that he did not deny, but rather aimed to define, the Church's infallibility. Eybel took the safe option of softening rather than repudiating *Unigenitus* (1713), the controversial papal bull prohibiting Jansenism: we are to obey it as a papal ordinance, not as an article of faith.[75]

In keeping with Riegger's theory of "mutual independence," Eybel asserted the state's power alongside the bishops' and councils': "No papal or extraordinary ambassadorial right can extend so far that, contrary to natural and revealed divine law, it impairs sovereign prerogative, the well-being of entire states or the original episcopal right and the well-being of individual churches." In civil affairs papal decrees are valid only to the extent that sovereigns accept them.[76]

In his reform Catholic agenda based on natural law, Episcopalism, and conciliariasm, Eybel supplied the blueprint for the state church that Maria Theresa, Kaunitz, and Joseph II considered integral to transforming the Habsburg monarchy into a unified state. In the 1770s, however, Eybel's ideas were a step ahead of the monarchy's public

---

[71] Ibid., 3:202–3, 207, 209–32, 290–91. Riegger also thought bishops alone had the power to award benefices. See Seifert, *Paul Joseph Riegger*, 283.

[72] *Einleitung*, 3:100, 115. On papal infallibility, see 3:77–78. Infallibility "extends only to principles of belief that exceed reason, and the ethical teachings required for salvation." See 2:79. Cf. 2:115–16.

[73] Ibid., 3:268.

[74] Ibid., 3:135, 150. Against Bellarmine's arguments for papal monarchy, see 3:156–60.

[75] For Febronius, ibid., 3:165–66. For the Gallican model, 3:90, 141, 151, 264, 276. For *Unigenitus*, 3:207.

[76] Ibid., quotation at 3:340. Cf. 3:235.

policy. In the 1780s, in contrast, Eybel was in step with Joseph II and played a conspicuous role.

LINZ AND JOSEPH II

Eybel's arrival (1779) as district magistrate (*Landsrat*) in Linz, a major commercial and manufacturing city in Upper Austria, coincided with a new era in the Habsburg monarchy. With Maria Theresa's death, on November 29, 1780, Joseph II succeeded to sole rule and immediately embarked on a comprehensive program of reform at a frantic pace—some seven hundred edicts per year—whose keystone was Church reform. Eybel played so crucial a role in publicly advocating and implementing these reforms that he became thoroughly identified with Josephism. He once asked, "Without Joseph II, where would I be?"[77]

Joseph aimed to realize reform Catholicism's dual agenda of pastoral care, by curtailing Baroque piety and promoting cure of souls, and a state church, by curtailing papal power and promoting episcopal and state power. His program constituted the third series of reforms of the Habsburg monarchy since 1740. He put into practice ideas that dated from Maria Theresa's sole reign and the co-regency, especially those that had been tested in Lombardy. Maria Theresa was "not only the mother of Joseph II but also of Josephism."[78]

The tempo of Joseph's reforms was stunning: within a year he had prohibited publication of papal bulls without his prior approval, placed monasteries under the jurisdiction of local bishops and required them to sever contact with heads of orders abroad, asserted his sovereign right to make all appointments to benefices, abolished the papal delegation handling issues of marriage, and issued edicts extending limited toleration to Protestants and Jews.[79]

[77] Cited in Sturmberger, "Zwischen Barock und Romantik," 170. For Joseph's edicts, see Harm Klueting, "Kaunitz, die Kirche und der Josephinismus: Protestantisches landesherrliches Kirchenregiment, rationaler Territorialismus und theresianisch-josephinisches Staatskirchentum," in *Staatskanzler Wenzel Anton von Kaunitz-Rietberg, 1711–1794; Neue Perspektiven zu Politik und Kultur der europäischen Aufklärung,* ed. Grete Klingenstein and Franz A. J. Szabo (Graz and Estergom, 1996), 170–71. For Maria Theresa's average of 100 edicts per year, see Ingrao, *The Habsburg Monarchy,* 197.

[78] Ferdinand Maass, *Der Frühjosephinismus* (Vienna, 1969), 9. Similarly, Hittmair, *Der Josefinische Klostersturm,* 3: "Maria Theresa . . . was already a Josephist." Cf. Georgine Holzknecht, *Ursprung und Herkunft der Reformideen Kaiser Josefs II. auf kirchlichem Gebiete* (Innsbruck, 1914), 55. On three periods of reform, see Szabo, *Kaunitz and Enlightened Absolutism,* 209–57.

[79] Blanning, *Joseph II,* 92–101. For fiscal constraints, see P.G.M. Dickson, "Joseph II's Reshaping of the Austrian Church," *The Historical Journal* 36, no. 1 (1993): 89–114. For the

By enacting so many laws so quickly and without papal approval, Joseph produced the most radical package of Church reforms eighteenth-century Catholic Europe would see from a sitting monarch. Joseph's reforms were to be surpassed only by revolutionary France's Civil Constitution of the Clergy (1790). Yet we should be careful to define precisely Joseph's radicalness. From the point of view of Reform Catholics and high Habsburg officials, he was implementing predictable plans that had long circulated in Habsburg chancelleries. In contrast, the tempo, scope, and unilateralism were radical. We should avoid the common misconception that his radical policies departed from his mother's conservative ones, so as to capture his true radicalness, his accelerated pace of autocratic rule.[80]

Eybel publicly advocated Joseph's reforms in a series of famous pamphlets. Eybel sharpened his formulations, and in some cases radicalized his positions of the 1770s. In the case of monasticism, Eybel had raised some questions and suggested some minor reforms in the *Introduction to Catholic Ecclesiastical Law*. He had also acknowledged the sovereign's right to reapportion church property to attain "greater utility for the church and promote the welfare of souls."[81]

In contrast, in 1781 he produced one of the best argued and most influential cases for a thoroughgoing reform. *Seven Chapters on Monks* paved the way for Joseph's legislation dissolving monasteries, diverting funds to charity and raising the number of secular clergy devoted to the cure of souls (January 12 and 29, 1782): "my intention is only to show that the contemporary monastic estate is at odds with the principles of the old church discipline and that the sovereigns, according to the oldest church laws, have sufficient cause, authority and duty to abolish them."[82] Eybel employed stock Reform Catholic ideas. He cited the early Church to establish an historical alternative: in the first centuries monks were not priests but merely individuals who wished to retreat from society. Against monastic life he appealed to the higher criterion of "cure of souls": the Church must give priority to the people's need for religious education and pastoral care. "In the future educate not monks but priests for the world and turn the cloisters into priests'

Vienna Archdiocese, see William Bowman, *Priest and Parish in Vienna, 1780–1880* (Boston, 1999).

[80] Derek Beales, "Joseph II and Josephism," in idem, *Enlightenment and Reform in Eighteenth-Century Europe* (London, 2005), 287–308.

[81] *Einleitung*, 2:225. Cf. 4:319–74.

[82] *Sieben Kapitel von Klosterleuten* (Vienna, 1781), 46.

houses."[83] He emphasized the sovereign's authority to implement these changes: to serve the best interests of "religion and state," natural right empowers him to abrogate existing vows and charters. Eybel subordinated the secular criteria of social utility and productivity to his Reform Catholic framework: only "penitents," "spiritual convalescents" and other "individuals dispensable to state and religion" are eligible to be monks.[84] Monasticism is contrary to Jesus's spirit and the Apostles' ministry:

> Christ, his apostles and youths were the founders of pastoral care . . . in the midst of societal life they helped to promote and fulfill duties to God and themselves, their fellow men and the state. . . . for that reason the mode of life of all those communities that under the veil of religion withdraw from societal life and do not serve the state, do not resemble the life of our savior.[85]

At year's end Eybel published a pamphlet on marriage law that prepared the way for Joseph II's legislation (January 16, 1783). Marriage law was "the fundamental, perhaps indeed . . . the essential component of the entire Josephist system." For Catholic sovereigns, wresting control of marriage impediments from, and stopping the flow of cash for dispensations to, Rome were a sine qua non for erecting a state church. It was equally important for Episcopalism, since local bishops would now exercise those powers.[86] Marriage impediments and dispensations were the one issue for which Riegger had publicly advocated reform, urging the state to reclaim its authority. As early as 1753 Maria Theresa had begun to introduce minor reforms concerning betrothals, and during the co-regency she had forbidden subjects to ask Rome for dispensations (September 27, 1777), ordering them to address their bishop. The papacy vigorously resisted such efforts. Not

---

[83] Ibid., 63. Cf. 23, 27–28.

[84] Ibid., 105. Cf. 1–16, 97. For the priority of religious criteria, see 25, 26, 45, 101, 105, 119–20.

[85] Ibid., 30–31.

[86] Johannes Mühlsteiger, *Der Geist des Josephinischen Eherechtes, Forschungen zur Kirchengeschichte Österreichs* 5 (Vienna, 1967), 8. On Joseph's rejection of civil marriage, see Hermann Conrad, "Staatliche Theorie und kirchliche Dogmatik im Ringen um die Ehegesetzgebung Josephs II," in *Wahrheit und Verkündigung: Michael Schmaus zum 70. Geburtstag*, ed. Leo Scheffczyk, Werner Dettloff, and Richard Heinzmann 2 vols. (Munich, 1967), 2:1171–87. For marriage law in Portugal, see Samuel J. Miller, *Portugal and Rome, c. 1748–1830: An Aspect of the Catholic Enlightenment* (Rome, 1978), 171–76, 208–16; for the Rhenish Bishops' Punctation at Ems (1786), see Matthias Höhler, ed., *Heinrich Aloys Arnoldi Tagebuch über die zu Ems gehaltene Zusammenkunft der vier Erzbischöflichen deutschen Herrn Deputirten*, (Mainz, 1915), 173 (Article II).

surprisingly, Eybel's work quickly found a place on the Index (January 20, 1783).[87]

In his *Introduction to Church Law*, following Riegger, Eybel had been conciliatory, attempting to reconcile marriage as sacrament with marriage as civil contract (though some considered the very distinction a "gallican-regalist maxim").[88] The Church can set obstacles to marriage as a sacrament—for example, the priest as "spiritual judge" can question the proposed partners' faith, with the state doing the same for marriage as a civil contract. Marriage as sacrament and civil contract must not conflict, and no promise may be made or contract agreed that is injurious to the state. Nevertheless, Eybel insisted that the authority to establish impediments derived from the state: "The church can only exercise this jurisdiction in the name of the temporal sovereign."[89]

In his pamphlet, Eybel highlighted the sovereign's uncontested power. In the early centuries the temporal sovereign exercised complete control over marriage law. Only in its notorious "middle age" did the Church usurp these powers from lax sovereigns. Yet the state did not cede this authority. The state merely "delegated" it, and therefore can revoke it:

Anytime the sovereign finds it necessary or useful for the state, he can withdraw from the Church the right to determine impediments that destroy the marriage contract. Also at anytime he can entirely abolish, limit or grant dispensations for, those impediments to marriage that do not have a basis in natural or divinely revealed law. In this he cannot be hampered by anyone including Church leaders, since the Church has received no greater power from God in recent times than it had at its inception, and Church leaders today have no less duty to follow civil law than Church leaders proved in the earliest times.[90]

The state should now reclaim its authority. The Church dishonors itself by regulating marriage law, especially by granting dispensations for payment. The laws injure the states by impeding population growth

[87] Brandl, *Der Kanonist Joseph Valentin Eybel*, 154. For Maria Theresa, see Mühlsteiger, *Der Geist des Josephinischen Eherechtes*, 29–31, 43–44. For Riegger, see Seifert, *Paul Joseph Riegger*, 290–94, 340.

[88] Mühlsteiger, *Der Geist des Josephinischen Eherechtes*, 13–22, 36; Conrad, "Staatliche Theorie und kirchliche Dogmatik im Ringen um die Ehegesetzgebung Josephs II," 1172.

[89] *Einleitung*, 2:111–12, 126–28, 3:272–73, 4:408, 460. Cf. Roderick Phillips, *Putting Asunder: A History of Divorce in Western Society* (Cambridge, 1988), 5–9.

[90] *Nichts Mehreres von Ehedispensen als was Religion, Recht, Nutzen, Klugheit und Pflicht fordert* (n.p., 1782), 80. Cf. 30–31; 48–49; 63.

and sending abroad funds that should be used for charity. Eybel emphasized the urgency of returning to early Church discipline:

"the sovereign has the power and the duty to return, as much as is possible, to the simplicity and purity of the earliest Church discipline. Thus the earliest times will reemerge by themselves, in which the clergy adjudicated in marriage contracts according to civil law, without making new laws or assessing taxes for dispensations.[91]

In a quartet of pamphlets that appeared in 1782, *What Is the Pope? What Is a Bishop? What Is a Priest? What Is an Indulgence?*, Eybel popularized the positions he had articulated in his *Introduction to Catholic Ecclesiastical Law* while also advancing more radical conclusions sanctioned by the ideas of "cure of souls" and "penitence." While the origins of his pamphlets on monasticism and marriage law are unclear, Eybel patently wrote the quartet at the government's bidding. This was clearest in regard to *What Is the Pope?*, the pamphlet that made his reputation. Franz Joseph Heinke, Eybel's longstanding sponsor now at the Imperial Ecclesiastical Commission, invited him to Vienna in the months prior to Pope Pius's visit (March 22–April 22, 1782). During this period Eybel wrote that pamphlet and probably the other three.[92] Although not coordinated with a single event, his other pamphlets supported Joseph II's reforms and appeared with the government's connivance.

Joseph had relaxed censorship rather than lifting it (February and July 1781). The full range of deceptive ancien régime practices therefore remained in play. For example, Eybel's *What Is the Pope?*—indeed most of Eybel's pamphlets from the 1780s—appeared anonymously (some also had a false place of publication). Joseph wanted to shield the government from having to approve controversial works for publication, yet also to have such works further his policies. Joseph manipulated the new public sphere he had allowed to emerge by orchestrating a campaign for his own agenda, especially Church reform.[93]

What Is the Pope? addressed Pius VI's sensational month-long visit to Vienna in 1782 (March 22–April 22), the first time in three centuries a pope had left Italy. The most obvious explanation for the pope's

---

[91] Ibid., 120. Cf. 86–87, 92–3, 111, 116–18, 125–6.

[92] Brandl, *Der Kanonist Joseph Valentin Eybel*, 118.

[93] Ernst Wangermann argues that this was only new for domestic policy. See *Die Waffen der Publizität: Zum Funktionswandel der politischen Literatur unter Joseph II* (Vienna, 2004), 13–15; Leslie Bodi, *Tauwetter in Wien: Zur Prosa der österreichischen Aufklärung, 1781–1795*, 2nd ed. (Vienna, 1995) 53; and E. Kovács, "Der Besuch Papst Pius VI. im Spiegel josephinischer Broschüren," *Archivum Historiae Pontificiae* 20 (1982), 165f. The pamphlet that carried Eybel's name was *Pilgrims to Vienna* (1783).

unprecedented and hastily planned trip was that he came to remon-
strate with Joseph II over his unilateral legislation in the hope of per-
suading him to desist or, better still, retreat. Another and comple-
mentary possibility was that he wished to avoid turning a tense
situation into an open conflict. The papal nuncio, Guiseppe Garampi,
may have achieved this had he acted on his threat to refuse the
emperor the sacraments on Maundy Thursday. In the event, the
pope administered the sacraments while Garampi celebrated Mass
elsewhere.[94]

The visit monopolized public attention, and Eybel's pamphlet was
front and center. The pamphlet was written in a direct conversational
style unusual for the time. It was so controversial and widely read as
to make Eybel a household name. It elicited some seventy responses
within three months and was quickly translated into numerous languages. It was condemned and placed on the papal Index (itself a minor diplomatic scandal: the Habsburg government exiled the papal
nuncio who released the papal brief).[95]

Eybel heightened his Episcopalist and conciliarist arguments. Bishops, like the pope, receive their authority directly from God. They are
"equal brothers in office," and "every Bishop is authorized by the Holy
Spirit to rule the Church and has no less authority than the Pope."[96]
Councils are the supreme arbiter of Church doctrine, the pope is subject to them, and Christ, rather than the pope, rules the Church: "The
Pope is no ruling sovereign, but rather a serving leader designated to
maintain unity who receives his energy, resolution and support from
the entire body of the Church."[97]

The papal monarchy began in the ninth century when the pope
began to see himself as the Church's "Father" and bishops began to see
his authority mediating theirs. A significant change occurred in the
fourteenth century when confirmation was separated from ordination
and both were brought under papal control. Such factors as bishops

[94] Derek Beales, "The Origins of the Pope's Visit to Joseph II in 1782," in idem, Enlightenment and Reform in Eighteenth-Century Europe, 256–61.

[95] Bodi, Tauwetter in Wien, 125; Sturmberger, "Zwischen Barock und Romantik," 178;
Elisabeth Kovács, Der Pabst in Teutschland: Die Reise Pius VI. im Jahre 1782 (Munich,
1983), 156. Wangermann asserts Joseph II was unhappy the Censorship Commission
had approved the book's publication. See Die Waffen der Publizität, 73–74. For the opposition, see Kovács, "Der Besuch Papst Pius VI. im Spiegel josephinischer Broschüren,"
172ff.; Brandl, Der Kanonist Joseph Valentin Eybel, 186–98; and Ludwig Freiherr v. Pastor,
Geschichte der Päpste, 12th ed., 16 vols. (Freiburg, 1955–61), 16, 3: 395.

[96] Was ist der Pabst? (Vienna, 1782), 16, 34.

[97] Ibid., 18. Cf. 12–15.

and sovereigns neither exercising nor knowing their rights, the false Isidorean decrees, the use of the Index to enforce ignorance and the Inquisition to stifle criticism, the disorder of the Crusades, and the "Roman chancellery's" undue influence and power allowed "the Pope to be considered something that he is not."[98]

Eybel's inflammatory conclusion was that "every reasonable person who gives the matter due consideration must see the need for a Reformation" and called on Europe's sovereigns to lead the way. In particular, reiterating the contents of his pamphlet of 1781, *On the Election of Religious Officials*, Eybel advocated returning to the early Church's practice of the people and clergy participating in electing bishops and the pope (Joseph II did not adopt this suggestion; revolutionary France did).[99]

Eybel deepened his call for reform (*What Is a Bishop?*) by excoriating the mistaken notions of Papal supremacy and infallibility:

> He who today considers the Pope the supreme judge in matters of faith, or who regards him as infallible in this respect, will be seen as a man who knows nothing of Holy Scripture, the teachings of tradition, Church fathers, or Church history, and who speaks so either because he does not comprehend the proper use of the requisite scholarly knowledge or else simply wants to assert such positions.

On the grounds that "the bishops and their ancestors have never explicitly nor implicitly renounced their God given authority and the episcopal rights and duties that flow from them," they should reclaim their rights over confirmation, resignation, dismissal, and translation to another see of fellow bishops.[100]

Eybel developed the idea of cure of souls (*What Is a Priest?*) by discussing "instruction" and toleration. Drawing on Muratori and other reform Catholics, he pitted the ideal of proper instruction in beliefs and practices against Baroque piety: "the main duty of every pastor is to give the people a true and reliable instruction":

> Right-thinking pastors are concerned to give their people a clear, comprehensible and congenial instruction that is genuine and distinct, that pertains only to actual doctrines of belief and morality, and that are necessary for a good Christian and a good subject to

[98] Ibid., 30. Cf. 19, 23, 26–30.
[99] Ibid., 32–33. Cf. 36. See *Etwas von den Wahlen der Religionsdiener*, aus dem lateinischen Werke Herrn Joseph Valentin Eybels, k.k. wirklichen Raths bei der Landstelle ob der Enß. trs. W.S. Heinz (Vienna, 1781).
[100] *Was ist ein Bischof?* (Pressburg, 1782) 18, 31.

know. Otherwise the people . . . will learn neither its belief nor its other duties.[101]

Pastors must be resident in their parishes, may not hold pluralities, and each week must preach, instruct, and offer sacraments. Parishes must be small so that the pastor can be in close contact with parishioners and "the necessary and genuine instruction (*Unterricht*) of Christians takes place, and from it the fortification of faith and good morals." The division of parishes is the sovereign's responsibility. In the interest of freeing the priest's time to engage more effectively in instruction, Eybel made the radical recommendation of ending celibacy: wives would take full responsibility for domestic chores (Joseph II did not adopt this suggestion).[102]

Supporting Joseph II's edicts on Protestants and Jews (1781), Eybel understood the teaching of toleration to be a sine qua non of pastoral care. It belonged to being a good Christian: "[intolerance] is contrary to natural law, civic duties, the Gospel, original Church discipline, the examples of moral Christians, in consequence is contrary to God, love of fellow-man, and humaneness, and detrimental to religion and all human and civic society."[103] As in his *Introduction to Church Law*, Eybel did not specify which religious groups were to be accorded toleration. He recognized that social harmony required it and proper "instruction" inculcated it:

> History teaches us that the majority of disorders, disturbances and devastations of entire regions result not from toleration but from intolerance. If there have also frequently been those sorts of disorders in tolerant lands, so the cause of these has been that despite the sovereign's toleration the subjects and pastors of different religions have provoked each other and fed mutual hatred. This will all be improved by a better instruction, a well chosen clergy, an alert sovereign, and the daily improvements in thought that come with the Enlightenment.[104]

Crucial to Eybel's ideal of proper instruction was a restoration of authentic penitence in which indulgences figured prominently. Joseph II

---

[101] *Was ist ein Pfarrer?* (Vienna, 1782) 42, 45–46.

[102] Ibid., 21–22, 28–30.

[103] Ibid., 64–65. The main toleration tract was M.A. Wittola, *Schreiben eines österreichischen Pfarrers über die Toleranz nach den Grundsätzen der katholischen Kirche* (Vienna, 1781). See O'Brien, *Ideas of Religious Toleration at the Time of Joseph II*.

[104] *Was ist ein Pfarrer?* 62. In the *Einleitung* Eybel also did not specify groups to be tolerated. See 2:84–85, 131–33, 187–90. For Joseph II as toleration's paragon, see *Die Pilgrime nach Wien* (Vienna, 1783), 9.

ordered an end to abuses in indulgences (as well as brotherhoods and other devotionals, on November 27, 1781), and the Ecclesiastical Commission voted in September 1782 to limit the number of indulgences and for the Church to teach their proper meaning.[105] In that spirit, Eybel attacked indulgences (*What Is an Indulgence?* 1782) as characteristic of the Church's "corrupted middle age" and one of Baroque piety's most egregious acts of "false devotion":

> One would have to be perverse not to let these indulgences stand had they a legitimate basis. Then what could be easier than to win an indulgence by pronouncing the prayer "our father," an Ave Maria or another simple-minded one, by procuring a consecrated rosary, by kissing certain pictures, by visiting particular statues, or by enrolling in certain brotherhoods and performing lesser brotherhood duties.[106]

Indulgences are ineffective for the individual and deleterious for the Church.[107] He asks fellow Catholics to accept that indulgences are simply inadmissible:

> To the objection, that according to this view there is today no longer a true indulgence, because sins can only be released through the sacrament of penitence and divine punishments through serious acts of contrition; and that no other forms of penitence in the church are known and in use except those delineated by the father confessors; . . . this objection does not frighten an honest Catholic; he rather acknowledges with van Espen and Fleury and other pious and learned men that Church discipline is in disrepair.[108]

Eybel aspired to the "true conversion of the heart" which, typical of the early Church, reveals "the real striving for improvement precisely from the eagerness for penitence." He aimed to restore Church discipline by reintroducing the correct notion of true devotion, namely, "remission [through] prescribed acts of penance" an emphasis on contrition redolent of neo-Jansenism.[109]

That Eybel was committed to a renewal of core beliefs and practices further emerged in his second most famous pamphlet, *What Do the*

---

[105] Holzknecht, *Ursprung und Herkunft der Reformideen Kaiser Josefs II*, 58–59; Brandl, *Der Kanonist Joseph Valentin Eybel*, 161.

[106] *Was ist ein Ablaß?* (Vienna, 1782), 35–36. Cf. 17, 56. For the "middle corrupted age," see 61, 12, 21. For "instruction," see 4, 6, 17, 58.

[107] Ibid., 38.

[108] Ibid., 24–25.

[109] Ibid., 27, 38. The formula is "Nachlassung auferlegter Bußwerke"; cf. 49, 59. On contrition versus attrition, see William Doyle, *Jansenism* (Houndmills, UK, 2000), 22–23.

Sources of Ancient Christianity Say about Auricular Confession? (1784), which, like that on the papacy, evoked a papal condemnation (November 21, 1784).[110] Eybel questioned auricular confession's historical origins and contemporary efficacy.

The early Church knew nothing of confession as absolution since it maintained a clear distinction between reconciliation with the Church and God. Its forms of "public canonical penitence" aimed exclusively at reconciliation with the Church. The fourth Lateran Council first prescribed annual confession for both sexes and the annual taking of sacraments, while the Council of Trent made annual confession obligatory and deemed it heretical to question either the obligation or its origins.[111]

Eybel doubted whether oral confession actually promoted contrition. Most confessors were insufficiently trained to administer it properly. They did not prepare the soul for true contrition, usually requiring only confession of the sin and superficial penance. Eybel's answer was neither to revive early Church practices ("canonical penance") nor to endorse an "exaggerated rigorist enthusiasm" but to seek the "avowal of sins" as a step to "true guidance in penitence."[112]

Eybel's solution was vague because he was caught on the horns of a dilemma: a committed conciliarist, he viewed the council rulings (Lateran, Trent) on this issue as inauthentic and pernicious. His characteristically Reform Catholic response was to remain faithful to his historical sources, insisting on the practice's late origins while bowing to Trent's authority. He only hoped that the Church would find a satisfactory answer.[113]

Eybel's bureaucratic praxis outdid his theory. Joseph's reforms in Upper Austria focused on two issues: abolishing monasteries and creating a new diocese of Linz by separating Upper Austria from Passau. In implementing both of these reforms, Eybel exceeded official policy.

Erecting a new Linz diocese was characteristic of Joseph's reforms. He effected longstanding Habsburg plans to create a diocese coincident with the administrative province, a policy integral to the idea of a "state church." Moreover, he did so unilaterally, only retroactively securing the Church's permission. Joseph took the death of the sitting prelate (Cardinal Firmian; March 1783) as his signal to act. The government immediately froze the diocese's machinery in Upper Austria and put Eybel in

[110] Pastor, *Geschichte der Päpste*, 16,3:241.

[111] *Was enthalten die Urkunden des christlichen Alterthums von der Ohrenbeichte?* (Vienna, 1784), 18, 20, 23, 35, 52, 70–71, 75–79.

[112] For training confessors, ibid., 45. For true versus superficial penance, 80–87.

[113] Ibid., 84–85.

charge. In July 1784 Joseph II reached agreement with the new Bishop of Passau, Joseph Anton Auersperg (in office, 1783–95), who renounced his jurisdictional rights to Upper and Lower Austria, an arrangement which the Pope confirmed later that year (November 1784). The first bishop of the new Linz diocese was Ernest Johann Graf von Herberstein (1731–88), who, although an outspoken Josephist, was sufficiently cautious not to assume his post until he was certain the pope would approve the new diocese and his appointment (January 28 and February 14, 1785).[114]

Herberstein was an effective administrator; Eybel was a problem. While the bishop's office remained vacant, Eybel had performed its duties; after Herberstein's investiture, he did the same. As the consistory pointedly put it:

> The government counselor Eybel became accustomed during the controversy with Passau to assume the role of Bishop of Upper Austria. He wants to continue to do so; this is the true cause of all difficulties. Two bishops in one city only leads to trouble. We request . . . that you consider whether Eybel is capable of representing the office of a Bishop in the Catholic Church.

Herberstein went further. On April 23, 1785, he wrote to the chair of the Imperial Ecclesiastical Commission asking him to rein Eybel in so that he (Herberstein) could fulfill his duties without interference.

> The aforementioned ecclesiastical expert [Eybel] is not accustomed to having a Bishop by his side and his behavior shows this. . . . Since. . . I wish to avoid a public collision with [Eybel], [yet] cannot view all this indifferently without violating my duties, so I take the liberty of . . . [asking] your Excellency . . . to avoid future misunderstandings by holding the temporal authorities to a normal rule of conduct in their behavior to the Vicar Generals in matters of ecclesiastical discipline as well as the degree to which they intervene in such matters.

Herberstein and Eybel also clashed over the substance of two reforms. Herberstein adhered to the letter of Joseph's reform (September 1782) in reducing drastically the number of indulgences. Eybel wanted to abolish indulgences altogether. Moreover, while Herberstein supported Joseph II's toleration edicts, circulating a pastoral letter imploring his clergy to respect the tolerated religions, he objected

[114] Rudolf Zinnhobler, "Josephinismus am Beispiel der Gründung des Bistums Linz," *Zeitschrift für Kirchengeschichte* 93 (1982): 295–311; Klueting, "Kaunitz, die Kirche und der Josephinismus," 172–73.

to a Protestant tract that insulted Catholicism and wanted the bookseller to withdraw it from circulation. Eybel backed the bookseller, questioning the bishop's right to search his premises.[115]

Eybel's role in closing monasteries in Upper Austria and redirecting their funds to cure of souls, education, and charity gained him notoriety. One member of a two-man commission created to implement these policies (the other member closed his own monastery), Eybel notoriously exceeded the law: he never saw a monastery or cloister he was not happy to shut. At one point the government felt compelled to address his behavior: the emperor rebuked Eybel for overstepping official policy by closing cloisters the Imperial Commission had not authorized.[116] In addition, there was a question of malfeasance: had Eybel misappropriated property from two cloisters, Gleink and Baumgartenberg, for his own benefit? Joseph II ordered an inquiry, presumably to absolve Eybel. Under oath, the priors of the two cloisters exonerated Eybel. From then on Eybel was careful to have priors certify that the inventories he produced were complete and without error.[117]

To be sure, there were other Church matters that won Eybel loyalty if not affection. For example, while closing down the cloister of Thalheim in October 1784, residents of a neighboring parish, Timelkam, asked him to assign a parish priest there for the first time. They claimed that the dean had sworn to them that within a year and a day they would have their own minister of souls. Eybel, always eager to improve pastoral care, replied: "I will not swear an oath as the Dean did, but I will write and you will receive what you wish."[118]

In the implementation of Church reforms, Eybel's excesses stained his reputation.[119] His notoriety ("the executioner"), whether or not deserved, highlights the differences between Linz's two generations of Reform Catholicism. In the figure of Plazidus Fixlmillner (1721–91) Linz had its own version of moderate, monastic Reform Catholicism emanating from Kremsmünster, the preeminent Benedictine monastery in Upper Austria. At Salzburg University Fixlmillner studied Wolff, mathematics, experimental science, and later theology, canon

---

[115] Quotations in Zinnhobler, "Josephinismus am Beispiel der Gründung des Bistums Linz,", 305. Cf. 306–9.

[116] Ferihumer, *Die kirchliche Gliederung*, 118–20; cf. 146. For the commission's other member, see Brandl, *Der Kanonist Joseph Valentin Eybel*, 120–21.

[117] Hittmair, *Der Josefinische Klostersturm*, 267–68.

[118] Ibid., 190.

[119] Ferihumer, *Die kirchliche Gliederung*, 362–63.

law, and history. He taught ecclesiastical law and history for half a century at the monastery's Academy for Nobles (Ritterakademie). He was also a mainstay of its observatory, which he directed for almost three decades (built in 1749, the observatory sat atop the cloister's eight-story "mathematical tower"). His observations plotting Uranus's course made him a major figure in European astronomy. He was, however, a quintessential moderate. While studying Wolf he retained scholasticism. He favored toleration yet opposed the idea of natural religion. He rejected Febronius as too radical. In sum, "he was enlightened, without allowing himself to be overwhelmed by the Enlightenment."[120]

"True Devotion"

Eybel published two multivolume devotional works between 1784 and 1791 designed to wean Catholics from harmful reading matter. His commitment to Reform Catholicism was not theoretical: just as he implemented Joseph's policies in Upper Austria, so he actually wrote thousands of pages of proper devotion.

Eybel may have written his *Christian-Catholic Family Devotion Useful for All Sundays and Holiday Epistles and Gospels of the Entire Year* (five volumes, 1784–87) during the interim period when he performed the bishop's duties in the new Linz diocese (1783–85); indeed, he may have first delivered it orally. This would account for a work so ostensibly unlike his others.[121] Yet the book's prolix subtitle tells another tale: *Directed Against all Sunday and Holiday Abuses: For the Instruction, Consolation, and Use of all those interested in true devotion, genuine Divine Worship, and purified religious concepts; and also for the benefit of all Pastors and Those responsible for cure of souls, indeed even for some Bishops.* The book contains the weekly New Testament reading followed by an "application." The application is homiletical rather than exegetical: Eybel uses the text to discuss contemporary issues in Reform Catholic perspective.

[120]Sturmberger, "Zwischen Barock und Romantik," 153–62, quotation at 162. On Kremsmünster see Beales, *Prosperity and Plunder*, 55–57.

[121]*Christkatholische nützliche Haus-Postill. Auf alle Sonn- und Feyrtägliche Epistel und Evangelien des ganzen Jahres, gegen alle Sonn- und Feyrtägliche Mißbräuche eingerichtet; Allen der wahren Andacht, des ächten Gottesdienstes, und reiner Religions-Begriffe begierigen Seelen zum Unterrichte, Trost und Nutzen; wie auch allen Pfarrherren und Seelsorgern, ja sogar manchem Bischofe zum Behufe,* 5 vols. (1784–87).

There is a question of authorship. Sturmberger, "Zwischen Barock und Romantik," 177, attributes it to Eybel. Brandl, *Der Kanonist Joseph Valentin Eybel*, does not mention it.

Eybel used some readings to legitimate Joseph's reforms. The wedding Jesus attended at Cana (John 2:1–12) allows him to argue that the ideal primitive Church left marriage law to the state. The reading that includes "love your neighbor as yourself" (Romans 13:8–11) confirms the need for a toleration that recognizes "no difference in estate or religion." Joseph II's edict agrees with the Gospel.[122]

Eybel used other readings to reinforce his Reform Catholic agenda. He uses the twelve-year-old Jesus listening to instruction in the Temple (Luke 2:42–52) to criticize cloister seminaries: their inferior teachers, by inculcating misguided scholastic theology, have "condemned and uprooted genuine divine worship, true devotion, morals and the knowledge of civic duties."[123] Jesus's healing of a sick child (Matthew 8:1–14) offers a model for monks and nuns: "The majority of miracles that our Savior performed were for the sick. Can a Christian imitate his savior in a more pleasing manner than by caring for the poor and the impoverished sick with all his might?"[124] Similarly, the reading that enjoins "pity" (Letter to the Colossians 3:12–18) elicits a diatribe against monasteries and Baroque piety for not aiding the needy:

> O my Christians! All these [circumstances: poverty, ill health] demand holy, beloved and heartfelt pity. Perfection is to be found only in this pity, not in a bequest to a cloister or brotherhood—not in an endowed devotion. Love alone is the bond of perfection.[125]

Eybel sees hope for regeneration in the parable of the weeds and wheat (Matthew 13:24–31). The founders of the Church were the sowers of wheat. The sowers of weeds are money, meddling sovereigns, and popes who act as a "universal monarch." The "weeds" result in such abuses as the multiplication of cloisters and the creation of huge dioceses that provide enormous incomes for indolent bishops and cathedral canons. Nonetheless, "Joseph II does not sleep." He will clear the weeds while preserving the wheat. Witness "the solicitude that he applies day and night for religion, for pastors, for schools, for the care of the poor."[126]

Each application conveys Eybel's Reform Catholic ideas vis-à-vis the New Testament lection in five to ten printed pages. The applica-

---

[122] *Christkatholische nützliche Haus-Postill*, 2:63, 65.
[123] Ibid., 2:28–36, 17.
[124] Ibid., 2:53.
[125] Ibid., 2:78.
[126] Ibid., 2:85. Cf. 82–84.

tions are designed for easy reading and oral comprehension; there are no difficult concepts, no elaborate definitions, no abstruse interpretations.

Eybel continued his devotional efforts by challenging the popular view of the saints (*The People's Understanding of the Saints*, four volumes, 1791). Using the Enlightenment's popular genre of didactic dialogue, he has a representative of Reform Catholicism converse with a range of recognizable figures. The spokesperson for Reform Catholicism, usually a priest, sometimes an abbess, makes clear the extent to which reading the saints' lives has inculcated erroneous notions of piety, devotion, and morality.

Eybel tried to do for the saints what he earlier did for canon law: remove centuries of fabrication and invention to restore the pristine ideal. "I will attack not the honor of any saint but only the dishonor that the legend writers have brought to them." Predictably, Eybel saw monks as the culprits: "the monks were, from the start, the main cause and continue to be so of us having such legends."[127]

> If I were to show you that legend writers have invented the entire lives of some saints; that for other saints the true [aspect of their lives] was made suspicious and dishonored by mythical additions and perceptible lies; that for many saints those deeds that are opposed to reason, Gospel morality, man's purpose, and the duties of individual societies as well as the well-being of entire states and nations, are presented as meritorious and worthy of imitation and, indeed, as the reason why this or that saint had deserved glory in Heaven.[128]

For Eybel, the saints' lives had caused unspeakable damage. The saints' legends stupefy readers, giving rise, for example, to "a sheer delusion that the saints have specific powers and that one is not secure in the face of plague or fire when there is no statue or picture of a specific saint in the Church or at home"[129] A priest pointedly asks: "Are we pagans or Christians?"[130] Some of the supposed miracles blasphemously contradict creation.[131]

---

[127] *Die Heiligen nach den Volksbegriffen*, 4 vols.(Leipzig, 1791), 1:21, 54.

[128] Ibid., 1:17. Popularizing the Maurists' and Bollandists' scholarly scrutiny of saints' lives to "bring historical knowledge to the public" (Koller, "Joseph Valentin Eybel als Historiker," 260–61), Eybel cites Mabillon, 1:105–6; Fleury, 116; Bolland, 188; Baillet, 64, 69; Maurists, 193ff.

[129] *Die Heiligen*, quotation at 1:467. Cf. 1:381, 238.

[130] Ibid., 1:454, 472. This dialogue cites Muratori. Cf. 1:459, 461, 469, 472, 475, 478, 480–81.

[131] Ibid., 1:297.

Inspired by Muratori, Eybel questioned the emphasis on miracles and legends, instead stressing the saints' virtues, the simple human truth that can serve as a model for emulation: "saintliness is measured only by the virtuous conduct of life": "not every action is saintly because it is committed by a saint; rather saintliness is to be measured in those actions that have the imprint of reasonable and Gospel concepts."[132] Eybel wanted Catholics to replace the saints' legends with works that convey Muratori's devotional ideal of "instruction" and "edification"[133]:

> These [books] will give you not false inventions but rather, on the basis of healthy reason and the holy Gospel, enlightenment [Aufklärung], consolation and ease of mind. A good legend is proper, for example, when all ignorance is omitted and the fable is presented to emphasize how this or that saint endeavored to fulfill his duties to God, himself, his fellow men, his duties of estate and office according to the natural laws and the Gospel doctrine, so that we may imitate him in all this. Such a legend is edifying and useful.[134]

In one dialogue a sculptor rejects a monk's paintings of the saints' legends in favor of works of "useful edification, admonition and teaching" that would impart the "fruit of true contrition" and encourage readers to live "like other reasonable people who have edifying and honorable lives."[135]

> Had your Excellency painted a collection of pictures in which one saw the saints extending charity to the poor, or [giving] instruction to children thirsty for instruction or in another [offering] the same to working peasants or burghers, responsible housemasters and housewives, in another deferential subjects eager for the welfare of the fatherland willingly paying taxes to their sovereign; and not just showing these for admiration but actually inspiring imitation in the hearts of viewers; such work would I gladly undertake.[136]

Similarly, a priest who advocates a "reasonable and Christian design for an altar painting" plans to paint the crucifixion on the altar and Christ's deeds on the side walls:

---

[132] Ibid., 1:310, 32. The entire book reflects Muratori's influence, beginning with Pope Clement's alleged endorsement of Muratori's "True Devotion" (1:3).

[133] For the ideal of instruction (*Unterricht*), see *Die Heiligen* 1:119; for edification (*Erbauung*), see 1:9, 202, 238, 243.

[134] Quotations at ibid., 1:238, 202.

[135] Ibid., 1:265, 276.

[136] Ibid., 1:311.

There for the eyes of all are presented for imitation—from Christ's teaching and deeds—[the virtues of] toleration, ministering to the poor, instruction of children and solicitude for them.[137]

Eybel prepared the way for Joseph II's legislation of July 26, 1786, abolishing side altars and prohibiting unnecessary pictures and lights.

Eybel carefully distinguished his agenda from the secular Enlightenment's. The sculptor who represents Reform Catholicism takes issue with a purported miracle but also the philosophers' view of it:

PRIEST: "Today's philosophers do not understand things as did the holy legend writers."

SCULPTOR: "I am not a philosopher. Yet not only healthy reason but also our holy religion . . . is against the trustworthiness of such a [miracle]."[138]

Eybel was even more critical of monastic life than in his earlier pamphlet (*Seven Chapters on Monks*), attacking the monks' callous indifference to fellow Christians. He recognized that the early Benedictines engaged in a serious "civilizing" mission, working as artisans and scholars. Yet

they subsequently contributed to the preservation of nonsensical books and the continuation of superstitious, mythical matters, especially the legends. They gave up doing useful work, sought to procure gold and goods from all directions; lived well behind their cloister walls; arrogantly, often cruelly, augmented their well being; and under the pretense of prayer, which consisted preeminently in the choir, ignored the sins of all other members of the polity who wallowed in need and poverty.[139]

An abbess insists that her nuns should serve the poor by staffing the hospital rather than wasting their time with excessive prayer, singing, and tending of relics. (These ideas reinforce Joseph II's legislation of April 28, 1784, that included a prohibition on illuminating relics.) The abbess recommends Scripture over legends: "The sister should read Holy Scripture rather than the legends; it contains the best legends."[140]

---

[137] Ibid., 1:488–89, 500.
[138] Ibid., 1:262.
[139] Ibid., 1:371.
[140] Ibid., 1:447.

REVOLUTION

Joseph II's death ended the intense decade in which Eybel advocated and implemented Church reform and produced devotional works. The French Revolution challenged him to defend Joseph's legacy.

Eybel had been fully aware that the 1780s were an inordinately propitious time for enlightened absolutist reform. In 1782 he discerned support for reforms across the estates and the bureaucracy. Furthermore, the diplomatic alliance of Catholic states made the cause irresistible. In consequence, change could be introduced peacefully.

> One should really express endless thanks to God that the time and opportunity have come to introduce adjustments without ferment or confusion in the state. The Catholic Church's prayer for peace and unity among Christian rulers has been heard. Every potentate devotes himself to being a father to his people, and almost all share the same sentiments and proposals to make their subjects happy. All of them endeavor to fortify true religion and to exclude abuses and whatever else is injurious to the state. That they join forces rather than hindering each other so that the good is more certain of being attained, and that in religion as well as in other spheres they are not hindered by those divisions that in the middle age perplexed the church and the kingdoms, so is this unity of views a dam which the malcontents can no longer surmount. The malcontents see all of their desires frustrated in the future as well. They see among almost every Catholic nation a series of rulers, ministers, advisors and civil servants . . . who will follow each other with similar opinions.

All ranks of the clergy similarly favored reform:

> And what is best, the Catholic Church now boasts a clergy that itself detests the principles of the middle age and rejects propagating it among others, and distinguishes the true in religion from the appearance and disguise and teaches this distinction as well. The lower clergy no less than all the other believers is informed with a sense of duty to the sovereign and in brief, helps to promote the general good through the principles of religion.[141]

Eybel knew that as a reformer in the 1780s he was living at an auspicious moment.

---

[141] *Nichts Mehreres von Ehedispensen* (1782), 110–11. For a similar passage, see *Christkatholische nützliche Haus-Postill*, 2:46.

In his *Divine Dialogues against the Jacobins* (1794), Eybel faced the fact that the French Revolution had entirely displaced the cause of reform. How was he to understand it? His book was primarily war propaganda. Eybel denounced the Jacobins to rally support for the "united powers" (the first Coalition of Great Britain, Prussia, Austria, and other German states, 1793–95); by the book's conclusion he had celebrated Robespierre's execution and the Jacobin's fall. The book transcended mere propaganda, however, because he enunciated his own principles. To counter the Jacobins as heirs of the Enlightenment and representatives of popular sovereignty and a Republic, he offered his credo as a Reform Catholic devoted to absolutist monarchy.

Eybel first rescued the Enlightenment from the Jacobins. The Jacobins represented a "false Enlightenment" ("Afteraufklärung") responsible for the revolution. The writers who raised the "torch of Freedom and equality" by taking a position "against all positive religion, . . . against all rulers, all monarchs, all current forms of government," "are truly the source of the present disaster."[142] The antireligious and dissident Enlightenment was the villain; he consigned Voltaire and Rousseau to the furies. The Jacobins made this brand of Enlightenment a "fanaticism without religion" which, like earlier religious fanaticism, yielded regicide. The Jacobins undermine all morality: "I never heard of a righteous man becoming a Jacobin or being sympathetic to the Jacobins."[143] They discredit all values and knowledge, debase the language by reversing the meaning of words (as Vernet contended about the philosophes), and undermine natural law:

> under superstition they [the Jacobins] understand every essential and useful religious regulation. For them ignorance and pedantry means any discipline that imposes order on reason. State for them means anarchy . . . . The right of war and nations is directed towards the expropriation and destruction of all nations. And all this together designates the temple of wisdom, nature and reason that the Jacobin philosophers have built.[144]

The "struggle against the Jacobins . . . is a struggle for religion itself."[145]

---

[142] *Göttergespräche gegen die Jakobiner* (Linz, 1794) 2, 12, 13, 435, 480–84. For German responses to the First Coalition, see Thomas P. Saine, *Black Bread-White Bread: German Intellectuals and the French Revolution* (Columbia, SC, 1988).

[143] *Göttergespräche*, 1:187–88, 61, 312.

[144] Ibid., 1:256–57. Cf. 91–97, 116, 324.

[145] Ibid., 1:243. Cf. 362–63.

Eybel also exposed the false principle of sovereignty and a republic. Human weakness makes republics inadequate. The people are incapable of ruling themselves and susceptible to the worst forms of deception and misrule. The philosophers are unable to determine what is practical and useful. Sovereignty and equality therefore lead to oppression by the few and enslavement of the many. Republics ineluctably fail, degenerating into tyranny and despotism:

> Thus is the sovereignty of the people the most oppressive and cruelest [of governments], which allows the most upright of men who serve the state to be sacrificed to the people's anger, as is evident in the history of the Greek and Roman republics and in the most recent history of the false French republic.[146]

A republic cannot conduct a foreign policy that promotes domestic peace and its neighbors' well-being.

> A republic is always condemned to destruction either by a bellicose barbarity which makes it attack others but ultimately ends in its own subjugation, or by a weakness [effeminacy] which makes it perplexed and impotent as to how to defend itself against every threat, and destroys the happiness of the individual through uprisings and factions.[147]

Jacobin France is worse than just an egregious failed republic. The Jacobins have the most evil intentions: sovereignty serves them as a thin disguise for "the cruelest tyranny, the most horrible despotism," indeed, "the worst despotism which has no equivalent in the history of tyrants." They exploit the slogan of sovereignty: "the Jacobins . . . desire an unthinking populace which allows itself to be deceived with the name sovereignty."[148] They are a band of unscrupulous and evil robbers, murderers, assassins and regicides; believe only in their own power and profit; and function as a conspiratorial club employing the most heinous means. Their wicked and unprincipled rule takes tyranny and despotism to the depths of anarchy. Moreover, their "cult of reason" makes them "new pagans" who wage war against Christianity.[149]

Against the Jacobins' false enlightenment and illusory republic Eybel championed true enlightenment and divine right monarchy. True

---

[146] Ibid., 1:480 cf. 13–14.
[147] Ibid., 1:414.
[148] Ibid., 1:5, 11, 201.
[149] Quotation at ibid., 1: 564. Cf. 1:25, 76, 90.

enlightenment is one "that contributes to the true glory of religion, the security and maintenance of states and monarchies, and the peaceful well-being of every individual."[150] True enlightenment was a middle ground. At one extreme was the anti-Christian and dissident enlightenment responsible for the revolution; at the other extreme were those thinkers who adhered to "guild authority" to justify the church-state status quo. The middle ground of true enlightenment, in contrast, consisted of "those [thinkers] who, complying with the laws of religion and state, wrote only against abuses that were in opposition to religious and state regulations, and who based their writing on the natural and positive divine laws and the wisest regulations of righteous legislators of ancient and modern times."[151]

True Enlightenment is his Reform Catholicism, which, loyal to Church and state, advocates reforms consistent with natural and divine law.[152]

Eybel thought monarchy the form of government best able to vouch-safe its citizens the "true and undisturbed happiness" that is predicated on "freedom from danger" and the protection of "law and property." It alone can realize the "true freedom," not the Jacobins' illusory "total" freedom, that consists in obedience to the law and the ability to chose the lesser evil.[153] Monarchy recognizes the inherent inequality among mankind ("nature itself . . . rests on plenitude and inequality") and the inescapable need for authority and hierarchy to secure peace and security. A republic based on equality is a "chimera of enthusiastic fools."[154]

Eybel endorsed divine right dynastic monarchy. God establishes the monarch whose person is inviolable. Whereas representative government is subject to coercion and factions, a monarchy is stable. A monarch is able to make the hard decisions needed to promote his subjects' happiness and well-being while succession is secure.[155]

[150] Ibid., 1:12.

[151] Ibid., 1:435–56.

[152] Eybel did not mention the Civil Constitution of the Clergy and misunderstood Fauchet (1:270).

[153] Ibid., 1:414, 436–37, 157, 437.

[154] Ibid., 1:44–45, 48–49, 437. For the link between plenitude and inequality in the "great chain of being," see Arthur Lovejoy, *The Great Chain of Being: A Study in the History of an Idea* (Cambridge, MA, 1936). For the revolution as "enthusiasm" see Anthony J. La Vopa, "The Philosopher and the *Schwärmer*: On the Career of a German Epithet from Luther to Kant," in *Enthusiasm and Enlightenment in Europe, 1650–1850*, ed. Lawrence E. Klein and Anthony J. La Vopa (San Marino, CA, 1998), 103–5.

[155] *Göttergespräche*, 429, 432, 477, 481.

True enlightenment and monarchy converge in acquiescence to authority. Eybel vindicated his advocacy of Church reform under an absolutist state.

> Genuine Enlightenment and reason point to the necessity of religion and positive religious ordinances. . . . Genuine Enlightenment establishes the state and shows the necessity of subordinating oneself to the state's higher authority. Genuine Enlightenment perfects the idea of the form of government, and confirms the thesis that monarchy is the best form.[156]

Eybel's embrace of authority was not counterrevolutionary. Unlike de Bonald and de Maistre he did not ground it in the papacy but was consistent with his earlier commitments: he explicitly defended his position of enlightened divine right monarchy and Reform Catholicism as a middle way between the extremes.[157] Eybel was one of an "army of civil officials" in the 1790s who struggled to remain true to the Enlightenment and Joseph II's legacy.[158]

Conclusion

Joseph's decade of rule represented a high-water mark for the alliance of enlightened absolutism and reform Catholicism, or at least Eybel's version of it. This was not a story of unmitigated success. More radical secular Enlightenment thinkers criticized Joseph's limits on freedom of the press and many of his policies. A conservative opposition began to grow more articulate and organized. Moderate Reform Catholics withdrew from government service to protest radical policies. Joseph withdrew some reforms, clamped down on freedom of the press, and, feeling unappreciated, grew frustrated and bitter.[159]

Joseph's successors had other concerns. Leopold II (1790–92) worked frantically to avert the monarchy's collapse. To protect the monarchy from dismemberment, Francis II (1792–1835) adopted conservative policies that overturned Joseph's. Association with the French Revolution rendered the Enlightenment suspect. In consequence, while Reform Catholicism remained a factor in state and church, it was never to get

---

[156] Ibid., 12.

[157] Ibid., 527, 572–73. He legitimated his multiple commitments: "I have obligations as a man, a Christian, a subject and a civil servant." Ibid., 577.

[158] Ingrao, *The Habsburg Monarchy*, 224.

[159] Ibid., 197–209; Ernst Wangermann, "The Austrian Enlightenment," in *The Enlightenment in National Context*, 136–40.

as far as it had in the halcyon days of the 1770s and 1780s, when it had not only succeeded in introducing an enlightened theology but also aspired to create an enlightened church—a presumptuous and perhaps vain ambition.[160]

The combination of Joseph II's death and the French Revolution spelled the end of Habsburg Reform Catholicism's decade of accelerated reform. In the next chapter we will see how the revolution first propelled and then destroyed the possibility of Reform Catholicism in France.

[160] On the Revolution's radicalizing impact, see Bradley and van Kley, "Introduction," *Religion and Politics in Enlightenment Europe*, 1–45. On an enlightened Church, see Hersche, *Der Spätjansenismus*, 390–404.

Opposite: Adrien Lamourette. Frontispiece, *Prônes civiques, ou Le Pasteur patriote* (Toulouse, 1792). Courtesy of Princeton University Library.

CHAPTER SIX

Toul-Paris-Lyon

Adrien Lamourette's "Luminous Side of Faith"

What set France apart? Why was its Enlightenment so famously anti-clerical? Why did it not develop a version of religious Enlightenment? France developed a peculiar historical configuration after the Wars of Religion that persisted until the 1770s.

The battered House of Bourbon that survived the Wars of Religion reconstituted itself as a sacral monarchy based on religious unity hostile to religious controversy, dissent, or reform. Louis XIV imposed that policy on the eighteenth century by cementing the Crown's alliance with the Jesuits and requesting a papal bull *Unigenitus*, in 1713 to suppress Jansenism—the "movement toward a new Counter-Reformation" that emphasized man's depravity, irresistible grace (predestination), the integrity of individual conscience, and a rigorous morality.[1] Louis XIV considered Jansenism "a republican party in Church and State" that threatened to revive the Fronde, the challenge to absolutist rule that had irrupted into civil war during his minority (1648–53). Louis XV in 1730 radicalized his predecessor's policy of excluding church reform by promulgating *Unigenitus* and requiring ecclesiastical appointees to subscribe to an anti-Jansenist Formulary. He drew battle lines between Jansenists and Jesuits and, using the power of patronage, largely succeeded in purging the episcopate of Jansenists and their sympathizers.[2]

Louis XV's anti-Jansenist campaign aroused the Parlement, the courts that were the nobility of the robe's institutional home. Given that the Estates General had not convened since 1614, the Parlement considered themselves the nation's only legally constituted representatives and defenders of its liberties. The Parlement resisted not only because of Jansenist sympathies but also, and perhaps more so, because

---

[1] John McManners, *Church and Society in Eighteenth-Century France*, 2 vols. (Oxford, 1998), 2:345. For Jansenism as a failed "second Reformation," see Dale Van Kley, *The Religious Origins of the French Revolution: From Calvin to the Civil Constitution, 1560–1791* (New Haven, 1996), 372. For theology, see Nigel Abercrombie, *The Origins of Jansenism* (Oxford, 1936).

[2] Louis XV put patronage (*feuilles de bénéfices*) in the hands first of the hardline Archbishop Fleury, 1726–43, and then Bishop Boyer, 1743–55. The appointment of the "*tiers parti*" La Rouchefoucauld (1755) shifted policy. See McManners, *Church and Society*, 1:50–51, 2:481, 502.

of the arbitrary, despotic means the monarchy used to implement its policy: *évocation*, to remove cases from the Parlement to the Royal Council's judicial side, the *lit de justice*, to suspend temporarily the Parlement's authority in order to impose laws it refused to register, and the *lettre de cachet*, to exile or imprison recalcitrant magistrates and clergy. Those means threatened to undermine not only French liberties but also the Church's Gallican liberties, that is, the monarch and Parlement's right to scrutinize papal decrees. By aligning crown and curia, Louis XV seemed to abdicate guardianship of the Gallican liberties. This was a situation Louis XIV had wisely avoided by insisting on scrutinizing the very bull he had requested.[3]

The "eighteenth century may be as plausibly christened the century of *Unigenitus* as of *lumières.*"[4] The struggle over *Unigenitus* largely shaped French religious and political culture, giving rise to a protracted conflict throughout the reign of Louis XV (1715–74) that pitted Jansenists against Jesuits (the *parti dévot*). A so-called "third party" (*tiers parti*) of neutral bishops and clergy emerged whose influence peaked during the papacy of the moderate Benedict XIV (1740–58), yet was rendered largely ineffective after mid-century.[5] At that point the philosophes joined the fray. In addition, a form of "judicial Jansenism" emerged, combining Jansenist ideas and sensibilities with the Parlement's opposition to absolutism, whose power waxed as Louis XV's waned (1750–74).

The struggle over *Unigenitus* transformed Jansenism from "a body of doctrine" into "a series of historical situations."[6] The first was the dispute over the bull's acceptance (1715–32), which the monarchy appeared to win through suppression. The next was the "refusal of sacraments" (especially extreme unction) to those who lacked a *billet de confession* because they rejected *Unigenitus* (1749–58). At this point the conflict ceased to be merely theological and became that of "a national party with constitutional demands set against an absolutist party tied to the churchmen and their bull."[7] The conflict virtually froze the state's machinery when the crown exiled the Parlement and the magistrates resigned en masse. Subsequently the Parlement took the lead in sup-

---

[3] Julian Swann, *Politics and the Parlement of Paris under Louis XV, 1754–1774* (New York, 1996).

[4] William Doyle, *Jansenism* (Houndmills, Basingstoke, UK, 2000), 87.

[5] Emile Appolis, *Entre Jansénistes et Zelanti: Le "Tiers Parti" catholique au XVIIIe siècle* (Paris, 1960).

[6] Dale Van Kley, "Catholic Conciliar Reform in an Age of Anti-Catholic Revolution: France, Italy, and the Netherlands, 1758–1801," in *Religion and Politics in Enlightenment Europe*, ed. James E. Bradley and Dale K. Van Kley (Notre Dame, IN, 2001), 60.

[7] McManners, *Church and Society*, 2:501.

pressing the Jesuits (1758–63). Indeed, a provincial Parlement issued the first orders of suppression, and a rising tide of such rulings forced Louis XV's hand in November 1764. Finally, in Maupeou's coup of 1771–74, Louis XV's chief minister attempted to destroy the Parlements by installing new magistrates. This controversy encouraged Jansenists to rally to the Parlements by pooling their networks of organization and publicity. The Parlement again triumphed when the newly crowned Louis XVI recalled the magistrates to their posts.[8]

The monarchy's policy of systematic persecution exasperated the Jansenist movement, propelling some to a fateful embrace of miracles and prophecy. At the height of Cardinal Fleury's campaign of persecution in Paris in the 1720s and 1730s, Jansenists attested to miracles of healing at the cemetery of Saint-Médard (Jacob Vernet examined one of these in his first book). In the 1730s, in response to increased persecution from church and state, some Jansenists, already in underground conventicles and prayer circles, developed a convulsionary tendency. This "enthusiastic" turn distanced most philosophes from the Jansenists throughout Louis XV's reign, fundamentally differentiating it from religious reform movements in other countries, which generally rejected enthusiasm in favor of, or coopted it to, Enlightenment.[9]

This historical configuration, in which the state chose not to sponsor a movement of religious reform but to suppress it, as a result of which the reform movement became identified with enthusiasm rather than Enlightenment, set France apart from the other European countries we have examined. France was the "great anomaly."[10] The consequence of this historical configuration was a peculiarly French polarization between religion and Enlightenment. As Adrien Lamourette put it, "in

---

[8] For the Maupeou controversy, see Durand Echeverria, *The Maupeou Revolution: A Study in the History of Libertarianism, France, 1770–1774* (Baton Rouge, 1985), and Keith Michael Baker, ed., *The Maupeou Revolution: The Transformation of French Politics at the End of the Old Regime, Historical Reflections* 18, no. 2 (Summer, 1992). For "judicial Jansenism," see Van Kley, *Religious Origins*.

[9] Monique Cottret, *Jansénismes et Lumières: Pour un autre XVIIIe siècle* (Paris, 1998). For convulsionism, see McManners, *Church and Society*, 2:440–41, and B. Robert Kreiser, *Miracles, Convulsions and Ecclesiastical Politics in Early Eighteenth-Century Paris* (Princeton, 1978).

[10] Roy Porter, *The Enlightenment*, 2nd ed. (Houndmills, Basingstoke, UK, 2001), 55. See also Ernst Cassirer, *The Philosophy of the Enlightenment* (Princeton, 1951), 134; W. R. Ward, *Christianity under the Ancien Régime, 1648–1789* (Cambridge, 1999), 171; and Alasdair MacIntyre, *After Virtue*, 2nd ed. (Nortre Dame, IN, 2003), 37. For the historical configuration, see McManners, *Church and Society*, 2:348, 364, and Nigel Aston, *Religion and Revolution in France, 1780–1804* (Washington, DC, 2000), 81. For France as the radical Enlightenment's headquarters after 1720, see Jonathan Israel, *Enlightenment Contested: Philosophy, Modernity and the Emancipation of Man, 1670–1752* (Oxford, 2006), 699–862.

the eighteenth century Philosophy has become the opposite of Christianity, and [philosophy] needed to be impious and blasphemous to merit the honor of figuring in the [mental] picture of the wise."[11]

This configuration predominated throughout Louis XV's reign, preventing the emergence of Reform Catholicism. The configuration and resulting polarization seemed to decline in the 1780s when Louis XVI implemented reforms and inklings of Reform Catholicism emerged. During the early years of the revolution (1789–90), the polarization seemed to disappear. With the controversy over the Civil Constitution of the Clergy, followed by laicization and de-Christianization, however, the polarization returned. France re-experienced an extreme division between the secular and the religious that undermined, and finally with Napoleon's Concordat foreclosed, Reform Catholicism in France.[12]

CATHOLICISM

Adrien Lamourette (1742–94) is usually accorded a passing reference in histories of the French Revolution for his "kiss," or a line in histories of political thought, for coining the term "Christian democracy" (*démocratie chrétienne*). Yet he played an intriguing role in fashioning and bringing to fruition a Reform Catholic theology. A member of the Lazarist order and a sometime seminary professor, seminary director, and parish priest, Lamourette devised a theology that combined reasonable religion and Rousseauist sentimentalism on the basis of a moderate fideist skepticism. Lamourette belonged to a loose circle of writers and theologians who, opposed to the radical philosophes, combined fidelity to Church and monarchy (although with the hope of constitutional reform). During the revolution Lamourette both articulated his ideas and influenced events. He wrote pamphlets and a journal, collaborated with Mirabeau, was elected bishop of Lyon, and served as a delegate to the Legislative Assembly. Broadly associated with the Girondins and a participant in the Lyon uprising (1793), Lamourette and his effort at Reform Catholicism were condemned to the guillotine in 1794.[13]

---

[11] *Les Délices de la Religion, ou le pouvoir de l'Évangile pour nous rendre heureux* (Paris, 1788), ix. Cf. *Pensées sur la Philosophie de l'Incrédulité, ou Reflexions sur l'esprit et le dessein des philosophes irréligieux de ce Siècle* (Paris, 1786), 253, 263.

[12] For the Jansenist-Molinist controversy and the revolution excluding moderation, see Cottret, *Jansénismes et Lumières*, 17.

[13] "Posterity maintains Lamourette only through the memory of the kiss that carries his name." See Z. Marchal's "Approbation" to Abbé Liebaut, *Prêtre et Évêque Assermenté* (Nancy, 1894), 3. For a misreading, see Robert Darnton, *The Kiss of Lamourette: Reflections*

Our knowledge of Lamourette's early life is sparse; despite his fleeting celebrity he remains an obscure figure. Born in 1742 as the oldest of five children to a humble family in the market town of Frévent (now the Department of Pas-de-Calais), where his father was a comb-maker, Lamourette showed an early aptitude for study, and his parents dedicated him to the Church. He entered the Lazarist order at seventeen (1759) and was ordained a decade later.[14]

Founded in 1625 by St. Vincent de Paul (1581–1660), the order consisted of secular priests who specialized in missions to the rural poor— it was also called the "Congregation of the Mission"—and the education of clergy according to the Council of Trent. The order was better known for good works than for intellectual rigor. Lamourette attended the central seminary at the order's Paris headquarters, the Maison Saint-Lazare (hence "Lazarist").

In 1760 there were 153 *grands séminaires* in France for training priests. Bishops had originally entrusted sixty to religious orders, including twenty to the Lazarists; by 1789 the Lazarists administered half the seminaries, having assumed control of many former Jesuit institutions. In the early seventeenth century the seminaries followed the Council of Trent's prescriptions and specialized in pastoral training (scriptures, singing, rites); later in the century they added systematic theology and philosophy, the original course growing from six months to as long as three years. Priests received their education exclusively within the seminary unless there was a local college or university with a Theology Faculty. Lamourette likely followed a twelve-year curriculum for aspiring seminary professors. During Lamourette's years of study the Maison Saint-Lazare apparently emphasized Jesuit theology (Molinism). Like the Jesuits, the Lazarists were "pillars of papal orthodoxy"— at least in the capital.[15]

---

in Cultural History (New York, 1990), 17. On Lamourette, see F. Z. Collombet, "L'Abbé Lamourette," *Revue du Lyonnais* 2 (1835): 195–212; Liebaut, *Prêtre et Évêque Assermenté*; André Monglond, *Le préromantisme française*, 2 vols. (Paris, 1966), 2:86–98; Daniele Menozzi, "*Philosophes*" e "*Chrétiens éclaires*": *Politica e religione nella collaborazione di G.H. Mirabeau e A. A. Lamourette (1774–1794)* (Brescia, 1976); Norman Ravitch, "Catholicism in Crisis: The Impact of the French Revolution on the Thought of the Abbé Lamourette," *Cahiers internationaux d'histoire économique et sociale* 9 (1978): 354–85; William R. Everdell, *Christian Apologetics in France, 1730–1790: The Roots of Romantic Religion* (Lewiston, 1987), 213–24; Caroline Blanc, "Adrien Lamourette: Une apologétique du bonheur," *Chrétiens et Sociétés (XVIe–XXe siècles)* 10 (2003): 47–68.

[14] Menozzi, "*Philosophes*" e "*Chrétiens éclaires*," 96 n. 4.

[15] Stafford Poole, *A History of the Congregation of the Mission, 1625–1843* (Santa Barbara, CA, 1973), viii–ix, 83–98, 101–30; McManners, *Church and Society*, 1:199–207, 519; L.W.B. Brockliss, *French Higher Education in the Seventeenth and Eighteenth Centuries: A Cultural History* (Oxford, 1987), 231–34. On seminaries, see A. Degert, *Histoire des séminaires*

In 1769–72 Lamourette taught philosophy in Metz, where the Abbé Grégoire was his student. In 1773 he was a professor at the Lazarist seminary in Toul (Lorraine). If Lamourette encountered Jesuit theology in Paris, he now found himself in a Jansenist heartland. Imported from Port Royal to the west and Utrecht to the north, Jansenism was attractive because it gave Catholics an effective means to address Lorraine's numerous Lutherans. The Toul seminary, Lazarist at its founding in 1678, assigned Jansenist textbooks, a curriculum that persisted until the 1740s, when the *parti dévot* introduced Molinist books endorsing *Unigenitus*.[16]

Jansenism survived in the Toul seminary, as generally in Lorraine, behind a "façade of submission" to *Unigenitus*.[17] Students read the new texts alongside the older ones. For two decades prior to Lamourette's arrival the diocese was bitterly divided between a *parti dévot* bishop (Drouas; 1754–73) who aggressively attacked Jansenism, and a Jansenist clergy that vigorously defended itself, even resorting to the courts. The bishop had difficulty finding a competent director for the Toul seminary. His penultimate appointee, Broquevielle, an "implacable enemy of Jansenists, Gallicans and parlementaires," was a disappointment as student discipline visibly declined. His successor, M. Ferris, fared no better. Worse still, the seminary divided over Ferris and Broquevielle.[18]

The next bishop, Champorcin (1721–1807), appointed Lamourette director of the seminary of Toul in 1776. He served for two years, to January 1, 1778. Most writers understand Lamourette's brief term in light of the Jansenist–*parti dévot* conflict. The actual cause may have been the diocese's and seminary's restructuring. In 1778 the inordinately large Toul diocese was divided into three dioceses, Toul, Nancy, and Saint-Dié, and the Toul seminary was associated with the new

---

français jusqu'à la Révolution, 2 vols. (Paris, 1912), 1:331, 2:97–208; on training seminary professors, see Raymond Darricau, *La Formation des professeurs de séminaire au début du XVIIIe siècle d'après un directoire de M. Jean Bonnet (1664–1735), Supérieur général de la congrégation de la mission* (Piacenza, 1966). On Lazarist ultramontanism, see Poole, ibid., 75–79.

[16] For the Toul seminary, see Degert, *Histoire des séminaires français*, 1:60, 318–20. For the Jansenist (Van Espen, 1646–1728; Gaspard Juénin, 1650–1713; Louis Habert, 1635–1718) and anti-Jansenist texts (Pierre Collet, 1693–1770), see Poole, *A History of the Congregation of the Mission*, 74–75; René Taveneaux, *Le Jansénisme en Lorraine, 1640–1789* (Paris, 1960), 196, 208, 257, 378–79, 637–38, 677–78; and Degert, *Histoire des séminaires français*, 2:243–62. Lamourette noted his relationship to Grégoire in *Observations sur l'état civil des juifs: Adressées a l'assemblée nationale* (Paris, 1790), 19.

[17] Taveneuax, *Le Jansénisme en Lorraine*, 653.

[18] Eugene Martin, *Histoire des Diocèses de Toul, de Nancy and de Saint-Dié*, 3 vols. (Nancy, 1900–1903), quotation at 2:558. Cf. 2:555–560, 625–28. For *richérism*, see Tavenaux, *Le Jansénisme en Lorraine*, 691–705, and Francis Oakley, *The Conciliarist Tradition: Constitutionalism in the Catholic Church, 1300–1870* (Oxford, 2003), 141–216.

University of Nancy.[19] Lamourette was probably appointed as a place-holder during the seminary's reorganization.

After his term as director, Lamourette found another post through Bishop Champorcin's good offices (further evidence for being a place-holder). Lamourette became a parish priest in Outremècourt (Haute-Marne), where he spent five formative years, from 1778 to 83. He con-scientiously discharged his responsibilities, maintaining excellent relations with the local gentry and studying assiduously. This experi-ence made a lasting impression: in his books Lamourette idealized the pious rural priest and his parish.[20]

Lamourette's movements become sketchy in the second half of the 1780s. He returned to the congregation of Saint-Lazare in 1784, and in 1785 apparently to his parish of origin, where he was appointed to the Arras Academy. His first book appeared in 1785. He spent time in Paris, serving as chaplain to a convent, Saint Perine, and frequenting the salon of Madame de Sillery, better known as Madame la Comtesse de Genlis (1746–1830), a prolific author. It is difficult to imagine the humble Lamourette mingling with Genlis's aristocrats, yet he obvi-ously had some impact, at least on her. As governess to the children of the duc d'Orléans she compiled an anthology of quotations for her charge's (later Louis Philippe) First Communion. Genlis quoted twice from Lamourette, and some critics alleged that the book was his.[21]

Lamourette was loosely associated with Genlis's salon during the an-cien régime's final decade; he maintained those connections during the Revolution. To appreciate the significance of those relationships, we must first look to the 1780s: Lamourette had emerged at an auspicious moment.

THE 1780s

The 1780s were a crucial juncture; Louis XVI's reign (1774) ended the era of *Unigenitus*. The Jansenist–*parti dévot* divide began to dissolve

---

[19] Martin, *Histoire des Diocèses*, 3:52, and Gérard Dessolle, *Étienne, François-Xavier des Michels de Champorcin (1721–1807): Prêtre provençal, évêque de Senez, évêque-comte de Toul, prince due Saint-Empire* (Haute-Provence, 2001), 65–66; Tavenaux, *Le Jansénisme en Lor-raine*,715. Leon Berthe has Lamourette teaching philosophy at the Seminaire Saint-Anne in 1772. See "Grégoire, élève de l'Abbé Lamourette," *Revue du Nord* 44 (1962): 45.

[20] For idealization of the poor and rural parish as Jansenist tropes, see Cottret, *Jansén-ismes et Lumières*, 244–50.

[21] Violet Wyndham, *Madame de Genlis: A biography* (London, 1958); Gabriel de Broglie, *Madame de Genlis* (Paris, 1985). Genlis's book was *La Religion considéré comme l'unique base du bonheur et de la véritable philosophie*, 2 vols. (Paris, 1788). She quoted Lamourette's *Pen-sées sur la philosophie de l'incrédulité* at 2:77–80 and 97–98.

with the Jesuits' suppression in 1764. Louis XVI's restoration of the Parlement after the Maupeou controversy (1774) concluded the monarchy's
alliance with the *parti dévot* and its dispute with the "judicial Jansenists." A political realignment ensued as the clergy and bishops began to ally with the Parlement. In 1780 the Parlement and the Faculties
of Theology cooperated in condemning the second edition of Raynal's
History of the Two Indies. Jansenist thinkers opened to new cultural possibilities by embracing some " 'enlightened' reformist currents such as
Rousseauism, physiocracy and the political activism of civic humanism."[22] The government began to implement reforms conducive to
Reform Catholicism, including the limited toleration granted to Protestants in 1787, which the Assembly of the Clergy opposed, and the
appointment of a commission to consider the Jews' status. The irony, of
course, was that these reforms came at a time of weakness. The monarchy lurched from one unsuccessful effort to another to address its crip-
pling deficit, each failure further eroding its power.[23]

The 1780s were conducive to new directions in thought, including
Reform Catholicism. As evident from previous chapters, the core components of the religious Enlightenment were the ideas of reasonableness and natural religion, natural law and toleration, which functioned
together to varying degrees. What set France apart throughout the era
of *Unigenitus* was that the triangular dispute of Jansenists, Jesuits, and
philosophes had cast these ideas in mutually irreconcilable forms and
dispersed them across the field of conflict.[24]

The usually paired ideas of reasonableness and natural religion, for
example, inhabited different sides of the Jansenist-Jesuit divide. Jesuits
endorsed the idea of natural religion, although with restrictions, but
rejected reasonableness as a pejorative associated with philosophes
and deists. Regarding nature as corrupt and sinful, Jansenists resisted
any idea of natural religion.[25]

---

[22] Dale Van Kley, "The Abbé Grégoire and the Quest for a Catholic Republic," in *The
Abbé Grégoire and His World*, ed. Jeremy Popkin and Richard Popkin (Dordrecht, 2000), 79.
On Raynal, see Cottret, *Jansénismes et Lumières*, 110, 143–78. For "judicial Jansenists," see
Van Kley, *Religious Origins*, 294.

[23] McManners, *Church and Society*, 2:644–744. Protestant marriages were legitimated;
they were still denied freedom of worship. For the clergy's opposition, see Nigel Aston,
The End of an Élite: The French Bishops and the Coming of the Revolution, 1786–1790 (Oxford,
1992), 90–98, 109.

[24] Van Kley, *Religious Origins*, 235.

[25] Catherine M. Northeast, *The Parisian Jesuits and the Enlightenment, 1700–1762, Studies
on Voltaire and the Eighteenth Century* 288 (Oxford, 1991), 51, 58–89, 89, 125 for reasonableness, 156–75 for natural religion. In the 1760s the Jansenist André Blonde (1734–94)
attacked Rousseau and the main apologist for the Gallican Church, Nicolas-Sylvestre
Bergier (1718–90), as Pelagians. See Cottret, *Jansénismes et Lumières*, 107–111.

A mid-century attempt to unite these ideas, representing incipient Reform Catholicism, had been suppressed. In the University of Paris's Theology Faculty a group centered around Luke Joseph Hooke (1714–96), a member of the Jacobite diaspora, engaged with "rationalism, natural religion, the status of revelation, the role of experimental science and Locke's empiricism." Hooke's major work had a structure typical of religious Enlightenment theology (treating first natural religion and natural law, then revealed religion—Judaism, Christianity, and finally Catholicism), was informed by natural law theory, and was influenced by such English Moderates as Bishop Butler and Samuel Clark. Conservative opponents, including Archbishop Beaumont, thwarted this group through the de Prades affair (1751): de Prades lost his degree and Hooke his teaching position.[26]

The ideas of natural law and toleration were also dispersed across the polemical field. Jansenists at first rejected toleration and natural law, celebrating the revocation of the Edict of Nantes. Similarly, Jansenist writers criticized Montesquieu's natural law ideas. Eighteenth-century persecution increasingly convinced Jansenists to identify with Protestants and embrace civil, but not theological, toleration. A crucial step was the mid-century effort to "Jansenize" natural law by deeming it "primitive law." Joseph II's 1781 edict offered a crucial Catholic example of "Christian toleration." Jansenists now began to idealize the Edict of Nantes as having created a golden era for Protestants and themselves. By the 1780s the Jansenists were fully in toleration's camp.[27] In contrast, the philosophes tended to embrace natural law and toleration without distinguishing between civil and theological forms. In this regard as well, Jansenists and philosophes differed throughout most of the eighteenth century, their dispositions first converging in the 1770s and 1780s.

The effort at reformulating and assembling key ideas can be seen in the work of the Abbé Grégoire (1750–1831), a student of Lamourette's.

---

[26] Thomas O'Connor, *An Irish Theologian in Enlightenment France: Luke Joseph Hooke, 1714–96* (Dublin, 1995), 60. For the de Prades affair, 61–86; for Butler and Clarke, 151, 158. For Oratorians conversant with contemporary philosophy and experimental science, see Ruth Graham, "The Enlightened and Revolutionary Oratorians in France," *British Journal for Eighteenth-Century Studies* 4, no. 2 (1981): 171–83. For the example of P.C.F. Daunou (1761–1840), see Gérard Minart, *Pierre Claude François Daunou, l'anti-Robespierre: De la Révolution à l'Empire, l'itinéraire d'un juste (1761–1840)* (Toulouse, 2001). For additional evidence of Reform Catholicism, see Daniele Menozzi, *Les Interprétations politiques de Jésus de l'Ancien régime à la Révolution* (Paris, 1983), 92–98.

[27] Cottret, *Jansénismes et Lumières*, 170, 179–218; Charles H. O'Brien, "Jansenists on Civil Toleration in Mid-eighteenth Century France," *Theologische Zeitschrift* 37 (1981): 71–93, and idem, "Jansenist Campaign for Toleration of Protestants in Late Eighteenth-Century France: Sacred or Secular?" *Journal of the History of Ideas* 46 (1985): 523–38; McManners, *Church and Society*, 2:626–60.

In advocating the Jews' emancipation, Grégoire recast natural law theory and toleration in the spirit of Reform Catholicism. In his *Essai sur la régénération physique, morale et politique des Juifs* (1789), which the Academy of Metz awarded a prize in 1788, Grégoire made the same arguments for emancipating the Jews that secular advocates had systematically presented at the beginning of the decade, especially mankind's equality and the primacy of environmental causes; he attributed the Jews' degraded condition to their oppression.[28] Like all mankind, they were educable and, ultimately, perfectible. "Amend their education to amend their hearts; it is a long time that one repeats that they are men like us before they are Jews." It was incumbent upon France, if not Christian Europe, to regenerate the Jews: "creators of their vices, become that of their virtues; acquit yourselves of your debt and your ancestors'."[29]

These ideas functioned within a framework of Reform Catholicism. Grégoire affirmed Catholicism's veracity and Judaism's incapacity. That the Jews were the first recipients of revelation only highlighted their abiding mistake. Their "obstinate attachment to belief," including a Pharisaic emphasis on ritual, "talmudic and cabbalistic daydreams," and "blind credulity" in rejecting Jesus and embracing false messiahs, prevented them from "substitut[ing] for an ecstasy of folly the fruits of a luminous reason," namely, the one true Catholic faith.[30]

Grégoire's understanding of equality was also Reform Catholic. Grégoire embraced ideas of natural law, the "imprescriptible rights of man," and liberty of conscience. Yet he maintained the inherited Catholic distinction between the sinner and the sin, endorsing civil and not theological toleration. The citizenship he would extend to the Jews included freedom of conscience and worship, but also obligatory instruction in Christianity. Joseph II was his model monarch.

---

[28] For the Metz Academy competition, "Are there means to render the Jews more useful and happier in France?" see Frances Malino, *A Jew in the French Revolution: The Life of Zalkind Hourwitz* (Oxford, 1996), 14–37. For Grégoire's 1778 essay from which his Metz submission largely derived, see Alyssa Sepinwall, *The Abbé Grégoire and the French Revolution: The Making of Modern Universalism* (Berkeley, 2005), 26. For other advocates of toleration, see Menozzi, *Les Interprétations politiques de Jésus*, 103–4.

[29] *Essai sur la régénération physique, morale et politique des Juifs* (1789), 108, 194. The most influential presentation was Christian Wilhelm Dohm (1751–1820), *Über die bürgerliche Verbesserung der Juden* (1781; French translation, 1782), which Grégoire repeatedly cited. Mirabeau disseminated Dohm's ideas in France. See *Sur Moses Mendelssohn, sur la réforme politique des Juifs* (1787). On Grégoire's ideas of equality, see Hans-Jürgen Lüsebrink, "Grégoire and the Anthropology of Emancipation," in *The Abbé Grégoire and His World*, 1–12. For the term "régénération" see Mona Ozouf, "Regeneration," in *A Critical Dictionary of the French Revolution*, ed. François Furet and Mona Ozouf, trans. Arthur Goldhammer (Cambridge, MA, 1989), 781–91.

[30] *Essai sur la régénération physique, morale et politique des Juifs*, 15, 28–29, 32, 183, 187.

Grégoire's ultimate aim was the Jews' conversion; citizenship was a means to it. "According complete religious liberty to the Jews would be a major step toward reforming them, and I dare say, toward converting them; for the truth is most persuasive when it is mild."[31] Conversion was not a pragmatic project: Grégoire discerned a divine plan in the Bible and history that put the Jews' conversion front and center. His interpretation derived from the "figurist" tradition that identified visible signs of God's inscrutable plan.[32]

Whereas Grégoire developed natural law theory in respect to Jews, other thinkers applied it to the Church. The Abbé Fauchet (1744–93), who studied at the Jesuit seminary in Bourges and became a successful preacher at Versailles, worked in the conciliarist tradition.[33] In a daring work published on the eve of the Estates General, De la religion nationale (1789), Fauchet proposed fundamental Church reform by combining a populist version of conciliarism ("richérism," from Edmond Richer, 1559–1631), focused on the selection of priests and bishops, with notions of national sovereignty.

Fauchet envisaged a Church of liberty and virtue. The people's will would serve as the new "spirit of liberty": "the voice of the people is the voice of God, because it is that of nature and of society." The Church would recognize virtue as the sole criterion for appointment, repudiating noble birth and the monarchy's misuse of Church wealth. His models were the primitive Church, from which he derived the Presbyterian view that parishioners should elect their priests ("deputies of believing people"), and the Pragmatic Sanction of Bourges (1438), from which, by having priests and the faithful nominate episcopal candidates, he would preclude the monarch using high ecclesiastical office to reward incompetent and impious aristocrats. He similarly envisioned a redistribution of Church income to parish priests, maintenance of buildings, and care of the poor.[34]

---

[31] Ibid., 132. On natural law, 88, 126, 132, 151; on toleration, 152; on Joseph II, 138, 156, 193.

[32] Rita Hermon-Belot, "The Abbé Grégoire's Program for the Jews: Social Reform and Spiritual Project," in The Abbé Grégoire and His World, 21–26.

[33] Oakley, The Conciliarist Tradition; Brian Tierney, Foundations of the Conciliar Theory: The Contributions of the Medieval Canonists from Gratian to the Great Schism (Cambridge, 1955).

[34] De la religion nationale (Paris, 1789), 8, 45, 29, 107–11, 117, 138. For "liberty," see 57, 75, 100, 223, 252. For "volonté publique," see 1–2, 26, 45, 61–63, 66, 168, 293; for "volonté générale," see 46, 58; for "voix publique," see 85, 96. Lamourette called this book a "masterwork of logic and eloquence" in Prônes civiques, ou Le Pasteur patriote, no. 1 (Paris, 1791): 20. For Fauchet, see J. Charrier, Claude Fauchet, Évêque constitutionnel du Calvados, Député à l'Assemblée Législative et à la Convention (1744–1793), 2 vols. (Paris, 1909); Norman Ravitch, "The Abbé Fauchet: Romantic Religion during the French Revolution," Journal of the

Fauchet blamed government, not the papacy, for the Church's failure to act according to liberty and virtue. He rebuked the aristocracy for France's worst faults, proposing reforms to overturn the privilege of birth, redistribute aristocratic wealth (especially agricultural land), and bring criminal aristocrats to book. These measures would "regenerate" the nation by turning the majority, who are now "subjects" dependent on aristocratic wealth and power, into true "citizens." Fauchet aimed to revive the estate system by creating a new aristocracy of merit and service.[35]

Fauchet thought the French monarchy was predicated on Catholic unity. He considered Catholicism "the most tolerant" of religions and endorsed freedom of conscience for, and civil toleration of, Protestants, including the right to private worship (he denied atheists toleration). He deplored the hypocrisy of Catholics who refused civil toleration to non-Catholics yet "observe an infamous toleration" for those Catholics, especially aristocrats, who violate "the sanctity of the true religion and the natural morality common to all religions with great crimes and abominable scandals."[36]

Neither Grégoire nor Fauchet succeeded in formulating a full-blown Reform Catholicism, but they did pave the way for, and then participated in, its great experiment during the early years of the revolution. Lamourette similarly spent the 1780s developing the theories that he revised and tried to realize during the revolution.

THEOLOGY

Lamourette's theology of the 1780s broke crucial new ground in addressing central issues of Reform Catholicism. He attempted to recast and reassemble some of the key ideas that had been fragmented among the contending parties during the eighteenth century. He developed his fundamental positions in opposition to the philosophes': the role of reason and sentiment (inspired by Rousseau) in faith, the relationship between revealed and natural religion, and Christianity as a political philosophy and social ethics.

American Academy of Religion 42 (1974): 247–62; Monglond, *Le préromantisme français,* 2:106–113; and H. Maier, *Revolution and Church: The Early History of Christian Democracy, 1798–1901* (South Bend, IN, 1969), 105–31.

[35] *De la religion nationale,* 24, 103. For noble privileges, 161–62; punishing aristocrats, 209–210; redistributing wealth, 222–224, 239; "citizens," 230; monarchy, 165, 243; the estates, 158–89.

[36] Ibid., 104. For "unity of national religion," 183–84, 285; toleration, 14, 180–97.

Lamourette tried to make a fresh theological start. As a student and teacher he had encountered the ideas of the various theological parties. Although no Molinist, he may well have learned about natural religion from Lazarist or other *parti dévot* advocates. While sympathetic to aspects of Jansenism, he was not an avowed Jansenist. Instead, he appropriated some elements of Molinism and many of Jansenism for a new theological position. The Jansenist-Jesuit conflict was as moot for him in the 1780s as the Pietist-Orthodox conflict had been for Baumgarten in the 1720s. Lamourette refers neither to the vast theological literature of the eighteenth century nor to medieval theology. He cites either the great figures of the ancient Church or those of the seventeenth century, such as Bossuet and Fénelon. He does not refer to Jansenism's founders. He mentions only one or two noteworthy eighteenth-century apologists, especially the Abbé Noël-Antoine Pluche (1688–1761), who defended biblical cosmogony with physico-theology and Warburton's theory of Greek mythology. As a biographer put it, Lamourette was trying to avoid the extremes of Jansenism, which destroyed piety, and philosophy, which undermined faith.[37]

The fresh start is already evident in his first work, *Reflections on the Spirit and Duties of the Monastic Life* (1785), which he wrote while serving as chaplain to the Convent of Saint Perine. The book defends monastic life, arguing that it aims to disconnect its adherents from the visible world. It first negates the self through recognition of the "burden of [our] pitiful nullity" that requires a "heroism of obedience." Next comes "the repose of all our faculties on God alone [that] is the great goal of faith and the true character of the Gospel's perfection." A monastery should embody this ideal by appearing as a "tomb" of silence or death that is "uniquely and immediately subordinated to the direction of [God's] sovereign will."[38]

In vindicating monastic life, Lamourette sounded three important themes. He understood Jesus and the divine to represent "the infinite."

---

[37] Liebaut, *Prêtre et évêque assermenté*, 43. Sepinwall suggests similarly eclectic influences for Grégoire. See *The Abbé Grégoire and the French Revolution*. For Lamourette's dismissal of medieval philosophy, see *Pensées sur la philosophie de la foi*, 258–59; *Le Décret de l'Assemblée nationale sur les biens du clergé: Considéré dans son rapport avec la nature et les lois de l'institution ecclésiastique* (Paris, 1790), 26; *Instruction pastorale de M. L'évêque du département de Rhône et Loire: Métropolitain du sud-est, à MM. les curés, vicaires et fonctionnaires ecclésiastiques de son Diocèse* (Lyon, 1791), 17; and *Prônes civiques*, v. 48.

Pluche's *Spectacle de la Nature* (1732), a bestseller, was followed by *L'histoire du ciel* (1739). See Robert R. Palmer, *Catholics and Unbelievers in Eighteenth-Century France* (Princeton, 1939), 106–7. Lamourette cites Pluche in *Pensées sur la Philosophie de l'Incrédulité*, 31, 38–40.

[38] *Considérations sur l'esprit et les devoirs de la vie religieuse*, 10, 137, 270, 237, 197–98.

He idealized poverty as the sine qua non of religious life and monasticism. Jesus exemplified poverty ("the hidden treasure for which it is worth sacrificing all the rest"), and the poor bear true Christian belief: "It is among the class of the poor that the saints of the earth reside; it is there that is found the rest of the elect." Finally, he articulated a conservative politics that valued subordination and authority over liberty. He ascribed the seditious exercise of liberty to the philosophes, who, the "true agitators of states and nations,"

> dare to examine whether our Masters have the right to our homage and who shake, by the seditious maxims of their desolate philosophy, all the principles that are the support, the surety and the happiness of all societies on earth.[39]

Lamourette offered his version of Reform Catholicism in three volumes that appeared between 1786 and 1789. It consisted of a moderate skepticism, well established in French Catholicism by Pascal, that he wielded against the philosophes. By considering such words as "revelation, miracle, mystery, and prophecy" incompatible with truthful analysis, the philosophes delude themselves into thinking that they are able to decipher everything but religion. In fact, they find nature impenetrable and cannot explain a drop of water's true character. The theologian's belief in the Trinity has the same basis as the philosopher's in geometry: perception, "*bon sens*," and reason. Theology qualifies as philosophy since it rests on true perception and reason: "everywhere philosophy consists in heeding reason and submitting to truth." It is "anti-philosophical" to cite as grounds for incredulity the obscurity of miracles and mysteries.[40]

Lamourette's skepticism restricts his notion of reason and especially science. While admiring two centuries of scientific achievement as exemplified by the work of Copernicus, Galileo, Cassini, Toricelli, Pascal, and Malphighi, he insists that it remains on the phenomena's surface. Nature's essence or final cause is as impenetrable as the divine mysteries: "it is . . . only in the Infinite that the true principles of differences

---

[39] For "subordination," see ibid., 174–75. For the infinite, see 7, 24, 62, 228, 271, 278, 289, esp. 18; for poverty see 97, 100–1, 111. On Lamourette's idealization of poverty, see Menozzi, "*Philosophes*" e "*chrétiens éclairés*," 110–17. Darrin M. McMahon mistook Lamourette's views for counter-Enlightenment. See *Enemies of the Enlightenment: The French Counter-Enlightenment and the Making of Modernity* (New York, 2001), 46, 73.

[40] *Pensées sur la Philosophie de l'Incrédulité*, 283, 14–15, 21–22. On Catholic skepticism, see Richard Popkin, *The History of Scepticism: From Erasmus to Descartes* (New York, 1964). On Grégoire and Pascal, see Rita Hermon-Belot, *L'Abbé Grégoire, la politique et la vérité* (Paris, 2000), 29.

that distinguish created substances are to be found hidden away." Man's task is to act, not to understand.[41]

From this skeptical restriction of science and equation of theology and philosophy, Lamourette made a fideist leap, redefining "enlightened man."

> For the enlightened man [l'homme éclairé] of good faith the collection of human knowledge carries a preconceived disposition to believe without understanding; and the reluctance to recognize as truth that which cannot be explained is an absurd ostentation which decisively proves mediocrity and ignorance.[42]

Philosophers should recognize not only that there are truths beyond reason (supra rationem), but that being so attests to their divine source:

> The [philosophes] are unjust, in that they always assume that one can only acknowledge as true that which can be fully conceived. For it is evident that there are truths whose principle is not in the circumference of human ideas; and in consequence the foundation of their credibility does not need to consist in their accord with the set of our perceptions and axioms. . . . Incomprehensibility, far from being a sufficient reason for incredulity, should be seen as a characteristic of truth when it is concerned with God.[43]

Lamourette wanted to recover the core truths of Christianity that transcended mere reason:

> I want to lead all the thinkers to recognize the necessity of guiding their belief by a less equivocal criterion than the agreement of faith with our ideas, and to bring them back, without giving short shrift to their taste for philosophical analysis, to the luminous side of faith.[44]

Lamourette inverted the philosophes' claim that "Christianity is a cruel and seditious religion" and a form of "religious fanaticism." The philosophes are the true fanatics. They aim to create "discord in the hearts of all peoples and combustion in the entire universe" by making "the philosophical spirit . . . as much the ruin of reason as the tomb of all virtue."[45]

Lamourette strove to overcome the polarity between religion and reason: "the philosophes of our century have shown themselves to be too

---

[41] Pensées sur la Philosophie de la foi, 100. Cf. 93–95, 98–99, 339, 103, 112–15.
[42] Pensées sur la Philosophie de l'Incrédulité, 16.
[43] Pensées sur la Philosophie de la foi, xviii, xx–xxi.
[44] Ibid., xxv–xxvi. My emphasis.
[45] Pensées sur la Philosophie de l'Incrédulité, 201, 208. Cf. 206–7.

anti-Theologian, and our other theologians have perhaps been a bit too *anti-Philosophes.*" This polarity is a human invention: "Reason and revelation get along infinitely better than their interpreters. . . . These two torches are taken from . . . the same light; they never . . . conflict except in the hands of man."[46] This false polarity can be avoided by finding a middle ground in which "the masters of theology would reduce less severely the rights of reason, and . . . the philosophes show more respect and consideration for those of revelation." Lamourette proposed undoing the polarization by having the Republic of Letters promote belief and piety and the universities employ pious writers to teach religion.[47]

Within his skeptical structure, Lamourette made sentiment a source of belief. Lamourette began to exhibit traces of Rousseau's sentimental understanding of religion in his second book (*Thoughts on the Philosophy of Unbelief, or Reflections on the Spirit and Design of the Irreligious Philosophers of Our Century,* 1786) where he wrote of the "sentiment of faith" and asserted that Catholicism not only elevated the spirit but also "contents the most capacious heart."[48] In his third book, *The Pleasures of Religion, or the Power of the Gospel to Make Us Happy* (1788), he elevated sentiment to a source of religious knowledge, combining the argument of reasonable religion with that of belief from sentiment: he aimed "to enlighten reason and interest feeling." The Gospel demonstrates that "our intimate sense [*sens intime*] is the first proof of the beauty of the Gospel and the strongest conjecture of its truth." The same holds for our perception of Jesus, which has the persuasive proof of science.

> It is not the demonstration of the internal truth of the *miracles* of Jesus Christ that determines my adoration and belief; but it is a proof of sentiment that draws its strength from the knowledge that I have of his character, the tissue of his actions, the infinity of local circumstances and persons, whose combination victoriously produces conviction in a healthy and reasonable mind, like all the evidence of a geometric proof.

Since reason is an equal source of belief, Lamourette argued that we must disengage ourselves from the "realm of passions" and submit to "reason" that is the "realm of God": "Therefore we see reason everywhere beginning the work of faith, and we are transported by the most natural gradations to the great wisdom of the Gospel."[49]

---

[46] *Pensées sur la Philosophie de la foi,* xviii–xix. Cf. *Pensées sur la Philosophie de l'Incrédulité,* 253, 263, and *Les Délices,* ix.

[47] *Pensées sur la Philosophie de l'Incrédulité,* 13, 263, 250, 267–68.

[48] *Pensées sur la Philosophie de l'Incrédulité,* 26–27, 78, 137.

[49] *Les Délices,* iii–iv, 272.

Whereas in his third book Lamourette had explicitly associated natural religion with rank unbelief ("the disciple of natural religion, the impious person who no longer sees God in the universe"), in his last book, *Thoughts on the Philosophy of Faith, or the System of Christianity* (1789), he linked it to reason in a manner characteristic of Reform Catholicism. Natural religion is identical with Christianity; there is no theism without revelation. True natural religion "pushes and inclines toward the Gospel."[50]

Lamourette vehemently attacked the philosophes' political philosophy, unmasking them as "a dark and malicious sect which . . . makes a study of corrupting men and freeing them of every sort of duty" as well as subverting all authority and undermining morality because there is no "middle route . . . between Christianity and atheism." Lamourette lambasted the philosophes' seditious politics: "One can never ascribe a virtuous intention to writers who continuously affect to sow republican maxims in the bosom of a nation subject to a monarchical government." The philosophes will incite the people "to dare to meditate on a revolution."[51]

Lamourette discerns similar "malignity" in the philosophes' view of society: by positing that men were originally solitary beings who want to devour each other, they promote an "egoism destructive of all social virtue" and sense of obligation.[52] The philosophes are, therefore, "as much an enemy of throne as of altar."

Lamourette had two political-social ideals. He examined an idyllic rural parish (Outremècourt, but this was also a trope of Jansenist literature) whose dedicated priest imbues it with faith:

> [A] rural parish becomes, through a virtuous and sensible pastor, the most beautiful and delightful spectacle that the entire grand theater of the world can offer. There one can see religion shining in all the glory of its triumph.[53]

In his third book he injected "sentiment," making the poor its true repository. He then combined this rural parish with his other ideal, the propertyless primitive Church.[54]

---

[50] *Pensées sur la Philosophie de la foi*, 2–3, 10–11, 272, 288, 291, 293. Cf. *Les Délices*, 105.

[51] *Pensées sur la Philosophie de l'Incrédulité*, 5–6, 30–31, 42, 230–34, 198–99, 89. For the philosophes as a "sect" or "cabal," 22–23, 42, 51, 55, 90, 105, 115, 124, 238, 244; for morality, 99, 112–16, 151.

[52] Ibid., 243 (italics in original). Cf. 48–49, 60–63, 75, 78–79.

[53] Ibid., 184. For idealization of the poor and the rural parish as Jansenist tropes, see Cottret, *Jansénismes et Lumières*, 244–50.

[54] *Les Délices*, 191–92. On Lamourette's idealization of the early Church, see Menozzi, *"Philosophes" e "Chrétiens éclaires,"* 95–104.

Lamourette sketched an alternative social philosophy. He attacked social contract theory's "first principle" of a "natural man" or "state of nature" as "an abstraction and a pure hypothesis," a "geometric *postulatum*." It is the equivalent in the social world of being emerging out of chaos in the physical world. Philosophers "cannot explain anything without chaos."

He argued instead that society is the "first state of humankind." Man is born into a "double relationship" with God and society, his relations with God yielding religion, those with his fellowmen morality. Both of these are embodied in the Gospel. The Gospel teaches the "lessons of respect and submission to the powers that be," that make Christians the "true and excellent philosophes."[55] Thus "society is the natural state of the human species." God creates man in society from the start. "The state of society is therefore a work of creation; it is a mode of human nature that does not rest at all on what one calls a pact or a contract."[56]

Christian society derives directly from its Creator and is invested with an authority that is neither man-made nor subject to human approval.[57] Christianity inculcates performance of obligations as the first step toward the "mystery of God's kingdom." It also entails a conservative acceptance of the established order, with divine society serving as the template for human society: "the infinitely perfect society of eternity is the origin and model of the profound idea that God used in conceiving and fashioning temporal society."[58] In this divinely ordained Christian social order, in which authority and obedience are foremost, the ideal government would be "a *theocratic régime*," but barring that "a monarchical regime."[59]

Christianity also creates the best society: it is "the unique system which is able to form a perfect society, and people the empire with true and incorruptible citizens" because it corresponds to the infinite's unity within plurality. In his 1789 book, *Thoughts on the Philosophy of Faith, or the System of Christianity*, Lamourette attempted to formulate a systematic theology of the infinite in which reasonableness and sentiment were equal sources of belief. The ideal of the primitive Church fortifies this notion of a Christian social order since, based on communal prop-

---

[55] *Pensées sur la Philosophie de l'Incrédulité*, 70–71, 63, 70–72. In a letter to Grégoire (Sept. 7, 1789), he wrote that the work contained "the elements of a political philosophy." See Leon Berthe, "Grégoire, élève de l' Abbé Lamourette," *Revue du Nord* 44 (1962): 43.

[56] *Pensées sur la Philosophie de la foi*, 3, 17–18, 30–31.

[57] Ibid., 29.

[58] *Les Délices*, 178–81, 250, 261, 147–48, 112, 110.

[59] *Pensées sur la Philosophie de la foi*, 121, 19, 29.

erty and a life devoted to prayer, it represented "all the characteristics of the most perfect and happiest society that could establish itself on earth," embodying the ideals of "equality" [*égalité*] and "sociability" [*sociabilité*][60]. By 1789 Lamourette had enunciated two of the revolution's three principles.

The idea of the infinite grounds Lamourette's social ethics. Man's very Christian potential depends on it: "a man is so great a being through the excellence of his nature and entirely by his capacity to know and to possess the Infinite." In contrast, the impious pursue the "false" infinity of luxury and sensual experience: "Luxury is none other than the inarticulate and confused search for the infinite that religion gives us. It is the sterile and deceptive supplement to the great force in which Jesus Christ comes to incorporate all of humankind."[61]

Here are the lineaments of a religious refutation of the important Enlightenment view, *"doux commerce,"* that trade and goods have a civilizing impact (Vernet's argument against it was republican). Proposed in a variety of forms by such diverse thinkers as Montesquieu and Hume, this doctrine held that free trade gave rise to a "commercial humanism" through a new sociability based either on the arts and sensibility or on manners and morals.[62]

Lamourette derisively labeled the philosophes' ethics the "regime of the passions." Based on the desire for the "false infinity" of objects, its ideal is "passionate man" (*"l'Homme passioné"*) who, acting solely from physical needs and "self-love," is incapable of benevolence and solidarity. Lamourette pits against "passionate man" the "moderate man" (*"l'Homme moderé"*) who understands that he is born into society in solidarity with his fellow men, subjects himself to the true infinity of Christ, and acts in "profoundly reasonable" ways.[63]

Lamourette's theology of the 1780s may be compared with that of another prominent writer of the decade we have already met, Madame Genlis. In her *Religion Treated as the Singular Basis of Happiness and True Philosophy*, Genlis drew much of her material from the same outstanding seventeenth-century thinkers as Lamourette, and invoked some

---

[60] Ibid., 221, 272, 223, 233–36. See Daniel Gordon, *Citizens without Sovereignty: Equality and Sociability in French Thought, 1670–1789* (Princeton, 1994).

[61] *Les Délices,* 183, 259. Cf. xxxvii, 159–60, 55–58, 345–47.

[62] A. O. Hirschman, *The Passions and the Interests: Political Arguments for Capitalism before Its Triumph* (Princeton, 1977); Laurence Dickey, "*Doux-Commerce* and Humanitarian Values: Free Trade, Sociability and Universal Benevolence in Eighteenth-Century Thinking," in *Hugo Grotius and the Stoa: Philosophy, Politics and Law,* ed. Hans Blom (Assen, 2004), 271–318; Christopher J. Berry, *The Idea of Luxury: A Conceptual and Historical Investigation* (Cambridge, 1994).

[63] *Pensées sur la Philosophie de la foi,* 204–11.

contemporary or near contemporary English ones: "The virtuous philosophers who make the maxims of the Gospel the base of their morality, Fénélon, Nicole, Pascal, Abadie, Massillon, Addisson, Clarcke, Richardson. . . ." She attacked the philosophes with many of the same arguments as Lamourette. They are perverse and act in bad faith, excite and value the passions, comprise a cabal or a sect, and in the end are the true fanatics who will undermine morality and destroy society. She was openly partisan in citing well-known Jesuit or *parti dévot* preachers.[64]

Genlis and Lamourette shared an opposition to the philosophes and a commitment to constitutional monarchy (Genlis was an Orléanist). Yet Genlis made no effort to use the philosophes' ideas to support the Gospel's superiority. In contrast, Lamourette tried to invent a theological middle ground that reconciled major features of Enlightenment thinking with the Gospel: reasonableness and natural religion, moderation and Rousseauist sentiment. While he embraced ideas of equality and sociability that presaged the revolution, he also held to notions of authority and obedience at odds with it.

What became of Lamourette's "luminous side of faith" during the Revolution? Who were his allies and adversaries? To what extent was he able to realize his version of Reform Catholicism?

THE REVOLUTION, 1789–91

In the early years of the revolution (1789–91), Lamourette played a public role through salons and clubs, association with Mirabeau, and pamphlets and addresses. In Paris during the Estates General, he continued to attend Madame Genlis's salon and also began to frequent Madame Anne-Catherine Helvétius's (1719–1800). Lamourette met Mirabeau at these salons, and they discussed such key issues as monarchy and religion's political and social utility. Mirabeau had been influenced by two versions of religious Enlightenment. During his stay in Switzerland, in Neuchâtel, he associated with "representant" preachers who argued for the social utility of enlightened religion. His subsequent study of

---

[64] Madame de Sillery, ci-devant Madame la Comtesse de Genlis, *La Religion considérée comme l'unique base du bonheur et de la véritable philosophie*, 2 vols. (Paris, 1788), quotation at 2:6. For the philosophes, see 1:198, 200, 208, 210–11. Cf. 2:32; 127; 1:227, 118; 2:93, 36–37; 1:195; 2:10. The preachers were Abbé Louis Bourdaloue (1632–1704), Martin Pallu (1661–1742), and Gabriel Gauchat (1709–79). Jean-Baptiste Massillon (1663–1742), an Oratorian and the only *"tiers parti"* figure she quotes regularly, was frequently taken for an anti-Jansenist. See Appolis, *Le "Tiers Parti,"* 76–79, 95–97.

Anglicanism convinced him of religion's importance for toleration. Lamourette was one among many members of the Helvétius salon who served in Mirabeau's "atelier" of thinkers and writers. During the heady years of the early revolution, the salon met so frequently that it was said to have three venues: in the morning Mirabeau's, during the day the Assembly, and in the evening Helvétius's. Mirabeau drew on Lamourette's expertise in ecclesiastical matters. The two became so friendly that Mirabeau asked to see Lamourette in his final hours.[65]

Lamourette also participated in the *Cercle Social*, the group around Nicolas Bonneville (1760–1828) that eventually became the Parisian Girondins' base. The Cercle Social first emerged as a faction in Paris politics advocating representative democracy (1789–90). Its members then founded a political club, the Confédération des Amis de la Vérité, in 1790, that examined such issues as civil religion and public education, property rights, and women's rights. Finally, it established a publishing house, Imprimerie du Cercle Social (1791–93) to champion the Girondin cause.

Lamourette was a member of the Cercle Social's Directory (1789–91). When he returned to Paris as a delegate to the Legislative Assembly (1791–92), the Cercle Social provided a congenial home in its equal commitment to the Civil Constitution of the Clergy and representative democracy (either constitutional monarchy or moderate republicanism). Fauchet, who as "preacher of the Paris Commune" and "an actor in most [events of the revolution] and an eye witness in almost everything," was a leader of the early Cercle Social (1789–91). He delivered to the Confédération his famous lectures on Rousseau's *Social Contract* trying to reconcile the Gospel and the revolution. Cercle Social connections helped both Lamourette and Fauchet gain election as bishops.[66]

Lamourette was one of the "patriotic" and "enlightened" clergy who emerged during the early years of the Revolution. These were priests who embraced the Revolution and Christianity, understanding them to

[65] For Mirabeau, see Menozzi, *"Philosophes" e "Chrétiens éclaires,"* 45–94. For Mirabeau and Lamourette, 183–87. On the Helvétius salon, see Antoine Guillois, *Le Salon de Madame Helvétius: Cabanis et les idéologues; ouvrage orné de deux portraits d'après des originaux inédits* (Paris, 1894), 76–77. On Mirabeau's atelier, see Oliver J. G. Welch, *Mirabeau: A Study of a Democratic Monarchist* (London, 1951), 211. For other salons, see Dena Goodman, *The Republic of Letters: A Cultural History of the French Enlightenment* (Ithaca, 1994), 75, 145, 227.

[66] *Journal des Amix* (1 Jan. 1793): 6, quoted in Charrier, *Claude Fauchet*, vi. Gary Kates, *The Cercle Social, the Girondins, and the French Revolution* (Princeton, NJ, 1985). Fauchet's lectures, "Discours sur la liberté Françoise," appeared in the Confederation's journal, *Bouche de Fer*. For a Namierite view of the Girondins, see M. J. Sydenham, *The Girondins* (London, 1961).

be mutually fulfilling: the Revolution realized the Gospel's central ideas, while the Gospel guaranteed the morality and belief indispensable to the Revolution's success. Neither a coterie nor a party, the "patriotic" or "enlightened" clergy formed a loose grouping professing equal loyalty to Christianity and the Revolution.[67]

Lamourette developed his version of Reform Catholicism by articulating this double loyalty during the early Revolution. His first public response to the revolution was a pamphlet about the assault on the Maison St-Lazare during the period of "the Great Fear" when the Parisian populace took to the streets. Two days before crowds attacked the Bastille (July 14), they broke into the Maison St-Lazare and, after a fourteen-hour rampage, left it a virtual ruin.

Lamourette approved of the revolution by distinguishing between the patriotic crowd that gathered to resist "despotism" and the "henchmen" without "public sentiment" who were out for "blood and booty." He expressed the period's characteristic fear of conspiracy and counterrevolution, seeing the miscreant crowd attempting to deceive king and people by plunging the kingdom into "combustion." The ruin of Saint-Lazare, a heroic sacrifice for the good of France, foiled these plans by raising the alarm among patriotic citizens: "It is the ruin of Saint-Lazare that saved Paris, that saved all of France."[68]

Lamourette next responded to the debate on whether non-Catholics—specifically Protestants and Jews, actors and executioners—should be admitted to the civic oath (the December 21–23 debate concluded with the Assembly admitting Protestants and actors but deferring a decision on Jews). Two clergymen, Abbé Maury and Bishop de la Fare, were among the Jews' staunchest opponents, while five patriotic clergy, François Mulot, Antoine Bertolio, and Fauchet in Paris, Grégoire in the Constituent Assembly, and Lamourette, were conspicuous advocates. Although Lamourette had not previously written about the Jews, he, like Grégoire, was familiar with them from Lorraine.[69]

---

[67] Mona Ozouf, "La Révolution française et l'idée de fraternité," in L'Homme régénéré: Essais sur la révolution française (Paris, 1989), 158–82, esp. 164; Hermon-Belot, L'Abbé Grégoire 63–129, 183–226. Hermon-Belot identified as "clergé patriote" or "éclairé" Grégoire, Fauchet, Lamourette, Bertolio, Jumel, Mulot, Chaix, Le Conte, and Delehelle. A definition is at p. 72. Daniele Menozzi labeled the precursors "chrétiens éclairés." See Les Interprétations politiques de Jésus, 92–114. Bernard Plongeron used the term "philosophe chrétien." See L'Abbé Grégoire (1750–1831), ou L'Arche de la fraternité (Paris, 1989), 40–41.

[68] Désastre de la Maison de Saint-Lazare (Paris, 1789), 13–14, 30–31. For the Maison and the attack, see Poole, A History of the Congregation of the Mission, 102–7, 348–51. For a translation of Lamourette's pamphlet, 433–43.

[69] Ozouf, "La Révolution française et l'idée de fraternité," 164; Rita Hermon-Belot, L'émancipation des juifs en France (Paris, 1999), 55; and Malino, A Jew in the French Revolution,

Lamourette now espoused the revolution's ideal of "liberty" (he had already embraced equality and fraternity). He understood the Jews' admission to "civil status" as an issue of principle. Citizenship was a legal and constitutional question that did not depend on utility or character: "The determination of our right of citizen is anterior to the evaluation of our influence on the general good." Practical considerations did not apply in a discussion of rights:

> One is justified in balancing advantages and disadvantages when it turns on according a privilege. But for declaring a right, and in giving its use, the only thing that is necessary is to ascertain the truth.[70]

Citizenship for the Jews is "a manifest consequence of the principles adopted by the nation." "You can no longer refuse their civil existence without shaking the very foundation of your political edifice and without falling into an inconsistency destructive of the very elements of your new constitution."[71]

By embracing the idea of the Jews' "natural and irrefragable rights," Lamourette achieved the pairing of natural right with toleration characteristic of religious Enlightenment, although he was now endorsing full citizenship. His argument was exceptional: no delegate to the assembly argued so lucidly from principle. Indeed, Lamourette took the Assembly to task for violating its own ideals.[72]

Lamourette's deepening revolutionary commitment is evident in his endorsement of the Civil Constitutional of the Clergy (12 July 1790).

80–82. For Jews in Alsace-Lorraine, see Paula Hyman, *The Jews of Modern France* (Berkeley and Los Angeles, 1998), 1–15; idem, *The Emancipation of the Jews of Alsace: Acculturation and Tradition in the Nineteenth Century* (New Haven, 1991), 11–16.

[70] *Observations sur l'état civil des juifs, adressées a l'assemblée nationale* (Paris, 1790), 3–4. For equality and fraternity, see *Pensées sur la Philosophie de la foi,* 233–36.

[71] *Observations sur l'état civil des juifs,* 19.

[72] For the debates, see Achille-Edmond Halphen, ed., *Recueil des lois, décrets, ordonnances, avis du conseil d'état, arrêtés et réglements concernant les israélites depuis la Révolution de 1789* (Paris, 1851), 180–94. For the novelty of Lamourette's argument, see Bernard Plongeron, "Permanence d'une idéologie de 'civilisation chrétienne' dans le clergé constitutionnel," *Studies in Eighteenth-Century Culture* 7 (1978): 282, and Hermon-Belot, *L'émancipation des juifs en France,* 55. For the "moralization of citizenship," see Ronald Schechter, *Obstinate Hebrews: Representations of Jews in France, 1715–1815* (Berkeley and Los Angeles, 2003), 163. Arthur Hertzberg misunderstood Lamourette's argument. See *The French Enlightenment and the Jews: The Origins of Modern Anti-Semitism* (New York, 1968), 362–63.

Lamourette subsumed the Jews' utility and character to the idea of France's "regeneration." *Observations sur l'état civil des juifs,* 5–7, 10. Liberty and equality would restore the will to work; fraternity would reshape their relationship to the larger society and religious practices. Ibid, 8–9, 13, 15, 17.

The Civil Constitution was a Reform Catholic restructuring of the Church. It reorganized dioceses and parishes to conform to population shifts and administrative needs (as had Joseph II and Karl Theodor in Bavaria), abrogated chapters and benefices without cure of souls (as had Joseph II), introduced a salary scale for parish priests according to responsibility, set fixed salaries for bishops and cardinals, had them elected by their diocese (recognizing the people's sovereignty), and required proper residence in the diocese. The Assembly expropriated Church lands to support this program (as had Joseph II, the Kingdom of Naples, and Friedrich Karl von Erthal in Mainz). The Constitutional Church's reforms had obvious precedents.[73]

In common with Reform Catholicism elsewhere, the Constitutional Church resulted from a lay-clerical alliance. The Ecclesiastical Committee that drafted the legislation comprised reformist clergy and able laymen, including Jansenist or Jansenist-minded lawyers. Yet such an alliance was fleeting. Momentary amity, compromise, or even unanimity swiftly gave way to misunderstanding and rancor. In revolutionary France, the alliance held long enough to conceive and enact the Civil Constitution, though considerable strains were evident throughout the process, as exemplified by the bishops and laymen who resigned from the original committee in protest and the considerable opposition during the Assembly's debates. The alliance began to unravel during implementation when large numbers of clergy refused the oath and divided the Church. It disintegrated entirely when the more radical Legislative Assembly and Convention repudiated the Constitutional Church in the name of civil religion and de-Christianization.[74]

The Civil Constitution aroused greater opposition than other Reform Catholic efforts. Other polities had introduced such reforms in a piecemeal fashion over an extended period. The Civil Constitution was a comprehensive program; in fact, it was Europe's most radical package of state-led Church reform. It was proposed by a legislature in the name of a sovereign nation or, in the eyes of the Pope and others, "subjects in revolt." Moreover, France was diplomatically isolated. In the 1770s and 1780s the pope had yielded to the Jesuits' abolition and Joseph II's reforms because he faced a formidable alliance of Catholic

[73] McManners, *The French Revolution and the Church*, 38–40. On the suppression of monasteries, see Derek Beales, *Prosperity and Plunder: European Catholics Monasteries in the Age of Revolution, 1650–1815* (Cambridge, 2003).

[74] Albert Mathiez, *Rome et le clergé français sous la Constituante: La Constitution civile du clergé, L'Affaire d'Avignon* (Paris, 1911), 77–124, 150–79. The *commission des réguliers* (1766–68) had also been composed of bishops and lay bureaucrats. See Beales, *Prosperity and Plunder*, 169–78.

monarchs (as Eybel indicated). In 1791 the Pope could count on Catholic monarchs to support his opposition. Finally, the revolution's challenge to papal rule in Avignon exacerbated matters.

For Lamourette, the Civil Constitution was "as necessary to the regeneration of the church as to that of the state," since it was "the sole revolution that can put an end to the ills of religion, and restore it to [its] ancient and austere majesty."[75] By promising to restore the early Church, the Civil Constitution raised millenarian hopes.

Lamourette endorsed a return to the propertyless primitive Church. Jesus had raised the "negation of property" to "the essential condition of the institution he came to found; as the verification of what the prophets said would be the nature of a Christian regime and the form of the Gospel ministry." The Church's acquisition of property in the fourth century was a fundamental mistake that the Church fathers rued. An end to property would mark a "rebirth of the Church's beautiful days."[76]

Lamourette recognized that Church wealth is the "root of depravation": "The experience of seventeen centuries shows us that wealth among the clergy destroys all the power of the Gospel ministry and undermines religion altogether." Freeing the Church of property would achieve Lamourette's twin ideals of the primitive and rural Church: it would "renew" the Church by reestablishing "in [their] dignity" the "virtuous and obscure priests" who have borne the church's mission without adequate remuneration. The reimposition of the early Church's "spirit of wisdom, simplicity and labor" would enable the virtuous rural pastor and his flock to flourish. The clergy will comprise "the healthiest, most incorruptible and venerable of all the people" and exhibit the virtues of "wise, moderate and industrious men."[77]

A propertyless Church would also regenerate France: "All the ills that afflict [the French] come from the corruption and vice of its priests and its teachers." The Church sets society's tone and goals: the people believe that "happiness [bonheur] consists in wealth because the men of God search for abundance." The government also seeks wealth, as a result becoming "tyrannical." The Church's wealth is the "root of universal corruption," its expropriation the key to national regeneration.[78]

---

[75] *Le Décret de l'Assemblée nationale sur les biens du clergé, considéré dans son rapport avec la nature et les lois de l'institution ecclésiastique* (Paris, 1790), 2. For Oratorians who supported the Civil Constitution, see Graham, "The Enlightened and Revolutionary Oratorians in France," 171–83.

[76] *Le Décret de l'Assemblée nationale*, 24, 37–38, 41–42, 47–50.

[77] Ibid., 25, 6–7, 54, 60–62, 55.

[78] Ibid., 52–53.

Lamourette justified expropriation using Reform Catholicism's natural law idea that the state is the steward of Church property: "the entire ecclesiastical order is subordinate to the state in all its civil relations." In consequence, "the wealth allocated to the church is a branch of the public resource and is imprescriptibly subsumed to the regime of public power." The nation can determine how churchmen are remunerated:

> [Wealth] is in the church but not of the church, and the nation can never forget that it possesses the invariable liberty to change the mode of circulation by which it provides for the subsistence of the ministers of the cult.[79]

Lamourette deepened his dedication to the revolution by espousing the "sovereignty of nations" and "their legislative power." "Sovereignty is . . . divine law in the body of each nation." He rejected his earlier commitment to divine right monarchy or constitutional monarchy. Quoting Fénélon, he reduced the king to the executor of law and power. Lamourette also invoked the concept of "natural law" alongside "divine law," insisting that the two should correspond by instilling morality in each estate; otherwise the nation will have "priests without religion and citizens without patriotism."[80]

Lamourette saw the revolution in stark partisan terms. The revolution represented justice and virtue, its opponents unpatriotic destruction; the revolutionary capital purveyed truth, the countryside rumors and plots. He advocated sending propaganda missions to the countryside to counter the alliance of aristocrats and clergy that would mislead common priests. He denounced clergy instigating plots threatening the "*patrie*," encouraging them to promote stability.[81]

Lamourette redirected his pre-1789 endorsement of subordination to the revolution. The new legislation is "a sacred law that is due the respect and obedience of every Frenchmen." The laws that injure clergy are to be accepted with "submission and patience." The ancien régime cannot be restored; the alternative is national disaster.[82]

---

[79] Ibid., 4. Cf. *Prônes civiques, ou Le Pasteur patriote*, no. 3 (Paris, 1791), 30. Poole estimates that only eighteen of some four hundred Lazarists took the oath. See *A History of the Congregation of the Mission*, 353.

[80] *Le Décret de l'Assemblée nationale*, 19–20, 11, 13–14, 19, 2–4, 68. For divine right monarchy, see *Pensées sur la Philosophie de la foi*, 19, 29. For patriotic priests rejecting divine right monarchy, see Hermon-Belot, *L'Abbé Grégoire*, 200–1.

[81] *Le Décret de l'Assemblée nationale*, 2–4, 20–21, 29–30.

[82] Ibid., 8, 10, 12–5, 21–22. For other patriotic clergy or enlightened Christians who emphasized obedience, see Hermon-Belot, *L'Abbé Grégoire*, 196, and Menozzi, *Les Interprétations politiques de Jésus*, 125–44.

The revolution so enraptured Lamourette that he, like other patriotic clergy, had millenarian visions: by fulfilling the Gospel's promise, the revolution would bring "prophetic" changes. In its "equality and unity in plurality," revolutionary society would emulate the "infinity" that is the model for human society ("harmony, unity and equality"). Revolutionary society would erase the polarity between religion and philosophy so that the "two torches [will] unite to enlighten men and make them good and happy," establishing an "eternal alliance of temple and school [lycée]." Justice and Christianity will converge in the National Assembly; the virtues of this world and the next will meet.[83]

Lamourette voiced utter confidence in the revolution's ability to regenerate the nation and Christianity. Do not believe those who anxiously claim a plot first to destroy the Church, by expropriating its property, and then to "banish Christianity from France."[84] Lamourette would live to reflect on those words.

Lamourette offered his most radical version of revolutionary Reform Catholicism in five popular sermons, the Civic Lessons, or the Patriotic Pastor (1791), which was his most widely reviewed and best-known work.

In the first three sermons ("The Revolution Envisaged in the Light of Religion"), he rewrote Christianity's history according to the revolution's ideals. Jesus was the champion of liberty, promoting the "principles of fraternity and equality" against Rome's tyranny. The "heads of the synagogue" who conspired against him represented the "spirit of domination and aristocracy." Thus "Jesus Christ died a victim of the synagogue's despots and Rome's tyrants."[85]

Christianity embodied the ideas of 1789, infusing the "principles of reason and nature" and the ideas of "the eternal laws of equality and egalitarianism [l'équité et l'égalité]" into every society, even despotic regimes. In promoting "equality, humility and the sacrifice of the passions," Christianity showed the "incompatibility of its rule with that of all unjust authority."[86]

---

[83] Le Décret de l'Assemblée nationale, 15–17, 59–60. Cf. Pensées sur la Philosophie de l'Incrédulité, 13, 253, 263, and Pensées sur la Philosophie de la foi, 223–36. For these ideas among the "patriotic clergy," see Hermon-Belot, L'Abbé Grégoire, 74f. For the Constitutional Church in general, see Aston, Religion and Revolution in France, 203.

[84] Le Décret de l'Assemblée nationale, 19–20.

[85] Prônes civiques, i–ii. For reviews, see Kates, The Cercle Social, 87 n. 23, and Menozzi, "Philosophes" e "Chrétiens éclaires," 261ff. Fauchet made a similar argument in his Sermons sur l'accord de la Religion et de la liberté. See Plongeron, L'Abbé Grégoire, 55, and Menozzi, Les Interprétations politiques de Jésus, 136–40. Rita Hermon-Belot treats the Prônes civiques as "patriotic sermons." See L'Abbé Grégoire, 63–68.

[86] Prônes civiques, no. 3, 19–20, quotation at 27.

Neither Jesus nor Christianity justify absolute rule. Jesus's call for obedience to pagan princes cannot be used to legitimate absolute monarchy let alone tyranny. On the contrary, government should create "justice." Resistance to oppression or even insurrection is justifiable only as a response to "all the cruelties and all the exactions of tyranny," and if it derives from "the corps of the societies and the will of nations." Yet anything is "preferable to the disorder of anarchy and license without goal."[87] As much as he loved the revolution, Lamourette hated anarchy—which would fuel his opposition to the Jacobins.

As Lamourette had argued vis-à-vis the Civil Constitution, the incursion of wealth and power initiated "the deplorable epoch of the degeneration of all the ideas and all the rules of the evangelical system." Constantine's adoption of Christianity corrupted the Church: "The world became Christian, continued to be enslaved and thereby to nourish all the vices that destroy Christianity." Church government was equally perverted: "alongside imperial despotism there arose . . . a priestly despotism . . . to establish an indivisible unity between the Church's pastors and the empire's leaders."[88]

Leaping directly from late antiquity, Lamourette asserted that ancien régime France was a "monstrous reversal of all principles." The regime's rank inequality and "endless suffering" excluded "true Christianity."

It is well known . . . that a bad government leads to the loss of religion and morals, and that the two extremes of domination and dependence are equally inhospitable to the penetration of the spirit of faith and to tasting the sublime and rigorous wisdom of the Gospel! It is well known already that there was no more faith in France, and that no political revolution could make the situation of religion worse than the one we had.[89]

By excoriating the ancien régime, Lamourette vindicated the revolution; condemning the entire ancien régime Church risked alienating the faithful.

The fourth sermon claimed fraternity and equality as fundamental to the early Church ("religion consecrates the common ancestry and fraternity of all who come from the stem of Adam"). That sense of unity is essential to such laudable and indispensable impulses as

---

[87] *Prônes civiques*, no. 1, 14–6, 22–23.

[88] *Prônes civiques*, no. 3, 28–30. For despotism in prerevolutionary pamphlets, see M.G. Hutt, "The Curés and the Third Estate: the Ideas of Reform in the Pamphlets of the French Lower Clergy in the period 1787–89," *Journal of Ecclesiastical History* 8 (1957): 89.

[89] *Prônes civiques*, no. 2, 29–32, 34–35. For this issue see Hermon-Belot, *L'Abbé Grégoire*, 193.

benevolence: "Everything that destroys the sentiment of equality in our souls at the same time stifles all benevolence." Pride, "a passion destructive of all bases of justice and religion," "has introduced distinctions, ranks, privileges in our social institutions" that are a "disorder to the eyes of reason, and sacrilege to the eyes of faith": "the just God . . . neither created nor inspired the iniquitous distinctions that you place beneath the feet of other men." Lamourette invited the privileged to renounce their titles and to "celebrate with [their fellow citizens] the fête of universal equality."[90]

The fifth sermon endorses taxation as imperative to liberty. Lamourette first defended taxation by invoking Jesus's famous dictum ("render unto Caesar"): even paying taxes to a despot is allowed. Yet Frenchmen are being asked to pay liberty's taxes. While taxation in general is "the essence" of society, without the present taxation the revolution may fail and France collapse into greater despotism. The people must recognize that "the only true riches are the riches of the state; because it is only those that guarantee liberty."[91]

Lamourette revised his understanding of the Enlightenment. In the 1780s he had assailed the radical philosophes as a seditious cabal promoting impiety. In addressing the Jews' civil status he first took a positive view, valorizing the Enlightenment's impact on Christianity by asserting its similar consequence for the Jews. "Do you believe that the philosophy that purified our Christianity will not immediately enlighten [éclairé] the Jews?"[92] He now recast the philosophes as defenders of liberty and freedom against the despotism of the ancien régime, including the Church's:

> Systematic unbelief has its primary origin in the hatred that reflective and sensitive spirits conceive against a theology that consecrates tyranny, that flatters the pride of agents of power, that makes it law for all peoples of the earth to suffer servitude and opens hell under the feet of whoever dares to say to his brother, "be free."

Lamourette understood the philosophes to have opposed tyranny in the service of the commonweal:

> The writers one calls irreligious were at bottom only the political philosophes who had the sole goal of restoring our government to the imprescriptible and inviolable principles of true association. . . . The more they felt indignation towards the iniquities and scandals

[90] *Prônes civiques*, no. 4, 2, 29, 32, 41–42, 46–47.
[91] *Prônes civiques*, no. 5, 5, 20, 34.
[92] *Observations sur l'état civil des juifs*, 13–15.

of the tyrannical regime that enslaved a nation so worthy of being free and happy, the more they summoned up all the forces of reason to combat every teaching that strengthened the despots' power and supported the blindness and stupidity of the people.[93]

The early Enlightenment was compatible with belief; indeed, the new philosophy (Descartes? Malebranche?) supported religion so that "it was neither possible to be a philosophe without Christianity nor to be a Christian without philosophy." This harmony sadly collapsed when the Church opted for "authority" against the "rights of people," treating "the struggle against oppression" as "an attack on divinity." Since the priests identified with an "aristocratic theology" that was "intolerant, turbulent and persecutorial," the philosophes could not distinguish between "the Gospel and superstition." They attacked the Church and rejected religion altogether. Like other patriotic clergy, Lamourette now held despotism, including the Church's, responsible for France's polarization: "the history of the entrance of unbelief in France . . . is, like so many other evils, an effect of despotism, and that religion has suffered as much as the patrie from all the forms of tyranny that for so long overwhelmed the French people."[94]

Lamourette remained a monarchist. In accounting for ancien régime despotism he consistently exonerated the king. The unscrupulous ministers and courtiers surrounding the king conspired to exploit the public purse and foster the growing tyranny that made him "the first slave of the intolerable despotism of your former government." Since "he was the most deceived," the "revolution was a grand deliverance" for him as well. He can now be "the first true king that France has had on its throne."[95]

Lamourette gave central aspects of his theology a revolutionary twist: he now understood the incarnation to be the basis for human equality: "the principle of excellence and equality of the entire human species consists . . . principally in that we are created according to the model of Christ the Lord, preordained of all eternity to be the heart, the center and the support of all creation."[96]

The incarnation helps "achieve . . . the divinity of man that palpably commenced with his creation, through the relationship that exists between his faculties and divine perfection" and that sustains man's relationship to the infinite and the eternal. This relationship to the son

[93] *Prônes civiques*, no. 3, 30–32.
[94] *Prônes civiques*, no. 3, 32–36. For the patriotic clergy see Hermon-Belot, *L'Abbé Grégoire*, 94–95.
[95] *Prônes civiques*, no. 1, 23–24; no. 2, 27–28; no. 5, 29–32.
[96] *Prônes civiques*, no. 1, 5; no. 3, 38–39; no. 4, 7, 37.

"joined together the most mysterious truths of your belief with the best known principles of your reason."[97]

In his first three sermons Lamourette envisioned a regenerated Church. The revolution was creating "the moment of regeneration": "prepare in all quarters for the most brilliant triumph that the Gospel has ever attained in the world." By the final sermon he was cautiously pleading for time: the revolution cannot succeed overnight, "regeneration" and the "reestablishment of justice" are protracted processes. Perhaps only today's children will eventually see "liberty shine on the horizon of France in all the brightness of its glory and magnificence." Nonetheless, he remained confident of liberty's inevitable triumph.[98]

Lamourette's early revolutionary activities culminated in ghostwriting two important speeches for Mirabeau. Mirabeau delivered his speech of November 27, 1790, in the tense period after the Assembly had enacted the Civil Constitution (July 12) yet had not realized that it could divide the nation. By November there was mounting uncertainty. Would the new regulations be implemented? Would the king sanction them? The pope approve them? The clergy accept them? Would they stoke the fires of counterrevolution?

Mirabeau/Lamourette deplored the danger of a "counterrevolution" resulting in a "schism" between "Catholic France and free France." Mirabeau/Lamourette identified the revolution with Christianity, the counterrevolution with ancien régime despotism. If the clergy accepted "the spirit of revolution and liberty" they could play a positive role; if they persist in "decry[ing] liberty in the name of the Gospel" they risk the "horrors of a religious war." Mirabeau/Lamourette invoked the primitive Church to justify the Civil Constitution. They also characteristically emphasized the need for subordination, though now in the service of "liberty": the episcopacy should be teaching the "current duties of its citizens, the necessity of subordination, the benefits that come of liberty."[99] In the end, Mirabeau/Lamourette

---

[97] Prônes civiques, no. 4, 10, 14, 33. Hermon-Belot sees this idea of man's co-creativity with God underpinning a notion of progress. See L'Abbé Grégoire, 106–7, 109–115. Cf. Dale Van Kley, "The Rejuvenation and Rejection of Jansenism in History and Historiography: Recent Literature on Eighteenth-Century Jansenism in French," French Historical Studies 29, no. 4 (2006): 678–80.

[98] Prônes civiques, no. 3, 36.; no. 2, 35; no. 5, 35, 42.

[99] "Séance du 27 Novembre," in M. Mérilhou, ed., Oeuvres de Mirabeau, précédées d'une notice sur sa vie et ses ouvrages, 9 vols.(Paris, 1825–27), 8:338–63, esp. 341, 353–54, 347, 343–44, 349, 350–51, 353–54. For Lamourette's authorship, see Etienne Dumont, Recollections of Mirabeau and of the Two First Legislative Assemblies of France (London, 1832), 212–13. For Mirabeau see Welch, Mirabeau, 298–305, and Menozzi, "Philosophes" e "Chrétiens éclaires," 271–85.

proposed punitive measures against nonjurors, which the Assembly accepted.

Two months later, on January 14, 1791, Mirabeau/Lamourette addressed the worsening situation: in response to the Civil Constitution (the king sanctioned the clerical oath on December 26, 1790, and administration began on January 2, 1791), France appeared even closer to a dangerous divide between "Catholic France," an antirevolutionary, pro-clerical party, and "Free France," a pro-revolutionary, anti-clerical party. Mirabeau/Lamourette endeavored to explode the notion that there was a fundamental "alternative" between "being Christian or [being] free." Whoever promotes this erroneous and dangerous polarity appears to be "resolved on the ruin of Christianity":

> the sole difference which distinguishes the irreligious doctrine from the ecclesiastical aristocracy is that the former doctrine yearns for the downfall of religion only in order to secure more firmly the triumph of the constitution and of liberty; and that the second is striding towards the destruction of the faith with no other hope than that of seeing it involve in its overthrow the liberty and constitution of the empire.[100]

Wholehearted adoption of the Civil Constitution could overcome this revolutionary reincarnation of France's polarization, enabling France to "teach the surrounding nations that the Gospel and liberty are the inseparable bases of all true legislation and the everlasting foundation of the most perfect state of man." Mirabeau/Lamourette appealed to the clergy not to oppose the Civil Constitution "upon false and arbitrary principles" by "confound[ing] human opinions and scholastic traditions with the Gospel's sacred and inviolable ordinances."[101]

To avert this polarization, Mirabeau and Lamourette tried to find a mediating group, which they significantly called "enlightened Christians." Echoing the *Civic Lessons*, they vehemently attacked the ancien régime Church and government:

> Enlightened Christians [*les chrétiens éclairés*] asked, whither had fled the august religion of their fathers, and the true religion of the Gospel was nowhere to be found. We were a nation without a

---

[100] "Séance du 14 Janvier," in M. Mérilhou, ed., *Oeuvres de Mirabeau*, 9:14–46, here 9:37, 39–41. English translation in *Speeches of M. de Mirabeau the Elder, pronounced in the National Assembly of France*, trans. James White 2, vols. (London, 1792), 2:265–331. I cite White's translation. On this speech see Menozzi, *"Philosophes" e "Chrétiens éclaires,"* 289–301.

[101] *Oeuvres de Mirabeau*, 9:38, 43.

country, a people without government and a church without character and discipline.[102]

With these assertions Mirabeau/Lamourette alienated the clergy on the right side of the Assembly: the majority rose in protest and departed the chamber. At the same time, the pro-revolutionary, anti-clerical party on the left rejected with catcalls the very notion of an "enlightened Christian."[103] There could not have been more striking testimony to the Civil Constitution's radicalizing impact.

Mirabeau and Lamourette had miscalculated: they had failed to recognize that aside from the few patriotic clergy there was no distinct pro-revolution, pro-Christian party that actively identified with the Enlightenment; a substantial group of "enlightened Christians" did not exist. They had failed to address how the Civil Constitution had alienated such potential allies among the lower clergy as the "richerists," by favoring lay over priestly Church governance, as well as many of the "judicial Jansenists," by its very radicality.[104] They had also failed to address the procedural objections: without prior approval from a National Council of clergy, the pope, or both, the majority of prelates and clergy felt compelled to refuse the oath. Moreover, the Assembly had exacerbated the clergy's dilemma by prohibiting the easy option of professing "reservations" while swearing the oath. Appealing to a constituency of "enlightened Christians" was so much wishful thinking.[105] Rather than averting the polarization, Mirabeau and Lamourette fell victim to it.

In the early days of the Revolution, Lamourette emerged as one of the patriotic clergy. He embraced the revolution's ideals of liberty in

---

[102] Ibid., 9:43. This was apparently the only time Lamourette used the term. For its use since mid-century, see Menozzi, *Les Interprétations politiques de Jésus*, 92ff.

[103] Menozzi, "Philosophes" e "Chrétiens éclaires," 294–300.

[104] Aston, *The End of an Élite*, 231–46; Mathiez, *Rome et le Clergé français sous la Constituante*, 164–66; Roland G. Bonnel, "Ecclesiological Insight at the 1790 National Assembly: An Assessment of the Contribution of Catholic Thought to the French Revolution," in *The French Revolution in Culture and Society, Contributions to the Study of World History* 23, ed. David G. Troyansky, Alfred Cismaru, and Norwood Andrews, Jr. (New York, 1991), 48–50; for the missing middle ground, see 54–55. For the "richérists," see E. Préclin, *Les Jansénistes du XVIIIe siècle et la Constitution civile du Clergé: Le développement du richérisme; Sa propagation dans le Bas Clergé (1713–1791)* (Paris, 1929), 463–540. For the "judicial Jansenists," see Van Kley, *The Religious Origins of the French Revolution*, 357–59. The Assembly later (in January and May, 1791) allowed reservations. See Tackett, *Religion, Revolution and Regional Culture*, 25–27.

[105] Ruth Graham, "The Revolutionary Bishops and the *Philosophes*," *Eighteenth-Century Studies* 16, no. 2 (Winter, 1982–83): 117–40. For pro-revolutionary and pro-Christian laypeople in the countryside, see Suzanne Desan, *Reclaiming the Sacred: Lay Religion and Popular Politics in Revolutionary France* (Ithaca, 1990), 22, 123, 146, 158.

defending the Jews' admission to the civic oath, and sovereignty in defending the Civil Constitution, as well as coming to a positive view of the philosophes (*Civic Lessons*). He joined forces with Mirabeau to try to arrest the polarization threatening France's revolutionary regeneration.

THE REVOLUTION, 1791–94

Lamourette became a public official of the revolution when he was elected constitutional bishop of Lyon in 1791. Mirabeau and members of the Cercle Social sponsored Lamourette. In the ancien régime it had been virtually unthinkable for someone of Lamourette's background to aspire to the prelacy: the only two non-nobles elevated under Louis XVI were, not surprisingly, appointed in 1789. Lamourette's publications were now official pronouncements.[106]

Lamourette's election was no gift. Lyon's populace was divided (artisans vs. owners). Its economy (silk-weaving, hat making, printing) was in decline, it was chronically at odds with the surrounding countryside, and Lamourette faced formidable opposition. Like other constitutional bishops, he had difficulty finding a sitting bishop to consecrate him. Once consecrated, he had to contend with the former bishop, the nonjuring Yves-Alexandre de Marbeuf (1734–1800), who personified the ancien régime's worst abuses: he had never set foot in his diocese. Marbeuf refused to relinquish his see and, with his vicar general, organized the nonjuring clergy by circulating his and other opposition publications. The civil authorities attempted to thwart these efforts by confiscating pamphlets, expelling nonjuring priests, and purging their strongholds.[107]

Once elected, on March 2, 1791, Lamourette became the focus of conflict: whether the clergy would accept a constitutional bishop and read his pastoral letters was the Civil Constitution's critical test. At Lyon's

---

[106] Kates, *The Cercle Social*, 135; Menozzi, *"Philosophes" e "Chrétiens éclaires,"* 304–8; Maurice Wahl, *Les premières années de la Révolution à Lyon, 1788–92* (Paris, 1894), 304–5; A. Kleinclausz, *Histoire de Lyon*, 3 vols. (1939–52), 2:265–66, 277. For episcopal appointments, see Aston, *The End of an Élite*, 11–12, and idem, *Religion and Revolution in France, 1780–1804*, 85.

[107] For Lyon, see W. D. Edmonds, *Jacobinism and the Revolt of Lyon, 1789–1793* (Oxford, 1990), 9–69. Jean-Baptiste Gobel (1727–94, formerly Bishop of Lydda and then Metropolitan of Paris) consecrated Lamourette (on March 27, 1791). See Liebaut, *Lamourette*, 25, and Menozzi, *"Philosophes" e "Chrétiens éclaires,"* 320ff. Gobel discussed consecration during the debate on the Civil Constitution. See Mathiez, *Rome et le Clergé français sous la Constituante*, 174–75. For consecrations, including Lamourette's, see Paul Pisani, *Répertoire biographique de l'Épiscopat Constitutionnel (1791–1802)* (Paris, 1907), 455–59.

Church of Saint Nizier, the priest Linsolas insisted in his instruction on March 13 that Lyon had an archbishop (Marbeuf), not a bishop (Lamourette), inciting a brawl that the civil authorities had to quell. Linsolas was jailed. The civil authorities caught the grand vicar with stacks of Marbeuf's publications and incarcerated him as well.[108]

Lamourette struck a pacific note in his first pastoral letter, sent from Paris on April 7, 1791. He called on his diocese to resist the growing polarity of "patrie" and "church." While the country "regenerat[es] itself," he would teach a Christianity that shows how to be "good citizens on earth" and "worthy of becoming citizens of heaven," a task the Gospel made easy, since it was the source of the revolution's ideals. He defended the Civil Constitution as altering only the Church's "exterior order," which had always been subject to the civil authorities. Moreover, the reforms are a "return to the spirit and, even more, the practice of the ancient Church." Christianity was not only compatible with the new government but was necessary for patriotism and a tranquil society: the "success of the regeneration of our civil society" must be based on religion, since "the attachment to religion preserves in our hearts love of the commonweal."[109]

Marbeuf replied, attacking the Civil Constitution as heretical and Lamourette as a usurper. He held any priest who cooperated with Lamourette complicit in schism.[110] Now in Lyon, Lamourette penned an angry response (*Directive to His Clergy*, May 12, 1791) in which he defended the sincerity of his vocation and attacked those who impugned his motives. He questioned the clergy's right to use personal judgement in regard to the Civil Constitution and to present their views as "an incontestable and evident truth." He accused them of sacrilege in doubting a bishop's authority and arrogance in making themselves the arbiters of salvation:

> You constitute yourselves . . . the supreme judges of a question whose irrefragable decision cannot proceed except by the judgement of the universal Church. You have your flock swear that they

---

[108] For Marbeuf's position, see *Déclaration de M. l'archevêque de Lyon, primat des Gaules, en réponse à la proclamation du département de Rhône-et-Loire concernant l'exécution des décrets sur la constitution civile du clergé* (Paris, 1790). Cf. Wahl, *Les premières années de la Révolution à Lyon*, 291ff., and Kleinclausz, *Histoire de Lyon*, 2:274–79. For the clergy's hostility to constitutional bishops, see Tackett, *Religion, Revolution, and Regional Culture*, 32.

[109] *Lettre pastorale de M. L'Evêque du département de Rhône et Loire. Métropolitain du sud-est, à tous les Fidèles de son Diocèse* (Lyon, 1791), 4, 8–11, 15–16, 14, 18–19, 20–21.

[110] *Lettre pastorale de M. l'Archevêque de Lyon, primat des Gaules, sur l'usurpation de son siège par le sieur Lamourette* (n.p., n.d.). See Wahl, *Les premières années de la Révolution à Lyon*, 325–29.

will follow only you; that is, you obligate them to avow that you cannot mislead them and that there is no salvation . . . except from you.

The nonjuring clergy have become "opinionated, dogmatic, and facile reasoners" who promote "irreverence and blasphemy." They will "plunge" the people into a "skepticism that is a thousand times worse than heresy," and foment a "religious insurrection." The activist nonjuring clergy had replaced the philosophes (as he had understood them in the 1780s) in promoting a polarization that threatened anarchy.[111]

Eight days later (*Pastoral Warning*, May 20, 1791) Lamourette was conciliatory. Alarming reports continued to reach him of clergy who "undermine, along with the constitution of the clergy, the entire constitution of the empire" by turning Churches into centers of "fanaticism and furor." Whereas such priests accuse others of the "crime of schism and heresy," they are risking anarchy by "rousing men against the law." They also act without "restraint" [*frein*], again resembling the philosophes (as he had understood them in the 1780s). He promised "severe and effective measures" against "all resistance to authority."

Desperate for unity, he retreated from his earlier rejection of the clergy's right to exercise judgement by proposing to recognize actions in good conscience: "your refusal to swear the oath ordered by the Public Minister of religion will never be a fault in our eyes provided you respect order and love peace." Willing to accept an honorable disagreement among "men of goodwill," he appealed to both sides to commit to a church dedicated to "creat[ing] Christians" and salvation:

"let us show all our brethren that we are in agreement on the foundation of religion and on all points bearing on the salvation of souls . . . and that which divides us only concerns . . . the accidental aspects foreign to the body and substance of the Gospel."

Anticipating his "kiss" of 1792, he appealed to priests of "good faith" who were free of "partisan spirit" ("*homme de bien*") to endorse "eternal fraternity" by embracing one another, accepting him as their bishop, and publicizing his letter to their parishioners.[112]

One month later, on June 29, Lamourette addressed his rural parishes about the infamous incident at Poleymieux in which a mob attacked

---

[111] *Instruction pastorale de M. L'évêque du département de Rhône et Loire. Métropolitain du sud-est, A MM. les Curés, Vicaires et Fonctionnaires Ecclésiastiques de son Diocèse* (Lyon, 1791), 9, 14–15, 17–23.

[112] *Avertissement pastoral de M. L'évêque du département de Rhône et Loire, Métropolitain du sud-est, aux Ecclésiastiques qui exercent dans son Diocèse, le ministère de la Confession* (May 20, 1791), 2–9, 12–13, 15–16.

the chateau of a rural seigneur suspected of promoting counterrevolution, sacking it and brutally murdering him. Lamourette condemned this "moment of forgetfulness and abandon" when "hands have been raised against liberty." He poignantly asked, "Is one worthy of being free, when one renounces innocence and tramples on the feet of justice?" He hoped to be "the pastor and father of a flock so wise and so much the friend of peace, order and justice."[113]

The print war continued: nonjurors published responses to Lamourette, containing libelous accusations alongside reasoned arguments, and Marbeuf issued an episcopal order on May 18, 1791, supporting the pope's condemnation of the Civil Constitution on May 4, 1791.[114]

Lamourette responded on July 16 with a defense of the Civil Constitution as embodying the primitive Church ideal and the conciliarist Gallican liberties. The pope has the same ordination as other bishops: "the public profession and the universal practice of the primitive church" confute the claim of "primacy." Moreover, it is "heresy" to suggest that there are two episcopates, Rome and others: the Apostles received, and subsequently each bishop receives, universal jurisdiction "immediately from Jesus Christ." Every bishop is consecrated as if by Christ himself.[115] A bishop's assignment to a particular diocese is "secondary and of purely ecclesiastical economy" since "his jurisdiction and mission" are universal. These assignments are exterior to the Church and subject to the secular authorities; the "state alone is the creator of the public existence of Christianity." Rome and St. Peter are a center of unity; the pope's "primacy of honor and jurisdiction" enable him to convene and preside over councils. The bishops as a body possess the actual "governing and administrative" power. The "ultramontane" papal monarchy is heretical, resting on the false decretals

---

[113] *Lettre circulaire de M. L'évêque du Département de Rhône et Loire, Métropolitain du sud-est, aux Municipalités, Gardes Nationales et Habitans des Paroisses rurales de son Diocèse* (Lyon, 1791), 1–4. See Wahl, *Les premières années de la Révolution à Lyon*, 387–91, and Kleinclausz, *Histoire de Lyon*, 2:281.

[114] *Lettre à M. Lamourette, sur son Instruction Pastorale, adressée aux Fonctionnaires publics* (n.p., n.d.) accused him of being "sometimes a subtle metaphysician, never an exact logician, even less an erudite theologian" and of displaying the "false spirit" of "innovators and heretics" (5). *Quelques observations en forme de lettre, à M. Adrien Lamourette, Évêque constitutionnel. Sur ses Prônes civiques, Lettres Pastorales & Avertissement Pastoral* (n.p., n.d.) accused him of lack of conviction, of inexact and false Scriptural quotations; of being a reformer and "an immoral and dissolute priest, a slave to perversity," p. 26. See Wahl, *Les premières années de la Révolution à Lyon*, 331–33.

[115] *Instruction pastorale de M. L'évêque du Département de Rhône et Loire, Métropolitain du sud-est, au Clergé et aux Fidèles de son Diocèse* (Lyon, 1791), 34–37, 42. Menozzi sees this as Lamourette's answer to the Pope. See *"Philosophes" e "Chrétiens éclaires,"* 331–46.

that substituted "scholastic and purely human traditions . . . for the wise and solid teaching of the primitive Church."[116]

Lamourette professed confidence in the revolution's providential nature as a third stage of history that will bring "the reign of faith by establishing the reign of liberty":

> It is by striking changes in human government that the Church came into being; it will achieve its last state following a new movement imprinted on the imposing mass of powers here. It was born amidst the profound silence of an enslaved world. It increased through the passions that the masters of an oppressed world multiplied. It may die and deploy itself in all its magnificence in the bosom of a happy and free world.

France is now the "cradle of mankind's liberty" and "the rallying point of all peoples for the holiness of the Gospel." As the "capital of the free universe," Paris will spread liberty and Christianity. Unlike religions ("idolatry and Islam") that promote despotism, the Gospel teaches all peoples "to form a society of mankind on the model of the eternal and indivisible society of the divine persons." Christianity's divine dispensation will enable it to resist the current tempest, revive the primitive Church, and bring Jesus's triumph. The Church's present divisions are the pope's fault for either exercising bad judgment or being misled by royalists to "establish the war of Catholicism versus liberty." Lamourette was confident that

> all of the citizens of France will recognize that the clergy of liberty and of the regenerative constitution are but the resurrection of the venerable clergy of the first age of religion; that all of the resistance of the pastors of the ancient servitude are . . . nothing but the struggle of the spirit of despotism against the deliverance of the people.[117]

Lamourette's official career in the revolution took another step when the Department of Saône-et-Loire elected him a delegate to the Legislative Assembly on September 4, 1791. Lamourette's decisive victory indicated the esteem he had won among the "moderate" and "enlightened" voters of his department.[118]

---

[116] *Instruction pastorale*, 48, 60, 43–44, 53, 58. Lamourette included extracts from Charrier, the Bishop of Rouen, and Arman Gaston Camus (1740–1804), a delegate to the Assembly and author of the Civil Constitution. Ibid., 71–100. Episcopal appointments divided older (Maultrot) from younger (Camus) Jansenists. See David C. Miller, "A.-G. Camus and the Civil Constitution of the Clergy," *Catholic Historical Review* 76 (July 1990): 481–505, esp. 486.

[117] *Instruction pastorale*, 7–8, 10, 12–13, 17, 19–20, 24–25, 28.

[118] Georges Guigue, ed., *Procès-verbaux des séances du Conseil Général du département de Rhône-et-Loire, 1790–93* (Lyon, 1895), 412; Lamourette's acceptance speech is at 427.

Before leaving for Paris, Lamourette issued an episcopal order allowing priests in rural parishes to celebrate mass twice on Sundays and holidays in order to accommodate farmers (an entire household could not attend mass at the same time). Even this minor matter was unavoidably implicated in the struggle over the Civil Constitution. Lamourette asserted that this innovation did not "overthrow religion"; it merely adjusted "discipline" to specific needs, leaving "faith" untouched.[119]

Lamourette may have been optimistic in returning to Paris. The Legislative Assembly (October 1, 1791) had been elected by a limited property franchise. The majority comprised a moderate center. The groupings at the extremes were small, the factions that were later to dominate the Convention, Girondins and Montagnards, had yet to emerge, although most of their salons and clubs already existed. For most of the Legislative Assembly's fifty-one weeks the delegates cooperated more than they clashed.

Nevertheless, the grounds for optimism quickly dissipated. The Legislative Assembly functioned in a profoundly flawed constitutional monarchy in which the indecisive and increasingly recalcitrant Louis XVI appointed ministers and vetoed legislation. The Legislative Assembly tried to make this imperfect arrangement work. Unsuccessful and increasingly frustrated, especially given the mounting pressures of war and the threat of counterrevolution, it was forced by a massive uprising to depose the king, on August 10, 1792. Moreover, the Legislative Assembly was more anti-clerical than its predecessor. The Constituent Assembly had contained large numbers of prominent clergy: their "revolt" brought the body into existence, and they then provided the Constitutional Party's "core" and leadership. Its successor, by law an entirely new body, included only twenty clergy, of whom sixteen were constitutional bishops and none could offer the distinguished leadership of the earlier body.[120]

A concantenation of events—the declaration of war, the fall of the throne, growing numbers of emigrés, plus the treatment of refractory clergy as a "fifth" column—further polarized the revolution and religion by branding as antirevolutionary the clergy and Catholicism. In its last month, the Legislative Assembly enacted this polarization by laicizing the registry of births, deaths, and marriages (*état civil*) and

[119] *Mandement de M. L'évêque du département de Rhône et Loire, Métropolitan du sud-est, Qui accorde provisoirement à MM. les curés des Paroisses rurales, la permission de célébrer deux fois le saint Sacrifice de la Messe, les jours de Dimanches et de Fêtes seulement* (Lyon, 1791), dated Sept. 16, 1791, 1–8.

[120] C. J. Mitchell, *The French Legislative Assembly of 1791* (Leiden, 1988); Aston, *The End of an Élite*, 3.

permitting divorce (September 20, 1792). The constitutional clergy protested these measures. The polarization also found expression in public celebrations. All of the revolution's early celebrations (1789–90) had
contained prominent religious elements, including the Mass. In contrast, Voltaire's burial in the Pantheon, on July 11, 1791, marked a secular turn. This trend culminated in the fête for the Civil Constitution
(August 10, 1793) and the deistic "cult of reason."[121]

When Lamourette entered the Legislative Assembly, his moderate
fusion of Catholicism and revolution had already failed in principle, if
not in practice. Fauchet resigned from the Cercle Social in May 1791, for
example, to protest the growing insistence on civil religion as a surro-
gate for Catholicism. On October 21, 1791, before the end of its first
month, the Legislative Assembly began a protracted debate over
church-state relations that pitted anticlerical deputies against constitutional bishops. Toward the end of that debate one deputy, François de
Neufchâteau (1750–1828), a minor poet whom Lamourette either knew
personally or by reputation from the Toul seminary, proposed elimi-
nating the Civil Constitution of the Clergy.[122] Lamourette understood
Neufchâteau's proposal to have two aims: to create "theism," which
Neufchâteau obviously regarded "as the perfection of the French revolution," and to reconcile the refractory clergy to the Constitution.[123]

Lamourette found both these aims so repellent that he produced the
most trenchant formulation of his ideas. Drawing on the *Civic Lessons*
and his episcopal pronouncements, he asserted that the Gospel is the
"ancient and unfailing root" of "unity, liberty and equality"; Christianity is a force against tyranny, a form of "evangelical democracy." He
posited a fundamental distinction between the "religion of theology,
which is the work of the aristocracy," and "the religion of the Gospel,
which is more democratic than even the constitution of the French."
"[T]he Sage of Nazareth, the true friend of the people" voiced not

---

[121] McManners, *The French Revolution and the Church*, 63–79. For a National Assembly
acting on principle, a Legislative Assembly on expediency, see Michael P. Fitzsimmons,
The Remaking of France: The National Assembly and the Constitution of 1791 (Cambridge,
1994). For Lyon's mediocre deputies, see Wahl, *Les premières années de la Révolution à
Lyon*, 424 n.1.

[122] Kates, *The Cercle Social*, 131–33. For Catholicism and representative democracy, see
Nicolas Bonneville, *De L'Esprit des religions* (Paris, 1792). For Neufchâteau, see Pierre Ma-
rot, *Recherches sur la vie de François de Neufchâteau à propos de ses lettres à son ami Poullain-
Grandprey* (Nancy, 1966), 52–54, and Mitchell, *The French Legislative Assembly of 1791*, 51.

[123] *Observations contre l'Article XV du Projet de décret du comité de législation sur les trou-
bles religieux; Prononcées le 21 novembre 1791, par M. Lamourette, Evêque du département de
Rhône et Loire*, 3, 7. Menozzi emphasizes Neufchâteau's desire for secularization; see
"Philosophes" e "Chrétiens éclaires," 347–64. Mitchell emphasizes tactical maneuvers; see
The French Legislative Assembly of 1791, 53.

"theology" but "the luminous principles of Christian democracy."[124] Here was Lamourette's enduring formulation.

"Christian democracy" covered a range of positions among the patriotic clergy. Fauchet held an almost socialist version emphasizing agrarian and property reform, Grégoire a radical egalitarian one in his opposition to the Legislative Assembly's tax-based franchise. An unwavering commitment to constitutional monarchy made Lamourette's understanding distinctly moderate.[125]

Lamourette argued against Neufchâteau's proposal: to separate the Constitution from the Gospel is a "rupture against nature." There are now priests in France who "for the first time . . . are enemies of despotism and supporters of public liberty." The Constitutional clergy are "elected by the *constitutional* law of the state" and "the people." They should be enabled to perform their jobs since they are also "one of the great forces that supports and guarantees the revolution."[126] Lamourette's objections were accepted and de Neufchâteau's proposal was shelved indefinitely.

Lamourette's "kiss" was his last effort to prevent the polarization threatening "Christian democracy." He made his proposal during the deepening political crisis (Roland's ministry had been dismissed on June 13, demonstrators had invaded the Tuilieres on June 20, the Assembly had debated whether Lafayette should be impeached) and after heated discussions over further restrictions on the Church—the suppression of teaching and missionary orders and the prohibition of clerical dress on April 6, 1792, a substitute religion for Catholicism on April 20–21, deportation of nonjuring clergy on May 26—Lamourette's motion, introduced on July 7, defended the status quo of constitutional monarchy and the Civil Constitution against alternatives from both ends of the political spectrum: the radicals' proposal of a republic, the conservatives' of a second legislative house.[127]

Lamourette identified France's current malady as the "disunion of the Assembly." The legislative body is the "true barometer of the state

[124] *Observations contre l'Article XV*, 4–5: "*Démocratie évangelique*" and "*Démocratie chrétienne.*"

[125] For Lamourette and Fauchet, see Menozzi, *Les Interprétations politiques de Jésus*, 176–85; for Lamourette and Grégoire, see Plongeron, *L'Abbé Grégoire*, 51–63. For the term see Maier, *Revolution and Church: The Early History of Christian Democracy, 1798–1901*, 113, 125.

[126] *Observations contre l'Article XV*, 4–7.

[127] *Projet de Réunion entre les membres de L'Assemblée nationale, par M. Lamourette, Député du Département de Rhône-et-Loire*. On this motion, see Sydenham, *The Girondins*, 112; Mitchell, *The French Legislative Assembly of 1791*, 57–60, 247; Everdell, *Christian Apologetics in France*, 237–38.

of the nation" since "here resides the lever that can drive the great machine of the State in the sense of unity and harmony." Convinced that "schism is never irremediable," he searched for points of consensus by appealing to "men of goodwill" and a shared attachment to "virtue," as he had in his own diocese. He asked his fellow delegates to show "unity of national representation" in the face of a deep divide:

> One section of the Assembly attributes to the other a seditious plan to undermine the monarchy and establish a republic; and the second ascribes to the first the crime of wanting the destruction of the egalitarian constitution by striving for the creation of two chambers.

To restore unity and safeguard the revolution he proposed "an irrevocable oath, striking down the republic and two chambers." The Assembly accepted this proposal. The delegates swore the oath, then celebrated by embracing and kissing. In the next two months many of them would vote to depose the king (on August 10) and to abolish the monarchy (on September 21, 1792).

Disheartened by the fractious polarization, Lamourette did not stand for election to the convention and returned to Lyon (the Legislative Assembly closed on September 20, 1792). Before leaving Paris he expressed his fears that the revolution was at a turning point: it could lead either to France's regeneration or its fall. He extolled the "triumph of reason" and liberty, yet he feared that the revolution could "degenerate" into a lack of "respect for law" and a "dangerous exaggeration of enthusiasm" that would engender a "spirit of anarchy and disorder." He abhorred the daily incitement of passions as a "homicidal movement." He called on men of letters to counter these developments by recovering the revolution's "liberty" and "goodness."[128]

In Lyon, Lamourette continued to defend "Christian democracy" by participating in a fateful conflict. Local Jacobins had gained control of the Lyon municipality (November 1792), governing in a high-handed and extralegal manner. The moderates who controlled the departmental government resisted these radicals. Supporters of the Civil Constitution (*patriotes*) opposed the lack of a proper municipal administration and the dictatorship of *"représentants en mission"*; they wanted to restore legal government. On May 29, 1793, a municipal uprising chased the Jacobins from the city. With the Jacobin coup d'état in Paris two days later (May 31–June 2), what was meant to be a local event suddenly looked like part of a Girondin or "federalist" conspiracy against

---

[128] "Discours sur les devoirs des gens de lettres envers leurs concitoyens, dans les tems de révolution," *Extrait du tribut de la société nationale des neuf soeurs, 14 August 1792*, no. 19 (Paris, 1792), 3–8.

Jacobin rule that included Bordeaux and Marseilles. The Lyon rebels tried to maintain good relations with the Convention to show that this was merely a local effort to restore order and legality.

The Jacobins could not countenance an open rebellion that they considered counterrevolutionary. The "revolutionary ideology" that pitted the people against an aristocratic plot underlay this perception. The Convention promulgated the new constitution of 1793 to satisfy the provinces' demands for order and legality, yet also needed to quell the rebellion and punish its leaders.[129]

Lamourette joined the rebellion.[130] In a funeral oration on June 12, 1793, for the martyrs he vindicated the May 29 uprising as "defending the sacred laws of equality and republican liberty against the oppression of anarchy." This local rebellion aimed to preserve the revolution from the fateful polarization, which he and Mirabeau resisted, that now (1793) appeared as a conflict between counterrevolution and the "anarchy" of continuing revolution.

The Jacobin municipal administration was "the monster of anarchy." Its members were "ferocious agitators" and "perfidious disrupters," informed with a "dark impiety." Their aim, in language reminiscent of Eybel's, was

[the] extinction of all principles in order to achieve their goal, which is to deliver everything up to combustion and pillage, to assassinate and to bathe in blood, to the point that there are only villains and monsters on the earth.

Lyon's citizens had been subjected to "a system of subversion and crime" that constituted "the most hideous and vile anarchy which ever sullied the history of revolutionary politics."

How had the revolution gone so awry? The revolution unleashed "all of the unregulated and voracious passions"—one of his criteria in the 1780s for understanding the philosophes—that were easily confused with the noble ones the times required. "In the setting of universal confusion and unrest, the cowardly and sordid passions appear as much in harmony with the noble and sublime enthusiasm of liberty." The revolution's initial needs enabled these passions to persist and,

[129] C. Riffaterre, *Le Mouvement antijacobin et antiparisien à Lyon et dans le Rhône-et-Loire en 1793 (29 Mai-15 Août)*, 2 vols. (Lyon, 1912–28); Edmonds, *Jacobinism and the Revolt of Lyon.*

[130] Georges Guigue, ed., *Registre du Secrétariat Général des sections de la Ville de Lyon, 2 Août–11 Octobre 1793 suivi des Délibérations de la section de Porte-Froc 26 Mai–10 Octobre 1793, Publié d'après les manuscrits originaux pour le Conseil Général du Rhône* (Lyon, 1907), 164, 169, 177, 181, 268.

ultimately, prevail. The "gangrenous and impure portion" of the nation gradually gained enough power that it was able to "produce revolutions upon revolutions."

Two additional problems exacerbated the continuing revolution of impure "passions." There was a lack of "true national representation." Lamourette was horrified by the current representatives, "an incendiary horde" who make the capital "a refuge of villains and a theater of great crimes." Moreover, these representatives enact "impractical legislation" based on "miserable speculations of a hollow and somnolent metaphysic." Disdaining "the wise and old lessons of experience," they are creating a situation of odious extremes: "For them the counterrevolution is the return of justice, morality and the virtues; for the others, every kind of constitution is evil, tyrannical, odious because it has the unpardonable fault of confronting them with authorities, laws and courts."

Lyon's rebels were "heroes of a true and wise liberty," "martyrs of law and public order." Citizens must vow "to maintain liberty, equality, the inviolable rights of the people, the unity and indivisibility of the republic" by enacting legislation that "combine[s] the theory of liberty with that of felicity," namely, "a legislation adapted to men, times and things, . . . which throughout admits sensible ideas and morals!" Lamourette wanted "a society reconstituted on the basis of eternal justice; there is the unshakable linchpin of liberty and national felicity."[131]

One month later, on July 14, 1793, Lamourette warned his rural parishioners not to allow the counterrevolution to hijack Lyon's rebellion. May 29 was not a victory of "aristocracy over the patriots"; ignore the aristocrats who oppose "liberty" and wish to "revive despotism and . . . the ancien régime." Those who helped to drive out "a faction of brigands and assassins" were "true and sincere friend[s] of . . . a single and indivisible Republic." The Jacobins' "anarchy" is a despotism of dangerous passions that "democratiz[es] all virtues and aristocratiz[es] all crimes."[132]

---

[131] "Discours prononcé le mercredi 12 juin, en l'église métropolitaine de Lyon, par Adrien Lamourette, évêque du département de Rhône-et-Loire, à l'occasion d'un service solemnel cèlébré pour les citoyens morts à la journée du 29 mai. . . ." in Georges Guigue, ed., *Registre du Secrétariat Général des sections de la Ville de Lyon, 2 Août–11 Octobre 1793 suivi des Délibérations de la section de Porte-Froc 26 Mai-10 Octobre 1793, Publié d'après les manuscrits originaux pour le Conseil Général du Rhône* (Lyon, 1907), 511–15. Other constitutional clergy described the Legislative Assembly's laws as "anarchy." See Plongeron, "Permanence d'une idéologie de 'civilisation chrétienne' dans le clergé constitutionnel," 269.
[132] "Lettre de Adrien Lamourette, évêque métropolitain du département de Rhône-et-Loire, aux habitants des campagnes de ce département," in George Guigue, ed.,

The Committee for Public Safety laid siege to Lyon in the summer of 1793. The siege lasted some nine weeks because General Kellermann's army was short of troops and armaments. The city capitulated on October 9. The Jacobins, and especially Robespierre, were determined to make an example of Lyon. Their representatives enforced a brutal repression that claimed some 1,800 victims. This was an "exercise in . . . high Jacobinism . . . which aimed . . . to consolidate the Republic by force."[133]

Lamourette was arrested and sent to Paris, where, appropriately, he shared a cell with his fellow patriotic priest Fauchet, who was executed on October 31, 1793. Lamourette was interrogated in October, condemned to death by the Tribunal on January 11, 1794, and, unusually, executed that same day.[134]

As a public functionary, Lamourette struggled against the revolution's growing polarization. In Lyon he defended the Civil Constitution and tried to maintain Church unity. In the Legislative Assembly he famously if in vain defended the middle ground by coining the term "Christian democracy" and proposing his "kiss." In Lyon he joined the municipal revolt to avoid the extremes of counterrevolution and continuing revolution.

Conclusion

A window opened in the 1780s that enabled Lamourette to assemble the components of a Reform Catholic theology composed of a number of original ideas. Aiming to overcome the French Enlightenment's endemic polarization of philosophy and Christianity, he joined the discourse of "reasonableness" to Rousseau's notion of sentiment through a moderate fideist skepticism. He was one of the patriotic clergy who welcomed the Revolution. Lamourette enthusiastically supported the constitutional monarchy and the Civil Constitution of the Clergy, in which Reform Catholicism was poised to enjoy its most spectacular success. The revolution's fusion of belief and politics aroused millenarian hopes.

Procès-verbaux des séances de la Commission Populaire républicaine et de salut public de Rhône-et-Loire 30 Juin-8 Octobre 1793 (Lyon, 1899), 395–97.

[133] Edmonds, *Jacobinism and the Revolt of Lyon, 1789–1793*, 302. Cf. Paul Mansfield, "The Repression of Lyon, 1793–4: Origins, Responsibility and Significance," *French History* 2, no. 1 (1988): 74–101.

[134] Lamourette's alleged prison cell recantation (Jan. 7, 1794) is probably counterfeit. See François Thérèse Panisset, Gabriel Deville, and Adrien Lamourette, *Rétractations de trois evêques constitutionnels* (Paris, 1796).

These hopes began to erode when the revolution's early divisiveness (1790–91) raised the specter of a new polarization between Christianity and liberty. The Legislative Assembly and the Convention convinced Lamourette that the Revolution's initial promise was disappearing in the conflict between counterrevolution and continuing revolution. With de-Christianization and the cult of reason, the Revolution repudiated the Constitutional Church. Lamourette joined the revolt against the "anarchy" of Lyon's Jacobin government, a decision that cost him his life.

Reinstated under the Directory, the Constitutional Church was a shadow of its former self. Despite Grégoire and the constitutional bishops' heroic efforts, and the Richerists' introduction of clerical rule at the Council of 1797, the Constitutional Church was undermined by the government's continuing oscillations. While partial freedom of worship reigned from 1795 to 1797, church and state were separated in 1795 and a new campaign of de-Christianization continued for two years (September 1797–December 1799).

Napoleon conclusively shut the window on the Constitutional Church and Reform Catholicism with the Concordat (1801). The Concordat legally ended the Constitutional Church while giving some of its cardinal features a more authoritarian form: nationalization of church property, a reduction in the number of dioceses and bishops, clergy as salaried state employees, religious toleration. Through a Ministry of Cults, Napoleon subjected the Church to even greater state supervision, including appointing an entirely new episcopate that wielded greater authority over the clergy through the power of appointment. Through the Organic Articles, which he appended unilaterally to the Concordat, Napoleon maintained the Gallican heritage of independence vis-à-vis the papacy while augmenting government control.[135]

The Revolution polarized not just France but all of Europe. Napoleon exported his policies to the empire. He negotiated a separate Concordat for the Italian Republic (1803) and elsewhere abolished monasteries, nationalized Church lands, suppressed festivals and brotherhoods, and introduced religious toleration. When Pope Pius VII balked at

---

[135] For the 1787 council as richerism's apogee, see Préclin, *Les Jansénistes du XVIIIe siècle et la Constitution civile du Clergé*, 535. For the post-Terror Constitutional Church, see A. Aulard, *Christianity and the French Revolution* (New York, 1966), 133–58. For Grégoire's role, see Plongeron *L'Abbé Grégoire*, 65–80, and Sepinwall, *The Abbé Grégoire and the French Revolution*, 144–49; for lay religion, see Desan, *Reclaiming the Sacred*; for the Concordat, see Martyn Lyons, *Napoleon Bonaparte and the Legacy of the French Revolution* (New York, 1994), 77–93.

Napoleon's political demands in 1809, imperial troops occupied Rome and held him prisoner until 1814. Napoleon's religious policies aroused opposition that contributed to his empire's collapse.[136]

The Glorious Revolution had ushered in the era of the religious Enlightenment by fashioning a middle way of an established Church and toleration, king and Parliament. By introducing a stark choice between old regime and new, Christianity and reason, revolution and counter-revolution, the French Revolution and Napoleon ushered it out.

[136] Bradley and Van Kley, eds., *Religion and Politics in Enlightenment Europe*, 4–11, 95; Stuart Woolf, *Napoleon's Integration of Europe* (London, 1991), 206–15; TCW Blanning, "The Role of Religion in European counter-revolution," in *History, Society and the Churches*, ed. D. Beales and G. Best (Cambridge, 1985), 195–214.

Epilogue

THE FRENCH REVOLUTION WAS "THAT volcano-crater," in Carlyle's words, that so forcefully jolted Europe as to constitute a seismic shift. Europe's political and cultural terrain was irrevocably altered, and in a manner that virtually eliminated the religious Enlightenment. France now inflicted its characteristic polarization on the rest of Europe, irreversibly separating it into two camps of implacable belligerents who divided over the Enlightenment and religion: the revolution's advocates claimed the Enlightenment, its adversaries claimed established religion. Enlightenment not only came to be associated with the revolution but, for many, became culpable for its worst excesses, while its actual achievements, especially the middle ground of incremental reform, or even its professed aspirations, were either traduced or wilfully forgotten. In consequence, if "in many places in the nineteenth century, the Enlightenment simply disappeared from the intellectual landscape," all the more so did the religious Enlightenment: it did not fit the new configuration of politics and religion, to the degree that it became virtually inconceivable. The revolution's "interpretational net" was utterly incapable of catching the religious Enlightenment, allowing it to fall into oblivion.[1]

Efforts to rehabilitate the Enlightenment in the nineteenth and twentieth centuries did not extend to the religious Enlightenment; indeed, they further complicated its retrieval. Two examples illustrate the point. The republicans who made the Enlightenment the mainstay of the French Third Republic (1870), canonizing it in the school curriculum, understood it to be not just secular but militantly anticlerical. They reinstated and sharpened the revolution's polarization.[2] Similarly, the twentieth-century scholars who raised the Enlightenment's banner against fascism, including Paul Hazard (1878–1944) and Ernst Cassirer (1874–1945) in the 1930s, but also Franco Venturi (1914–94) in the postwar era, treated it largely as an "ideological touchstone of liberal, humanist,

[1] James E. Bradley and Dale K.Van Kley, eds., *Religion and Politics in Enlightenment Europe* (Notre Dame, IN, 2001), 4–11; Lynn Hunt with Margaret Jacob, "Enlightenment Studies," in *Encyclopedia of the Enlightenment*, ed. Alan Charles Kors, 4 vols. (New York, 2003), 1:424. For the term in English see James Schmidt, "Inventing the Enlightenment: Anti-Jacobins, British Hegelians, and the Oxford English Dictionary," *Journal of the History of Ideas* 64 (2003): 421–43.

[2] Stephen Bird, *Reinventing Voltaire: The Politics of Commemoration in Nineteenth-Century France* (Oxford, 2000).

secular values."[3] Peter Gay (b. 1923), himself a refuge from Nazism, deepened the humanist, cosmopolitan image of the Enlightenment in fashioning his secularization narrative.[4] These scholars at best relegated institutional religion to the margins, at worst ostracized it. The religious Enlightenment could hardly find a place, let alone its rightful place.

The efforts of scholars to reclaim their tradition's version of religious Enlightenment remained hotly contested and confined to denominational discourse. For example, the liberal Catholic Wurzburg historian Sebastian Merkle (1862–1945), best known for his scholarship on the Council of Trent, delivered a forceful address at the International Congress for Historical Science in Berlin in 1908 in which he tried to rehabilitate the Catholic Enlightenment by redefining it as a "second humanist age" aiming to awaken the Church's intellectual resources. While the lecture aroused a storm of controversy among Catholic historians and journalists, it did not penetrate either the historical profession or the larger German intellectual scene.[5] Most German intellectuals and academics prior to and after the First World War continued to regard the Enlightenment as a shallow rationalism that historicism and idealism had transcended through the neo-humanist notion of self-cultivation (*Bildung*).[6]

To be sure, the various versions of the religious Enlightenment did not simply disappear in 1789. They survived in modified, attenuated,

---

[3] Hunt and Jacob, "Enlightenment Studies," 1:427. On Cassirer, see Johnson Kent Wright, "'A Bright Clear Mirror': Cassirer's *The Philosophy of the Enlightenment*," in *What's Left of Enlightenment? A Postmodern Question*, ed. Keith Michael Baker and Peter Hanns Reill (Stanford, 2001), 71–101; and David Lipton, *Ernst Cassirer: The Dilemma of a Liberal Intellectual in Germany, 1914–1933* (Toronto, 1978). For Venturi, who studied with Hazard, see John Robertson, "Franco Venturi's Enlightenment," *Past and Present* 137 (1992): 183–206, and Guiseppe Ricuperati, "The Historiographical Legacy of Franco Venturi (1914–1994)," *Journal of Modern Italian Studies* 2 (1997): 67–88.

[4] Peter Gay, *My German Question: Growing Up in Nazi Berlin* (New Haven, 1998). For his father's anticlerical notion of Enlightenment, see 50. Cf. Daniel Gordon, "Peter Gay," in *Encyclopedia of the Enlightenment*, 2:102–5.

[5] "Die katholische Beurteilung der Aufklärungszeitalters" and Merkle's reply to his critics, "Um die rechte Beurteilung der sogenannten Aufklärungszeit," in *Sebastian Merkle: Ausgewählte Reden und Aufsätze*, ed. Theobald Freudenberger (Würzburg, 1965), 361–420. On the controversy, see Freudenberger, "Sebastian Merkle: Ein Gelehrtenleben," 43–46, 79, and Joseph Lortz, "Sebastian Merkle: Gedächtnisrede," 88–89. Cf. Horst Stuke, "Aufklärung," in *Geschichtliche Grundbegriffe: Historisches Lexikon zur politisch-sozialen Sprache in Deutschland*, ed. Otto Brunner et al. 9 vols. (Stuttgart, 1972–92), 1:321–23.

[6] Jonathan Knudsen, "The Historicist Enlightenment," in *What's Left of Enlightenment? A Postmodern Question*, 39–49; Bernd Faulenbach, *Ideologie des deutschen Weges: Die deutsche Geschichte in der Historiographie zwischen Kaiserreich und Nationalsozialismus* (Munich, 1980), 130–41. For the term's history, see Stuke, "Aufklärung," 1:243–342.

or subterranean forms and in time recombined with new cultural and political impulses, often varieties of political liberalism. Moderation remained a party in the Church of England and produced such notable figures as William Paley (1743–1805), an imposing apologist in the tradition of physico-theology, as well as fueling the "liberal Anglicanism" of the 1830s.[7] It briefly captured the spotlight in a mid-century controversy that pitted "Broad Church" liberals (*Essays and Reviews*, 1860) against an alliance of conservatives, resulting in the liberals' condemnation by the ecclesiastical authorities (Convocation) yet their acquittal in court. Broad Churchmen subsequently faced recurrent persecution.[8]

The German "theological Enlightenment" reappeared in the Vormärz era (1830–48) as a form of "theological rationalism" that combined with and supported a version of popular liberalism that clashed with the Prussian state over matters of religious freedom and helped form the opposition in 1848. It also became an important strand of the "cultural Protestantism" (*Kulturprotestantismus*) that pervaded the nineteenth century.[9] The Haskalah gave way in the German states to an ideology of emancipation that inspired the emergence of the Jewish denominations—Reform, Positive-historical and Neo-orthodox—as well as the academic study of Judaism (*Wissenschaft des Judentums*). The Haskalah also played a significant if conventionally overlooked role in the articulation of Orthodoxy.[10] Habsburg Reform Catholicism survived the restoration and Metternich's repression, reemerging in Ferdinand I's reign (1835–48) among the "late Josephist" bureaucracy, the

[7] Peter Nockles, "Church Parties in the Pre-Tractarian Church of England, 1750–1833: The 'Orthodox.' Some problems of definition and identity," in *The Church of England c. 1689–c.1833: From Toleration to Tractarianism*, ed. John Walsh, Colin Haydon, and Stephen Taylor (Cambridge, 1993), 334–59; Richard Brent, *Liberal Anglican Politics: Whiggery, Religion and Reform, 1830–41* (Oxford, 1987).

[8] Gerald Parsons, "Reform, Revival and Realignment: The Experience of Victorian Anglicanism," in *Religion in Victorian Britain*, ed. Gerald Parsons, 4 vols. (Manchester, 1988), 1:40–45; M. A. Crowther, "Church Problems and Church Parties," ibid., 4:4–27. For *Essays and Reviews*, see Josef L. Althoz, "The Mind of Victorian Orthodoxy: Anglican Responses to 'Essays and Reviews,' 1860–1864," ibid., 4:28–40.

[9] Hans Rosenberg, *Politische Denkströmungen im deutschen Vormärz* (Göttingen, 1972), 18–68.

[10] David Sorkin, *The Transformation of German Jewry, 1780–1840* (New York, 1987); Michael Meyer, *Response to Modernity: A History of the Reform Movement in Judaism* (New York, 1988); Michael Meyer, ed., *Emancipation and Acculturation, 1780–1871*, vol. 4 of *German-Jewish History in Modern Times*, 4 vols. (New York, 1996–98). For the Haskalah and orthodoxy, see Edward Breuer, "Rabbinic Culture and the German Haskalah" (Hebrew), in *Ha-Haskalah le-Gevaneha*, ed. Israel Bartal and Shmuel Feiner (Jerusalem, 2005), 137–48.

clergy, and such influential figures as Bernard Bolzano (1781–1848). It dominated seminary education in Vienna until 1848 and fueled early liberalism.[1] In France, the Abbé Grégoire, who defied the odds in surviving the Terror, valiantly struggled to rebuild the Constitutional Church (1794–1801), only to see Napoleon destroy his efforts with the Concordat.[2] During the July monarchy Félicité Lammenais (1782–1854) and other liberal Catholics continued the effort to combine republicanism with Catholicism, while later in the century Catholic Modernists such as Alfred Loisy (1857–1940) championed theological renovation and ecclesiastical reform.[3]

All these later adherents were epigones of the religious Enlightenment. Individually or collectively, in scope and influence, power and prestige, they were pale shadows of the eighteenth-century movement. The revolution's polarization had radically diminished the nineteenth century's middle ground.

A fuller and more accurate understanding of the Enlightenment is of the utmost importance today. Both at home and abroad, the twenty-first century has begun with seemingly unbridgeable chasms between secularists and believers. One step in averting such a parlous situation is to recover the notion of an Enlightenment spectrum that, by including the religious Enlightenment, complicates our understanding of belief's critical and abiding role in modern culture.

[1] Eduard Winter, *Der Josefinismus: Die Geschichte der österreichischen Reformkatholizismus, 1740–1848* (Berlin, 1962), 286–98, and idem, *Frühliberalismus in der Donaumonarchie: Religiöse, nationale und wissenschaftliche Strömungen von 1790–1868* (Berlin, 1968); William D. Bowman, *Priest and Parish in Vienna, 1780 to 1880* (Boston, 1999), 114–25.

[2] Alyssa Goldstein Sepinwall, *The Abbé Grégoire and the French Revolution: The Making of Modern Universalism* (Berkeley, 2005).

[3] Bernard Reardon, *Liberalism and Tradition: Aspects of Catholic Thought in Nineteenth-Century France* (Cambridge, 1975), 62–112, 249–80.

Glossary

Accommodation — An exegetical principle. God "condescended" ("accommodated") to the mentality or limited understanding of mankind in general or a specific historical audience. In consequence, scripture has temporally conditioned contents.

Adiaphora — Religious practices scripture does not prescribe. As "matters of indifference," these could either be subject to state control or negotiation between confessions.

Arminianism — A revision of Calvinism that questioned predestination for an elect by stressing free will and universal salvation. It takes its name from Jacob Arminius (1560–1609), professor of theology at Leiden. Although the Synod of Dort (1618–19) condemned Arminianism, it became the most influential theology of reform in eighteenth-century Protestantism.

Baroque Catholicism — The ritual practices and doctrines of the Counter-Reformation Church, including pilgrimages, processions, multiple holy days, and brotherhoods. Usually associated with the Jesuits.

Collegialism — A natural law theory of church-state relations that envisaged the Church as a voluntary society without coercive powers. First proposed by the sect of Dutch Collegiants, a later Central European version (from 1670) competed with the more state-centered doctrine of territorialism.

Conciliarism — The doctrine that invested ultimate authority in a General Council rather than the pope. Dating from the thirteenth century, it endorsed episcopal power in opposition to papal monarchy.

Court Jews — Jews who served sovereigns during and after the Thirty Years War as bankers, minters, and army purveyors. Although especially conspicuous in the German states, court Jews functioned throughout Europe.

Deism — God as a creator ("clockmaker") who does not intervene in the world and requires adherence only to the ideas of natural religion. A repudiation of revealed religion and church authority.

Febronianism — The movement to augment episcopal authority in the Holy Roman Empire. It was named for the pseudonym ("Febronius") of Johann Nikolaus von Hontheim (1701–90), suffragan bishop of Trier, who in 1763 published a controversial treatise on church government.

Gallicanism — The doctrine contained in the Four Gallican Articles (1682). Approved by the Assembly of French Clergy, the articles asserted the authority of a General Council over the pope and the French Church's ancient liberties from Rome. Gallicanism was the eighteenth century's most influential version of conciliarism.

Halakha—The entire body of Jewish law contained in the Bible, Talmud, and subsequent literature (codes, commentaries, responsa).

Haskalah—The Jewish Enlightenment.

Jansenism—A revival of Augustinian theology stressing personal holiness and moral austerity, predestination and irresistible grace. It takes its name from Cornelis Jansen (1585–1638), bishop of Ypres. Two papal bulls (1705, 1713) condemned it.

Jesuits—The Society of Jesus, founded by Ignatius Loyola in 1534. The order exemplified Baroque Catholicism because of its near monopoly on education and ritual practice. The order's abolition in 1773 was a victory and a watershed for the Enlightenment and for Reform Catholicism.

Kabbalah—The mystical and esoteric teachings in Judaism.

Maskil (plural: maskilim)—Exponent of the Haskalah or Jewish Enlightenment.

Masoretes—The Jewish scholars and scribes who compiled the traditions (*masora*) meant to authenticate the Hebrew text of the Bible.

Mishnah—A compilation of Jewish law (second second century CE) that constitutes the first part of the Talmud.

Natural law—The law God implants in all mankind that is universally accessible to reason.

Natural religion—The basic beliefs (usually God, providence, and immortality of the soul) available to man through reason without revelation. Compare to "revealed religion."

Physico-theology—An argument for God's existence based on the purpose evident in creation. This "argument from design" flourished with the new science, especially Newton's physics.

Pietism—A movement of spiritual revival in German Lutheranism. Founded by Philip Jakob Spener (1635–1705) and August Hermann Francke (1663–1727), it emphasized personal experience and devotion rather than doctrinal assent and adherence to the established Church ("Orthodoxy").

Revealed religion—Religious truths and practices that God reveals to mankind and are not available to unaided reason.

Richerism—A populist version of Gallicanism in which parish priests are to help elect bishops and parishioners help select priests; named for Edmond Richer (1559–1631).

Socinianism—An anti-Trinitarian doctrine that denies Jesus's divinity, recognizing him as an inspired teacher or messenger. Named for the Italian theologian Faustus Sozini (1539–1604).

Scholasticism—The philosophy/theology of the medieval schoolmen who attempted to reconcile Aristotelian logic and Church tradition. Neoscholasticism served as the medium of confessional disputation in the post-Reformation era.

Territorialism—A version of ecclesiastical natural law theory that recognizes individual freedom of conscience and Church independence, yet also the "territorial" sovereign's ultimate control over the Church. Compare with Collegialism.

Unigenitus—The papal bull of 1713 condemning Jansenism.

Index

CPSIA information can be obtained at www.ICGtesting.com
Printed in the USA
BVOW020933210812

298140BV00006B/8/P